IN CAESAR'S SHADOW

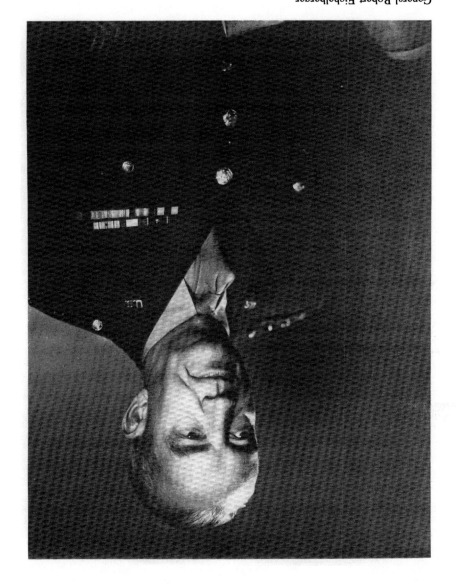

General Robert Eichelberger

(*Robert L. Eichelberger Papers, photograph Special Collections, Duke University Library*)

IN CAESAR'S SHADOW

The Life of General Robert Eichelberger

PAUL CHWIALKOWSKI

Contributions in Military Studies, Number 141

Greenwood Press
Westport, Connecticut • London

Library of Congress Cataloging-in-Publication Data

Chwialkowski, Paul.
　In Caesar's shadow : the life of General Robert Eichelberger /
Paul Chwialkowski.
　　　p.　　cm.—(Contributions in military studies, ISSN 0883-6884
; no. 141)
　Includes bibliographical references and index.
　ISBN 0-313-28605-1
　1. Eichelberger, Robert L.　2. Generals—United States—Biography.
3. United States.　Army—Biography.　　I. Title.　II. Series.
U53.E33C49　1993
355'.0092—dc20　　92-35928
　[B]

British Library Cataloguing in Publication Data is available.

Copyright © 1993 by Paul Chwialkowski

All rights reserved. No portion of this book may be
reproduced, by any process or technique, without the
express written consent of the publisher.

Library of Congress Catalog Card Number: 92-35928
ISBN: 0-313-28605-1
ISSN: 0883-6884

First published in 1993

Greenwood Press, 88 Post Road West, Westport, CT 06881
An imprint of Greenwood Publishing Group, Inc.

Printed in the United States of America

The paper used in this book complies with the
Permanent Paper Standard issued by the National
Information Standards Organization (Z39.48-1984).

P

In order to keep this title in print and available to the academic community, this edition was produced using digital reprint technology in a relatively short print run. This would not have been attainable using traditional methods. Although the cover has been changed from its original appearance, the text remains the same and all materials and methods used still conform to the highest book-making standards.

Contents

Acknowledgments		vii
Introduction		ix
1	Origins of a Military Career	1
2	Formation of a Personality	7
3	Siberia—A Personality Emerges	15
4	Paths to Promotion	29
5	Preparation for Wartime Command	43
6	Buna—The Pyrrhic Victory	57
7	Struggles from the Sidelines	81
8	Hollandia and Biak—Victory and Conflict	95
9	The Philippines—Competition with Krueger	109
10	Victory and Disappointment	131

| 11 | MILITARY OCCUPATION OF JAPAN | 149 |
| 12 | RETIREMENT—AND TURMOIL | 173 |

CONCLUSION   205

SOURCES   209

INDEX   221

ACKNOWLEDGMENTS

In this project, I am deeply grateful to professors Alex Roland and I. B. Holley. Dr. Roland provided continuing advice and guidance, while Dr. Holley nurtured the initial ideas that made this project possible. Special thanks also go to Dr. Martin Miller, who was a warm and encouraging friend during my stay at Duke University. Gerald Pierson provided valuable editorial assistance and Mary Lou Carr was kind enough to draw the maps. I am also indebted to William Meyer and Jeffrey Alvanos; both provided helpful insights into the psyche of Robert Eichelberger. Most of all, I would like to thank my wife, Mary Carr Chwialkowski, for her eternal patience and support during the trying times of this literary ordeal.

INTRODUCTION

Robert L. Eichelberger was, in the words of an editorial in the *Army and Navy Journal*, "one of the really great soldiers that America has produced."[1] A 1909 graduate of West Point, Eichelberger held a number of prominent positions during his military career, including Superintendent of West Point and Secretary to the General Staff of the War Department. He served as a division, corps, and army commander, and was part of the "American Expeditionary Force" that was stationed in Siberia during World War I.

During World War II, Eichelberger won a number of victories against the Japanese in the Pacific Theater. As commander of the I Corps and later the 8th Army, he successfully defeated the Japanese at Buna and Hollandia in New Guinea, and at Biak in the Schouten Islands. In 1944, he participated in the invasion of Luzon in the Philippines, and played a large role in the capture of Manila. During the early part of 1945, his 8th Army landed in rapid succession on Palawan, Panay, Negros, Cebu, and Mindanao, and successfully completed a series of brilliant strikes against the Japanese forces in the southern Philippines. Eichelberger was subsequently awarded a leading role in Operation Coronet (the proposed invasion of Japan) and, after the Japanese surrender, was placed in charge of the American forces that occupied Japan.

During these many assignments, Eichelberger advanced in rank from lieutenant to lieutenant general (in addition, he received a fourth star after his retirement from the army). He also received more than a dozen decorations, and served with a number of prominent officers, including Douglas MacArthur, George C. Marshall, Dwight D. Eisenhower, Omar N. Bradley, and George S. Patton. Eichelberger received high marks from his superiors during every part of his career, and retired from the army in 1948 with a sterling reputation for duty and gallantry.

Despite this distinguished career, Eichelberger has never received the attention and fame that would normally accrue to a man of his talents and accomplishments. For example, he is virtually ignored by most historians and scholars of military history. Russell F. Weigley makes no mention of him in the *History of the United States Army* nor do Guy Wint and Peter Calvocoressi in the 913-page volume *Total War: The Story of World War II*. Michael Howard, in his 1972 book *Grand Strategy: August 1942-September 1943*, fails to include any discussion of Eichelberger or his victories at Hollandia and Buna. Similarly, Martin Gilbert, in his 1989 book entitled *The Second World War: A Complete History*, omits any discussion of Eichelberger except for one brief passage about the Biak campaign.[2] Even Eichelberger's peers and former classmates have ignored him, and barely mention him in their memoirs and autobiographies.[3]

This lack of attention is surprising and puzzling, particularly since Eichelberger left an excellent set of papers upon his death in 1961. He fully expected that future historians would be interested in the details of his life and career, and he took great pains to save his personal letters, diaries, and other documents. In the mid-1950s, he left most of these papers to Duke University, where they have remained for over 30 years, virtually untouched by military scholars and historians.

However, John Shortal has made some use of these papers in *Forged by Fire: Robert L. Eichelberger and the Pacific War*.[4] Published in 1987, Shortal's book is not a biography, but covers Eichelberger's years in the Pacific during World War II. The study focuses on only a small portion of Eichelberger's papers, and emphasizes his training techniques with the I Corps and the 8th Army. *Forged by Fire* begins with the assumption that Robert Eichelberger was one of the greatest commanders of World War II; Shortal believes that Eichelberger was the most unappreciated commander of the Pacific War, and he dedicates his book to resurrecting the general's reputation.[5]

This present study has no such goal; it examines Eichelberger's entire life, and makes an exhaustive review of his personal papers. Its purpose is to explain the life and career of Robert Lawrence Eichelberger, a man whose own destructive personality and inner turmoil prevented him from achieving greatness.

NOTES

1. *Army and Navy Journal*, 21 August 1948, under the "Editorial" section (a copy of this editorial is included in the Robert L. Eichelberger Papers, located at the Perkins Library, Duke University, in Durham, North Carolina).

2. Russell F. Weigley, *History of the United States Army* (New York: Macmillan, 1967); Peter Calvocoressi and Guy Wint, *Total War: The Story of World War II* (New York: Pantheon Books, 1972); Michael Howard, *Grand Strategy: August 1942-September 1943*, Vol. IV of *History of the Second World War*, United Kingdom Military Series (London: Her Majesty's Stationery Office, 1972); Martin Gilbert, *The Second World War: A Complete History* (New York: Henry Holt and Company, 1989), 542-43.

3. For example, Dwight D. Eisenhower failed to make even a single mention of Eichelberger in his books *Crusade in Europe* and *At Ease: Stories I Tell to Friends*. Similarly, George Patton failed to mention his former schoolmate in *War As I Knew It*, and Omar Bradley made only one passing reference to Eichelberger in his book, *A Soldier's Story*. Even Douglas MacArthur (who made 10 references to Eichelberger in *Reminiscences*) only included one substantive passage about Bob in his autobiography. Dwight D. Eisenhower, *Crusade in Europe* (Garden City, N.Y.: Doubleday, 1949); Dwight D. Eisenhower, *At Ease: Stories I Tell to Friends* (Garden City, N.Y.: Doubleday, 1967); George S. Patton, *War As I Knew It* (Boston: Houghton Mifflin, 1947); Omar N. Bradley, *A Soldier's Story* (New York: Henry Holt and Company, 1951), 20–21; Douglas MacArthur, *Reminiscences* (New York: McGraw-Hill, 1964), 157.

4. Of lesser importance is Jay Luvaas's *Dear Miss Em*. Published in 1972, this is an edited compilation of Eichelberger's letters to his wife during World War II. Luvaas, *Dear Miss Em: General Eichelberger's War in the Pacific, 1942–1945* (Westport, Conn.: Greenwood Press, 1972).

5. John F. Shortal, *Forged by Fire: Robert L. Eichelberger and the Pacific War* (Columbia: University of South Carolina Press, 1987).

IN CAESAR'S SHADOW

1

ORIGINS OF A MILITARY CAREER

Robert Lawrence Eichelberger was born in Urbana, Ohio, on 9 March 1886. His father, George Maley Eichelberger, was a successful farmer and lawyer who had been educated at Ohio Wesleyan University. During the Civil War, George served several short enlistments with the Union army while on his summer breaks from college. After the war, he met Emma Ring, a southerner and Civil War refugee from Port Gibson, Mississippi. After a brief courtship, they were married and settled on a farm outside Urbana, Ohio.

Urbana in the 1880s was a railroad center and a trading crossroads for cattle, horses, and produce from the West. In this small, closely knit town, many of the residents were related and most were familiar with the people in the surrounding community. Schools and stores were within easy walking distance, and it was not necessary to use a horse and carriage except for destinations outside of Urbana. The Eichelberger farm, located exactly one mile east of the public square, was just beyond the outskirts of Urbana, and had easy access to the conveniences and amenities of the town.

The Eichelberger homestead, consisting of 235 acres, included a large two-story home, two barns, an ice house, a smoke house, carriage house, tool shed, hen house, and tobacco warehouse. The home itself was surrounded by a variety of fruit orchards, which in turn were surrounded by long wheat fields that stretched out along the perimeters of the farm. Although George Eichelberger raised a variety of crops, he considered the farm "more a place in which to raise his family than one to provide a livelihood." In 1890 he accepted a herd of small ponies as payment of a lawyer's fee to ensure that his children would be adequately entertained. This purchase made the Eichelberger farm a mecca for boys and girls of all ages, and battles of "cowboys and Indians" became a normal occurrence in the fields surrounding the family's homestead.[1]

These ponies and the "fullness of the outdoor life" were the fondest memories of childhood for Robert Eichelberger. The youngest of five children, Robert thoroughly enjoyed his outdoor activities with his sister (Sue) and three older brothers (George Jr., Frank, and Fred). With his siblings as his constant companions, Robert participated in a variety of organized "family diversions," including baseball and most recreational sports. The activities of young Robert were not limited to play, for he also helped in the fields during the harvest season. He held the grain sacks at the thresher, ran the hay rake, and drove the horses that furnished the power for the rig that elevated hay to the barn loft. Robert also fed and groomed the horses and, with the aid of his brothers, entered the mares in "horse circuses" and county fair competitions.[2]

Young Eichelberger described life during this period as "extremely pleasant." His father made a large income as a lawyer and, for a time, was successful in monopolizing most of the legal business of Urbana. As a result, Robert and his sister and brothers enjoyed the comforts of a large home complete with servants and distinguished guests. Friends and family from as far away as Massachusetts and New Orleans were entertained by the Eichelbergers, and these guests dazzled young Robert and his brothers with stories of distant cities and faraway places.[3]

This curiosity about new places was encouraged by the family's own travels. As a lawyer for the St. Lawrence Railway, George Eichelberger was entitled to free railway passes, which he used to take his family to Cleveland, Sandusky, Cincinnati, and Louisville. The family visited Washington, D.C., where they toured the Library of Congress and the Smithsonian Institution. Robert and his brother Frank also used these railroad passes to take trips into Michigan and Tennessee, as well as to Buffalo, New York, where they attended the Pan-American Exposition in 1901.[4]

In addition to these travels, the Eichelberger children increased their knowledge of faraway places by making use of their parents' extensive library. As a boy, Robert read many of the G. A. Henty and Oliver Optic writings; in later years, he read many of his father's books by Shakespeare, Dickens, Thackeray, and Bulwer-Lytton, as well as repeatedly reading Henry M. Stanley's *Through the Dark Continent*. Robert and his brothers also borrowed books from the libraries of their neighbors and friends, and continued their reading and "studies" at home under the careful tutelage of their parents.[5]

Both George and Emma Eichelberger were extremely interested in the education of their children. They encouraged their sons to become knowledgeable about outside events and foreign cultures. George, in particular, encouraged a "very active interest" in international affairs, and made it a practice to discuss and debate "world problems and peoples" around the dinner table. He fostered continuing and lively discussions about foreign events. Through these family talks, he made a healthy contribution to the education and political awareness of his three sons.[6]

George Eichelberger's influence was not always positive. His children were sometimes hurt by his critical attitudes and frequent absences from home. The success of George's law practice meant that he was busy and often away on business, and his fondness for travel added to his time away from Urbana. George took his children on some business trips and on pleasure vacations to nearby cities, but he was rarely present during the routine day-to-day activities of his children. He also had a keen interest in politics and a desire to run for Congress, but the expenses of his large family and the small pay then allotted to congressmen ($5,000 per year) frustrated his political ambitions. His law partner's successful campaign for a congressional seat in 1904 only intensified George's frustration, and led him to take out his disappointment on his family.[7]

George Eichelberger's frustration was particularly evident in his treatment of his sons. Without exception, George expected each of them to do well in academics, sports and their chosen professions. He became very disappointed when they did not perform up to par. Believing that his sons were lazy and spoiled, he felt that none of them fully appreciated the value of a dollar. The son who most closely met his expectations was George Jr., who was easily the most talented in the family. George Jr. was the only son to graduate from Ohio Wesleyan (George Sr.'s alma mater), and the only son to gain any measure of approval from his father.

In comparison, young Robert and his brother Frank competed for the unenviable position of the biggest family failure. While Robert was not as boisterous or troublesome as Frank, he did win his father's disapproval in 1898 when his "father tired of hearing reports that his twelve-year-old son was playing with the city's chess players in the back rooms of saloons and offices throughout the town." In 1903, George Eichelberger again expressed displeasure when he discovered that his youngest son had incurred a large personal debt in Columbus, Ohio. Angry and upset, George forced Robert to work five days on the farm, from dawn to dusk, to pay off his financial obligations.[8]

George Eichelberger was most upset, however, by the mediocre academic performance of his youngest son. Awed by the brilliance of his older brother, George Jr., Robert chose to devote his energies in high school to baseball and football, where he was a starter but not a star. In 1903, Robert entered Ohio State, where he again ignored his studies in favor of a thriving social life and his fraternity, Phi Gamma Delta.[9] By 1904, Robert's lackluster attitude and poor grades convinced his father that his son's only chance for success was to become a lawyer in his father's law office—a prospect Robert accepted with the enthusiasm of a condemned man.

Robert's brothers fared only slightly better, for George Eichelberger was equally critical of the abilities of his other children. Perhaps unwittingly, George exerted a strong negative influence on their personal development by continuously harping on their weaknesses without giving any compensatory praise. The evidence suggests that George's reluctance to give praise and affection caused his sons to compete for love, attention, and respect, with this competition eventually spilling over into all areas of their personal lives.

This intra-family rivalry for love and attention was accentuated by George Jr., who frustrated his brothers by winning most of the competitions. Robert noted that his oldest brother was "invincible in local riding circles" in their games of "cowboys and Indians." George Jr. was the best-looking and was pursued by many beautiful girls, including one woman who was queen of the Mardi Gras in New Orleans. He graduated from the state's most prestigious university (Ohio Wesleyan), while his brothers were students at either Urbana College or Ohio State. Even in sports, he was highly competitive, although athletics was his weakest talent. The family agreed that George Jr. had the most "powerful personality" and "scintillating mind," although Frank was reputed to be the "biggest talker" in a "family of big talkers." Robert stated in later years that George Jr. was his "favorite" brother and Frank his "least favorite," for he was in constant competition with Frank to gain his father's approval and to avoid the ignominy of being the least successful son in the Eichelberger clan.[10]

The end result of this fraternal competition was extremely unhealthy. It appears that all the Eichelberger children carried these intra-family rivalries into adulthood, and inherited a strong need for success, based on a personal sense of insecurity. By 1904, all of the Eichelberger children (except Robert) had left the homestead in desperate pursuit of personal fame and fortune. George Jr. endeavored to make his mark in law and politics, Frank, in the mining industry, and Fred in the entertainment business. Even sister Sue attempted to gain a measure of success by marrying a wealthy businessman from Cleveland. The changes in their location did nothing to decrease their personal antagonisms, for friends of the family remarked that the Eichelberger children were "quarrelsome devils" whose personal rivalries only increased with age.[11]

Robert was certainly no exception to this pattern, for he was also anxious to demonstrate his superiority over his siblings. By his second year at Ohio State, he was eager to join his brothers in their competition for success and fame, although he had no idea of what occupation he wished to pursue. He was certain, however, that he did not want to be left behind at home as the only son incapable of making his own way in the world. Nevertheless, he remarked that "I would probably have ended up practicing law with my father if his law partner, Judge William R. Warnock, had not been elected to Congress, thereby having an appointment to West Point to offer." This unexpected event excited Robert, for an appointment to West Point provided an "avenue of escape" from a boring law career in Urbana and an opportunity to make his mark in a profession distinct from his brothers.[12]

More importantly, the military represented one of the few areas of common interest shared by Robert and his parents. When Robert was a young boy, his mother Emma enjoyed telling him stories about the Civil War. John McClernand, a Union general, had made his headquarters in the Ring house during the Vicksburg campaign, and Emma and her sister had convinced the general to protect their family cow from the Yankee cooks. Emma also told Robert about her experiences at a Confederate hospital, where she had served as a volunteer by holding the basin when amputations were performed. Furthermore, she taught Robert several Confederate songs, and fostered his interest and reading on Civil War topics.[13]

Robert's father also approved of his son's interest in the military. A group of Civil War veterans met regularly in one of the rooms of George Eichelberger's law office, and George allowed his son to listen to the old men's stories of battles, wounds, and bloodshed. When Robert was 12, his father took him on a tour of the battlefields at Lookout Mountain and Missionary Ridge. In 1901, George bought Robert a "Rough Rider" suit and took him to Columbus, Ohio, to see Teddy Roosevelt. That same year, Robert attended the Pan-American Exposition in Buffalo, New York, where he watched the West Point Corps of Cadets drill and parade.[14]

These pleasant experiences for Robert made the prospect of a military career the most enticing alternative to a future in the legal profession. When an appointment to West Point became available in 1904, however, George Eichelberger deliberately failed to inform his son, although he must have known that Robert's appointment was assured due to his close friendship with Judge Warnock. Both he and Warnock had doubts about Robert's ability to be successful at West Point, especially since several Urbana boys had failed to graduate from the U.S. Military Academy in the past. Robert heard about the West Point opening only after Warnock had unsuccessfully tried to convince several of Robert's friends to accept the appointment. When Robert heard that the position was still unfilled, he "ran all the way to [Warnock's] office to ask him to give this appointment to me." Arriving out of breath, Robert pleaded with Warnock for the position. Obviously embarrassed by the situation, Warnock agreed to offer the appointment to Eichelberger after giving the excuse that he was unaware that Robert was interested in a military career. In retrospect, Robert concluded that Warnock had been extremely generous in offering him the appointment.[15]

Robert forgave Warnock for his indiscretions, but he never forgave his father for the lack of confidence in his abilities. After leaving for West Point, he rarely wrote or spoke about his father. Years later, after Robert became Superintendent of West Point, a friend is reported to have heard him whisper at his father's grave, "You said I wouldn't be appointed to West Point, you said I wouldn't make the grade at West Point and now I'm running the place."[16]

NOTES

1. Eichelberger Dictations, "Early Days," 6 July 1955, 1–2 (the Eichelberger "Dictations" are included in boxes 172, 174–78 of the Robert L. Eichelberger Papers, William R. Perkins Library, Duke University, Durham, North Carolina; hereafter, these dictations will be referred to as the Eichelberger Dictations).

2. Eichelberger Dictations, "General Eichelberger—Childhood to West Point," no date, 1–2 (included in Box 172 of Eichelberger Papers).
3. Eichelberger Dictations, "RLE—Personal History," 20 February 1961, 1–4.
4. Eichelberger Dictations, "Foreword," no date, 3.
5. Eichelberger Dictations, "Early Days," 6 July 1955, 2–4.
6. Ibid.
7. Eichelberger Dictations, "RLE—Personal History," 20 February 1961, 4.
8. Eichelberger Dictations, no title, but this piece begins with the statement, "Time lends a certain perspective to historical research", no date, 5–6.
9. Eichelberger Dictations, "General Eichelberger—Childhood to West Point," no date, 2–3.
10. Eichelberger Dictations, "RLE—Personal History," 20 February 1961, 2, 4; Eichelberger Dictations, "Foreword," no date, 3; Harold W. Houston to Robert L. Eichelberger, 3 October 1947, Eichelberger Papers.
11. George Maley Eichelberger to Robert L. Eichelberger, 7 July 1905, Eichelberger Papers.
12. Eichelberger Dictations, no title, but piece begins with the statement, "Time lends a certain perspective to historical research," no date, 6–7.
13. Robert Eichelberger to Kenneth Williams, 9 September 1955, Eichelberger Papers; Eichelberger Dictations, "Foreword," no date, 1–2; Eichelberger Dictations, "RLE—Personal History," 20 February 1961, 3; Eichelberger Dictations, "Chronological Data on Life of RLE," no date, 1 (box 172 of Eichelberger Papers).
14. Eichelberger Dictations, "Foreword," no date, 2–4; Eichelberger Dictations, no title, but piece begins with the statement, "Time lends a certain perspective to historical research," no date, 4, 7.
15. Eichelberger Dictations, "Foreword," no date, 2–4; Eichelberger Dictations, no title, but piece begins with the statement, "Time lends a certain perspective to historical research," no date, 4, 6–7; Eichelberger Dictations, "General Eichelberger—Childhood to West Point," (no date), 3.
16. *Urbana Daily Citizen*, 27 September 1961, 1 (Robert L. Eichelberger's obituary, included in Eichelberger Papers).

2

FORMATION OF A PERSONALITY

Robert Eichelberger entered West Point in June 1905. His first year was difficult emotionally, for he had to deal with the problems of a new environment as well as a rigorous academic program. His confidence was hindered by his father, who continued to express reservations about his abilities. George wrote that "you will find your chief difficulty in mathematics," and "one thing will help you though and that is [that] you do not apparently feel too much overconfidence . . .with your studies." George concluded that "if you don't [pass the studies] and come back we will be much happier than to have you away, for it is very lonesome for us . . . and I have looked forward to having you, the youngest, with us all the time until the end."[1]

Torn by the demands of school and home, Robert also suffered under the harshness of West Point life. He complained that the barracks were always cold and that he never got enough sleep. He was frequently ill with colds, tonsillitis, and flu. His life was made miserable by the upperclassmen, who chose the naive Ohio farmboy as the object of their pranks and hazing. Enraged by this ill-treatment, Robert was advised by his father to "ignore it," but "if any fellow makes himself too obnoxious give him an upper punch under the jaw."[2]

Robert's social problems were trivial in comparison to his academic difficulties. Unused to prolonged study and not interested in learning for pleasure, he quickly fell behind in his schoolwork and had difficulty in maintaining passing grades. As an excuse for his poor marks, he blamed his roommates, Wentworth Moss and William Mathues (both were football players who later flunked out of West Point). Eichelberger claimed that they would frequently take the books out of his hands and throw them on the floor and chastise him for "boning files on your classmates." Robert admitted, however, that he was usually more than happy to "surrender" his books, and that his interest in football and other diversions took precedence over his academic work.[3]

For the remainder of his stay at West Point, Eichelberger performed the minimum needed to receive passing marks. As a result, in 1909 he graduated with the disappointing rank of 68th out of 103 graduates. He later admitted, "It was not until after I had graduated . . . that I realized it was a lot of fun to try to stand near the top of the class."[4]

After graduation, Eichelberger was commissioned a Second Lieutenant of infantry and assigned to Company I of the 10th Infantry Regiment. For the next nine years, he was assigned to several different units and served in a variety of locations and outposts. He served with the 10th Infantry from the summer of 1909 to the winter of 1915. During this period, he was stationed at Fort Benjamin Harrison in Indiana; in San Antonio, Texas; and at Camp E. S. Otis in the Panama Canal Zone. In March 1915, he was reassigned to the 22d Infantry Regiment. He served with that unit at Fort Porter, New York; at Douglas, Arizona; and Fort Douglas, Utah; and at the Kemper Military School in Boonville, Missouri, as professor of military science and tactics. He was promoted to First Lieutenant in July 1916 and to Captain in May 1917. In August 1917, he was transferred to the 43d Infantry Regiment, in which he served as Provost Marshal and officer training instructor at Camp Pike, Arkansas. In February 1918, he was transferred to the War Plans Division of the War Department General Staff in Washington, D.C., where he served in the office of Brigadier General William S. Graves, executive assistant to the Chief of Staff.[5]

During these assignments, Eichelberger attempted to develop the characteristics of an outstanding military officer as well as his own style of leadership. The insecurities of his childhood, however, made him doubt his own judgment in determining the style, manner, and personality of a competent officer. His mediocre academic performance at West Point only served to increase his feelings of insecurity and inadequacy. Outside of a pleasant and engaging demeanor, he was not sure that he possessed the talent and ability to become a successful officer at all. Distrusting his own judgment and having no ideas of his own, Eichelberger attempted to become a respectable officer by copying the characteristics and mannerisms of his superiors. His peers and commanding officers in this early period, then, became the foundation upon which his personality was formed. Eichelberger's attempt to copy a personality fulfilled the prophecy of his critical father, who once stated that "the excuse I find for [the family's] peccadilloes is that they are all with the exception of you (Robert) and me persons of strong individuality."[6]

From 1909 to 1918, Eichelberger closely examined and imitated the behavior of his immediate superiors. His first role models were Sergeants James Collins and Frederick Schmidt, from Company I of the 10th Infantry Regiment. Eichelberger noted that these sergeants believed in iron discipline and "knew how to handle tough men." This quality was exceptionally important, for only a few of the soldiers were educated beyond the eighth grade, and most engaged in heavy drinking, gambling, and whoring. Despite these shortcomings, the men had great pride and would "march until they dropped." The sergeants expected the officers to demonstrate an equal toughness, or they would risk losing the respect of the troops.[7]

The commanding officer of Company I was Captain James Gowen. Eichelberger described him as modest, efficient, and sociable. He had an "intense interest in the men under his command from the first sergeants to the lowliest private" and "looked after . . . the ones who were sick, the ones who had troubles at pay day." Gowen emphasized attention to duty and discouraged his officers from wasting time by "playing cards all afternoon and evening." He had little patience with officers who were neglectful and lazy or those who were repeatedly absent from camp.[8]

The regimental commander, Colonel Henry A. Greene, was equally stern. A regular army officer with a fine record, Greene was described as a benevolent autocrat and born dictator. When Greene was asked, by the Inspector General, why his regiment had stopped during maneuvers, he replied, "By God, sir, because I commanded it." In Panama, Greene developed an active dislike for Colonel George Goethals, the chief engineer of construction work on the Panama Canal and a "man of deep prejudices." Eichelberger noted that the two men were excellent officers but "both were jealous of their positions and prerogatives in the post hierarchy." As the senior officer, Greene demanded unusual courtesies from Goethals, and Goethals responded by denying supplies to the 10th Infantry. Greene blamed Goethals for the delay in his promotion to Brigadier General, and criticized Goethals for stealing credit from his subordinates (especially John F. Stevens) during the building of the Panama Canal. In the dispute, Eichelberger sided with Greene, for Greene got along well with his officers and "anyone who did his duty promptly and was diplomatic had no trouble with the colonel."[9]

In Panama, Eichelberger also served with Captain E. L. Breckenridge, a compassionate man who "looked like a leader and was a leader." Breckenridge was a "proud Kentuckian" who received great affection from his troops and "was ready to fight for his men and his company." Eichelberger noted that he commanded an outstanding unit but "resented bitterly any criticism or any attempt to over-ride his authority."[10]

One more officer who made an impression on Eichelberger during this period was Captain John B. Schoeffel. A large, husky professional soldier, Schoeffel had tremendous drive and felt his troops always had "a lot more left in them" than they thought. Eichelberger noted that Schoeffel was not bothered by the tears caused by fatigue, and was impressed that Schoeffel's unit completed a 25-mile march "down a narrow, hot, steaming jungle trail" without any troops falling by the wayside.[11]

Eichelberger learned a variety of lessons from these officers. The first and most vital lesson was the importance of being on the job and showing interest in the men. He noted that an officer usually "received from his men the liking and backing which he deserved," and that the "hard-working officer who liked his men and looked after them in rain and shine was popular." As a result, Eichelberger never underestimated the importance of looking after the well-being of his troops, and through this attention to duty "I gained a reputation for being on the job and interested in my men which, in turn, affected my efficiency reports."[12]

A second important lesson was that the quality of the troops rose or fell in direct proportion to the respect the men had for their officers. Eichelberger learned this lesson the hard way during his first few months with the 10th Infantry Regiment. During a 20-mile hike, he found that he was walking on blisters because he had failed to break-in his new pair of shoes prior to the march. Rather than retire to an ambulance, he completed the hike on swollen feet. He stated, "I knew if I fell out I would never gain their respect," for "one officer who rode in an ambulance after his feet began to hurt never had any standing among the officers or the men after that."[13]

Respect from the troops, however, had to be maintained by iron discipline and strength of character. At times, harshness and even brutality were justified if they served to preserve the integrity of the unit. Collins, Schmidt, Greene, and Schoeffel were examples of officers who maintained their authority by severe discipline and an intimidating personality. Eichelberger noted that "discipline by rank rather than personality . . . met quick response in lowered morale and often in inefficiency," and that "the bullying-type officer [often succeeded] in that strong discipline induced fear."[14]

Eichelberger learned that a reputation as a "son-of-a-bitch" or "bastard" was not necessarily a hindrance to an officer's military career. He noted that the fainthearted officer often was ignored and pushed aside by his peers, while the domineering officer who protected his privileges and position usually rose in rank and prestige. It was important for an officer to "stand up for his rights," for other officers would attempt to take credit for his deeds and accomplishments. Colonel Goethals, for example, took credit for the work others had done on the Panama Canal, and other officers took advantage of their rank by gambling or "having the first sergeant bring the morning report to their bed to sign." When Eichelberger was assigned to the War Plans Division as the only captain, he observed that "I was the working member of the fraternity," for "some of the colonels felt that it was not up to them to work too hard when they had a captain who seemed willing and reasonably able."[15]

These conflicts and petty jealousies led Eichelberger to believe that personality clashes and intraservice rivalries were a natural and inevitable part of military service. As protection against hostile rivals, he concluded that a prudent officer should cultivate friendly relations with his commanding officer. He also believed that an officer's career was based on efficiency reports and the influence of friends in Washington, D.C. A prudent officer, he believed, should always develop contacts with potential supporters in high places.

In August 1915, Eichelberger received a letter from the Adjutant General of the army "asking if I had used influence in getting stationed with the 22nd Infantry." The letter indicated that "Lieutenant Eichelberger" had been unexpectedly shifted to Fort Porter (a beautiful post near Urbana complete "with tennis courts and a nice care-taking establishment"), while the rest of his regiment was sent to Douglas, Arizona, to quell the uprising of Mexican bandits. The letter stated that Senator John Overman of North Carolina had been active in pursuing this matter. Eichelberger replied, "I had used no influence but I had a big suspicion that my father-in-law, Judge H. A. Gudger of the Panama Canal Zone, was involved." He added, "While I did not know Senator Overman and had never seen him . . . I was happy indeed to know that I had a good friend in Senator Overman."[16]

Eichelberger's preoccupation with contacts and efficiency reports prevented him from pursuing more intellectual interests such as reading and the study of languages. He believed that education was less important than a forceful personality or highly placed friends. Many of his superiors, he observed, had little or no formal education and still attained high rank and the respect of their fellow officers. In 1910, this careless attitude toward his intellectual development caused him to fail one of his first garrison courses, on military topography. He subsequently offered the excuse that the instructor was "hostile to West Point graduates," but the commanding officer, Colonel Greene, bawled him out for his laziness and warned him that he would accept no excuses in the future. "From that time on," Eichelberger stated, "I worked hard in the garrison schools, and if I didn't stand number one I was within the first two or three."[17]

This improved attitude was motivated by a desire for promotion, not by a new-found appreciation for learning or intellectual growth. Eichelberger stated that the benefit of his improved grades was that "under the rules of that day, when I took my promotion examinations I only had to present a bunch of certificates." Eichelberger's motives were apparent in 1916–1917 during his service as professor of military science and tactics at Boonville, Missouri. The only significance that he attributed to this assignment was that "for the first time in my career I made over $200 a month" and "I was made a First Lieutenant that summer after seven years of service." His letters and memoranda from 1909 to 1918 fail to mention even a single book that he had read during this period.[18]

By his own choice, Eichelberger's education during these years was limited to his personal experiences, duties, and travels. His military assignments allowed him to see different parts of the United States and Central America. He was present during the construction of the Panama Canal and observed the difficulties firsthand. In Panama, he experienced a "taste of what jungle warfare would be like" when he was ordered on a mapping expedition to mark the trails leading to the canal. He also learned a lesson in foreign policy when he was forced to rescue his troops from houses of prostitution, thereby preventing their execution by Panamanian police. In Douglas, Arizona, he gained his first taste of combat when he observed a battle between Pancho Villa and opposing Mexican forces only a hundred yards from the Mexican border. In 1911 in Texas, he met for the first time the "reserved, aloof" Captain Douglas MacArthur and the "high brow lieutenant," George C. Marshall.[19]

Despite these experiences, Eichelberger had a desire for even greater adventure and excitement. In 1911, shortly after seeing his first airplane in San Antonio, he volunteered to be a pilot at a flying school in Texas. His commanding officer, Captain Gowen, pigeonholed this application until he was transferred to Panama. Eichelberger later admitted that his commander's decision had been a wise one, for the mortality rate among new pilots was over 50%, and two of his closest friends had died in crashes within three months of their enlistments.[20]

This brief flirtation with flying demonstrated Eichelberger's immaturity and lack of direction. He admitted that he was restless, impatient, and ambitious during this period. His uneasiness and dissatisfaction were fueled by several factors. As always, he felt a keen sense of inferiority caused by his failures as a son, student, and athlete. This feeling was exacerbated by the success of his brothers, who had already made their fortunes in business, politics, and law while he was still struggling for his first promotion. Furthermore, in 1913, Eichelberger married Emma Gudger, an attractive North Carolinian whose father was Judge H. A. Gudger, Chief Justice of the Canal Zone in Panama. Thereafter, his feelings of inadequacy were inflamed by his father-in-law, who repeatedly wrote to his daughter asking "if Robert had made Captain yet." Eichelberger's marriage also put a strain on his finances, for each time he was transferred, he had to borrow money from his family to pay for his expenses. In 1915, he borrowed $300 from his father to pay for his transfer to Douglas, Arizona. Even then, he could only afford to rent a "shack" for his wife.[21]

Under these circumstances, the brewing war clouds in Europe seemed like a welcome salvation from the deprivations and boredom of the peacetime army. Additionally, they provided the best opportunity for Eichelberger to overcome his lack of finances, self-esteem, and rank. He was not displeased, then, when America declared war against Germany in April 1917. In the spring of 1918, he reported to the War Plans Division in Washington, D.C., where he was placed under the command of Brigadier General William S. Graves, and given the responsibility of assigning overseas duty to officers above the rank of Captain. In July, Graves was ordered to France as a division commander, and he informed Eichelberger that he would accompany the division as either a unit commander or a member of the division staff. Eichelberger was excited and elated, for it seemed that finally providence had granted him an opportunity to prove his mettle and to finally amount to something.[22]

NOTES

1. George M. Eichelberger to Robert Eichelberger, 11 September and 6 October 1905, Eichelberger Papers.
2. George M. Eichelberger to Robert Eichelberger, 14 July 1905, Eichelberger Papers.
3. Eichelberger Dictations, "Foreword," no date; George M. Eichelberger to Robert Eichelberger, 31 October 1905, Eichelberger Papers.
4. Eichelberger Dictations, "Foreword," no date.
5. Personal military service records, box 52, Eichelberger Papers.
6. George Maley Eichelberger to Robert L. Eichelberger, 7 July 1905, Eichelberger Papers.
7. Eichelberger Dictations, "On Service Personnel," 25 March 1955; Eichelberger Dictations, "The American Soldier as I Have Known Him," 12 September 1958.
8. Eichelberger Dictations, "Notes on Leadership," 14 October 1957.
9. Eichelberger Dictations, "Foreword," no date; Eichelberger Dictations, "Notes on Leadership," 14 October 1957; Eichelberger Dictations, "On Service Personnel," 25 March 1955.
10. Eichelberger Dictations, "Notes on Leadership," 14 October 1957; Eichelberger Dictations, "On Service Personnel," 25 March 1955.
11. Eichelberger Dictations, "The American Soldier As I Have Known Him," 12 September 1958.
12. Eichelberger Dictations, "Notes on Leadership," 14 October 1957; Eichelberger Dictations, "The American Soldier As I Have Known Him," 12 September 1958.
13. Eichelberger Dictations, "Foreword," no date.
14. Eichelberger Dictations, "On Service Personnel," 25 March 1955.
15. Eichelberger Dictations, "Foreword," no date.
16. Eichelberger Dictations "The American Soldier As I Have Known Him," 12 September 1958, 1-3.
17. Efficiency records of Robert L. Eichelberger, entitled "Standing at Service Schools and in Examinations for Appointment or Promotion," no date, National Personnel Records Center, St. Louis, Missouri; Eichelberger Dictations, "The American Soldier As I Have Known Him," 12 September 1958.
18. Efficiency records of Robert L. Eichelberger, entitled "Standing at Service Schools and in Examinations for Appointment or Promotion," no date, National Personnel Records Center, St. Louis, Missouri; Eichelberger Dictations, "The American Soldier As I Have Known Him," 12 September 1958; Robert L. Eichelberger and Milton MacKaye, *Our Jungle Road To Tokyo* (New York: Viking Press, 1950), introduction.
19. Eichelberger Dictations, "Service on the Mexican Border," no date, 1-5; Eichelberger Dictations, "Foreword" no date, 1-9.
20. Eichelberger Dictations, "The American Soldier As I Have Known Him," 12 September 1958, 1-10; Eichelberger Dictations, "Service on the Mexican Border," no date, 1-3.

21. Eichelberger Dictations, "Service on the Mexican Border," no date; Eichelberger, "Introduction" to *Our Jungle Road to Tokyo*; H. A. Gudger to Emma Eichelberger, 16 August 1917, Eichelberger Papers (box 1).

22. Eichelberger Dictations, "Foreword," no date.

3

SIBERIA—A PERSONALITY EMERGES

In July 1918, General Graves instructed Eichelberger to "cut orders" for their transfer to France and to "pick us out a division which will go soon." The two available units were the 6th and 8th Divisions; the 6th Division was scheduled to sail for France in three days, while the 8th Division (stationed in Palo Alto, California) was to leave in 30 days. Eichelberger selected the 8th Division. Two weeks later, as Eichelberger was en route to Palo Alto, he learned from Graves that their orders had unexpectedly been changed, and that they were to sail for Siberia instead.[1]

The reasons for American intervention in Siberia were complex and controversial. In July 1918, the Allies were alarmed by the strength of the German offensives in France. They feared that the western front would collapse unless some efforts were made to restore the eastern front in Russia. The Russian Revolution and the Treaty of Brest-Litovsk in March 1918 eliminated Tsarist Russia as a fighting force in the East; the French and British feared that the growing power of the Bolsheviks would create a political atmosphere hostile to Allied military and economic interests. In order to preserve their economic claims and aid those elements willing to continue the war against Germany, the French and British planned armed expeditions into Russia and encouraged the Japanese to stake their claims in eastern Siberia.[2]

The British used the Japanese as an excuse for American participation; they argued that American involvement was necessary to protect against Japanese threats to the Open Door Policy in China. The British added that American troops were needed to protect the "vast military stores [which] had been sent into Russia from the United States for the use of the Czarist government." For "humanitarian reasons," the French urged American intervention to protect 65,000 Czech soldiers (deserters from the Austro-Hungarian army and colonists from the old Russian Empire); the French claimed that this "Czech Legion" had been stranded in eastern Russia after the collapse of the Tsarist government, and that this unit was being attacked by an army corps of German and Austro-Hungarian prisoners who had been released by the Bolsheviks.[3]

On 6 July 1918, President Wilson reluctantly agreed to commit American troops to a limited intervention in Russia. He repudiated any direct military interference with the internal affairs of the Russian nation. The purposes of the American expedition were limited to protecting the military stores at Vladivostok, providing assistance to the Czechs in "consolidating their forces," and supporting "any efforts at self-government or self-defense in which the Russians themselves might be willing to accept assistance." General Graves was chosen to head this delicate diplomatic expedition. His only orders were in a vaguely worded "aide-memoire" written by Secretary of War Newton D. Baker. Before he left for Siberia, Graves was warned that "his mission would be more political than military," and that he must "maintain strict neutrality" among the various factions in Russia.[4]

On 15 August 1918, Graves and Eichelberger sailed from San Francisco with two regiments of American troops. Both men regretted their change in destination—especially Eichelberger, who was eager to see action in the trenches in France. The Siberian expedition, however, proved to be a valuable experience. In retrospect, Eichelberger admitted that his experiences in Russia had strengthened his personality and set the tone for the rest of his career. In many ways, the strengths, weaknesses, and emotions that emerged from Russia remained unchanged for the rest of his life. By the end of the expedition in 1920, the basic outline of Eichelberger's personality, with its multitude of strengths and flaws, had emerged in final form.

The most dramatic change in Eichelberger's personality was an increase in confidence. He was pleased that his superiors in Washington were impressed with his work, and he was even more flattered that he was made Assistant Chief of Staff of the expedition. Upon arriving in Siberia, he was appointed to the Inter-Allied Military Council, a 10-nation committee that debated and formulated Allied policy for Siberia and eastern Russia. Eichelberger wrote his wife, "[This appointment] will prove to be a great experience for me," for "I am constantly being thrown with men who are well known in the military and political life of the Far East."[5]

Eichelberger's confidence received another boost when he was made chief intelligence officer of the American forces in March 1919. In this position, he examined such diverse questions as the size and intent of the Japanese forces; current prices and Russian economic conditions; motor transportation and the condition of roads; the strengths and weaknesses of the Red and White factions in Siberia; and the extent of counter-espionage. He interviewed hundreds of Russians, including "everything from a Baron to a prostitute." By 1920, his intelligence network extended over 5000 miles into the Ural Mountains. Impressed by this work, General Graves allowed Eichelberger to send frank reports and cablegrams to the War Department in Washington. Eichelberger treasured this duty because "half the cablegrams on conditions here . . . are written by me" and "the General . . . seldom changes even my wording."[6]

Content with his duties, Eichelberger's letters to his wife reflected his confidence and satisfaction in his new position. He wrote, "In many ways I prefer my new job because it is more independent than the other (Assistant Chief-of-Staff) and I am the biggest man in this office no matter how small I may be out of it." He added, "I am less of an office boy and find men of importance coming in for information, etc. and it makes me feel that I am really doing something."[7]

Because of his new position, Eichelberger discovered that he had the ability to simplify and interpret even the most complex of situations. Although he received contradictory information from hundreds of sources, he stated, "I am getting to be a regular newspaper reporter when sorting out what is a real news item and what is bunk." Even the Russians turned to him for information about the changing political situation. In November 1919, a Russian lieutenant-general asked him to determine the official Omsk representative of the Russian people.[8]

His most important duty, however, was determining a consistent American policy amidst competing signals from the U.S. State Department, the U.S. War Department, the various Russian leaders of the Red and White factions, and the representatives of the French, British, and Japanese governments. For the first nine months of the expedition, he struggled through the tangled web of information and data supplied by Allied representatives and Russian peasants. By March 1919, he was convinced that the British and French had deceived the American government; the Czech unit "was not" attacked by the Reds, and there "never was" a German army corps composed of prisoners released from the prison camps. Furthermore, Eichelberger was convinced that the Japanese were seeking a military takeover of Siberia, and that the British and French were supporting them. The British and French, he felt, were actively seeking the overthrow of the Bolshevik government; in pursuit of that end, they were providing financial and military assistance to the White forces under Admiral Alexander Kolchak.[9]

Eichelberger was also confused and angered by the directives from the U.S. State Department and the Department of War. The State Department favored indirect support of the Kolchak government. The War Department advocated "strict neutrality" in the dealings with the Russian people. Both departments agreed that the American forces should guard and protect the Siberian Railroad and the Suchan mines (which provided the coal for the operation of the railroads). The American government considered these installations necessary for the economic relief of the Russian people.[10]

Eichelberger disagreed. The Siberian Railroad was a "military road" only, he argued, and the areas around the railroad were controlled exclusively by Kolchak's forces. Furthermore, he reported that the White forces used the railroad for their periodic recruiting expeditions; during these excursions, Kolchak's troops killed, branded, or tortured any peasant who refused to join their ranks. These punitive expeditions "drove the Russian peasants into the ranks of the Bolsheviks," a result that "America contributed to" by guarding the railroad that made this oppression possible.[11]

The American presence in Siberia, Eichelberger concluded, provided support to "a rotten, monarchistic" government (Kolchak) that "has the sympathy of only a very few of the people." In his intelligence reports, he stated that the Bolsheviks were preferable to the "murderers" and "cutthroats" of the Kolchak regime. "There is more chance that the Bolsheviks will alter their principles for the better," he stated, "than that this small group of men . . . will sincerely try to do good for the people." Writing that "it is a dirty place for Americans to be," Eichelberger recommended the withdrawal of American troops from Russia.[12]

Eichelberger's observations were not far from the truth. Most historians agree that the American expedition was a mistake. The U.S. troops were sent to Siberia for a variety of reasons: to help establish an eastern front, to hinder the spread of Bolshevism, and to prevent the Japanese from gaining control over eastern Russia. The original intention—to save the Czech Legion—turned out to be a fraud, for the Czechs were more concerned with attacking the Bolsheviks than escaping from Russia. President Wilson himself was uncertain about the reasons for Allied intervention, and his official policies demonstrated his personal confusion and ambiguity.[13]

In this political vacuum, Graves was forced to decide American policy on a day-to-day basis. The American units eventually followed a policy of strict non-interference, although they were instructed to keep open the Siberian Railroad. As Eichelberger noted, this had severe negative repercussions. The pro-Japanese forces (under Kolchak) used the railroads as a device to terrorize the population. The continued American presence therefore had the opposite effect of Wilson's intentions—it served to spread Japanese influence in Siberia, contributed to military chaos and confusion, and caused strong Russian resentment against the American forces.[14]

Richard Goldhurst, in *The Midnight War: The American Intervention in Russia*, concludes that the Siberian expedition "was certainly folly in that it failed abysmally." George F. Kennan and Betty M. Unterberger (in *Russia and the West under Lenin and Stalin* and *American Intervention in the Russian Civil War*, respectively) both agree that the American intervention was a "pathetic and ill-conceived venture." General Graves wrote his own book about Siberia after World War I, and stated that the U.S. expedition was a mistake from its very inception.[15]

Graves, even in 1919, agreed with Eichelberger's recommendations. Like his young subordinate, he was concerned about the hardships of the peasants that were caused by the Kolchak regime. Graves resisted pressure from the Allies and the State Department to provide economic and military aid to the Kolchak forces. In response, the British and Japanese representatives petitioned the American government for Graves's relief, stating that "General Graves refused to cooperate with the Allies" and "is decidedly incapable of meeting the responsibilities of that delicate mission thrust upon him here."[16]

Eichelberger admired General Graves for his principled stand. "It has taken a man with the courage of his convictions," he stated, "to stand up for what he believed to be right." On his own initiative, he sent cablegrams to Washington, D.C., arguing that "had it not been for General Graves, the United States would have given whole-hearted but entirely hopeless support to Kolchak, and that as a result America . . . would have earned the hatred of the Russian people." He warned his superiors in the Military Intelligence Division that the French, British, and Japanese representatives would attempt to discredit General Graves. These candid reports were read by Secretary of War Newton D. Baker; Baker reportedly used them to convince President Wilson to retain Graves as the American Siberian commander.[17]

General Graves strongly appreciated Eichelberger's support. Because of their similarity of views, he gradually came to respect and rely on Eichelberger's judgment. As the pressure on Graves increased, due to his refusal to support the Kolchak forces, he turned more and more to his young subordinate as his advisor and confidant. In time, the two men became close friends; they enjoyed mutual interests and needed companionship to insulate them from their common worries and loneliness.

As a reward for his loyalty, Graves took Eichelberger under his wing and made him his personal assistant. The two men ate, roomed, and exercised together. Both officers climbed over the hills that come down to the shore in Vladivostok. During these walks, Eichelberger listened to Graves's problems and his observations on life. "I am very fortunate . . . to be able to profit by his talks," Eichelberger stated, "[for General Graves] doesn't advise as a rule but lets me exercise my own initiative and criticizes later when necessary."[18]

Eichelberger learned a variety of lessons from Graves. He admitted that Graves "was a man whom I admired extravagantly and his character made a very definite impression on me—probably more so than any officer with whom I have served." From his superior, Eichelberger learned the importance of setting a steady course and of resisting pressure from competing groups. He learned how to eat and sleep under enormous stress. In March 1919, Eichelberger commented that "General Graves is certainly a dandy—he goes serenely on his way, no matter what pressure is brought to bear."[19]

Eichelberger also noted that General Graves had a ferocious temper, especially when he felt that he was being betrayed by his superiors in Washington. Graves frequently complained that his orders were contradictory, that his authority was undercut by the State Department, and that the criticism of his policies in Siberia was "made without appreciation of the situation and present difficulties." He believed that his enemies in Washington had prevented his transfer to France and were responsible for the delay in his promotion to Major General. He was upset that the Inspector General had given him an unfavorable efficiency report because one of his units had mistakenly fired on some Red civilians. Graves periodically "boiled over" in response to these frustrations; he yelled at his staff and the Allied commanders, and denounced his critics in Washington.[20]

As Graves's confidant, Eichelberger witnessed his superior's outbursts on more than one occasion. In one instance, Graves "cussed out" the members of his staff for their inefficiency and called his chief of staff (Colonel P. O. Robinson) a "vindictive liar." He repeatedly lost his temper with the local Japanese and British commanders, and called them "liars" and "cutthroats." Shortly after the withdrawal from Siberia, Graves wrote Eichelberger that "if it were not for the money involved, I feel like I would like to tell them to go to hell with their two stars should it even be offered to me."[21]

As Graves's closest friend and admirer, Eichelberger seemed to inherit the pugnacious manner of his chief. The evidence suggests that he, perhaps unknowingly, imitated Graves's bouts of temper. "Some of these Russians make me so darn mad," Eichelberger stated, "that I finally explode and tell them what I think of them." Asked to investigate a newspaper accused of writing anti-American propaganda, he reported that his aide "wanted to be diplomatic but I got rid of this precious thought." In February 1919, Eichelberger got into a fight at a YMCA dance when he bumped into a passing couple and was shoved back. "I finally got so mad," he stated, "that I . . . [yelled], 'You damned ass, you are not large enough to shove me.'"[22]

Eichelberger seemed to imitate his chief in other ways besides his temperament. General Graves had a great love for education, and he encouraged his young protégé to read widely and study Russian as "the best insurance that an officer could make in his future." Mostly to appease Graves, Eichelberger hired a Russian tutor and spent an hour each evening studying Russian vocabulary and grammar. After one year, he reported that his Russian was still mediocre. He eventually became frustrated and quit altogether. Offering the excuse that he was "rather old to start to learn a language," Eichelberger stated that "it would be too much of a task for me to try to learn much Russian beyond what I will naturally pick up." He also refused to read English books and articles. "It is not often," he stated, "that I get a chance to read—I don't know how long it has been since I have read a novel."[23]

To occupy his free time, Eichelberger pursued a wide variety of interests in lieu of reading and study. He swam, lifted weights, and boxed. He played bridge for money, and made several hundred dollars. To settle his nerves, he started to smoke and drink. Although drinking was forbidden by General Graves, Eichelberger offered the excuse that alcohol was necessary for his intelligence work. "Some of the best information I have been able to get here," Eichelberger stated, "is when I have let Russians drink about five times to my one and then have them get confidential." He told his wife that "General Graves understands it [the drinking]," but privately he admitted that Graves was disappointed in his personal habits.[24]

SIBERIA—A PERSONALITY EMERGES

To regain the good graces of General Graves, Eichelberger adopted a more aggressive attitude toward his work. Instead of waiting for intelligence information to come to him, he actively acquired information by accompanying American patrols into the Russian countryside. He volunteered for Japanese and American expeditions against Red bandits in the interior of Russia; he often accompanied these units as a "mere private." In these excursions, he found a companion in Sidney Graves, General Graves's son. Sidney had been decorated in France and had earned a reputation as the daredevil of the 1st Division; Eichelberger noted that General Graves's friends had sent Sidney to Siberia "to save his life" because the young man was inclined to expose himself to enemy fire.[25]

With Sidney as his guide, Eichelberger stated he "was young enough and adventurous enough . . . to find pleasure in a variety of hairbreadth adventures." In April 1919, he was captured by Kolchak's forces when he attempted to stop a battle between Red and White units at Pyratino. He was released after one day. On 28 June 1919, at the request of General Graves, he effected the release of four American prisoners who had been held hostage by the Bolsheviks. In this encounter, he acted as intermediary in an exchange of prisoners with Red leaders. In retaliation for the murder of U.S. soldiers, Eichelberger also participated in a punitive attack against Bolshevik headquarters on 2–3 July 1919. In this action, he covered the withdrawal of an American patrol after the platoon leader had been wounded, and assisted in establishing a firing line to eliminate Bolshevik forces entrenched in a mountain pass.[26]

Excited by these adventures, Eichelberger admitted that "it seems ridiculous that" he "should be running around this way." He wrote his wife "I enjoyed our little engagements thoroughly" and "had a wonderful time." He added, "I proved to myself that I could stand up and laugh while bullets were passing and other men old enough to know better had eyes as big as full moons." In May 1919, he exclaimed, "I don't know what has come over me but I feel like I would like to have a bunch of trained men and then start something."[27]

Eichelberger's reckless enthusiasm was motivated in part by his restlessness and unhappiness during this period. Depressed about being in Siberia instead of in France, he complained that "with the greatest war in history going on, we have not heard a shot fired." He was also troubled by rumors that the officers would not be allowed to return to the United States in the immediate future because they had been tainted by communism. In a moment of despair, he wrote his wife that "sometimes I feel that I would like to get out of the Army if I had an opportunity in business that would give you a decent living."[28]

Delays in his promotion contributed to Eichelberger's unhappiness. He was concerned that his service in Siberia had delayed his promotion to Major. He was also upset by General Graves's reluctance to promote his staff members; he stated that "General Graves is very ticklish about promotion—he has had it denied to him in Washington so many years that he has often told me that if he finds a man that is trying to get himself promoted . . . he likes to keep him from it." Largely because of Graves's attitude, Eichelberger wrote his wife in February 1919 that he had probably "lost [his] lieutenant-colonelcy."[29]

Despite these fears, Eichelberger was promoted to Major (temporary) on 3 June 1918, and to Lieutenant Colonel (temporary) on 28 March 1919. These promotions did not satisfy him. He felt that he deserved an even higher rank. He noted that General Graves was authorized to make his own promotions subject to confirmation by the War Department, but that Graves favored promotion only "where there were vacancies and where it was *necessary* to promote in order that officers could properly perform their duties." Stating that Graves's "point of view hurts . . . like the dickens," he complained, "I don't imagine that [Graves] believes that we are entitled to any more than we have gotten."[30]

Eichelberger was also upset that he did not receive more decorations from General Graves. He did receive the Distinguished Service Medal [DSM] and the Distinguished Service Cross [DSC] for his bravery under fire from 28 June to 3 July 1919, and for his role in rescuing the four American hostages. This put him in select company; only nine officers in World War I received both the DSC and DSM. Nevertheless, he was jealous that two fellow officers received a decoration for rescuing a Russian family during a Bolshevik attack. Eichelberger had played a small part in the action but was not recommended for a medal. He wrote his wife, "I feel . . . very bad about the decoration—not so much that I deserved it but . . . I deserved it more than the rest." He was also upset that he did not receive any decorations for his role as a member of the Inter-Allied Military Council. All of the other members received the French Legion of Honor and the British Distinguished Service Order. General Graves prevented him from receiving these foreign decorations. Angry and irritated, Eichelberger complained that "except for General Graves' opposition, I would have had . . . a very proud group of decorations at a time when these would have meant a lot to me in my service record."[31]

The lack of publicity surrounding the Siberian expedition was also disturbing. Since the size and purposes of the expedition were classified, there was little newspaper coverage of the American forces in Russia. The war in Europe attracted most of the press attention. Few journalists were interested in traveling to the desolate environment of Siberia. Eichelberger was not authorized to inform his friends of his whereabouts or of the importance of the Siberian mission, and he was embarrassed that his wife was repeatedly asked by his classmates—"Whatever happened to Bob?" In an effort to gain some recognition for his services, Eichelberger tried to insert himself into the background of publicity photographs of General Graves. He admitted, "I managed to get in quite a bunch . . . by skillful placing of myself at opportune moments."[32]

The publicity problem was not the greatest source of unhappiness. A more serious problem was Eichelberger's conflict with Colonel O. P. Robinson, the chief of staff of the American expedition. The two men got off to a bad start on the trip to Siberia; Robinson asked Eichelberger to do his shipboard duties for him, and acted in a pompous fashion toward the members of the staff. After their arrival in Siberia, Robinson tried to censor Eichelberger's letters to his wife, and accused him of excessive drinking and "having a tummy." Robinson also tried to get Eichelberger relieved; he apparently believed that there was no need for two General Staff officers on the expedition. The conflict continued until Robinson was relieved in October 1919, allegedly for taking a Russian prostitute to an army-navy dance and for having affairs with Red Cross nurses.[33]

Robinson's presence made Eichelberger nervous and miserable. He stated that Robinson "insults everyone's intelligence" and "sticks his nose into everything," with the result that "everyone hates the sight of him." Furthermore, the investigation into the chief of staff's immorality contributed to the darkening mood; Eichelberger had to acknowledge that a list of witnesses against Robinson contained his name. The whole investigation turned into a "dirty mud-slinging proposition." The affair was so divisive that General Graves threatened to replace the entire staff and send them back to the United States.[34]

Although the Robinson affair was probably Eichelberger's greatest worry, he was also angered and irritated by the Russian people's antagonism toward the American troops. Eichelberger felt that the Russian people and their leaders should be grateful for the American presence in Siberia; American troops, he believed, prevented atrocities by the Japanese and resisted Allied attempts to influence internal events in Russia. He was surprised and angered when the Russian newspapers criticized the American troops and questioned the motives of the American intervention. He was amazed that the Russian peasants resented the presence of American troops and treated them with the same disdain they showed for the Japanese, British, and French forces. Complaining that "it is impossible to imagine a more illogical crowd," he wrote his wife that "we will never get any thanks from that crowd." He added, "This is the best school in Americanism I have ever seen; . . . any half-American coming over here would be turned into a real patriot because some of the biggest liars and crooks in the world are all assembled here and they are all knocking us."[35]

Eichelberger admitted that the American intervention was based on faulty premises (i.e., the Czech Legion incident), but he still believed that America's motivations were superior to the selfish interests of the Japanese, British, and French. He was puzzled that the Russian people could not perceive America's moral superiority. He concluded that this failure was due to the corruption and inferiority of Russian society itself. "Nearly every nation in the world is represented here," he declared, and the "best of all of course are the Americans and then the Canadians." He stated, "There is present in this country little of the good, solid blood which characterized the men who settled the United States." In the winter of 1918, he commented that "all the inhabitants are dirty and smell like billy goats," and "the average place here is so unsanitary and dirty that no white person could live in it." He concluded, "Few of the men or women seem to possess any of the solid virtues which have made America a great country."[36]

The Russian population in Vladivostok was a favorite subject of Eichelberger's prejudices. This "mongrel crowd" included "too many" Jews, "ugly women," "Chinks," and even "niggers." Two of Eichelberger's favorite expressions were "That woman would be safe in a lumber camp," and "He's a nice fellow even if he is a Jew." These groups, in Eichelberger's opinion, made Vladivostok and the Russian nation a "hotbed of murder and oriental intrigue."[37]

Eichelberger's most scathing comments were reserved for the Japanese. "My outstanding feeling was one of hatred for the Japanese military," he stated, "for the Japanese High Command . . . managed to achieve for itself [in Siberia] a record of complete perfidy, of the blackest and most heinous double-dealing." Eichelberger's perceptions were largely correct. The Japanese promised to send to Siberia only 12,000 troops, but instead sent 120,000. They supported Cossack leaders who tortured and abused the peasants. Eichelberger correctly believed that the aim of the Japanese High Command was the complete conquest of eastern Siberia; to achieve this end, the Japanese military lied not only to the Allies but to their own government. The Japanese officers in 1919 were already discussing a future war with the United States for control of eastern Asia, and they deliberately fostered an attitude of rudeness and hostility toward their American counterparts. In letters to his wife, Eichelberger observed, "Officially we are friends of Japan—beneath the surface we are waging a bitter war or rather having one waged against us."[38]

This internal conflict reached a climax during the last six months of the American expedition. By the end of 1919, the Red forces were advancing triumphantly throughout Russia. On 7 January 1920, Admiral Kolchak was captured and executed by the Communists. In February 1920, the Bolshevik forces entered Vladivostok; President Wilson subsequently ordered the recall of the American force. Secure in the knowledge that American units could no longer thwart their plans of conquest, the Japanese launched a surprise attack against the Bolsheviks in eastern Siberia on 4 April 1920, only three days after the withdrawal of the American units.[39]

Eichelberger witnessed the first few days of this conflict immediately before his departure from Vladivostok. He left Siberia convinced that "Japanese militarism had as its firm purpose the conquest of all Asia."

He also left with the feeling that he had missed the greatest opportunity of his career—the war in France. From 1920 on, he attempted to find a way to redress this disadvantage. Eichelberger now believed, however, that he had the ability to overcome this deficiency. No longer the shy, timid farm boy of his early career years, he was more confident, aggressive, and "unafraid in combat." He had a greater understanding of the role of personalities within the army and a strong prejudice in favor of American culture and character. He had gained a strong friend and role model in the person of General Graves. In many ways, Eichelberger modeled his career after Graves; both men were competent career officers who complained that they had been treated unfairly and that "invisible forces" were arrayed against them. After Siberia, Eichelberger developed an "us-against-them" attitude, and he disdainfully referred to those officers who fought in France as the "fair-haired boys from Europe."[40]

NOTES

1. Eichelberger Dictations, "On Siberia," 19 July 1961, 1–7.
2. George Kennan, *Russia and the West Under Lenin and Stalin* (Boston: Little, Brown and Company, 1960), 97–105; Betty M. Unterberger, *America's Siberian Expedition, 1918-1920* (Durham, N.C.: Duke University Press, 1956), 65–70.
3. Kennan, *Russia and the West Under Lenin and Stalin*, 97–105; Unterberger, *America's Siberian Expedition*, 65–70; "Notes Prepared for Col. R. P. Reeder on the AEF, Siberia by General R. L. Eichelberger," Eichelberger Papers, 16 September 1960; Michael J. Carley, *Revolution and Intervention: The French Government and the Russian Civil War* (Montreal: McGill-Queen's University Press, 1983), 72–89; Arthur Bullard, *The Russian Pendulum* (New York: Macmillan, 1919), 164–73.
4. Robert L. Eichelberger, "The Siberian Expedition, August, 1918 to April, 1920," 9 January 1923 (confidential), Eichelberger Papers, Duke University; Eichelberger Dictations, "On Siberia," 19 July 1961, 1–2; Sylvian G. Kindall, *American Soldiers in Siberia* (New York: Richard R. Smith Company, 1945), 19–20; Paul Dotsenko, *The Struggle for a Democracy in Siberia, 1917-1920* (Stanford, Calif.: Hoover Institution Press, 1983), 122–23; Unterberger, *America's Siberian Expedition*, 67–70.
5. Robert L. Eichelberger to Emma Eichelberger, 12 November 1918, Eichelberger Papers, Duke University.
6. Robert L. Eichelberger to Emma Eichelberger, 1 April 1919 and 6 October 1919, Eichelberger Papers; Eichelberger Dictations, "Thoughts on Military Intelligence," 16 March 1959.
7. Robert L. Eichelberger to Emma Eichelberger, 25 March 1919 and 5 April 1919, Eichelberger Papers.
8. Robert L. Eichelberger to Emma Eichelberger, 11 August 1919 and 3 November 1919, Eichelberger Papers.
9. Robert L. Eichelberger to Julian Dana, 2 May 1955, Eichelberger Papers; Eichelberger Dictations, "On the Rise of Communism During World War I," 16 March 1955.
10. Eichelberger Dictations, "Notes on Siberia," 1946, 5, 13–16; Robert L. Eichelberger to Colonel Lloyd R. Moses, 28 August 1952, Eichelberger Papers.
11. Eichelberger Dictations, "Notes on Siberia," 1946, 5, 13–16; Robert L. Eichelberger to Colonel Lloyd R. Moses, 28 August 1952, Eichelberger Papers.
12. Robert Eichelberger to Emma Eichelberger, 14 November 1919, 23 October 1919 and 19 November 1919, Eichelberger Papers; Robert Eichelberger, "Conditions in Siberia" and "Report to Colonel Eichelberger," 9 October 1919 (intelligence reports), box 54, Eichelberger Papers.
13. Bullard, *The Russian Pendulum*, 148–52; Unterberger, *America's Siberian Expedition*, 67–70; Ernest M. Halliday, *The Ignorant Armies* (New York: Harper, 1960), 19–24.

14. John Albert White, *The Siberian Intervention* (Princeton, N.J.: Princeton University Press, 1950), 186–88, 270–75; Dotsenko, *The Struggle for a Democracy in Siberia*, 122–23; Carl W. Ackerman, *Trailing the Bolsheviki* (New York: Charles Scribner's Sons, 1919), 164–73.

15. Richard Goldhurst, *The Midnight War: The American Intervention in Russia, 1918-1920* (New York: McGraw-Hill, 1978), 269–89 (conclusion); Kennan, *Russia and the West*, 105–19; Betty M. Unterberger, *American Intervention in the Russian Civil War* (Lexington, Mass.: D.C. Heath and Co., 1969), 61; William S. Graves, *America's Siberian Adventure, 1918–1920* (New York: Jonathan Cape and Harrison Smith, 1931), 1–24.

16. White, *The Siberian Intervention*, 270–75; Robert Eichelberger, "Conditions in Siberia" and "Report to Colonel Eichelberger," 19 October 1919 (intelligence reports), box 54, Eichelberger Papers.

17. White, *The Siberian Intervention*, 270–75; Robert Eichelberger, "Conditions in Siberia" and "Report to Colonel Eichelberger," 19 October 1919 (intelligence reports), box 54, Eichelberger Papers; Eichelberger, "The Siberian Expedition," 9 January 1923; Robert L. Eichelberger to Emma Eichelberger, 14 March 1919, Eichelberger Papers; Robert L. Eichelberger, Intelligence Report, no date, no title, box 54, Eichelberger Papers.

18. Eichelberger Dictations, "Additional Memorandum on Siberia (Semenoff)," 7 February 1948, 1–2; Robert L. Eichelberger to Emma Eichelberger, 2 November 1918 and 28 March 1919, Eichelberger Papers.

19. Eichelberger Dictations, "Additional Memorandum on Siberia (Semenoff)," 7 February 1948, 1–2; Robert L. Eichelberger to Emma Eichelberger, 2 November 1918 and 28 March 1919, Eichelberger Papers; Robert L. Eichelberger to Emma Eichelberger, 15 April 1919 and 5 March 1919, Eichelberger Papers.

20. Graves, *America's Siberian Adventure*, 84–96; Kindall, *American Soldiers in Siberia*, 19–20; William S. Graves to Robert L. Eichelberger, 22 September 1924 and 12 May 1932, Eichelberger Papers.

21. Graves, *America's Siberian Adventure*, 84–96; Kindall, *American Soldiers in Siberia*, 19–20; William S. Graves to Robert L. Eichelberger, 22 September 1924, 12 May 1932, and 8 December 1924, Eichelberger Papers; Robert L. Eichelberger to Emma Eichelberger, 8 September 1919, Eichelberger Papers.

22. Robert L. Eichelberger to Emma Eichelberger, 10 June 1919, 29 August 1919, and 23 February 1919, Eichelberger Papers.

23. Robert L. Eichelberger to Emma Eichelberger, 17 February 1919, 30 July 1919, 11 September 1918, and 12 May 1919, Eichelberger Papers.

24. Robert L. Eichelberger to Emma Eichelberger, 21 August 1919, 14 June 1919, and 3 October 1919, Eichelberger Papers.

25. Eichelberger Dictations, "Additional Memoranda on Siberia," 19 February 1948; Eichelberger Dictations, "Service in Siberia," 23 August 1954.

26. Ackerman, *Trailing the Bolsheviki*, 164–73; Eichelberger, *Our Jungle Road to Tokyo*, xiii; Robert L. Eichelberger to Emma Eichelberger, 2 May 1919 and 25 April 1919, Eichelberger Papers; Distinguished Service Cross Citation for 28 June to 3 July 1919, Eichelberger Papers.

27. Robert L. Eichelberger to Emma Eichelberger, 29 June 1919, 1 May 1919, 7 July 1919, and 2 May 1919, Eichelberger Papers.

28. Robert Eichelberger to Emma Eichelberger, 9 June 1919, 16 January 1919, 19 November 1918, and 13 December 1919, Eichelberger Papers.
29. Robert L. Eichelberger to Emma Eichelberger, 4 November 1918, 25 October 1918, and 6 February 1919, Eichelberger Papers.
30. Robert L. Eichelberger to Emma Eichelberger, 22 March 1919 and 15 May 1919, Eichelberger Papers; personal military service records, box 52, Eichelberger Papers; biographical material, box 172, Eichelberger Papers.
31. Distinguished Service Cross and Distinguished Service Medal citations, 30 December 1922 and 23 March 1923, Eichelberger Papers; Eichelberger Dictations, "Notes for a Possible Historian with some Thoughts on my Career as it Developed," 27 January 1961, 1–10; Robert Eichelberger to Emma Eichelberger, 12 December 1919 and 1 January 1920, Eichelberger Papers; Eichelberger Dictations, "More Data About Siberian Expedition," 26 July 1961, 1–5.
32. Robert L. Eichelberger to Emma Eichelberger, 11 July 1919, Eichelberger Papers.
33. Robert L. Eichelberger to Emma Eichelberger, 22 August 1918, 31 August 1918, 14 August 1919, 19 October 1918, and 11 September 1919, Eichelberger Papers.
34. Robert L. Eichelberger to Emma Eichelberger, 14 August 1919, 10 September 1919, and 23 September 1919, Eichelberger Papers.
35. Robert L. Eichelberger to Emma Eichelberger, 4 May 1919 and 27 October 1918, Eichelberger Papers.
36. Ibid.; Robert Eichelberger to Emma Eichelberger, 4 May 1918, 17 May 1919, 27 October 1919, 27 December 1918, 4 September 1918, 12 January 1919, and 13 December 1918, Eichelberger Papers.
37. Robert L. Eichelberger to Emma Eichelberger, 11 June 1919, 2 October 1919, 11 December 1919, 28 January 1919, and 24 December 1918, Eichelberger Papers.
38. White, *The Siberian Intervention*, 258–59; Dotsenko, *The Struggle for a Democracy in Siberia*, 122–23; Eichelberger Dictations, "On the Rise of Communism During World War I; Japan's Attitude," 16 March 1955; Eichelberger, *Our Jungle Road to Tokyo*, xii–xiii; Robert L. Eichelberger to Emma Eichelberger, 6 October 1919, Eichelberger Papers.
39. Canfield F. Smith, *Vladivostok Under Red and White Rule* (Seattle: University of Washington Press, 1975), 39–41; Russell E. Snow, *The Bolsheviks in Siberia, 1917-1918* (London: Associated University Presses, 1977), 187–220; Eichelberger Dictations, "Notes Prepared for Colonel R. P. Reeder on the AEF, Siberia by General R. L. Eichelberger," 16 September 1960; Eichelberger Dictations, "Notes on Siberia," 1946.
40. Eichelberger, *Our Jungle Road to Tokyo*, xiv; William S. Graves to Robert L. Eichelberger, 16 June 1932, 24 February 1933, 4 September 1933, 18 January 1934, and 3 August 1937, Eichelberger Papers.

4

PATHS TO PROMOTION

After Siberia, Eichelberger was assigned to the Philippine Department in Manila as Assistant Chief of Staff and Chief of Intelligence. His duties in Manila were the same as his duties in Siberia: to observe and report on Japanese activities in the Far East. He prepared a monograph on China and recommended that the United States prepare contingency plans for a possible war against Japan. For the most part, his new assignment was a relaxing change from the tense days in Siberia; he enjoyed a comfortable home with large, well-ventilated rooms, and every afternoon he played golf with his fellow officers on a public course outside of Manila.[1]

He was not totally satisfied with his new assignment. He stated that "it is a little difficult to understand now why" he "should have been ordered to the tropics after leaving Siberia after spending nearly two years there in war time." He added, "I cannot imagine worse torture than to be thrown into the tropics after a Siberian winter wearing heavy woolen uniforms." He was upset that Colonel Ralph H. Van Deman, a "fair-haired boy" from France, had plotted to take his place as the chief U.S. intelligence officer in the Philippines. Van Deman's friends successfully revoked Eichelberger's orders to Manila, and would have kept him from his new job if it were not for the intervention of General Peyton March, the Chief of Staff. Eichelberger noted that March "was not too friendly with the European group and had my orders reissued."[2]

Eichelberger was also unhappy that he had been reduced in rank from Lieutenant Colonel (temporary) to Major (permanent) on 1 July 1920. He bemoaned the loss of his wartime rank and complained that the intelligence work in Manila was "not as vitally interesting as the work" in Siberia. "In many ways I was sorry to leave Siberia," he stated, for "the work there . . . was more interesting than I am liable to get in the future in the army."[3]

His concerns about his future duties were ill-founded. In October 1920, he was ordered to China to establish intelligence offices in Peking and Tientsin.

Bragging that "no young army officer ever had a better job or one under more interesting conditions," Eichelberger was allowed to issue his own orders and to travel throughout China. He visited Shanghai, Hong Kong, Nanking, and Peking, and met General Joseph Stilwell and Sun Yat Sen, the first president of the Republic of China.[4]

This assignment had several drawbacks. Eichelberger felt inadequate for this position. His knowledge of China was "very superficial," and he was expected to send detailed reports to the commanding general of the Philippine Department. To offset this lack of expertise, he was forced to obtain assistance from foreign experts and correspondents. The most important of these was Roy Anderson, the son of a missionary, who spoke Mandarin Chinese and some of the dialects. Anderson was a "likable character" and did favors for the American intelligence network, but the American officers distrusted him and tried to convince Eichelberger to find other sources of information. Eichelberger admitted that Anderson "was a sort of entrepreneur in the employ, from time to time, of rather doubtful Chinese provincial leaders."[5]

The reliability of the sources of information was only one of Eichelberger's problems. He was concerned about his future as an intelligence and staff officer. Prior to his departure for China, he learned that he had failed to make the "general staff eligible list." This was a disappointing blow, for the eligible list determined future advancement and promotion. Failure to make the list prevented an officer from advancing to the higher ranks, and usually eliminated an officer from consideration for the best positions. After an initial failure to make the list, the only avenue to general staff eligibility was completion of the program at the Command and General Staff School at Fort Leavenworth.[6]

This failure to make the eligible list did not immediately affect Eichelberger's career. In August 1921, after 10 months service in China, he was assigned to the Far Eastern Section of the General Staff's Military Intelligence Division in Washington, D.C. He was assigned the task of preparing intelligence reports on China, the Philippines, and Siberia. Eichelberger credited General Graves for this new position, for Graves had requested his services at Fort Dix prior to his transfer from China to Washington.[7]

Eichelberger's new assignment was "very interesting." One of his tasks was to prepare a "short, workable history on China for the uninitiated." He also prepared a confidential study on the activities of the American forces in Siberia and a report on "The Problem of Reduction of European Land Armaments with Particular Reference to a Possible Aggression from Soviet Russia."[8]

The most interesting event of his tour of duty in Washington was the Limitation of Armaments Conference in the winter of 1921-22. Due to his experiences in the Far East, Eichelberger served as the military aide to the Chinese delegation. Stating that he enjoyed "every minute" of his participation, he later admitted that the conference was dominated by "taffy-warm hopes" to "reduce the armaments of the world and bring eternal peace." Nevertheless, as a young officer, he was dazzled by the spectacular conference, with its panoply of rank and full-dress uniforms. He noted that there was "more gold braid than Washington had seen in all its history," and there was a formal ball every night. He was excited to be seated in Constitution Hall when Charles Evans Hughes announced that the United States would destroy part of its fleet to meet the "5-5-3" naval apportionment agreement. Afterwards, at the White House party for foreign delegates, Eichelberger felt his "first doubts" about the conference when he observed the exuberance of the Japanese delegates over the sinking of a large part of the American fleet. He concluded that "any agreement that made the Japanese so happy might possibly not be one . . . in the interests of the United States."[9]

The conference left some other lasting impressions on him. The treaties signed at the conference substantially reduced American armaments, a trend that had continued unabated since the end of World War I. In 1922, the U.S. government voted to reduce the regular army from 280,000 men to 125,000 men. Combat organizations were reduced to skeleton strength, and infantry battalions drilled with "hardly more than a platoon present." This reduction in manpower was accompanied by massive military budget cuts. In 1920, the budget for the Manila Intelligence Department was cut to a sum lower than the cost of paying the office force in the Intelligence Department in Washington. Furthermore, there seemed to be no possibility of additional monies or manpower in the future. At the end of the Washington conference in 1922, Eichelberger stated that "war seemed very remote" and "it looked as though future wars would not occur in my time."[10]

The prospects of promotion in the infantry also seemed dim. The army of the post-war period had only 20 brigadier generals, and most did not achieve this rank until they neared retirement. The rank of Major General and selection to the Army War College were usually reserved for officers in their 50s and 60s who were nearing the end of their military careers. Officers who failed to make the general staff eligible list and who were not selected to attend the Command and General Staff School (the majority of the officers in the infantry) faced the possibility of retiring as lieutenant colonels, if they were even that fortunate.[11]

Eichelberger concluded that "there was very little incentive to stay with the Infantry under those conditions." In the spring of 1924, he began to investigate the possibility of transferring to the Adjutant General's Corps (AGC). This option seemed to offer several advantages that were not available in the infantry. Promotions seemed to be easier in the AGC, and an officer was more likely to achieve general rank in that department. Eichelberger believed that he had the real possibility of becoming the Adjutant General (AG) of the army, which was second in importance to the Chief of Staff. He frankly admitted that "my best chance for promotion would be to become the Adjutant General."[12]

These ambitions were encouraged by General Robert C. Davis, the current AG. Davis was impressed by Eichelberger's fine service record, the overall excellence of his efficiency reports, and the decorations that he had received in Siberia.

He felt that Eichelberger would make a fine addition to the AGC; he promised Bob that if he transferred from the infantry he would get the opportunity to attend the Command and General Staff School and, if he were successful there, the Army War College. Davis knew that his offer was generous, for Eichelberger's failure to make the "eligible list" in 1920 made it questionable whether he would be permitted to attend these schools in the future as an infantry officer. More importantly, Davis know that his offer touched a raw nerve in the ambitious young major, for it provided a tempting opportunity to catch up in rank with the "fair-haired boys from Europe."[13]

In July 1924, Eichelberger accepted Davis's offer, and agreed to transfer to the AGC if he "were sent to school." General Davis kept his promise, and, shortly after Eichelberger's transfer, sent him to the Command and General Staff School at Fort Leavenworth, Kansas. Faced with his "big chance," Eichelberger was determined to make the most of this opportunity, and to atone for his poor academic performance at West Point. The pressure to do well academically was intense, particularly since "all officers were working hard and behind them were the ambitious wives, urging them on to greater efforts."[14]

The problem-oriented curriculum at Fort Leavenworth, Eichelberger discovered, was more interesting and practical than the academic atmosphere of West Point. The class of 248 officers was divided into committees of 20, with two instructors assigned to each committee. Instruction was offered in the medical, ordnance, quartermaster, and signal services, as well as in the operation of the fighting arms. Each committee was assigned problems under the case-study method, and each officer was required to prepare a plan of operations against a proposed enemy. There were "no examinations, no tests of memory."[15]

Under this format, Eichelberger enjoyed his studies for the first time. He could appreciate the practical utility of his courses and their application to his experiences in the field. "I learned more at thirty-nine [years of age at Fort Leavenworth]," he stated, "than I ever learned at twenty-one [at West Point]." His grades were also much better. In 1926, he graduated from Fort Leavenworth and was on the Distinguished Graduates List, with a ranking in the top 25% of the class. The top graduate was Dwight D. Eisenhower, a "pleasant" officer who sat next to Eichelberger (due to the alphabetical seating of the students).[16]

Eichelberger's fine performance attracted the attention of General Davis, and marked him as a rising star in the AGC. He was selected as adjutant general and instructor at the Command and General Staff School at Fort Leavenworth. From 1926 to 1929, he served as AG for General Eddy King and as part-time instructor in administrative work. In 1929, his excellent record at Fort Leavenworth gained him a selection to the Army War College. This was a major accomplishment, for only one in five of the Leavenworth men were selected to attend the War College in Washington, D.C.[17]

The program in Washington provided a year "of postgraduate inquiry into military strategy." The courses were demanding, although the format was similar to that of the Command and General Staff School. Most of the courses were divided into two parts, the preparation for war stage and the conduct of war phase. Each student participated in the writing of four staff studies related to the preparation for war, and completed two historical analyses of past military campaigns (Eichelberger gave a report on General Sherman's campaign from Dalton to Atlanta, Georgia, during the Civil War). The students contributed to the drafting of a hypothetical war plan, completed three month-long map maneuvers or war games, and participated in a command post exercise and in a strategic reconnaissance. Each student also prepared a study on a "live issue" for the "betterment of the Army." The instruction was supplemented by lectures on various subjects delivered by senior generals, War Department General Staff officers, the Army War College faculty, other students, and non-army experts.[18]

This experience was invigorating. Eichelberger made good use of his new knowledge, stating that "Caesar, Napoleon, Wellington, Sherman—a clear understanding of their military tactics has never handicapped a green officer in the field." He was discouraged, however, by the pressure and intensity of the educational experience. Some officers committed suicide, he noted, if they performed poorly or failed to gain admission to the War College. Eichelberger concluded that "officers gave a rather inflated value to Army education."[19]

In 1930, he graduated from the War College with a superior rating. His fine performance brought him to the attention of Major General William D. Connor, the Commandant of the Army War College. His splendid academic record also attracted the attention of Major General James McKinley, then Adjutant General of the army (replacing General Robert C. Davis). McKinley selected Eichelberger as the secretary of the Academic Board and as the AG at West Point.

From 1931 to 1935, Eichelberger served at the Military Academy under Major General William D. Connor (who was transferred from the Army War College shortly after Eichelberger's transfer to West Point). His position as AG and secretary of the Academic Board allowed him to work in close cooperation with the superintendent and to gain experience with the inner workings of West Point. General Connor took an immediate liking to his young subordinate, and reported that Eichelberger was "reliable and dependable, energetic and enthusiastic, an excellent adjutant who carries out plans of [his] Commanding Officer faithfully and ably." In a letter to Adjutant General James F. McKinley, Connor stated, "I have a very high regard for him [Eichelberger] personally and for his ability, which feelings I gathered from your statement you share with me."[20]

In May 1933, General Connor wrote McKinley that "I would hate like six to lose" Eichelberger . He informed McKinley that he planned to retain his young subordinate as Commandant of Cadets upon completion of Eichelberger's duties as AG at West Point. Connor wrote Eichelberger that "I have asked for you as my choice as Commandant of Cadets." He admitted that Eichelberger's age was "slightly against him for this particular duty," and that the request for the detail of a staff officer to the position of Commandant "is admittedly unusual."

Nevertheless, he submitted a list of preferred candidates to the War Department. Eichelberger topped the list, with Lieutenant Colonel Dwight D. Eisenhower the fourth choice and Lieutenant Colonel George Patton the fifth. Partly because he was not enthusiastic about the position, Eichelberger was not appointed as Commandant, but General Connor's fine recommendation facilitated his promotion to Lieutenant Colonel on 1 August 1934.[21]

General McKinley had his own plans for Eichelberger. He was somewhat suspicious of General Connor's ploy to make Bob the Commandant of Cadets at West Point. Believing that this move probably would have necessitated Eichelberger's transfer back to the infantry, McKinley was more concerned with using the young colonel as a vehicle to increase the prestige of the Adjutant General's department. Throughout 1934, McKinley worked with Major General Hugh Drum to have Eichelberger appointed as secretary to the War Department General Staff, a position no member of the AG department had held up to that time.[22] In September 1934, McKinley sent Eichelberger the following message:

> I have good news for you. Unless something unforeseen happens, you will come to Washington next year on the War Dept. General Staff, and I think it's the best job there is for a lieutenant colonel or colonel on the War Department General Staff; that is, Secretary to the General Staff. . . . It seems they have a policy in there of promoting officers within the section to the position of Secretary but that policy will be waived this year and General Drum has asked me to red tag you for this position. I am very happy about it because it will bring you in very close contact with all the higher-ups, which will mean a lot to you in the future.[23]

Eichelberger replied that he was "highly honored . . . that you . . . feel that I am qualified for the position." He did not underestimate his own contributions in gaining this post. Stating that "I have seen my efficiency reports during this period," he concluded that "this detail was based on the record I had made at the C & GS School, Adjutant General at Fort Leavenworth and instructor there, and as Adjutant General of West Point." He was adamant in refusing to give any credit to General Drum (Drum was a member of the General Staff who "was scheming" to become Chief of Staff). Convinced that Drum was a "cuff-snapper" who was only "concerned with himself and his comforts," he complained that the general "took credit for my detail but I always gave General McKinley who was my warm friend the credit for having selected me."[24]

In the spring of 1935, he began his new assignment as secretary to the General Staff. His new position was a key job in the War Department, for the secretary was exposed to the most intimate problems of army planning and administration. Eichelberger stated, "It would be silly for me to pretend that I took this appointment calmly in my stride; I was vastly pleased, and my ego, if not my hatband, had to be let out several inches."[25]

He was particularly impressed by the quality of personnel in his new office. His first "boss" was the "already legendary" General Douglas MacArthur, who served as Chief of Staff for the first three months of Eichelberger's assignment in Washington. One of Eichelberger's duties was to summarize the studies and reports of the General Staff, and to make a presentation of these materials to MacArthur. MacArthur approved or rejected these studies the next day, and the secretary was responsible for making notes about the Chief of Staff's decisions and clipping them to the appropriate studies.[26]

This task was made difficult by MacArthur's irregular hours. He had no stated time for receiving the studies; one day he might ring Eichelberger shortly after his arrival in the office, and another day not until he had returned from his afternoon nap or rest at Fort Meyer in Virginia. Eichelberger complained that the uncertainty "kept me on pins and needles" since "it was something of a task to present papers to the Chief of Staff."[27]

MacArthur demonstrated other peculiarities. He had strong prejudices against certain individuals. On one occasion, Eichelberger mentioned that George Catlett Marshall was "up for promotion." MacArthur retorted, "He'll never be a brigadier general as long as I am Chief of Staff, Eich, he is the most over-rated man in the United States Army." MacArthur repeatedly neglected to promote young officers. His practice of promoting only the senior officer off the eligible list meant that the majority of the appointees were approaching retirement age. MacArthur also demonstrated dramatic ability at unexpected moments. One morning, Eichelberger listened alone in silence for over an hour as MacArthur delivered a passionate oration in defense of old army horses, arguing that "these horses were our best friends and should be retired to pasture and live to an honorable end."[28]

Despite these quirks, Eichelberger stated that "my impressions [of MacArthur] were mostly favorable and I had a great admiration for him as a man." He noted that General MacArthur had a "scintillating" mind and was "very friendly and extremely courteous." He stated that MacArthur was "outstanding in his ability to quickly analyze the high points of a study," and that "often General MacArthur would signify his approval of the study before I had finished my presentation."[29]

MacArthur was equally impressed with the talents of his able secretary. He was appreciative of Eichelberger's diligent work. When MacArthur was sent to the Philippines in the summer of 1935, he entrusted his secretary with writing the history of his five years as Chief of Staff and asked him to assist his replacement. After his departure from Washington in September 1935, he sent Eichelberger the following message:

> Though only a short time has elapsed since your designation as Secretary of the War Dept. General Staff you have, from the first,

conclusively demonstrated that your selection for that important post was a most fortunate one. I have been particularly impressed with your comprehensive grasp of the Army's major problems and of War Department functioning, as well as with your tact, loyalty, intelligence and initiative . . . I shall watch your future career with keen interest.[30]

General Malin Craig, MacArthur's successor as Chief of Staff, was equally impressed with Eichelberger's abilities. General Craig had a reputation as a "Pershing protégé," strict disciplinarian, and great practical joker. He quickly developed an affection for his secretary, for Eichelberger also appreciated good humor and worked hard to ensure a smooth transition between the two administrations. For his part, Eichelberger appreciated Craig's kindly and considerate manner. Craig, unlike MacArthur, looked at the staff papers "the first thing in the morning." He was concerned about the health of his subordinates, and sent officers home if they looked tired and overworked. Interested in bringing new blood into the higher ranks, he promoted officers to general rank who were as young as 55 years of age.[31]

Eichelberger's respect for his superior increased when he learned of the problems of the Chief of Staff. Craig was indirectly involved in a personal feud between Secretary of War Harold Woodring and Louis Johnson, Woodring's assistant secretary. Johnson had ambitions to be Secretary of War, and engaged in an open fight to undermine the reputation of his boss. This struggle eventually affected the office of the Chief of Staff, for Craig received conflicting orders from these two men "and was in doubt about which to carry out." Craig was also depressed by the deteriorating health of his wife. "From the time of Mrs. Craig's death [in late 1937]," Eichelberger noted, "it seemed to me that General Craig no longer cared about living." The Chief of Staff was troubled by health problems of his own, and his tendency to punish himself contributed to his poor physical condition.[32]

Under these circumstances, General Craig was receptive to the friendly and sympathetic gestures of his young secretary. Eichelberger was concerned about his boss, and was a willing and patient listener. For over three years, he lunched almost daily with Craig in his office and listened to his personal problems. "I used to sit at a table in his main office facing a large photograph of General William Tecumseh Sherman," Eichelberger stated, with a meal that "usually consisted of a sandwich and a glass of milk." The atmosphere of these lunches was admittedly grim, although these meals marked the beginning of a close friendship that lasted until Craig's death in 1945.[33]

Besides Craig and MacArthur, Eichelberger met other prominent personalities during his tour as secretary to the General Staff. One of these was Major General G. S. Simonds, who served as Deputy Chief of Staff under MacArthur. Eichelberger stated, "I had known General Simonds from the time he was a tac officer at West Point and, like everyone else who had known him, I admired him extravagantly."[34]

He also admired General Edwin "Pa" Watson, the military aide and secretary to President Franklin D. Roosevelt. The two men first met when they were asked to serve as models for a new-style "blue" military uniform. Both men were inspected by President Roosevelt. The President made several "good-natured jibes" comparing the size and shape of the corpulent Watson and his more slender companion. The inspection ended on "a note of high good humor," and afterwards Eichelberger and "Pa" Watson became close friends.[35]

During the summer of 1935, Eichelberger became reacquainted with his old classmate from Fort Leavenworth, Major Dwight D. Eisenhower. Eisenhower occupied an office next to Eichelberger, and served as MacArthur's senior aide and confidant. Because of their proximity, the two men saw each other daily. Eichelberger reported that his former classmate always "received me with friendship and the utmost cordiality."[36]

In the spring of 1937, Eichelberger also met Major General George C. Marshall. Marshall was groomed by General Craig to be his successor as Chief of Staff. He was promoted to Major General and made Deputy Chief of Staff in the last several months of Eichelberger's term as secretary. Marshall made very few friends, although he did treat Eichelberger and the members of his office in an amiable manner.[37]

By mid-1937, Eichelberger had amassed an imposing array of friends, allies, and acquaintances. Impressed by Eichelberger's abilities and talents, most of these men were committed to his advancement and promotion. General "Pa" Watson wanted to make Eichelberger the next Adjutant General of the army. General Simonds stated that "I am for you [Eichelberger] and will do anything I can to boost you along—on two counts: one—the interests of the service and two—our friendship which I highly prize." General Connor was even more effusive; he wrote Eichelberger that "every little communication, even those of a carbon copy nature, that comes from you brings joy and happiness to my soul."[38]

This outpouring of support and praise was caused by several factors. First, Eichelberger was devoted to his duty, and he performed his assignments in an exemplary fashion. MacArthur noticed that Eichelberger studied all of the papers produced by the General Staff, even though he was responsible for presenting only half of them to the Chief of Staff. Simonds was impressed when Eichelberger requested a return to duty in 1936 before his 30-day leave of absence was completed (he admonished Bob to "go out on the beach . . . and forget all about us"). General Craig frequently slept in his office when there was an abundance of work, and he noticed that his secretary followed his example and brought in cots so that the working members of the staff could get some sleep.[39]

Second, Eichelberger took good care of his superiors and did special favors for them. He had lunches with them, listened to their problems, looked at pictures of their children, and commiserated with them in times of crisis. He wrote General Simonds a warm letter upon his retirement; Simonds responded that "you have my heartfelt gratitude," for "letters such as yours are bound to be really appreciated at this significant period of a soldier's life." When Eichelberger discovered that General McKinley's son was having academic problems at West Point, he quietly made inquiries and reported back to General McKinley. He assisted one of General Simonds's relatives in gaining entrance to West Point; a grateful Simonds wrote Eichelberger that "you certainly prepared the way by your usual discreet and effective methods, for which I am most appreciative."[40]

Third, and most importantly, Eichelberger gained the goodwill of his superiors by virtue of his own personality. Ambitious, brooding, and ill-tempered in private, he could also be deferential, optimistic, and good-humored at work. As the youngest and quietest child in a family of "big talkers," he learned at an early age that the quickest way to gain acceptance was to defer to one's elders and to spread good cheer through jokes and humorous anecdotes. A shared sense of conviviality was clearly at the center of his relationships with Generals Craig and Watson; General Connor remarked that Eichelberger "brings enough sunshine and joy . . . to make up for anything untoward that may happen."[41]

This deference and optimistic good humor paid dividends in Eichelberger's efficiency reports. Of the 13 reports filed from 1928 to 1937, seven mentioned that Eichelberger had a "pleasing" or "attractive" personality. The remaining six commented on his "unusual loyalty" or on his willingness to "carry out the plans of his Commanding Officer faithfully and ably." Not surprisingly, his efficiency reports as a whole were uniformly excellent, although he regularly received his poorest marks for "physical activity" (defined as "agility; ability to work rapidly") and for "physical endurance" (defined as "capacity for prolonged exertion"). He also received higher marks from the older officers (such as Generals Craig, Connor and Simonds); the younger officers (such as MacArthur, Marshall and Eisenhower) were relatively less impressed by his abilities. While Eichelberger's efficiency reports repeatedly emphasized his "resourcefulness," no specific talents or skills were mentioned except for one ambiguous comment (that he had "a splendid flair for the public reaction to his chief's acts and policies").[42]

Despite these deficiencies, Eichelberger was pleased by his efficiency reports and the obvious devotion of his elders. He had carefully cultivated this support and, in so doing, admitted that he had been less than honest in his emotional dealings with his superiors. He later stated, for example, that General Craig "was hard to take in those days" and that Craig's practical jokes "hurt many feelings." He also dropped, "like a hot potato," his relationships with Generals Connor, Simonds, and Graves when it became clear that they could no longer help him in his career (i.e., in the early 1940s). His attitude was particularly devastating to the older officers, who wondered what happened to their "darling Bobby" when their letters went unanswered during the Second World War.[43] This philosophy was totally consistent with Eichelberger's intentions, for he stated that "there seemed to be a lure drawing officers in [to Washington, D.C.] to serve under senior officers with perhaps the hope that these senior officers will be helpful in the future."[44]

By 1937, however, Eichelberger still had his full panoply of friends and allies, and he was prepared to use them to improve his position. He had spent 16 consecutive years in staff positions. He had advanced as far as he could go in the AGC, with the exception of the Adjutant General's position. Furthermore, the remilitarization of Nazi Germany by Adolf Hitler and the creation of the Anti-Comintern Pact convinced him that another war was on the horizon. He did not wish to "miss out" on this conflict, as he had in World War I. Eichelberger knew that he needed his new friends to increase his bargaining position for this next war, and he knew that a change must come soon if he hoped to gain wartime command.

NOTES

1. Robert Eichelberger to Major James E. Ware, 23 June 1920, Eichelberger Papers; Robert Eichelberger to Colonel Marlborough Churchill, 7 September 1920, Eichelberger Papers; Robert Eichelberger to Captain John E. Ewell, 3 June 1920, Eichelberger Papers; Eichelberger Dictations, "Post-Siberia Assignment," 3 August 1955, 1.

2. Eichelberger Dictations, "Post-Siberia Assignment," 3 August 1955, 1; Ralph E. Weber, ed., *The Final Memoranda: Major General Ralph M. Van Deman, USA Ret. 1865-1952, Father of U.S. Military Intelligence* (Wilmington, Del.: Scholarly Resources, 1988), xx–xxii.

3. Robert Eichelberger to Colonel Albert J. Gelen, 16 June 1920, Eichelberger Papers; Robert Eichelberger to Major James E. Ware, 23 June 1920, Eichelberger Papers.

4. Eichelberger Dictations, "Post-Siberia Assignment," 3 August 1955, 1–3; Eichelberger Dictations, "Notes on Life in China, 1920–1921," 12 June 1961, 2.

5. Eichelberger Dictations, "Roy Anderson and Others Whom I Knew in China in 1920–21," 15 September 1961, 1.

6. Eichelberger Dictations, "Roy Anderson and Others Whom I Knew in China in 1920–21," 15 September 1961, 1; William S. Graves to Robert Eichelberger, 8 October 1920, Eichelberger Papers.

7. Eichelberger Dictations, "Post-Siberia Assignment," 5, "Days Immediately Following Siberia," 3, "Thoughts on Military Intelligence," 4, "Roy Anderson and Others Whom I Knew in China in 1920-21," 4.

8. Eichelberger report on Soviet Russia, 1 February 1922, box 2, Eichelberger Papers; memorandum for Major Eichelberger from M. E. Locke, 30 December 1922, Eichelberger Papers.

9. Eichelberger, *Our Jungle Road to Tokyo*, xiv; Eichelberger Dictations, "Roy Anderson and Others Whom I Knew in China in 1920-21," 15 September 1961, 4; Eichelberger Dictations, "Post-Siberia Assignment," 3 August 1955, 5.

10. Eichelberger Dictations, "RLE and AG Dept.," 31 July 1961, 1–5; Eichelberger Dictations, "Memorandum on Leadership," no date, 1–4; Robert L. Eichelberger to Captain J. E. Ewell, 15 June 1920, Eichelberger Papers; Russell F. Weigley, *Towards an American Army: Military Thought from Washington to Marshall* (New York: Columbia University Press, 1962), 240.

11. Shortal, *Forged By Fire: Robert L. Eichelberger and the Pacific War*, 18–30; Eichelberger Dictations, "Woodring's Fight with Johnson (and my) Service with General Craig," 12 August 1954, 4–5.

12. Eichelberger Dictations, "RLE and AG Dept.," 31 July 1961, 1; Eichelberger Dictations, "Memorandum on Leadership," no date, 1.

13. Eichelberger Dictations, "RLE and AG Dept.," 31 July 1961, 1; Eichelberger Dictations, "Memorandum on Leadership," no date, 1; Shortal, "The Evolution of a Combat Commander," 22; Memorandum Number 1, Office of the Chief of Infantry, Washington, D.C., 7 August 1920, Eichelberger Papers.

14. Eichelberger Dictations, "RLE and AG Dept.." 31 July 1961, 1; Eichelberger Dictations, "Some Additional Thoughts On Men I Have Known," 10 August 1959, 5.

15. Dwight D. Eisenhower, *At Ease: Stories I Tell to Friends* (Garden City, N.Y.: Doubleday, 1967), 202.

16. Eichelberger, *Our Jungle Road to Tokyo*, xv; Eichelberger Dictations, "RLE and AG Dept.," 31 July 1961, 1. (For some reason, Eichelberger stated in 1961 that he, and not Eisenhower, "came out number one in the Distinguished Graduates List.")

17. Eichelberger Dictations, "RLE and AG Dept.," 31 July 1961, 1; Eichelberger Dictations, "Some Additional Thoughts on Men I Have Known," 10 August 1959, 5.

18. Eichelberger, *Our Jungle Road to Tokyo*, xv; Harry P. Ball, *Of Responsible Command: A History of the U.S. Army War College* (Carlisle Barracks, Penn.: The Alumni Association of the United States Army War College, 1984), 212, 218.

19. Eichelberger, *Our Jungle Road to Tokyo*, xv; Ball, *Of Responsible Command*, 212, 218; Eichelberger Dictations, "Some Additional Thoughts on Men I Have Known," 10 August 1959, 1, 3–4, 5.

20. Eichelberger Dictations, "RLE and AG Dept.," 31 July 1961, 1, 2; efficiency report of Robert L. Eichelberger, 28 July 1933, St. Louis; William Connor to James F. McKinley, 2 May 1933, Eichelberger Papers.

21. Eichelberger Dictations, "RLE and AG Dept.," 31 July 1961, 1, 2; efficiency report of Robert L. Eichelberger, 28 July 1933, St. Louis; William Connor to James F. McKinley, 2 May 1933, Eichelberger Papers; William Connor to Robert Eichelberger, 28 January 1936, Eichelberger Papers; William D. Connor to Adjutant General, War Department, 27 October 1936, Eichelberger Papers.

22. Eichelberger Dictations, "Opin. (Opinions)," 28 March 1955, 2.

23. James F. McKinley to Robert L. Eichelberger, 18 September 1934, Eichelberger Papers.

24. Robert L. Eichelberger to James F. McKinley, 19 September 1934, Eichelberger Papers; Eichelberger Dictations, "Opin. (Opinions)," 28 March 1955, 2; Eichelberger Dictations, "Some Questions Raised by Dictation of August 10, 1959 and RLE's Answers to Them," 17 August 1959, 1.

25. Eichelberger, *Our Jungle Road to Tokyo*, xvi.
26. Eichelberger Dictations, "Opin. (Opinions)," 28 March 1955, 3; Eichelberger Dictations, "Some Additional Thoughts on Men I Have Known," 10 August 1959, 1, 2.
27. Eichelberger Dictations, "Opin. (Opinions)," 28 March 1955, 3; Eichelberger Dictations, "Some Additional Thoughts on Men I Have Known," 10 August 1959, 1, 2.
28. Eichelberger Dictations, "Opin. (Opinions)," 28 March 1955, 3; Eichelberger Dictations, "Some Additional Thoughts on Men I Have Known," 10 August 1959, 1, 2; Eichelberger Dictations, "Woodring's Fight with Johnson; Service with General Craig," 12 August 1954, 4, 5.
29. Eichelberger Dictations, "Opin. (Opinions)," 28 March 1955, 3; Eichelberger Dictations, "Some Additional Thoughts on Men I Have Known," 10 August 1959, 1, 2; Eichelberger Dictations, "Woodring's Fight with Johnson; Service with General Craig," 12 August 1954, 4, 5
30. Douglas MacArthur to Robert L. Eichelberger, 20 September 1935, Eichelberger Papers; Eichelberger Dictations, "Some Additional Thoughts on Men I Have Known," 10 August 1959, 1, 2.
31. Eichelberger Dictations, "Woodring's Fight with Johnson; Service with General Craig," 12 August 1954, 1–4; Eichelberger Dictations, "Some Additional Thoughts on Men I Have Known," 10 August 1959, 2; Eichelberger, *Our Jungle Road to Tokyo*, xvi–xvii.
32. Eichelberger Dictations, "Woodring's Fight with Johnson; Service with General Craig," 12 August 1954, 1–4; Eichelberger Dictations, "Some Additional Thoughts on Men I Have Known," 10 August 1959, 2; Eichelberger, *Our Jungle Road to Tokyo*, xvi–xvii.
33. Eichelberger Dictations, "Woodring's Fight with Johnson; Service with General Craig," 12 August 1954, 1–4; Eichelberger Dictations, "Some Additional Thoughts on Men I Have Known," 10 August 1959, 2; Eichelberger, *Our Jungle Road to Tokyo*, xvi–xvii.
34. Eichelberger Dictations, "Some Additional Thoughts on Men I Have Known," 10 August 1959, 3; Eichelberger, *Our Jungle Road to Tokyo*, xvi.
35. Eichelberger, *Our Jungle Road to Tokyo*, xvi; Eichelberger Dictations, "Foreword," no date, 6–8.
36. Eichelberger Dictations, "Opin. (Opinions)," 28 March 1955, 3; Eichelberger, *Our Jungle Road to Tokyo*, xvi.
37. Eichelberger Dictations, "Woodring's Fight with Johnson; Service with General Craig," 12 August 1954, 5–6; Eichelberger Dictations, "Some Additional Thoughts on Men I Have Known," 10 August 1959, 3.
38. William D. Connor to Robert L. Eichelberger, 4 June 1937, Eichelberger Papers; Major General George S. Simonds to Robert L. Eichelberger, 22 March 1938, Eichelberger Papers.
39. Eichelberger Dictations, "Some Additional Thoughts on Men I Have Known," 10 August 1959, 1; War Department, Office of Chief of Staff to Robert L. Eichelberger, 18 July 1936, Eichelberger Papers; Eichelberger Dictations, "Woodring's Fight with Johnson; Service with General Craig," 12 August 1954, 3.

40. General George S. Simonds to Robert L. Eichelberger, 22 March 1938 and 9 February 1937, Eichelberger Papers; General James F. McKinley to Robert L. Eichelberger, 26 September 1934, Eichelberger Papers.

41. General William D. Connor to Robert Eichelberger, 4 June 1937, Eichelberger Papers.

42. Efficiency reports of Robert L. Eichelberger, 10 July 1928, 9 July 1929, 11 July 1930, 27 January 1931, 16 July 1931, 12 May 1932, 28 July 1932, 28 July 1933, 10 July 1934, 15 July 1935, 29 May 1936, 24 July 1936, and 16 July 1937.

43. General William D. Connor to Robert Eichelberger, 6 May 1944 and 9 August 1944, Eichelberger Papers; General George S. Simonds to Robert Eichelberger, 5 July 1942, Eichelberger Papers.

44. Robert L. Eichelberger to Emma Eichelberger, 2 August 1945, Eichelberger Papers; Eichelberger Dictations, "Some Additional Thoughts on Men I Have Known," 10 August 1959, 2; Eichelberger Dictations, no title, 2 November 1955, 1.

5

PREPARATION FOR WARTIME COMMAND

In September 1936, Eichelberger wrote to Generals Connor, Simonds, and Craig about a possible transfer to the infantry. Responding that "a transfer would be worthwhile taking a chance on," Simonds stated that "there is no doubt as to your qualifications to be a combat commander." General Connor agreed, stating that "I would make the move if I were you at the earliest moment that I could and, as you intimate, use the next two years to let the few who would notice it have time to forget it." General Craig also supported Eichelberger's transfer, with the provision that he remain as secretary to the General Staff for an additional year.[1]

In August 1937, Eichelberger submitted a one-line request for a transfer from the AGC to the infantry. This was a difficult decision; the Adjutant General's Department had treated him wonderfully and had invested a great deal of time and effort in his advancement and promotion. General James McKinley (the Adjutant General) and General Frank Burnett (the assistant AG) were both upset by the request. Nevertheless, Eichelberger convinced them to approve his transfer, and means were found to have him retained as secretary to the General Staff for an additional 15 months (as an infantry officer).[2]

In the meantime, Generals Craig, Simonds, Graves, and Connor attempted to find him an appropriate unit to command upon the completion of his duties in Washington. This was a difficult task; there were only a few regiments in the U.S. Army, and command experience was in high demand. General Craig eventually decided to give Eichelberger the 29th Infantry Regiment, an elite show regiment stationed at Fort Benning. After some deliberation, Eichelberger turned down the assignment "because I felt it would produce jealousy among aspiring infantry officers who know I had been out of the infantry for some years." Instead, he accepted the command of the 30th Infantry Regiment, stationed at the Presidio in San Francisco. Even this more modest assignment did not insulate him from the jealousy of his peers; one bitter army wife complained that "Bob can't possibly be given command of a regiment at his age (52)—there are old colonels who have not had the opportunity of commanding a regiment."[3]

In addition to this new command, Eichelberger was promoted to full Colonel in August 1938. In October, he attended a short refresher course at the infantry school at Fort Benning. In December, he assumed command of the 30th Infantry in San Francisco. Before he departed, General George C. Marshall (then Deputy Chief of Staff) instructed him to "go out to the Presidio and stop that hatred which has been going on in that regiment ever since Phillipson took command." Marshall explained that Colonel Irving J. Phillipson (a former staff officer) had created great hatred in the regiment by his heavy-handed efforts to control the personal lives of the troops. He added that "his wife (Flossie) assists him in raising hell" with the regiment. Marshall admonished Eichelberger to improve the morale of the garrison.[4]

Anxious to please Marshall, Eichelberger felt that this assignment was a test to determine if he was capable of handling troops. He knew that his peers questioned his ability to command a regiment after 17 consecutive years of staff duty. He realized that his friends had "pulled a lot of strings" to gain him this command, and that his rapid advancement had antagonized many junior and senior officers. His performance with the 30th Infantry would be closely scrutinized, and a sterling performance was necessary if he hoped to gain the respect of Marshall and his peers.

With these considerations in mind, Eichelberger set out to accomplish his first task: the elimination of poor morale in the 30th Infantry. Upon his arrival in San Francisco in January 1939, he discovered that Marshall's claims had not been exaggerated. The officers were upset over their ill-treatment at the hands of Phillipson and his wife. The morale of the unit was very low; the officers expressed their disapproval of Phillipson's policies by boycotting the Officers' Club.[5]

Eichelberger adopted a variety of methods to eliminate the hostilities in the unit. He allowed the officers to spend their off-duty time in San Francisco instead of at camp. He prevented his wife Emma from interfering in the personal lives of the officers and their families (the biggest complaint against Phillipson and his wife Flossie).[6]

On a more positive note, he sponsored Sunday night suppers (at a cost of only 35 cents) to help bring the officers together. He supported the regimental boxing, pistol, and rifle teams, and used WPA (Works Progress Administration) workers to build a motion picture house and to renovate the Officers' Club. Insisting that the officers rise before dawn to look after their men, he made it mandatory for them to inspect the preparation of food every morning. Largely because of these measures, he successfully eliminated much of the hatred within the regiment and introduced "a lot of friendship" among the men.[7]

During his two-year assignment with the 30th Infantry, he participated in a wide range of other activities. Throughout 1939, the 3d Division (consisting of three regiments, including the 30th Infantry) was involved in almost continuous maneuvers at Fort Ord, Camp Roberts, Pasa Robles, and Fort Lewis in the state of Washington. Details were assigned by rotation during these maneuvers, and Eichelberger had the opportunity to serve in a variety of positions, including regimental commander, division commander, assistant division commander, operations officer, and chief of staff.[8]

He was particularly successful in two of these maneuvers. In the summer of 1939, he participated in a command post exercise at the Presidio which attracted high-ranking officers from all over the United States. Besides participating in the exercise itself, he was responsible for the housekeeping and arrangements for the exercise. In the winter of 1940, he participated in a combined army-navy amphibious exercise near Fort Ord in California. This maneuver included "one of the greatest shore landings in our peacetime history." In this exercise, Eichelberger commanded the shore troops against an amphibious assault by two National Guard Divisions and various elements of the 3d Division.[9]

Eichelberger attracted the attention of several of his peers during these exercises. Colonel Dwight D. Eisenhower (a battalion commander in the 3d Division) and Colonel Mark Clark (the G-3 of the 3d Division) both made favorable comments about him after the maneuvers. General W. C. Sweeney, the commanding officer of the 3d Division, noted the fine performance of his able regimental commander and gave Eichelberger high marks in his efficiency reports (Eichelberger claimed that his ability to beat Sweeney and Clark in craps using their "famous pair of dice" contributed to his high standing). General Courtney B. Hodges complimented Bob for his superior performance at the command post exercise at the Presidio; he commented that "your instructions had to be most thorough, and your leadership of the highest degree to have obtained such results." Another officer remarked, "Upon reviewing the events of the short period I spent recently at the Presidio, I do not recall anything that gave me more satisfaction than the inspection of your post and command." Even George C. Marshall, who had witnessed Eichelberger's performance in the army-navy amphibious exercise, was favorably impressed by the colonel's abilities and the fine performance of the 30th Infantry.[10]

The success of these performances led to Eichelberger's promotion to brigadier general in October 1940. His wife Emma was moved to tears by this happy event, and George Patton (a West Point classmate who also was promoted to brigadier general) wrote Eichelberger, "At last they have had sense enough to promote the two best damn officers in the U.S. Army." Eichelberger attributed his promotion to a variety of factors—his "success" with the 30th Infantry, General Marshall's approval of his performance during the amphibious exercise, and General Craig's influence in Washington (General Craig talked with Marshall prior to Eichelberger's promotion). He added, "In all modesty, I have seen [his efficiency reports] in the War Department and all of my superiors in every chain of command recommended me for promotion."[11]

In November 1940, Eichelberger was assigned to the 7th Division as assistant division commander under General Joseph Stilwell. Before he could report for duty, he learned that his orders had been changed; he had been made corps commander of the VII Corps stationed in Columbus, Ohio. While en route to this post, he learned that his orders had again been changed, and that he had been appointed as the Superintendent of the Military Academy at West Point.

Eichelberger discovered that his good friend, General "Pa" Watson (secretary and military aide to President Franklin Roosevelt), was primarily responsible for this new assignment. Watson was directed by the President to fill the Superintendent's position (the President considered the positions of Chief of Staff, Inspector General, and Superintendent of West Point to be under his personal supervision); he chose Eichelberger as his compromise choice. "Quite a few names [were] bandied around," Eichelberger learned, with the deciding vote cast by Mrs. Watson, who rejected one candidate with the statement, "Would you send that woman to West Point when you could have that fine Mrs. Eichelberger?"[12]

In October 1940, Eichelberger left for his new post, and met briefly with General Marshall (who was now Chief of Staff) while en route to West Point. During this visit, Marshall emphasized the importance of tightening the discipline at West Point and of preparing the cadets for an impending war. Marshall stated, "When I was senior cadet captain at VMI [Virginia Military Institute] I held the corps under strict discipline at the time when West Point cadets were pointing the reveille gun at the Superintendent's quarters." Marshall mentioned that he had dramatically shortened the programs at the Command and Staff School at Leavenworth and at the Army War College in Washington; he intimated that "the same fate would befall West Point" unless discipline was improved and the curriculum tightened to meet the needs of wartime.[13]

Eichelberger left Marshall's office with "the idea that I had better work fast when I assumed the role of Supt. or I would find the West Point course reduced and the Academy practically ruined as was done in World War I when the course was reduced to one year." Upon his arrival at West Point, he used Marshall's warnings "to scare the Academic Board into producing at the Academy a picture which the Congress and the people would favor."[14]

In particular, Eichelberger proposed a dramatic change in the public relations image of West Point. Under his direction, there were "no more polite newspaper photographs of cadets jumping horses over hurdles." He discontinued "photographs of cadets smiling at pretty young women"; in their place, he substituted "pictures of cadets making river crossings under smoke barrages."[15] Fatigue uniforms were introduced, and "hours given over to training were increased" at "some expense to academic work." Horseback riding, formal ceremonies, and close-order drills were decreased. The cadets, as part of their instruction, were required to participate in maneuvers with National Guard units in New Jersey.[16]

PREPARATION FOR WARTIME COMMAND

The most controversial change was the introduction of flight training. Eichelberger explained that "my idea in this case was to get the support of the air corps behind West Point with, of course, the idea of preserving the integrity of the Academy in wartime." This idea was supported by General Marshall, who approved the plan over the opposition of the War Department General Staff.[17]

With the help of Major General Henry "Hap" Arnold (chief of the Army Air Forces), Eichelberger initiated a program requiring each eligible cadet to accrue 400 flight hours prior to graduation. Under his direction, the Military Academy purchased nearby Stewart Field in Newburgh, New York, and gathered 25 airplanes and 20 instructors. The stated goal of the program was to allow cadets to "earn their wings" during their four years at West Point by flight instruction four days a week. The plan was designed, as Eichelberger stated, to "bring West Point into the twentieth century" and to ensure that West Point cadets did not lag behind in the advancing technology of modern warfare.[18]

Eichelberger considered his air program vital to West Point's future, but he did not consider it his most noteworthy achievement as Superintendent. Oddly enough, he was most proud of the reforms that he instituted in the West Point football program. In response to the many criticisms of his excessive interest in this game, Eichelberger responded, "I do not apologize." Unlike his critics, he did not find football "frivolous and inconsequential."[19]

"My first afternoon as Superintendent," Eichelberger stated, "was spent at Franklin Field [Philadelphia], where I saw the University of Pennsylvania football team demolish Army 48–0." After the game, he decided that the cadets deserved a team "which would teach them to be good winners." He reasoned that a successful football team was necessary for high morale, and that "the concept of graceful losing can be overdone; in combat warfare there may be no game next week."[20]

After a lengthy argument with the West Point Academic Board, he decided that the Academy needed a new coach, and that Earl "Red" Blaik (the coach at Dartmouth) was the ideal choice to rejuvenate West Point football. In order to persuade Blaik to leave Dartmouth, he initiated a wide variety of changes to make West Point more competitive with other football powers. He abolished the rule that required the coach to be an army officer on active duty. He promised "Red" and his wife that the Army Athletic Association would build them a house near Fort Willis, New York. He also promised Blaik that his entire Dartmouth staff (and the trainer) would be hired at West Point.[21]

More importantly, he took measures to waive the army weight limits; these restrictions stated that a man six feet tall could not weigh over 160 pounds (with only a 10% variation for build or athletic body type). Although these limits were based on the Surgeon General's determination that "life expectancy is greater for a slender man," Eichelberger argued that these limitations made it practically impossible to recruit football stars with "fine, athletic builds." When the Surgeon General refused to change these limits, Eichelberger turned to General "Pa"

Watson for help. (The Surgeon General was Watson's personal friend, and Watson was "largely responsible" for appointing him to his present post). With Watson's assistance, the Surgeon General was persuaded to allow exceptions above the weight limits "provided a cadet was overweight due to athletic build rather than to obesity." This new ruling convinced Blaik to accept the coaching position at West Point, and allowed the army squad to field bigger and stronger football teams.[22]

West Point football had a profound impact on Eichelberger's military career. The evidence suggests that General Watson chose Eichelberger as Superintendent specifically for the purpose of revitalizing the football program. In October 1940, Watson wrote a friend, "We are going to send Eichelberger up there as Superintendent and I am going to fill him full of the idea of getting some real honest-to-God non-graduate full time coaches." "There is no real excuse," he added, "why we should not have the first team in the country."[23]

Watson was elated by the changes that Eichelberger made in the football program. He was particularly pleased by the selection of Blaik as head coach. The accumulation of victories on the football field represented a personal triumph, for "it was widely known that the Navy had been fleecing General Watson on his trips with the President by inducing him to bet considerable monies on the Army team at a time when the Army had little or no chance of winning." Watson was therefore pleased with the improvements in the army's gridiron record, and he told Eichelberger that he would be retained as Superintendent until the rejuvenation of the football program was completed.[24]

Watson's plan to keep Eichelberger at West Point was opposed by Lieutenant General Lesley J. McNair (chief of the Army Ground Forces) and Colonel Mark Wayne Clark (McNair's chief of staff). McNair and Clark had witnessed Eichelberger's fine performance with the 30th Infantry at the Presidio; both men felt that Eichelberger's talents were wasted at West Point. They believed that Eichelberger was qualified to command a division in the army, and they put pressure on Marshall to release him from the Academy so that he could assume more important duties. Marshall agreed with McNair and Clark, but Marshall's requests to transfer Eichelberger were repeatedly denied by Watson. Watson continued to argue that Eichelberger was needed at West Point. In private, Watson assured Bob that he was performing a great service for his country by remaining at the Military Academy, and he argued, "How can you be sure that if you go out with a division that you will make good?"[25]

"This was rather a ticklish position for me," Eichelberger stated, "because Watson, speaking for the President, wanted me to stay there while General Marshall sincerely wanted to get me away." He did not wish to antagonize either party. He admitted, "I was over a barrel because whichever decision I might make might produce an enemy." He therefore chose not to make any decision whatsoever; he left both men in the dark as to his true inclinations. This strategy almost backfired in June 1941, when Marshall and Watson, in the midst of an argument, telephoned Eichelberger's office to find out whether he preferred to command a division or remain at West Point. "Fortunately," Eichelberger stated, "I was not in the office" when the call arrived.

Marshall and Watson continued their argument in Watson's office. Marshall stormed out in a rage, retorting, "You're ruining Eichelberger's record [by] not allowing [him] to earn two stars by [commanding] a division." Upset by Marshall's accusations, Watson had on his desk a War Department list of proposed promotions to the grade of major general. He quickly added Eichelberger's name to the list, and took the paper to the President for approval. Later that afternoon, Watson telephoned Eichelberger and told him that he "had been a major general since 11:30 that morning."[26]

Elated by this turn of events, Eichelberger felt that his promotion was a great advantage because it increased his chances of getting a division or corps command. He continued to assure Watson that he was more than satisfied with his duties as Superintendent. Privately, however, he wrote Marshall, "We like it here [West Point] of course but sometime I hope you will find a tent for me."[27]

The bombing of Pearl Harbor by the Japanese in December 1941 finally allowed Eichelberger to express his true feelings. With Marshall's approval, he requested a troop command, and McNair and Clark arranged for his transfer to the 77th Division (stationed at Fort Jackson, South Carolina). This command was an experimental unit formed from pre-trained cadres of enlisted men and noncommissioned officers. Because of the novelty of this organization, Eichelberger was informed that the unit would enjoy the constant backing of General Lesley McNair, chief of the army ground forces.[28]

Excited by his new assignment, Eichelberger was thankful that McNair had selected him for this important job. He soon discovered that his peers were somewhat less impressed with his qualifications for the new post. One of his friends wrote him that "I heard some rumors to the effect that 'the powers that be' would make an effort to have you assigned to a field command but I did not take much stock in this . . . However, with this present war situation all messed up, as I really believe it is, the General Staff will take desperate measures to accomplish a solution."[29]

Eichelberger ignored these comments, and assumed command of the 77th Division in January 1942. He liked his new assignment, although he noted that the enlisted men "at first . . . seemed a bit discouraging" since "they were at the bottom of the draft barrel." His troops included young, married farmers from upper New York State, college students from New England, and others who, for various reasons, had been deferred in the draft. The average age of the division was 32; this was an advantage, Eichelberger discovered, because the men were "more mature and more desirous of learning the art of war."[30]

From January to June 1942, Eichelberger worked diligently to prepare the 77th Division for combat. He developed discipline by requiring proper saluting and a neat appearance. He steadily increased the hours of training, and reminded the troops that "preparation for war is no part-time job." He required each company officer to spend "eight to ten" hours per day with his unit on the training field; he ordered all married officers to spend at least three nights a week in camp and to hold night schools for the instruction of the enlisted men. In addition, each officer was required to attend two-hour classes in officer training at least three nights per week.[31]

The officers were also required to "turn out before reveille" to inspect their units and supervise the preparation of food for the troops. This practice was started by Eichelberger, who habitually rose before dawn to examine the messes. The battalion and company commanders felt compelled to imitate his example, and most of the officers were forced to rise early to attend to the needs of the troops.[32]

These new requirements made Eichelberger, in his own words, the "area's least popular man," although he noted that these measures were necessary to "get away from the 8-hour concept of soldiering" that was then prevalent. His demands at first were resented by some of the married officers and their wives, but the value of these changes soon became apparent. The night schools functioned perfectly; the officers were on hand at reveille to inspect messes and the early morning drills. Saluting, military appearance, and mess standards surpassed those of other divisions in the same camp.[33]

In May 1942, the reputation of the unit began to spread, and delegations of visitors arrived from other divisions and the War Department. Among these visitors were Generals Eisenhower, McNair, and Clark; these men were pleasantly surprised by the progress of the 77th Division. They were impressed by the quality and efficiency of the division's motor pool and ordnance. (Eichelberger stated that "through the good graces of his friends in Washington, he had already been able to secure—in the short time that he had been down there—more strategic ordnance equipment than some organizations that had been activated for a year and a half.")[34] The visiting dignitaries were also impressed by the discipline of the 77th Division, which was markedly superior to the "unruly behavior" of the adjoining units (Eichelberger referred to the neighboring 30th and 8th Divisions as "a bunch of tramps in uniform" distinguished by "general sloppiness" and "little or no saluting").[35]

Vice-Admiral Lord Louis Mountbatten, who accompanied one visiting delegation, was delighted by the overall efficiency of the 77th Division. He stated, "Of the many remarkable and inspiring sights I saw on the tour, the one that made the greatest impression was the sight of the 77th Division marching by in review order like veterans." He reported these impressions to Prime Minister Winston Churchill, and added that this high state of efficiency was achieved in only a few months of training. Churchill, who was skeptical about America's ability to quickly train an army for a cross-channel invasion of Europe, requested permission to inspect this division during his June 1942 tour of the United States.[36]

Generals Eisenhower and McNair were more than happy to agree to Churchill's request. They decided to arrange a corps demonstration for the benefit of the British high command. Since Eichelberger had demonstrated a high degree of proficiency in the training of the 77th Division, Marshall, Eisenhower, and McNair selected him to command the corps demonstration. On 18 June 1942, Eichelberger was ordered to report to Washington; upon his arrival, he was informed by Marshall that he had been made commanding officer of I Corps stationed in Columbia, South Carolina (consisting of the 77th, 8th, and 30th Divisions). He was informed that he had four days to prepare a corps demonstration for the Prime Minister of England, Sir Winston Churchill.[37]

"I am not sure," Eichelberger stated, "that [General Marshall] realized what a task he was giving me." He was ordered to have a review and honor guard in the demonstration and to display a "firing problem with ball ammunition." He was also required to include a paratroop drop (with ground-to-air radio communication) with 600 troops, as well as a flanking maneuver with 65 tanks. Eichelberger stated, "This seemed like quite a job to me," particularly since a similar demonstration at Fort Benning "was the result of some months of work with the best troops in the United States."[38]

Nevertheless, Eichelberger was determined to make a fine show for his superiors, and he attempted to assure the success of the demonstration by leaving nothing to chance. His troops drilled nonstop prior to Churchill's arrival, and the roads in the camp were treated with chemicals to hold down the dust during the demonstration. An automobile dealer in Columbia was persuaded to loan the military a convertible coupe so that Churchill would be spared the spinal rigors of a jeep ride.[39]

These preparations paid dividends on 24 June 1942, the date of Churchill's visit. The demonstration went exceptionally well, considering the time allowed for preparation. Eichelberger stated that "the individual members gave a magnificent account of themselves," and that "Churchill saw recruits perform like veterans." Afterwards, he stated that "if we had [had] a month to prepare for this demonstration it could not have been better."[40]

Other observers noted some flaws in the exhibition. General McNair stated that there were too many casual spectators "at or near the post of the reviewing party." Another observer noted that "there were several bad injuries right in front of" Churchill during the parachute drop, and that the first words exchanged over the radio in air-to-ground communications were, "God damn it, I told you what to do!" Field Marshall Sir Alan Brook, Churchill's chief of staff, concluded that the demonstration was a "stirring show" but "ventured the opinion that it would be murder to pit them against continental soldiery."[41]

Eichelberger also received some embarrassing criticisms from his peers, who questioned his influence in gaining the I Corps command. Several colonels noted that Major General Charles Thompson, the former commander of the I Corps, was relieved from his post only one week before the demonstration, allegedly because "he was a bit old for high command in combat." Furthermore, Lieutenant General Ben Lear, the Second Army commander and Eichelberger's immediate superior, was "directed *not* to come to this demonstration" by the "top brass" in Washington. Several officers became suspicious when Generals Bill Marley and Mathew Russell, commanders of the 8th and 30th Divisions, were relieved from their posts shortly after the corps demonstration. Many officers concluded that Eichelberger had used his contacts in Washington to criticize the "unruly behavior" of the 8th and 30th Divisions, thereby causing the demotion of Marley and Russell.[42]

Despite these rumors, most of the higher-ranking officers were pleased with Eichelberger's advancement and were "very satisfied" with his performance in the corps demonstration. General McNair wrote Eichelberger that "You, your staff, and the troops involved have performed a distinct public service of which the Army and even the country should be proud." Churchill commented that the "grim determination which was everywhere manifest not only in the seasoned troops, but in the newly drafted, bodes ill for our enemies." General Marshall was also pleased, and stated that "the training shown by these new soldiers has lifted a weight off my shoulders equaled only by the winning of the recent battle in the Pacific (the Coral Sea)."[43]

These superb reviews of Eichelberger's performance led to greater responsibilities. In July 1942, he was selected by Marshall and McNair to command an amphibious corps for Operation Torch, the Allied invasion of North Africa. For this task, he was given command of the 3d, 9th, and 30th Divisions, and ordered to attend amphibious operations in Chesapeake Bay with Admiral Henry K. Hewitt.[44]

After three weeks of maneuvers, Eichelberger reported to Washington on 9 August for a final briefing on the African operation. Upon his arrival, he was informed that "a new crisis had arisen" and that his orders had been changed. In a meeting with the chief of operations, General Thomas T. Handy, Eichelberger was notified that he and his staff had been assigned to the Southwest Pacific command under General MacArthur, and that they were scheduled to depart for Australia in 10 days.[45]

Unknown to Eichelberger, this change of plans was caused by an unusual series of events. In July 1942, MacArthur suggested that "the time had probably come to form" an American corps in the Southwest Pacific; he requested that Marshall select an officer to command this new position. Marshall recommended Major General Robert C. Richardson, a senior officer who had handled War Department press relations. MacArthur agreed with Marshall's choice, and stated, "I would be delighted to have General Richardson." When Richardson learned of his new assignment, however, he balked at the suggestion that he serve under Australian General Thomas A. Blamey (MacArthur's Allied Land Forces commander), adding that "Blamey was not capable of handling" his present duties. Marshall replied that, under the circumstances, Richardson was not the proper man for the command. He informed MacArthur that "Richardson's intense feelings regarding service under Australian command made his assignment appear unwise."[46]

On 30 July 1942, Marshall informed MacArthur that "[General Oscar W.] Griswold or Eichelberger" were available as alternatives to Richardson. Marshall asked MacArthur to "please let me have your reaction [to these two men];" he added that "Griswold has had more experience in corps command," but "Eichelberger's work as a division commander was so impressive that he was made a corps commander." But MacArthur was never allowed to express a preference. On 3 August, Marshall notified MacArthur's headquarters that "I have selected Eichelberger to replace Richardson as your corps commander."[47]

Eichelberger was extremely unhappy with this new assignment, especially when he learned that Richardson had "talked himself out of" the corps command. He angrily noted that this refusal would have ruined the career of most officers, but because Richardson had the support of Secretary of War Henry Stimson, he was awarded the prestigious Hawaiian command after his row with Marshall. Eichelberger was also disappointed that he would be unable to participate in the North African landing. He admitted, "It was a very abrupt change when I found that I was to fly out to Australia to join MacArthur and in no sense a pleasing change." Eichelberger stated, "I saw General McNair and he said it was the hardest decision he had to make during the war and that he had spent most of Sunday trying to see if some other decision could have been made so that I could go to Africa."[48]

Besides his disappointment over the African landing, Eichelberger had some uneasy feelings about serving under MacArthur. One week before Eichelberger's departure, McNair warned him that MacArthur "had been sending his high ranking officers home." MacArthur had relieved his chief infantry officer, General Julian F. Barnes, and his leading air officer, General George H. Brett (MacArthur relieved Brett because "he [was] naturally inclined toward more or less harmless intrigue and has a bent . . . for social entertainment").[49] McNair cautioned Eichelberger "to try to get along with MacArthur," and General Marshall added that "one reason it was felt that [Eichelberger] would be suitable was that [he] had served with General MacArthur as Secretary, General Staff and for that reason [he] might be able to get along with him." Eichelberger had his doubts; "I knew General MacArthur well enough to realize that he was going to be difficult to get along with." These apprehensions were supported by General Craig, who warned his old friend that MacArthur was "selfish and at times vindictive."[50]

Nevertheless, on 20 August 1942, Eichelberger and his staff left for Australia in high spirits, aboard a converted B-24. "It was a long uncomfortable flight," Eichelberger noted, "and we would not have been happy if we had known what was ahead of us in Australia, and I don't mean the enemy alone." He later added, "And so I went to the slaughterhouse like a little white woolly lamb."[51]

NOTES

1. General George S. Simonds to Robert L. Eichelberger, 12 September 1936, Eichelberger Papers; General William D. Connor to Robert L. Eichelberger, 17 September 1936, Eichelberger Papers.
2. Eichelberger Dictations, "Notes for a Possible Historian," 27 January 1961, 6; Eichelberger Dictations, "Memories of Time and Men," 7 December 1954, 2.
3. Eichelberger Dictations, "RLE and AG Dept.," 31 July 1961, 2; Eichelberger Dictations, "Memorandum," 15 October 1953, 5.
4. Eichelberger Dictations, "Some Thoughts about General Marshall," 24 April 1961, 2; Eichelberger Dictations, "Notes for a Possible Historian," 27 January 1961, 7.
5. Eichelberger Dictations, "With the 30th Infantry," 31 July 1961, 1.
6. Ibid.
7. General George C. Marshall to Colonel Robert Eichelberger, 2 October 1940, box 66, George C. Marshall Papers, Lexington, Virginia; Eichelberger Dictations, "Some Memories of George Catlett Marshall," 25 November 1957, 4.
8. Eichelberger Dictations, "With the 30th Infantry," 31 July 1961, 1–2.
9. Eichelberger Dictations, "AGD and Later Service," 1 August 1960, 2; Eichelberger Dictations, "Memorandum (For Dr. Luvaas or any other person who may work on my papers)," 15 October 1956, 2.
10. Eichelberger Dictations, "Notes for a Possible Historian with Some Thoughts on my Career as it Developed," 27 January 1961, 8–9; C. S. Hodges to Robert Eichelberger, 16 August 1939, Eichelberger Papers; Walter E. Prosser to Robert Eichelberger, 21 August 1939, Eichelberger Papers.
11. Eichelberger, *Our Jungle Road to Tokyo*, xviii; Eichelberger Dictations, "With the 30th Infantry," 31 July 1961, 2.
12. Eichelberger Dictations, "How I Came To Be Selected Superintendent, USMA", 8 September 1961, 1; Eichelberger Dictations, "Notes for a Possible Historian," 27 January 1961, 9–10.
13. Eichelberger Dictations, "Memories of Time and Men," 7 December 1954, 3; Eichelberger Dictations, "Some Memories of George Catlett Marshall," 25 November 1967, 6.
14. Eichelberger Dictations, "Memories of Time and Men," 7 December 1954, 3; Eichelberger Dictations, "Some Memories of George Catlett Marshall," 25 November 1967, 6.
15. Eichelberger, *Our Jungle Road to Tokyo*, xviii.
16. Eichelberger Dictations, "Memories of Time and Men," 7 December 1954, 3–5.
17. Eichelberger Dictations, "Some Thoughts About General Marshall," 24 April 1961, 3; Eichelberger Dictations, "Some Memories of George Catlett Marshall," 25 November 1957, 6.
18. Henry "Hap" Arnold to Robert Eichelberger, 24 October 1941, and Robert Eichelberger to H. H. Arnold, 7 November 1941, General H. H. Arnold Papers, container #12, Library of Congress, Washington, D.C.
19. Eichelberger, *Our Jungle Road to Tokyo*, xx.
20. Ibid., xix.

PREPARATION FOR WARTIME COMMAND 55

21. Blaik asked Eichelberger what rank he would hold at West Point (if he accepted the position). Eichelberger told him to go to the army barber, and to pay special attention to the amount of time that the barber spent cutting his hair. (The barber was a good judge of rank and character, Eichelberger observed, and gave longer haircuts to men of higher rank, and to persons who were highly respected.) When Blaik returned with this information, Eichelberger responded that Blaik would hold the rank of colonel, for only the Superintendent received a "longer" haircut. Eichelberger Dictations, "With Thoughts of Colonel Earl "Red" Blaik," 20 July 1959, 1-7; Robert Eichelberger to Edwin Pope (included with this letter is a memorandum "With Reference to Colonel Earl Blaik and United States Military Academy Football"), 27 February 1954, 1-5, Eichelberger Papers.

22. Eichelberger Dictations, "With Thoughts of Colonel Earl "Red" Blaik," 20 July 1959, 1-7; Robert Eichelberger to Edwin Pope (included with this letter is a memorandum "With Reference to Colonel Earl Blaik and United States Military Academy Football"), 27 February 1954, 1-5, Eichelberger Papers; also Eichelberger, *Our Jungle Road to Tokyo*, xix-xx.

23. Edwin M. Watson to Colonel T. J. J. Christian, 17 October 1940, Edwin M. Watson Papers, Alderman Library, University of Virginia, Charlottesville.

24. Eichelberger Dictations, "With Thoughts of Colonel Earl "Red" Blaik," 20 July 1959, 4-5.

25. Eichelberger Dictations, "Data on Departure from West Point," 18 February 1948, 1; Eichelberger, *Our Jungle Road to Tokyo*, xxi; Eichelberger Dictations, "Some Memories of George Catlett Marshall," 25 November 1957, 7-8.

26. Eichelberger, *Our Jungle Road to Tokyo*, xxi; Eichelberger Dictations, "Notes For a Possible Historian With Some Thoughts on my Career as it Developed," 27 January 1961, 10; Eichelberger Dictations, "Some Memories of George Catlett Marshall," 25 November 1957, 7-8.

27. Robert Eichelberger to General George C. Marshall, 14 July 1941, George C. Marshall Papers, George C. Marshall Research Library, Lexington, Virginia.

28. Eichelberger Dictations, "AGD and Later Service," 1 August 1960, 4-5; Eichelberger Dictations, "Winston Churchill's Visit," no date, 1.

29. Lt. Col. Wentworth H. Moss to Robert Eichelberger, 15 January 1942, Eichelberger Papers.

30. Eichelberger Dictations, no title, 26 June 1959, 1.

31. Eichelberger, *Our Jungle Road to Tokyo*, xxiii; Eichelberger Dictations, "AGD and Later Service," 1 August 1960, 6.

32. Eichelberger Dictations, "77th Division and Churchill's Visit to Ft. Jackson," 23 November 1954, 1.

33. Eichelberger Dictations, "Winston Churchill's Visit," no date, 2; Eichelberger, *Our Jungle Road to Tokyo*, xxiii.

34. Lt. Col. Henry T. Blair to Major General Edwin Watson, 30 May 1942, Edwin M. Watson Papers, University of Virginia.

35. Eichelberger Dictations, "Winston Churchill's Visit," no date, 2; Eichelberger Dictations, "AGD and Later Service," 1 August 1960, 6; Eichelberger Dictations, "American Army Divisions: 77th and Others," 24 January 1958, 3.

36. General George C. Marshall to Robert Eichelberger, 29 June 1942, George C. Marshall Papers, George C. Marshall Research Library, Lexington, Virginia.

37. Eichelberger, *Our Jungle Road to Tokyo*, xxiii.
38. Eichelberger Dictations, "Memories of Time and Men," 7 December 1954, 7; Eichelberger Dictations, "77th Division and Churchill's Visit to Ft. Jackson," 23 November 1954, 4–5.
39. Eichelberger, *Our Jungle Road to Tokyo*, xxiv–xxv.
40. Ibid.; also Eichelberger Dictations, "Winston Churchill's Visit," no date, 3.
41. Luvaas, *Dear Miss Em*, 15; Lt. Gen. L. J. McNair to Robert Eichelberger, 25 June 1942, Eichelberger Papers; Eichelberger Dictations, "77th Division and Churchill's Visit to Ft. Jackson," 23 November 1954, 6; Eichelberger, *Our Jungle Road to Tokyo*, xxv.
42. Eichelberger Dictations, "AGD and Later Service," 1 August 1960, 6–7; Eichelberger Dictations, "Short Dictations on Various Subjects," 25 February 1957, 2; Eichelberger Dictations, "77th Division and Churchill's Visit to Ft. Jackson," 23 November 1954, 3.
43. Lt. Gen. L. J. McNair to Robert Eichelberger, 25 June 1942, Eichelberger Papers; Commendation to Commanding Generals, 8th, 30th, and 77th Divisions, 27 June 1942, Eichelberger Papers; Shortal, *Forged By Fire: Robert L. Eichelberger and the Pacific War*, 38, 40–50.
44. Eichelberger Dictations, "Winston Churchill's Visit," no date, 5.
45. Ibid.; Eichelberger, *Our Jungle Road to Tokyo*, xxvi.
46. General George C. Marshall to General Douglas MacArthur, 30 July 1942, War Department Correspondence, RG-4: USAFPAC, WD 132 and WD 143, Douglas MacArthur Memorial Archives, Norfolk, Virginia; Forrest C. Pogue, *George C. Marshall: Organizer of Victory* (New York: Viking Press, 1966), 116.
47. General George C. Marshall to General Douglas MacArthur, 30 July 1942, and 3 August 1942, War Department Correspondence, RG-4: USAFPAC, WD 132, WD 174, and WD 143, Douglas MacArthur Memorial Archives, Norfolk, Virginia; Forrest C. Pogue, *George C. Marshall: Organizer of Victory* (New York: Viking Press, 1966), 116.
48. Eichelberger Dictations, "Winston Churchill's Visit," no date, 5; Eichelberger Dictations, "Some Additional Thoughts on Men I Have Known," 10 August 1959, 5; Eichelberger Dictations, "AGD and Later Service," 1 August 1960, 9; Eichelberger Dictations, "Some Memories of George Catlett Marshall," 25 November 1957, 9.
49. General MacArthur to General George C. Marshall, 30 June 1942, War Department Correspondence, RG-4: USAFPAC, WD 132, Douglas MacArthur Memorial Archives, Norfolk, Virginia.
50. Eichelberger Dictations, "Some Thoughts About General Marshall," 24 April 1961, 4; Eichelberger Dictations, "Some Additional Thoughts on Men I Have Known," 10 August 1959, 5–6; Eichelberger Dictation, "George C. Marshall," no date, 9; Luvaas, *Dear Miss Em*, 15.
51. Eichelberger Dictations, "AGD and Later Service," 1 August 1960, 9; Eichelberger Dictations, "George C. Marshall," no date, 9.

6

BUNA—THE PYRRHIC VICTORY

On 25 August 1942, Eichelberger and his staff arrived in Brisbane, Australia. After a short briefing by MacArthur, Eichelberger learned that he would command I Corps, consisting of the 41st Division under Major General Horace Fuller, and the 32d Division, under Major General Forrest Harding. His units were assigned to the Australian 1st Army, under General Sir John Lavarak. His primary assignment was to train the two divisions for future operations in the Southwest Pacific.

Eichelberger had barely begun his training program when the 32d Division was ordered to New Guinea in September 1942. This unit remained under the command of General Harding, the division commander. Eichelberger was prohibited from accompanying the unit to New Guinea, except for a brief visit on 25 September. From October through November, his sole task was to prepare his remaining unit, the 41st Division, for future combat assignments against the Japanese. He attempted to accomplish this mission by "hardening" the men through continuous maneuvers, tightening their discipline, and emphasizing exercises in night attacks and jungle tactics. On 23 October, while the 41st Division was engaged in these training exercises, Eichelberger was awarded a third star; he attributed his promotion to the influence of his old mentor, General Malin Craig.[1]

From his headquarters in Rockhampton, Australia, Eichelberger closely monitored his own troops and the fighting in New Guinea. Anxious to see action and to abandon his "training role," he watched with interest the activities of the 32d Division and its commander, General Harding. From discussions with other officers in Australia, Eichelberger learned that the 32d Division was to be part of a joint American-Australian effort to dislodge the Japanese from Buna, a small government outpost on the northeast coast of Papua, New Guinea. Since Buna was only 120 miles from the Allied base at Port Moresby, its occupation would be essential if the Allies were to retain their toehold in New Guinea and prevent an invasion of the Australian mainland.[2]

In October 1942, Eichelberger and Harding exchanged correspondence concerning the 32d Division's role in the Buna campaign. "I am confident," Harding wrote, "that we can take Buna . . . without too much difficulty." Eichelberger replied, "You are doing a grand job, going places and doing things." In November 1942, however, Eichelberger heard rumors that the 32d Division was having difficulties in the fighting around Papua. He was not surprised when he was hurriedly summoned to MacArthur's headquarters on the evening of 29 November 1942.[3]

On 30 November Eichelberger arrived with members of his staff at Port Moresby, New Guinea. He immediately proceeded to MacArthur's headquarters. He was briefed by MacArthur in the presence of General Richard Sutherland, MacArthur's chief of staff, and General George Kenney, commander of the Army Air Forces in New Guinea. MacArthur was visibly upset, and he paced the floor as he outlined the situation at Buna. MacArthur emphasized that the officers and men of the 32d Division had failed miserably. He was humiliated by reports that the men were dropping their weapons and running from the enemy. The officers were not performing their jobs, and much of the blame could be found in the ineffective leadership of General Harding. The troops were sick and were inadequately trained for jungle warfare; the climate was wearing them out. "A real leader," MacArthur suggested, "could take these same men and capture Buna."[4]

MacArthur instructed Eichelberger to relieve Harding, and all other officers "who won't fight." Take "personal command" at Buna, he ordered, and "put sergeants in charge of battalions and corporals in charge of companies—anyone who will fight." He added, "Time is of the essence," for the Japanese were expecting reinforcements within the next week. At the conclusion of the briefing, MacArthur looked at Eichelberger and stated, "I want you to take Buna, or not come back alive."[5]

The next morning at breakfast, MacArthur's mood softened considerably. Eichelberger reminded him of their pleasant service together in Washington (when Eichelberger was secretary to the General Staff); both men laughed as they exchanged jokes about their service. Afterwards, MacArthur put his arm around Eichelberger and said, "Now, Bob, I have no illusions about your personal courage, but remember that you are no use to me dead." Taking him aside, MacArthur promised him the Distinguished Service Cross and prominent press coverage if he succeeded in his assignment.[6]

On this more promising note, Eichelberger and his staff left for Buna on 1 December 1942. Arriving by plane that same afternoon, he quickly conferred with the leading infantry commanders and made a quick study of the situation. He informed General Harding, "I have been ordered to relieve you but get behind me and I'll see if I can't hold you here." Eichelberger's first impression was that Harding was doing a reasonably fine job under very difficult conditions. "There is no lack of fight," he stated, "in anybody I have seen out there." Eichelberger was impressed by the difficulty of the terrain, and he sympathized with Harding's problems in overcoming the natural strength of the Japanese defensive positions. He described the enemy positions as follows:

> The Jap utilization of terrain was admirable. At their back was the sea. Their left flank also rested on the ocean while on their right were two unfordable streams—the Girua River and tidal Entrance Creek. Almost the entire Japanese position was in a coconut plantation in which they had built up a series of concealed bunkers and connecting trenches. . . . In front of the enemy were the morasses where Michigan and Wisconsin boys hunched themselves above water on extruded tree roots to eat their rations. Since American advances from the morasses could only be made on a few known trails or tracks, it was simple enough for Japanese machine guns to cover them with fields of fire.[7]

On 2 December 1942, Eichelberger and Harding made a personal inspection of the American infantry units in the Buna area. This inspection shocked Eichelberger, and destroyed the rosy impression that Harding had created the previous day. Eichelberger discovered that the men were exhausted, hungry, and depressed. Many had eaten little or nothing for the last several days. The men refused to salute, called their officers by their first names, and had long beards and torn uniforms. Most of the units were badly scrambled. The rear areas were full of stragglers and skulkers who were avoiding combat. In Eichelberger's opinion, most of the troops looked like they had given up, and were either "feeling sorry for themselves" or were resting in the rear.[8]

The troops in the forward outposts were in the most deplorable state. The men were sloppy and lazy; they neglected to dig foxholes or provide cover for their machine guns. Since the Japanese rarely fired their guns, unless attacked or fired upon, many of the men refused to shoot at the Japanese bunkers and snipers. Orders to attack the enemy positions were either ignored or performed in a half-hearted fashion. The American dead were left rotting on the battlefield. The units made no attempt to determine the exact location of the enemy bunkers and snipers. The men were reluctant to engage in patrolling beyond their own perimeter. Eichelberger offered a medal to any soldier who would advance 50 yards down a jungle trail; he received no response except incredulous looks.[9]

Outraged by these conditions, Eichelberger expressed his feelings to General Harding, and added that the division command post was too far from the front lines. His angry outburst was cut short by Harding and Colonel John Mott, one of Harding's regimental commanders; they retorted that Eichelberger was making hasty judgments based upon misleading evidence. Harding argued that the troops had indeed fought well, but were now worn out after a month of continuous combat. As for Eichelberger's observations, Harding stated that the valor of the men had been proven by the large number of casualties and the numerous decorations awarded posthumously for bravery. It was impossible to dig-in, Mott argued, because of the high water table in the area. Most of the so-called "skulkers" were either sick men or engineers working in the rear. The men had attacked bravely for several weeks, despite enormous numbers of casualties. The troops were naturally reluctant, Mott added, to advance along a trail just "for a piece of ribbon," when "they knew definitely that enemy machine guns were posted up the track [and] their company commander lay . . . forward in the bushes dead."[10]

Eichelberger was not in the mood for excuses, and he relieved Mott and Harding after they twice lost their tempers in an argument concerning the positioning of troops on the left flank. Eichelberger informed Harding that MacArthur had demanded his immediate relief. He admitted afterwards that he would "have retained [Harding] at any risk provided he would put his shoulder behind me instead of feeling sorry about John Mott whose dispositions on the left flank were miserable ones." Harding's loss of temper was the deciding factor. "When I was trying to correct Colonel Mott . . .," Eichelberger stated, "General Harding should have kept silent and then when we were alone expressed his opinions." Eichelberger added, "I had a job to do and while I am a reasonable man, I would not allow subordinates to run it over me."[11]

After Harding was relieved, Eichelberger on 3–4 December 1942 reorganized the front and correcting the mistakes of his predecessor. He personally assumed authority over the Buna area and replaced a majority of the battalion and regimental commanders. Members of his staff were sent to the front to serve as troop commanders, advisors, and intelligence officers. The chain of command was strengthened at every level. The units were "unscrambled" and assigned a segment of the front to patrol.

The troops were given an opportunity to supplement their diet and gain a well-deserved rest. Eichelberger felt that an occasional bath and a hot meal were great morale builders; he encouraged each officer to provide additional rations for his men and to maintain cleanliness and neatness in the units. At the same time, the troops were required to salute properly, to be clean-shaven, and to address their superiors in the proper fashion. The soldiers in each unit were given a pep talk. They were encouraged to "stop feeling sorry for themselves" and to abandon the hope of being relieved by other units.[12]

These morale builders were completed on the evening of 4 December 1942. On 5 December, two regiments attacked both flanks of the Japanese positions at Buna. This frontal assault was met by a hail of enemy fire. The attacks on both fronts failed after creating a large number of casualties. Eichelberger was shaken by this failure. His aide and General Albert Waldron, the acting division commander, were shot during the attack. In a letter to his wife, Eichelberger understated his disappointment when he wrote, "I tried to do so much and while I know I accomplished some things I didn't do all I had hoped for."[13]

BUNA—THE PYRRHIC VICTORY

From 6 December to 12 December, Eichelberger changed his tactics and licked his wounds from the abortive attack of 5 December. Convinced that massed frontal attacks were futile, he encouraged his troop commanders to infiltrate the enemy positions and pinpoint the exact location of the enemy bunkers. After the bunkers were located, artillery fire was massed on the positions, followed by immediate small-unit assaults against the enemy fortifications. In this fashion, Eichelberger continued the offensive with small probing actions along the entire front, supplemented by constant patrolling and night attacks.

In addition to this change of tactics, Eichelberger improved the division's logistics. He eliminated the confusion at the supply bases, increased the number of daily flights into the battle area, and doubled the stockpile of ammunition and food at the front lines. He requested flamethrowers, tanks, and heavy artillery. And he requested and received reinforcements, including a regiment of American infantry and a brigade of Australian troops.[14]

Despite these improvements, the 32d Division failed to dent the enemy lines during the second week of December. Meanwhile, the messages from headquarters indicated that MacArthur was exceedingly unhappy with the Buna operation and was disappointed at the lack of success under Eichelberger's leadership. To offset MacArthur's impatience, Eichelberger sent optimistic reports to headquarters, stating that the men were "learning a lot" and were becoming energized. MacArthur soon grew tired of these "moral victories."[15] On 13 December 1942, he sent Eichelberger the following message:

> Time is fleeting and our dangers increase with its passage. However admirable individual acts of courage may be; however splendid and electrical your presence has proven, remember that your mission is to take Buna. All other things are merely subsidiary to this. No alchemy is going to produce this for you; it can only be done in battle and sooner or later this battle must be engaged. Hasten your preparations and when you are ready—strike, for as I have said, time is working desperately against us.[16]

MacArthur's exhortations caused Eichelberger to renew his attacks. On 14 December, the 32d Division captured Buna Village, a small enemy outpost on the extreme left flank of the American lines. Delighted by this small but important success, Eichelberger commended his men for their initial victory. MacArthur was also encouraged; he sent Bob a note of congratulations. "Under your magnificent leadership," MacArthur stated, "the 32nd Division is coming into its own."[17]

From 15 December to 18 December, Eichelberger attempted to exploit his initial success by making small penetrating attacks along both fronts. On the left flank (known as the Urbana Front), he was successful on December 17th in overrunning the Grove, an enemy strongpoint consisting of interconnected bunkers. On the right flank (the Warren Front), his troops achieved a more decisive victory. On 18 December, a combined tank-infantry assault by Australian troops (an Australian brigade attached to Eichelberger's command) smashed through 150 Japanese bunkers and drove to the ocean near Cape Endaiadere. The attacking units suffered casualties of over fifty percent. The assault broke the Japanese resistance on the Warren Front, and earned the Australians a well-deserved reputation for bravery and heroism. "All our officers . . . are high in their praise of the valor of the Australians," Eichelberger stated, for "there have not been very many instances in this war of anybody pushing Japanese out of entrenched positions."[18]

From 19 December to 29 December, Eichelberger attempted to duplicate the Australian success by making repeated attacks on the Urbana Front. These attacks were blunted by enemy strongpoints in the Triangle area and at the Government Gardens. Protected by swamps on both flanks, these positions consisted of a system of supporting reinforced bunkers that dominated the avenues of attack. The infantry of the 32d Division repeatedly bogged down in successive attacks. On 27 December, Eichelberger reported that his troops "will not and could not advance" against the enemy strongpoints.[19]

The 32d Division's lack of success was noted by the Australian observers; they felt the American attacks paled in comparison to the heroic efforts of the Australians on the Warren Front. They reported to MacArthur that the American troops were inferior to the Australians, lacked bravery and fortitude, and were incapable of defeating the Japanese on the Urbana Front (despite a seven-to-one superiority in numbers). These reports infuriated and humiliated MacArthur. He considered the American soldier to be the best fighter in the world. Convinced that the 32d Division's failures were the results of errors of command, MacArthur sent the following sharply worded message to Eichelberger:

> One word of advice on your fighting: it is being done with gallantry, but with much too little concentration of force on your front. Your problem is to apply your full power on our front line rather than limit it to two or three companies. Where you have a company on your firing line, you should have a battalion; and where you have a battalion, you should have a regiment. And your attacks, instead of being made by two or three hundred rifles, should be made by two or three thousand. Your problem is to find ways and means of getting two or three thousand in the front line so their fire power can beat the enemy down. It has reached a stage now where attrition will have to apply. It will be an eye for an eye and a tooth for a tooth—and a casualty on your side for a casualty on his. Every additional day you give him to dig in is going to cost you just that many more men to dig him out. Get everything you can on the line; hit with its fire power and keep on hitting. The sooner you do it, the fewer casualties you will have and the less danger of

some great counter stroke from the outside by him which is my constant anxiety. You have probably eight or nine times the strength of the enemy. Use it in unison and you will be surprised how soon victory will be yours. Your battle casualties to date compared with your total strength are slight so that you have a big margin still to work with. I beg of you to throw every ounce of energy you have into carrying out this word of advice from me, as I feel convinced that our time is strictly limited and that if results are not achieved shortly, the whole picture may radically change.[20]

The difficulty of the terrain made it impossible, as MacArthur instructed, to mass any large force in a particular area. MacArthur's message did, however, motivate Eichelberger to renew his attacks with increased vigor. On 29 December, elements of the 32d Division broke through the Japanese lines on the Urbana Front and drove to the sea. On 30 and 31 December, the American forces engaged in furious fighting against isolated pockets of enemy resistance. On 2 January, the last of the Japanese strongpoints fell. The following day, Eichelberger congratulated his men for their "hard-fought campaign." On 8 January, MacArthur sent his congratulations to the 32d Division. He said to Bob that "I am so glad that you were not injured in the fighting."[21]

Unfortunately for Eichelberger, his duties were not yet completed. On 12 January 1943, he was placed in command of the joint American-Australian effort to capture Sanananda, a small Japanese outpost 10 miles to the northwest of Buna. This was discouraging news. Eichelberger had lost 20 pounds during the Buna campaign; he was exhausted after a month of continuous exertion. Aware that the Australians had failed to capture Sanananda after six weeks of hard fighting, he felt that the Japanese defenses in the area were comparable to the Buna fortifications. Although Sanananda was reportedly a rest station for sick and wounded Japanese, reports from the front indicated that the Japanese were "far from licked" and were capable of resisting Allied attacks indefinitely. The Sanananda operation had the potential to be just as difficult and costly as the Buna campaign.

On 13 January 1943, Eichelberger met with his Australian infantry commanders. They confirmed that the outlook for a speedy victory was pessimistic. Arguing against a direct attack, they recommended that Eichelberger "surround the area and hammer it to pieces as well as starve the Japanese out." Eichelberger agreed. He sent out patrols "to find out exactly where the Japanese were, how they were getting their supplies, and whether we could find any high ground on which to put bunkers."[22]

These patrols revealed that the Japanese were retreating "with full packs" and were beginning a naval evacuation of their able-bodied troops. Eichelberger immediately ordered a two-pronged attack. The Australian forces harassed the enemy's front, while the Americans attacked the Japanese left flank from the direction of Buna. This offensive successfully split the enemy defenses, and isolated the remaining pockets of Japanese resistance. By 22 January, the last vestiges of enemy resistance were eliminated. On 24 January, general headquarters (GHQ) declared that the campaign was officially concluded.

Upon completion of the Papuan operation, Eichelberger was ordered back to Rockhampton (ostensibly for the purpose of directing the training of the 24th Division). Before his departure, he made a brief visit to Australian headquarters in Port Moresby, where he was hailed as a "hero" at a press conference. After receiving numerous accolades from the Australian press (including the title of "savior" of the "American reputation" in New Guinea), Eichelberger returned to his headquarters in Rockhampton, where he resumed the training of American infantry units.[23]

Historians have not fully analyzed the Buna and Sanananda campaigns. Many historians have ignored these operations completely. Peter Calvocoressi's 960-page volume *Total War: The Story of World War II* makes no mention of Buna or Sanananda. The most recent histories, such as John Keegan's *The Second World War* (1989) and Martin Gilbert's *The Second World War: A Complete History* (1989), describe the Buna campaign in less than a paragraph. These books make no attempt to analyze the operation, but merely state that the Buna campaign was one of the initial victories in the Allied drive across New Guinea.[24]

The most complete descriptions of these events are included in Samuel Milner's *Victory in Papua* and in Lida Mayo's *Bloody Buna*. These authors agree that the Buna campaign was fought under appalling conditions. Disease, starvation, and the rainy climate took a horrible toll on both sides. Buna was a "victory" for the Allies, but a tainted one. The American troops were ill-trained and were pushed haphazardly against strong enemy positions. Many of the casualties (totaling over 8,500) were unnecessary. Buna and Sanananda were important for several reasons. These campaigns, along with Guadalcanal, ended the advance of the Japanese armies, and took the initiative away from the enemy. They also convinced MacArthur that head-on attacks were too costly; he subsequently developed his successful island-hopping strategy.[25]

Neither Milner nor Mayo makes a complete evaluation of Eichelberger's contributions. They note that many mistakes were made in the campaign. Most of these mistakes were caused by MacArthur, who was anxious to gain a speedy victory at any cost. Both Eichelberger and Harding were pressured by MacArthur to make direct attacks against formidable enemy fortifications. Neither had adequate supplies, weapons, or troops. Harding and Eichelberger rushed unprepared soldiers into combat, continued costly frontal attacks, and demonstrated a shocking disregard for the welfare of their troops. Under the circumstances, these mistakes can be excused, for MacArthur continuously pressured them for immediate results.[26]

Eichelberger had his own opinions about these events. From his corps headquarters in Rockhampton, Australia, he reflected on his role in the Buna-Sanananda operation. In retrospect, he described this campaign as a nightmare and a "terrible fight—the worst in the Pacific War." His most vivid memories were not of the actual combat, but of the "clash of personalities" arising from the campaign. Complaining that conflicts with his follow officers were "more bothersome than the enemy," he stated that "the battle of personalities growing out of Buna was almost as important as the actual fighting."[27]

In particular, Eichelberger was troubled by personal differences with General Forrest Harding, the commander of the 32d Division. Harding and Eichelberger were West Point classmates. Prior to Buna, they were close and intimate friends. They respected each other's abilities, and were delighted by the prospect of serving together in Australia and New Guinea. From September to October 1942, Eichelberger complimented Harding for his handling of the 32d Division. He gave Harding favorable marks for his diligence in the training of this unit in Australia.[28]

However, this amicable relationship suffered its first setback on 25 September 1942, when Eichelberger and his staff made a surprise inspection of the 32d Division in New Guinea. Harding reported that Eichelberger and his staff were critical and arrogant, and demonstrated a lack of respect for the division's officers. Giving the impression that he was "looking for something to command," Eichelberger kept Harding's aides "up all hours going over the situation." Harding was willing to overlook this experience; he informed his wife that, for the moment, he was completely satisfied with his "immediate boss."[29]

Relations between the two men remained cordial throughout the early stages of the Papuan campaign, but took an abrupt turn for the worse when Eichelberger arrived at Buna on 1 December 1942. In Harding's opinion, Eichelberger arrived in a critical mood; he was unappreciative "of what the men had been through or of the spirit shown by most of them." Harding was offended by Eichelberger's harsh criticisms of the 32d Division. He felt these complaints demonstrated an "ignorance of jungle warfare and conditions at the front." Harding also objected to Eichelberger's decision to replace Mott and the regimental commanders. His own dismissal, he believed, was caused by Eichelberger's vanity and pigheadedness. Arguing that Bob was personally responsible for his dismissal, Harding rejected Eichelberger's claim that MacArthur gave him no choice in the decision. "No officer," he retorted, would "have held MacArthur's order in abeyance for 36 hours while he conducted an investigation to determine whether or not it should be executed!"[30]

Events after Buna strengthened Harding's conviction that he had been mistreated. After his removal, he visited MacArthur's headquarters in Port Moresby. He bluntly requested the reasons for his dismissal. MacArthur responded, "I haven't the slightest idea" of the reasons, and added that he would recommend Harding for a combat division in another theater (MacArthur subsequently ordered

Eichelberger to prepare a memorandum for the War Department on the subject of Harding's relief). MacArthur rejected Harding's request for a return to the 32d Division. Arguing that "spiteful Bob Eichelberger" would "get you for something else," MacArthur suggested that Harding "go to Australia, get rested, and then come back, and he would be given a job."[31]

With MacArthur's approval, Harding received the command of a division in Panama. Afterwards, he was sent to Washington, where he served in the Historical Section of the War Department. Ironically, one of Harding's first assignments was to review an official history of the Papuan campaign that had been prepared by Eichelberger and his aides. This job provided Harding an ideal forum to renew his personal grievances and explain his "failure" at Buna.[32]

In this endeavor, Harding was assisted by E. J. Kahn, a former staff member of the 32d Division. With Harding's approval, Kahn wrote an article for the *Saturday Evening Post* entitled the "Terrible Days of Company E." This article described the hardships of an infantry unit at Buna, including the lack of food, the unhealthy climate, and the superiority of the enemy's positions. The article criticized an "anonymous general," who contributed to the men's misery by ordering infantry charges against enemy bunkers. This same general reportedly passed out vitamins instead of food to the starving soldiers, and scampered to the rear at the first sound of enemy mortars.[33]

Besides giving this thinly veiled criticism of Eichelberger, Kahn and Harding talked to other officers and writers who were interested in the Buna operation. Harding explained his version of events to Samuel Milner, a historian preparing a study of the Papuan campaign. His troops had performed admirably at Buna, Harding argued, but the strength of the Japanese positions made victory impossible without additional infantrymen, armor, and artillery. Prior to Eichelberger's arrival, the 32d Division had been denied any reinforcements; after the change of command, tanks and two battalions of men were flown into Buna. Even then, Harding insisted, Eichelberger achieved victory only at a tremendous cost. His frontal attacks and unimaginative tactics antagonized the troops and increased the "slaughter" of depleted units. The majority of the 32d Division's casualties occurred after Eichelberger took command. As the casualties mounted, the enlisted men nicknamed their commander "Bobby the Butcher" and threatened to shoot him in the back. Eichelberger's heavy-handed methods, Harding concluded, succeeded only in filling the American cemetery outside Buna, a place the enlisted men sarcastically referred to as "Eichelberger Square."[34]

There is some truth to Harding's allegations. Although Harding was unsuccessful in his attacks, both Milner and Mayo (in *Victory in Papua* and *Bloody Buna*, respectively) agree that Harding was less willing than Eichelberger to sacrifice his troops in head-on assaults. Furthermore, Milner and Mayo believe that Harding was treated unfairly at Buna. Mayo states that Harding was relieved "just when conditions were beginning to improve." Mayo argues that, had Harding remained in command, he would have captured Buna in the same time period as

Eichelberger had, with perhaps fewer casualties (provided he received the same amount of reinforcements and armor).

Mayo also states that Eichelberger seemed to "take pleasure" in pushing his troops forward. On at least one occasion, he ordered an unplanned attack, allegedly for the purpose of impressing MacArthur's advisors. When the attacks failed, Eichelberger threw tantrums and screamed at his subordinates. The Mayo book draws a negative portrait of Eichelberger's leadership, and suggests that Harding's accusations may be partially true.[35]

Eichelberger was fully aware of Harding's criticisms, although there was little he could do to refute the charges from his headquarters in Australia. He did have a member of his staff write to Brigadier General Philip E. Brown, of the Inspector General's Department, asking Brown to "tighten up" censorship on Kahn and requesting that members of Harding's staff be forbidden from publishing articles "containing derogatory remarks about other general officers." Eichelberger repeatedly denied that there was any substance to any of Harding's charges. He wrote to his friends in the United States, including George C. Marshall, to soften the effect of Harding's complaints. "Harding is a fine chap," Eichelberger commented, "but the man who gave him a combat command should have his head examined."[36]

Harding was not the only object of Eichelberger's disfavor. He had equally strong feelings toward General Richard Sutherland, MacArthur's chief of staff. Sutherland, in Eichelberger's opinion, had an unusually strong relationship with MacArthur, and used this relationship to eliminate any potential rivals for his privileged position. Eichelberger received a warning to this effect in August 1942; Sutherland informed him that he had personally "rid" MacArthur's staff of Dwight D. Eisenhower (Eisenhower was MacArthur's aide in the Philippines before the war).

From the moment of his arrival in Australia, Eichelberger believed that Sutherland was determined to minimize his rank and responsibilities. Sutherland was allegedly responsible for preventing him from accompanying the 32d Division to New Guinea in September 1942. In October 1942, MacArthur's chief of staff attempted to prevent Eichelberger from becoming a Lieutenant General by "doctoring" the promotion recommendation. After his promotion, Sutherland reportedly became antagonistic and jealous, and sought to gain vengeance against Eichelberger by taking over command of his I Corps.[37]

The final break occurred on 14 November 1942. On that date, Eichelberger flew to Port Moresby with several members of his staff. He intended to "hitch" a ride over the mountains to observe the fighting at Buna. While at the airfield, he was told by Brigadier General Ennis Whitehead that Sutherland had threatened to "run him out" of New Guinea. Puzzled and confused, he immediately returned to MacArthur's headquarters; at GHQ, Sutherland informed him that he was to return to Australia and pick out a camp site for the incoming 25th Division. Eichelberger asked if he could leave the next day in a bomber, but was refused.

Sutherland informed him that he was to return that night in a two-engined courier plane.[38]

This was a shocking order. The weather broadcast called for a violent storm. Only two weeks earlier, Eichelberger noted, Sutherland had told him that "he would never cross the Coral Sea in anything but a four-engine" plane. These precautions were justified. The flight back to Australia was made in a terrible storm. After a passenger suffered a heart attack, the plane made an emergency landing at Rockhampton. Eichelberger gladly disembarked. Before he left, the pilot informed him that his orders were to leave his "distinguished passenger" in Brisbane, over 300 miles from I Corps headquarters.

Interpreting these actions as a deliberate slight, Eichelberger concluded that Sutherland "was having fun tearing the wings off a fly." "No man treats a man of any pride the way Sutherland treated me," Eichelberger stated, "without arousing a bitterness akin to hatred." He added, "Certainly a man of Sutherland's ability and knowledge would realize that to the day of death I would despise him."[39]

The events at Buna only intensified his bitterness. Eichelberger felt that Sutherland deliberately hampered his efforts to reorganize the 32d Division. Sutherland insisted that the division "follow the rule book" in transferring or "busting" officers, although he was fully aware that Eichelberger had extraordinary authority to make changes in command. He attempted to reduce the size of the I Corps staff. He limited Eichelberger's authority to decorate his own troops. Sutherland stated that the powerful enemy defenses at the Triangle were only hasty field fortifications; he criticized the 32d Division for failing to destroy them with artillery. Despite these criticisms, he refused to serve as a troop leader, although he was offered the opportunity to command the Urbana Front on 23 December 1942. The following day, he fled over the mountains to the comforts of Port Moresby after spending only one afternoon at the front.[40]

From these experiences, Eichelberger concluded that Sutherland was intelligent and able, but mean, vindictive, and unscrupulous. He unequivocally stated that Sutherland was "far, far from being my friend," but noted that Sutherland's enormous influence with MacArthur made him a dangerous adversary. After Buna, Eichelberger made a special effort to "watch his rear." He felt he would receive no aid or sympathy from MacArthur's headquarters staff.[41]

It is difficult to determine if Eichelberger's feelings had any basis in fact. There is no adequate biography of Richard Sutherland. Historians have placed him in MacArthur's shadow, and have failed to adequately discuss his role in the Southwest Pacific. There is little evidence concerning his relations with Eichelberger. Sutherland was undoubtedly a tough chief of staff; some officers, such as General George Kenney, felt that he was egotistical and hard to get along with. Eichelberger clearly disliked him, and blamed him for many of the difficulties of the Buna campaign.[42]

Despite his problems with Sutherland, Eichelberger reserved his greatest ire for his commander-in-chief, Douglas MacArthur. In Eichelberger's opinion,

BUNA—THE PYRRHIC VICTORY

MacArthur was misinformed about the hardships and difficulties of the Buna operation; he consequently failed to appreciate the 32d Division's enormous efforts on the battlefield. Faulty intelligence reports were partly responsible for MacArthur's "misconceptions," for these reports underestimated enemy numbers by 50% and grossly miscalculated the strength of the Japanese defenses. MacArthur's failure to visit Buna, either before or after the battle, contributed to his "ignorance" of conditions at the front.

For example, Eichelberger felt that MacArthur's orders during the Buna operation proved that "the Big Chief put his head in the clouds and knew little of details." On 25 December 1942, MacArthur ordered the 32d Division to launch mass attacks against the enemy bunkers, ignoring the fact that the nature of the jungle terrain made it impossible to mass more than a company of troops at any one position. MacArthur ordered the American command to bypass the Australians and to report directly to Port Moresby; Eichelberger deliberately ignored this order since his air support and supplies were controlled by the Australians. Believing that the Americans outnumbered the Japanese by an eight-to-one margin, MacArthur encouraged attrition tactics at Buna. This ratio was misleading, for this figure included engineers, supply troops, air support groups, and other rear elements that could not be used in combat. Eichelberger claimed that, contrary to MacArthur's figures, he was "actually attacking Buna with fewer troops than the Japanese."[43]

These misconceptions, in Eichelberger's opinion, were partly responsible for MacArthur's rude behavior after Buna. For six days after the operation, Eichelberger received no thanks from his commander in chief. (On 6 January 1943, Eichelberger remarked that "a good many days have passed and as yet I have not received a 'thank you dog.'") When MacArthur finally did respond on 8 January 1943, he merely informed Bob that he deserved a "hearty slap on the back." "I always feared," MacArthur added, "that your incessant exposure [to the enemy] might result fatally." (Eichelberger later commented that these words "didn't ring true to me in view of the fact that he told me to capture Buna or not come out alive.")[44]

In addition, MacArthur failed to adequately reward Eichelberger for his services at Buna. Although MacArthur did recommend him for a Distinguished Service Cross, five other officers who had not served at the front (including Sutherland) received the same award. The citations did not differentiate between "marked efficiency" and "conduct under fire." Eichelberger complained that his citation was "worded exactly like the others."[45]

Eichelberger also complained that MacArthur's press releases and communiqués minimized his role in the Papuan campaign. For example, MacArthur announced to the press, on 25 December 1942, that "our activities were limited to routine safety precautions." On 8 January 1943, a GHQ communiqué declared that the "Papuan campaign is in its final closing phase," and "can now be regarded as accomplished" except for "mopping up." Finally, at the close of all hostilities in Papua on 28 January 1943, MacArthur stated that "our losses . . . are low" because "the time element in this case was of little importance" and "there was no necessity to hurry the attack."[46]

These communiqués, in Eichelberger's opinion, "were the worst [thing] that happened to me in six long years in the Pacific." Contrary to MacArthur's announcement of 25 December 1942, the 32d Division was engaged in "desperate" fighting along the Buna front. As for the GHQ communiqué of 8 January 1943, this was an excuse since at that time there was no indication of any progress at Sanananda. MacArthur's use of the term "mopping up" was unfair; the newspapers were reluctant to cover a campaign that had already been declared finished. Eichelberger was angry that he received little credit for the fighting at Sanananda. "Nobody commands a 'Mopping Up,'" he noted, "there just ain't no such animal!"[47]

The communiqué of 28 January 1943 was the most upsetting. "One can understand my feelings," Eichelberger stated, "when I look back on how I pushed the attacks on Buna even to the extent that I was supposed to lose my life and then find 'the losses were small because there was no hurry.'" Contrary to MacArthur's communiqué, the attacks were rushed and uncoordinated. Eichelberger noted that "the losses were heavy and to some extent because General MacArthur continuously urged me towards aggressive action." (Samuel Milner, the official historian of the Buna campaign, states that losses were indeed "high," and estimates that American and Australian casualties in the Papuan campaign totaled over 3,000 killed and 5,400 wounded).[48]

Besides the communiqués, Eichelberger was troubled by some of MacArthur's "press policies." While in Australia, he was instructed to avoid all reporters and to clear press matters with GHQ. Sutherland informed him that "there is one thing that General MacArthur handles himself, and that is publicity."[49]

In the months before the Buna operation, Eichelberger discovered that MacArthur had used his control over the press to keep him "off the record." Reporters were forbidden to announce Eichelberger's presence in Australia. "I had seen in the *Army-Navy Journal*," Eichelberger remarked, "the assignment of all Lt. Generals with only a blank after my name." Puzzled and angry, he considered confronting MacArthur but decided to "let it rest" after consulting his friends in the United States. (In 1939, Dwight D. Eisenhower warned Eichelberger that he had been sent home from the Philippines after MacArthur accused him of "stealing his publicity because some writer had written an article praising him.")[50]

After the completion of the Buna campaign, MacArthur finally released Eichelberger's name to the press. Reporters flocked to interview this "unknown hero." *Life* magazine and *The Saturday Evening Post* ran feature articles on "Uncle Bob," and numerous local newspapers in the United States wrote glowing stories about the "historic" victory at Buna.[51]

In these articles, Eichelberger was depicted as a heroic, swashbuckling figure who was "one of the finest American officers yet to wage battle against the Japs." One correspondent described him as follows: "With a tommy-gun in one hand . . . and an optimistic smile always present on his friendly, understanding visage, he . . . spent night after night with the enlisted men in their foxholes and himself led a number of charges against Japanese positions." Another correspondent wrote that "General Bob" was the "guiding light" of the Buna campaign. The *Philadelphia Inquirer* reported that "when the story of the New Guinea campaign can be told, a tall lantern-jawed, badger-thatched United States Army officer by the name of Lieutenant General Robert L. Eichelberger will figure in it very prominently."[52]

MacArthur (as might be expected from his experience with Eisenhower) was less than thrilled with this new wave of publicity. In February 1943, Eichelberger was summoned to MacArthur's headquarters in Brisbane, where MacArthur abruptly informed him, "Do you realize I could reduce you to the grade of colonel tomorrow and send you home?" Eichelberger stated that "I knew exactly what he was talking about and my answer was 'Of course you could.'" MacArthur replied, "Well, I won't do it." MacArthur's message was explicit. Eichelberger left Brisbane with the impression that even a small amount of publicity in his favor would be perceived by his chief as a personal insult.[53]

In the weeks following this meeting, Eichelberger attempted to discover a plausible explanation for MacArthur's reluctance to publicize his subordinates. After long deliberation, he concluded that MacArthur "had to win the war every morning in his communiqués." Only sustained victories with minimal casualties, under a "central charismatic figure," would catch the public's attention. Eichelberger believed that MacArthur used this "public relations ploy" to force President Roosevelt and the Chief of Staff to divert more resources to the Southwest Pacific. The Pacific command was currently starved for troops and supplies under the President's "Europe First" policy. Eichelberger explained that "MacArthur always had the feeling that practically everyone was in opposition to him and . . . the fact that he was at the end of a supply line gave him some basis for this feeling."[54]

More importantly, Eichelberger believed that sheer vanity was the predominant reason for MacArthur's attempt to conceal his subordinates. "The only possible reason for this attitude," Eichelberger stated, "was to insure that he himself [MacArthur] would receive all the credit for anything successful in the Southwest Pacific." MacArthur didn't "intend to have any figures rise up between him and his place in history." He was not satisfied that he was the "overall Inter-Allied Commander in Australia . . . he wanted also to be known as the Commanding General of the units fighting in the area." To accomplish this end, MacArthur allowed headlines to go out from Port Moresby "saying, in effect, 'MacArthur at the front personally leading his troops,' which was magnified by some into 'Leading Charges.'" Moreover, MacArthur forced his subordinates to acknowledge these false reports and to verify his presence on the battlefield. Eichelberger's part in this "charade" became evident several weeks after the conclusion of the campaign. During a chance meeting, MacArthur casually remarked, "Those were terrible days when you and I were fighting at Buna, Bob." This was a clear indication to Eichelberger that he was expected to support MacArthur's "fabrications" concerning his battlefield leadership.[55]

MacArthur's "lies" proved to be too much for Eichelberger to handle. In the weeks following Buna, he suffered from extreme emotional distress. He admitted that "in February [1943] . . . I couldn't sleep and spent my days feeling sorry for myself." In his calmer moments, he wrote long, depressing letters to his wife and friends, explaining the injustice of serving under MacArthur and the hopelessness of his present situation. He sent one of these letters to Major General V. L. Peterson, the Inspector General and an old friend. After outlining a long litany of complaints against his chief, Eichelberger ended his letter to Peterson with the following foreboding message:

> Maybe I tell you these things because I want one friend to have a full picture should the question ever arise. You know I shall do everything in my power to fulfill my mission here and retain the good will of all my associates but I must be honest and admit a fear that there may be an open break, hence this long epistle.[56]

Eichelberger had good reason to be depressed, for many of his allegations were true. Mayo, in *Bloody Buna*, states that MacArthur's ignorance of the Buna terrain caused him to make "impossible demands" on his front-line officers. MacArthur never went to the battlefield, and depended solely on Sutherland's observations for his intelligence. John Costello, in *The Pacific War*, agrees with Mayo's conclusions, and states that Eichelberger was goaded by MacArthur into continuing his attacks, despite the heavy casualties. Milner, in *Victory in Papua*, states that MacArthur's communiqués were indeed untrue. MacArthur's statement that there was "no hurry" to capture Buna was patently false, and most GHQ communiqués were "distortions" designed to give a favorable picture of the fighting. There is little evidence concerning MacArthur's "manipulation" of the press immediately after the Buna campaign. It is not inconceivable that MacArthur deliberately attempted to prevent Eichelberger from gaining publicity. As D. Clayton James notes in *The Years of MacArthur*, MacArthur was indeed sensitive to press matters, and was jealous of publicity awarded to his subordinates. James's analysis suggests that Eichelberger's claims contain an element of truth, and that Eichelberger had good reason to be dissatisfied with his superior's behavior.[57]

MacArthur, for his part, was equally displeased with Eichelberger's conduct during the Papuan campaign. In MacArthur's opinion, Eichelberger's performance at Buna was mediocre at best. Although victory was finally achieved, the

BUNA—THE PYRRHIC VICTORY

costs were high—a delay of over a month, an enormous number of casualties, the exhaustion of irreplaceable men and supplies, the loss of American pride, and the humiliation of Australian criticism. Furthermore, MacArthur felt that he had unjustly favored Eichelberger over Harding. Harding had been denied the tanks and reinforcements that Eichelberger received after his arrival in Papua. Even then, Buna was captured only after the enemy was weakened by starvation; Sanananda fell after the disease-ridden Japanese were ordered to withdraw by their own officers. With all these advantages, Eichelberger admitted that he was just lucky to defeat the Japanese. MacArthur apparently agreed with the evaluation of Samuel Milner, who concluded that the victory in Papua was a "bitter anticlimax, partaking more of tragedy than of triumph."[58]

Eichelberger's failure to use tactics of attrition was also a disappointment. Instead of reports of vigorous assaults, MacArthur complained that he received only excuses and rationalizations from Buna. He soon grew tired of the unending reports of daily progress or, worse yet, of Eichelberger's dramatic statements concerning his personal bravery (on one occasion, Eichelberger wrote MacArthur that "you know me well enough now to know that if I could have laid down my life in leading American troops to a victory . . . you would have it at once"). Instead of these front-line heroics, MacArthur wanted results, and in quick fashion. Through indirect channels, MacArthur informed the 32d Division that the campaign was not being waged according to high standards, and that GHQ expected bolder attacks and more aggressive leadership. At the end of the campaign, Eichelberger acknowledged these criticisms. In a letter to MacArthur, he stated that "I realize that . . . some of the fighting has not been up to what you [MacArthur] had hoped for."[59]

MacArthur was particularly irritated that Eichelberger chose to ignore his advice concerning the Australians. Instead of disregarding the Australian commanders, Eichelberger eagerly sought their counsel and bragged that "my relations with the Australian high command have been very cordial." In letters to GHQ, he added that "I have absolutely no difficulty" with the Australian generals, and "we appreciate one another's problems." These comments alone may not have posed a problem, but the publicized "celebration" at Australian headquarters at the conclusion of the Papuan campaign certainly drew MacArthur's attention.[60]

Eichelberger's propensity for gaining press coverage, however, was the greatest source of conflict. MacArthur was willing to grant minimal publicity to his subordinates, but he was not prepared to share the spotlight with someone as publicity-conscious as himself. MacArthur noted with alarm the charming, easygoing relationship that Eichelberger had with the press; many reporters thought that Bob was the most colorful and quotable officer in the Southwest Pacific. Furthermore, Eichelberger willingly took reporters with him to the front lines. He granted them unprecedented access to his staff and troops. He treated the press with the utmost courtesy, unlike members of MacArthur's staff, who were often arrogant and bullying toward reporters.

MacArthur noted that Eichelberger had his own press officer. And MacArthur was aware that his I Corps commander had powerful friends in Washington (including a nephew who was a director of the Time-Life organization) who were able to provide immediate publicity. Furthermore, Eichelberger's reaction to the communiqués and his relations with the Australians indicated that he would not blindly follow GHQ directives, but would instead seek personal fame and glory at MacArthur's expense.[61]

MacArthur's fears were confirmed by a single event after Buna. Immediately after the campaign, the I Corps chief of staff (Brigadier General Clovis Byers) recommended Eichelberger for a Congressional Medal of Honor. The necessary documents were sent to GHQ. MacArthur quietly pigeonholed this recommendation, only to discover that Eichelberger had resubmitted the papers to the War Department through a member of his staff (Colonel Gordon Rogers). Convinced that Eichelberger was working behind his back, MacArthur sent the following fiery telegram to the Adjutant General:

> There was submitted a recommendation for award of Medal of Honor when Colonel Rogers was here on the staff of General Eichelberger . . . The matter was carefully investigated and considered at that time, I myself being personally familiar with all the elements of General Eichelberger's activities during the Papuan campaign [Stop] It was determined that the award was not, repeat, not appropriate [Stop] I awarded General Eichelberger the Distinguished Service Cross for the actions upon which Colonel Rogers based his recommendation for a Medal of Honor [Stop] Among many outside the immediate staff of this officer, there was criticism of his conduct of operations which while not detracting from his personal gallantry led to grave consideration at one time of his relief from the command [Stop] These and other factors known only to myself which I do not care to make of official record unless necessary would make this award most untimely [Stop] The fact that it was fully investigated and not approved at that time and is now revived through outside channels by an officer who was intimately connected with the recipient could not, repeat, not fail to arouse grave criticism and doubt throughout the command [Stop] I therefore not only do not, repeat, not approve the award but urgently recommend against it [Stop] Nothing is so injurious to morale as a belief that favoritism and privilege are exercised by high authority in such matters [Stop] There have been a number of cases similar to this one where officers relieved from this command have instigated awards already thoroughly investigated here at the time and disapproved [Stop] I deprecate such action on the part of officers who thus seek to avoid proper command channels and

recommend that the War Department discourage such action as being subversive of military discipline.[62]

Partly because of this incident, MacArthur became convinced after Buna that Eichelberger lacked the loyalty of other members of the GHQ staff. Although his I Corps commander had courage and was an excellent fighter, MacArthur decided that it would be best to let Eichelberger sit on the sidelines until he learned to play by the rules. In the meantime, MacArthur requested the transfer of Lieutenant General Walter Krueger, and the 6th Army headquarters staff, to Australia. Krueger was untested in combat, but MacArthur felt that he would be a better choice than Eichelberger for future campaigns. Krueger had a reputation as a colorless, hard-boiled commander who followed his orders to the letter and, more importantly, disdained both publicity and the press.[63]

NOTES

1. Robert Eichelberger to Emma Eichelberger, 23 October 1942, Eichelberger Papers.

2. Lida Mayo, *Bloody Buna* (Garden City, N.Y.: Doubleday and Co., 1974), 45–58; Luvaas, *Dear Miss Em*, 26–27; Eichelberger, *Our Jungle Road to Tokyo*, 11–14.

3. Major General Edwin Forrest Harding to Robert Eichelberger, 27 October 1942, Eichelberger Papers; Leslie Anders, *Gentle Knight: The Life and Times of Major General Edwin Forrest Harding* (Kent, Ohio: Kent State University Press, 1985), 233; Mayo, *Bloody Buna*, 98–110; Major General Courtney Whitney, *MacArthur: His Rendezvous With History* (Westport, Conn.: Greenwood Press, 1977), 79–82.

4. Eichelberger, *Our Jungle Road To Tokyo*, 21; D. Clayton James, *The Years of MacArthur, Volume II* (Boston: Houghton-Mifflin Company, 1975), 243–44; George C. Kenney, *General Kenney Reports* (New York: Duell, Sloan and Pearce, 1949), 157–58; Samuel Milner, *Victory in Papua* (United States Army in World War II: The War in the Pacific, Washington, D.C.: Office of the Chief of Military History, Department of the Army, 1967), 204; Mayo, *Bloody Buna*, 111–14; Whitney, *MacArthur: His Rendezvous with History*, 82–84.

5. Eichelberger, *Our Jungle Road To Tokyo*, 21; D. Clayton James, *The Years of MacArthur, Volume II* (Boston: Houghton-Mifflin Company, 1975), 243–44; George C. Kenney, *General Kenney Reports* (New York: Duell, Sloan and Pearce, 1949), 157–58; Samuel Milner, *Victory in Papua* (United States Army in World War II: The War in the Pacific, Washington, D.C.: Office of the Chief of Military History, Department of the Army, 1967), 204; Mayo, *Bloody Buna*, 111–14; Whitney, *MacArthur: His Rendezvous with History*, 82–84.

6. James, *The Years of MacArthur, Volume II*, 244; Kenney, *General Kenney Reports*, 158; Major General S. Woodburn Kirby, *The War Against Japan: India's Most Dangerous Hour* (History of the Second World War, United Kingdom Military Series, London: Her Majesty's Stationery Office, 1958), 288–90; Douglas MacArthur, *Reminiscences* (New York: McGraw-Hill, 1964), 162–65.

7. Eichelberger, *Our Jungle Road to Tokyo*, 24; Robert Eichelberger to General Richard Sutherland, 1 December 1942, Eichelberger Papers; Eichelberger Dictations, "Memorandum on Victory in Papua," 24 June 1957, 1.

8. Milner, *Victory in Papua*, 208-11; Eichelberger, *Our Jungle Road to Tokyo*, 24-25; Mayo, *Bloody Buna*, 118-20.

9. Milner, *Victory in Papua*, 208-11; Eichelberger, *Our Jungle Road to Tokyo*, 24-25; Mayo, *Bloody Buna*, 118-20; memorandum attached to letter, Colonel Gordon Rogers to Robert Eichelberger, 20 July 1948, 1, Eichelberger Papers.

10. Anders, *Gentle Knight*, 263-66, 268; Milner, Victory in Papua, 209-12.

11. Eichelberger Dictations, "Memorandum on Victory in Papua, Pages 208-209," 26 July 1957, 2; Eichelberger Dictations, "Memorandum on Victory in Papua," 24 June 1957, 5; Eichelberger Dictations, "Additional Memoranda on Some Phases of Victory in Papua," 31 May 1967, 2.

12. Eichelberger, *Our Jungle Road to Tokyo*, 25-30; Shortal, "The Evolution of a Combat Commander," 73-75.

13. Mayo, *Bloody Buna*, 124-28; Robert Eichelberger to Emma Eichelberger, 5 December 1942, Eichelberger Papers.

14. Report of the Commanding General, Buna Forces, "History of the Buna Campaign," 1943, 23-24, included in Eichelberger Papers; General H. W. Blakeley, "History of the 32d Infantry Division in World War II," manuscript, 1953, 56, 59, included in Eichelberger Papers, box 66; Milner, *Victory in Papua*, 245.

15. Robert Eichelberger to General Richard Sutherland, 8 December 1942, Eichelberger Papers; memorandum from General Sutherland to Robert Eichelberger, 9 December 1942, Eichelberger Papers.

16. General Douglas MacArthur to Robert Eichelberger, 13 December 1942, Eichelberger Papers.

17. Message from General Douglas MacArthur to Robert Eichelberger, 14 December 1942, Eichelberger Papers.

18. Robert Eichelberger to General R. Sutherland, 18 December 1942, Eichelberger Papers; Eichelberger, *Our Jungle Road to Tokyo*, 44-45.

19. Robert Eichelberger to General R. Sutherland, 27 December 1942 (the letter was never sent), Eichelberger Papers; report of the commanding general, Buna forces, "History of the Buna Campaign," 29-32.

20. General Douglas MacArthur to Lt. Gen. Robert Eichelberger, 25 December 1942, Eichelberger Papers; Eichelberger Dictations, "Conduct of the Men at Buna," 3 July 1948, 1-2; Lt. Gen. Eichelberger to General Douglas MacArthur, 25 December 1942, Eichelberger Papers; John Costello, *The Pacific War* (New York: Rawson, Wade, 1981), 377-79; Milner, *Victory in Papua*, 370-71.

21. General Douglas MacArthur to General R. L. Eichelberger, 8 January 1943, Eichelberger Papers; General Robert L. Eichelberger, memorandum to American troops in the Buna area, 3 January 1943, Eichelberger Papers.

22. Milner, *Victory in Papua*, 348-50; Mayo, *Bloody Buna*, 168-80; General Robert Eichelberger to General Richard Sutherland, 15 January 1943, Eichelberger Papers; Eichelberger Dictations, "Buna and Sanananda," 7 July 1948, 7-8.

23. Military report, Col. Hille, "Notes on the Buna-Sanananda Operation" (unpublished, 1946-47), 1-2 in sec. C, Eichelberger Papers, box 62; Eichelberger Dictations, "Buna and Sanananda," 7 July 1948, 8-9.

24. Calvocoressi and Wint, *Total War: The Story of World War II*, 1–959; John Keegan, *The Second World War* (New York: Viking Press, 1989), 296–97; Gilbert, *The Second World War: A Complete History*, 391.

25. Mayo, *Bloody Buna*, 180–88; Milner, *Victory in Papua*, 369–78; Kirby, *The War Against Japan: India's Most Dangerous Hour*, 288–90.

26. Mayo, *Bloody Buna*, 180–88; Milner, *Victory in Papua*, 369–78; Kirby, *The War Against Japan: India's Most Dangerous Hour*, 288–90; Costello, *The Pacific War*, 378–81.

27. Eichelberger Dictations, "Memorandum on Victory in Papua," 10 June 1957, 9; Eichelberger Dictations, "Memorandum on War Days," 20 March 1957, 1.

28. Anders, *Gentle Knight*, 221, 233.

29. Ibid., 238.

30. Ibid., 266, 276; Eichelberger Dictations, "Additional Memoranda on Some Phases of Victory in Papua," 31 May 1957, 2-3.

31. Eichelberger Dictations, "Explanation of Certain Statements During the Buna Period Carried in the 'History of the 32nd Inf. Div. in World War II,'" 17 October 1953, 3-4; Anders, *Gentle Knight*, 275; Kenney, *General Kenney Reports*, 159; radiogram from MacArthur to General Eichelberger, 17 February 1943, Eichelberger Papers.

32. Anders, *Gentle Knight*, 277, 283, 284, 297.

33. E. J. Kahn Jr., "The Terrible Days of Company E," *Saturday Evening Post*, 8 January 1944.

34. Anders, *Gentle Knight*, 271–74, 284, 296; David G. Witters, "These Are the Generals—Eichelberger," *Saturday Evening Post*, 20 February 1943, 1; General Robert L. Eichelberger to General Sir Edmund Herring, 26 August 1959, Eichelberger Papers; "Nightmare in Mud," *Chicago Tribune*, 7 July 1957, included in the Eichelberger Papers.

35. Mayo, *Bloody Buna*, 153, 159–60; Milner, *Victory in Papua*, 211–12, 369–70; Costello, *The Pacific War*, 378–80.

36. Eddie Grose to Brigadier General Philip E. Brown, 22 February 1944, Eichelberger Papers; Robert Eichelberger to Emma Eichelberger, 19 February 1944, 21 February 1944, and 26 March 1944, Eichelberger Papers; Eichelberger Dictations, "Fuller," 29 July 1957, 1-2; Robert Eichelberger to General George C. Marshall, 31 December 1942 and 11 March 1943, George C. Marshall Papers, George C. Marshall Research Library, Lexington, Virginia, box 66.

37. Eichelberger Dictations, "Memorandum on Victory in Papua," 10 June 1957, 8; Eichelberger Dictations, "Memorandum to Accompany Carbon Copies of My Buna Letters to MacArthur and Sutherland," 31 May 1957, 2; Eichelberger Dictations, "Explanation of Certain Statements . . . ," 17 October 1953, 3.

38. Eichelberger Dictations, "Additional Notes on Buna," Spring of 1946, 1-2; Eichelberger Dictations, "Notes from General Eichelberger on Buna," 21 September 1948, 2-4; Eichelberger Dictations, "Memorandum to Accompany Carbon Copies of My Buna Letters to MacArthur and Sutherland," 31 May 1957, 1; Eichelberger Dictations, "Memorandum on War Days," 20 March 1957, 4-5.

39. Eichelberger Dictations, "Additional Memoranda on Some Phases of Victory in Papua," 3 May 1957, 1; Eichelberger Dictations, "Notes from General Eichelberger on Buna," 21 September 1948, 3-4.

40. R. K. Sutherland to Robert Eichelberger, 18 December 1942, Papers of Lt. Gen. Richard K. Sutherland, Record Group 30, included with Papers of Douglas MacArthur, MacArthur Memorial Library and Archives, Norfolk, Virginia; Memorandum, R. K. Sutherland to R. L. Eichelberger, 9 December 1942, R. K. Sutherland Papers; R. L. Eichelberger to R. K. Sutherland, 23 December 1942, R. K. Sutherland Papers; Eichelberger Dictations, "Memorandum on Victory in Papua," 10 June 1957, 8, 10; Eichelberger Dictations, "Memorandum on One of Sutherland's Visits on or about 23 December 1942," 28 June 1957, 1; Eichelberger Dictations, "Memorandum on War Days," 20 March 1957, 3; R. L. Eichelberger to R. K. Sutherland, 18 December 1942, Sutherland Papers.

41. Eichelberger Dictations, "Memorandum on Victory in Papua," 10 June 1957, 8; Eichelberger Dictations, "Memorandum on War Days," 20 March 1957, 5.

42. Oral reminiscences of Major General Charles A. Willoughby, an interview with D. Clayton James conducted in Naples, Florida, on 30 July 1971, included in the Charles A. Willoughby Papers at the MacArthur Memorial in Norfolk, Virginia, Record Group 23, 3-12; Kenney, *General Kenney Reports*, 26-28, 33, 47-48, 52-53, and 124.

43. Eichelberger Dictations, "Memorandum on Failure of General MacArthur and General Kenney to Come to Buna in the Early Fighting in Papua," 4 October 1957, 1-2; Eichelberger Dictations, "Buna," 12 November 1954, 10; Eichelberger Dictations, "Buna Notes," 26 June 1961, 2; Eichelberger Dictations, "Buna and Sanananda," 7 July 1948, 2; Eichelberger Dictations, no title, 27 October 1955, 3-5; Eichelberger Dictations, "Additional Notes on Buna," spring 1946, 2-3; Eichelberger Dictations, "Memorandum for Emmalina," 22 October 1943, 5; Eichelberger Dictations, "Remarks on *Victory in Papua*, Official Army Military History of the SW Pacific," 27 May 1957, 2.

44. R. L. Eichelberger to Emma Eichelberger, 6 January 1943, Eichelberger Papers; General Douglas MacArthur to Robert Eichelberger, 8 January 1943, Eichelberger Papers; Eichelberger Dictations, "Buna & Sanananda," 7 July 1948, 1; James, *The Years of MacArthur, Volume II*, 270-75.

45. R. L. Eichelberger to Emma Eichelberger, 6 January 1943, Eichelberger Papers; General Douglas MacArthur to Robert Eichelberger, 8 January 1943, Eichelberger Papers; Eichelberger Dictations, "Buna & Sanananda," 7 July 1948, 1; James, *The Years of MacArthur, Volume II*, 270-75; Eichelberger Dictations, "Opinions," no date, 199 in dictation notebook; MacArthur, *Reminiscences*, 165 (footnote).

46. Eichelberger, *Our Jungle Road to Tokyo*, 47; Milner, *Victory in Papua*, 369; *The Telegraph* (Virginia), "Allied Losses in Papua Low," 29 January 1943, included in Eichelberger Papers.

47. Eichelberger Dictations, "Explanation of Certain Statements During the Buna Period Carried in the 'History of the 32nd Infantry Division in World War II,'" 17 October 1953, 5; James, *The Years of MacArthur, Volume II*, 271-74; Eichelberger Dictations, "Buna and Sanananda," 7 July 1948, 5-6; Eichelberger Dictations, "Memorandum for Emmalina," 22 October 1943, 2.

48. Eichelberger Dictations, "Explanation of Certain Statements During the Buna Period Carried in the 'History of the 32nd Infantry Division in World War II,'" 17 October 1953, 6; Eichelberger Dictations, "Memorandum for Emmalina," 22 October

1943, 2; Milner, *Victory in Papua*, 370–71; Eichelberger Dictations, "Opinions," no date, 11.

49. Eichelberger Dictations, "MacArthur's Views on Publicity," 9 September 1953, 1–4.

50. Ibid., 2; Eichelberger Dictations, "Opinions," no date, 6, 7.

51. Eichelberger Dictations, "MacArthur's Views on Publicity," 9 September 1953, 2; Eichelberger Dictations, "Opinions," no date, 6, 7; Eichelberger Dictations, "Public Relations Policies of GHQ, Particularly with Reference to Other Leaders Besides MacArthur," no date, 2.

52. John McCullough, "Gen. Eichelberger Helps Erase Defeat of Bataan," *Philadelphia Inquirer*, 24 January 1943, copy included in Eichelberger Papers; Frank Robertson, "Somewhere in New Guinea," 9 January 1943, included in most International News Service publications, and in Eichelberger Papers; Murlin Spencer, "Papuan Campaign is Tale of Heroism of Ohio's Sons," *Columbus Dispatch*, 4 July 1943, copy included in Eichelberger Papers.

53. Eichelberger Dictations, "MacArthur's Views on Publicity," 9 September 1953, 5–6; Eichelberger Dictations, "Opinions," no date, 8; James, *The Years of MacArthur, Volume II*, 276.

54. James, *The Years of MacArthur, Volume II*, 280–81; Robert L. Eichelberger to Samuel Milner, 8 March 1954, Eichelberger Papers.

55. Eichelberger Dictations, "MacArthur," 24 July 1961, 1; Eichelberger Dictations, "Opinions," no date, 6; Eichelberger Dictations, no title, 27 October 1955, 1, 5; Eichelberger Dictations, "Some Observations on . . . the Army Air Force," 13 January 1961, 5; Eichelberger Dictations, "MacArthur's Views on Publicity," 9 September 1953, 6.

56. R. L. Eichelberger to Maj. Gen. V. L. Peterson, 19 January 1943, Eichelberger Papers; R. L. Eichelberger to Emma Eichelberger, 30 May 1943, Eichelberger Papers.

57. Mayo, *Bloody Buna*, 180–88; Costello, *The Pacific War*, 380; Milner, *Victory in Papua*, 369–78; James, *The Years of MacArthur, Volume II*, 717–20.

58. Milner, *Victory in Papua*, 369, 374, 377; Robert Eichelberger to Brig. Gen. Floyd Parks (Chief of Staff, Army Ground Forces), 1 February 1943, Eichelberger Papers.

59. R. L. Eichelberger to Gen. Douglas MacArthur, 25 Dec. 1942, Eichelberger Papers; R. L. Eichelberger to Gen. Douglas MacArthur, 21 January 1943, R. K. Sutherland Papers (located at the MacArthur Memorial Library).

60. Robert Eichelberger to Gen. Richard K. Sutherland, 8 December 1942 and 18 December 1942, Eichelberger Papers.

61. James, *The Years of MacArthur, Volume II*, 276, 278, 429; Eichelberger Dictations, "MacArthur's Views on Publicity," 9 September 1953, 4, 6; Eichelberger Dictations, "Explanation of Certain Statements During the Buna Period . . . ," 17 October 1953, 6; Captain Robert M. White to R. L. Eichelberger, 10 January 1943, Eichelberger Papers; Roy White to Emma Eichelberger, 9 January 1943, Eichelberger Papers; Eichelberger Dictations, "Buna and Sanananda," 7 July 1948, 4–5.

62. General Douglas MacArthur to AGWAR (Washington), 23 August 1943, RG-4: USAFPAC, correspondence, War Department (WD 483), Papers of Douglas MacArthur, MacArthur Memorial Library and Archives, Norfolk, Virginia;

Eichelberger Dictations, "Opinions," (no date), 9-10; James, *The Years of MacArthur, Volume II*, 275-76.

63. Vice Admiral Daniel E. Barbey, *MacArthur's Amphibious Navy: Seventh Amphibious Force Operations 1943-1945* (Annapolis, Md.: U.S. Naval Institute, 1969), 26-27, 169-70; Eichelberger Dictations, no title, 20 March 1957, 1-2.

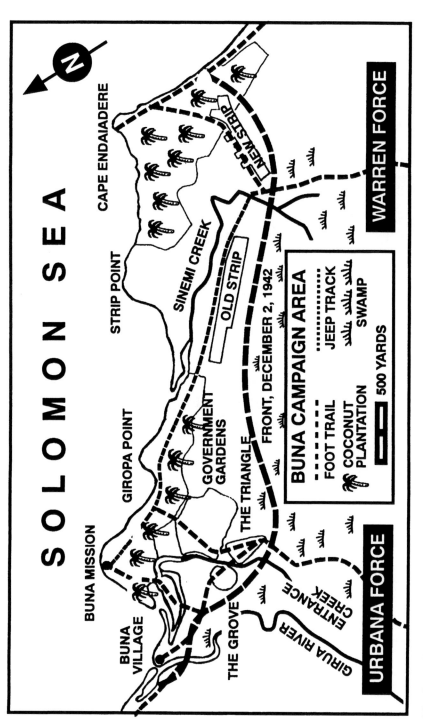

The Buna Campaign

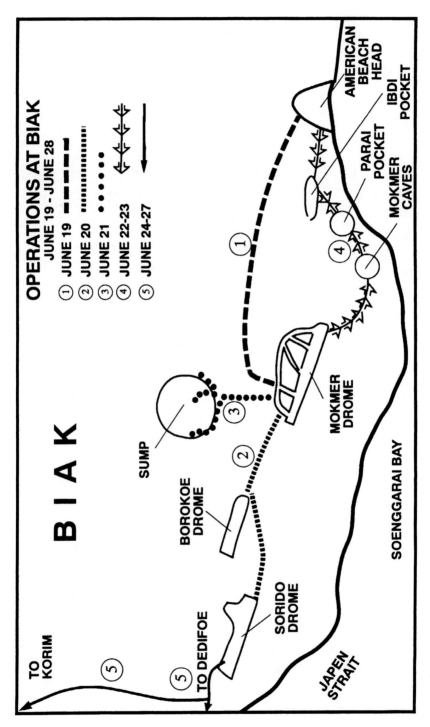

Operations on Biak

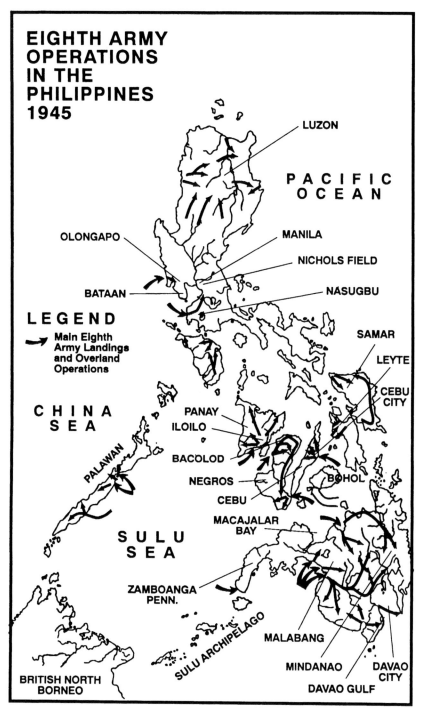

Eighth Army Operations in the Philippines

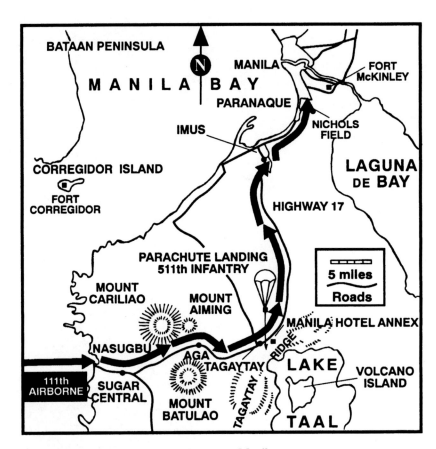

The Nasagbu Landing and the Advance to Manila

7

STRUGGLES FROM THE SIDELINES

Shortly after the Buna campaign, MacArthur decided to put his I Corps commander "on ice." From March 1943 to March 1944, Eichelberger spent his time in Australia, training the 32d, 41st, and 24th Divisions.

Eichelberger was puzzled and angry about this demotion. Although he was aware that MacArthur was displeased by some of his actions at Buna, he did not yet fully comprehend the complexities of his chief's personality. He could not understand how MacArthur could set him aside for merely personal reasons. In his daily letters to his wife in March 1943, Eichelberger expressed confusion and bitterness toward the "ingratitude" and insensitivity of MacArthur. "You have no idea," he wrote, "of the mental torture we endure and the body English we exert as we watch from the background." Eichelberger confessed, "I shall do my duty towards my country . . . but I shall not do it with quite the same élan and enthusiasm as I had last winter."[1]

His depression deepened when he discovered that MacArthur had requested the transfer of the 6th Army to the Southwest Pacific. After the arrival there of the 6th Army headquarters staff in February 1943, Eichelberger visited GHQ and asked MacArthur to define the role of I Corps. MacArthur replied that I Corps would be placed under the command of General Walter Krueger, the commander of the 6th Army. "Krueger," MacArthur stated, "is the one who will determine how and when you will fight." Several days later, Eichelberger asked Krueger for further clarification; Krueger replied that the directives from GHQ restricted the use of corps-sized units, and limited future corps operations to small combat teams under the jurisdiction of the 6th Army, which effectively ruled out any participation by I Corps in future operations. "How unfair," he added, "when one considers that he [MacArthur] brought General Krueger out to be an army commander and that I had been placed to a large extent out of the picture."[2]

In April 1943, another problem arose. It quickly became apparent that Eichelberger and Krueger had serious personality differences. This was an unpleasant surprise; Eichelberger had expected to get along with Walter. His old friend General Craig had assured him that Krueger was a "good man" and was "fearless, tireless and reasonably human." Within a month, however, Eichelberger decided that General Craig had made a gross error in judgment, and that Krueger was in fact an opinionated and stubborn "ball of pomposity." Eichelberger complained that Walter was a "know-it-all" who tried to impress his subordinates with his superior intelligence. He frequently was forced to listen in silence as Krueger detailed his experiences in the Louisiana maneuvers. On one occasion, he had to suffer through Krueger's analysis of the Sanananda campaign. Krueger "is a great talker," Eichelberger stated, "and I always find when I am thrown with him very closely that it really amounts to hard work."[3]

Krueger was also a harsh and critical officer, particularly toward his subordinates. On one occasion, Krueger rebuked Eichelberger for allowing his men to play baseball during their free time. He reprimanded off-duty soldiers for having their shirts off in the tropical heat. Krueger frequently inspected his troops at odd times. On one occasion, he made a surprise inspection of the I Corps late on a Saturday afternoon. Eichelberger complained that "no military command in the world would have been properly prepared for inspection [at that time in the week]."[4]

At the heart of Eichelberger's complaints was the painful realization that Krueger had been placed ahead of him (as the commander of the 6th Army), and that he would have to play second fiddle to this old soldier who had no combat experience in the war. Eichelberger felt even worse when he discovered that his friends in the War Department had recommended him for command of the 6th Army; MacArthur had ignored their recommendation in favor of Krueger. Eichelberger was further alarmed by his discussions with the 6th Army staff, which indicated that Krueger was ambitious and seemed determined to surpass him in combat experience. Krueger failed to brief him on the 6th Army operations, and left his headquarters in Australia for weeks at a time without informing his subordinates of his whereabouts. Fearful that Krueger was attempting to "hog all the glory," Eichelberger complained that it "would seem unbelievable that a force in the field wouldn't be kept informed about what was going on in adjacent combat units, but it was a fact and it was typical."[5]

This growing enmity between Krueger and Eichelberger was noted by several officers in the Southwest Pacific. General Charles A. Willoughby, MacArthur's chief of intelligence, explained the feud by contrasting the personal backgrounds of the two men. Willoughby, who probably held the same views as MacArthur, stated the following:

> Krueger was a hard-nosed professional who came up from the ranks. He was German born. . . . Krueger came from the bottom up [from the rank of private]. He had inherent talents that were not flamboyant. He was much better than he looked. He was tough and getting tougher with

each rise in command. He had a scholarly side to him also because he had been an instructor at Leavenworth. . . . He left translations of the leading German publications at the time. While he was a rough-looking character, more or less, he had a feeling for his profession. He was a first-class commander and a senior one. . . . There is a difference between Krueger and Eichelberger. Eichelberger was for many years the Secretary of the General Staff in Washington. That was a powerful position and a position which helped him to make friends in the political field. He was also Superintendent of West Point. He got that job because he had the other job. He was good-looking, smooth, polished, and socially the thing for Washington. That was another difference between him and Krueger. Once you go through these staff schools, and this applies to all armies including the Russian, this thing becomes a sausage-like chain performance almost. As long as they give you the troops, ammunition, and food, you are likely to make it because you are trained that way. But the other man, Krueger, was self-made.[6]

Admiral Daniel E. Barbey, the naval commander for many of MacArthur's amphibious operations, also noted the conflict between Krueger and Eichelberger. He made similar observations about the relative merits of the two men. Barbey believed that the personal feud was caused by the differences in their personalities and backgrounds:

Eichelberger, an able officer with a warm personality, was well liked by the press and not averse to friendly publicity. He had strong friends in the War Department and was known to be a close associate of Colonel Edwin M. (Pa) Watson, the military aide to the President. With a successful campaign behind him [Buna], and with all these other attributes, it was assumed he would be in the forefront of the leaders of all upcoming operations. But it didn't turn out that way. There was no place in the Southwest Pacific for two glamorous officers. For almost a year he fretted his time away in comparatively unimportant training roles in northeast Australia. An entirely different type of officer was Lieutenant General Walter Krueger who was assigned to command the Sixth Army, a job that Eichelberger had hoped to get. Krueger arrived from the States a few weeks after I did and set up his headquarters at Camp Columbia, a few miles outside of Brisbane. He was a taciturn Prussian type of officer of the no-nonsense sort who commenced his military career as a private. What his seniors wanted done, he wanted done—and well. He had an excellent military reputation. He shunned publicity, which was all to the good in the Southwest Pacific.[7]

These differences in personal style and background were a constant source of irritation between the two men. Eichelberger suffered the brunt of the emotional heartache due to his subordinate position. By May 1943, Eichelberger decided that his personality differences with Krueger (as well as with MacArthur) made it unlikely that he would receive fair treatment from his superiors as long as he remained in the Southwest Pacific. He subsequently decided to seek a different post in another theater of operations, with the help of his powerful friends in the United States. In this endeavor, he received the support and encouragement of General Malin Craig, his old mentor, who was the head of the Selection Board in Washington.[8]

Due to Craig's influence, Eichelberger quickly made progress in his efforts to find a new job. In mid-May, he heard rumors that he had been entered as a potential candidate for the position as commanding general of the 1st Army. These rumors were verified by GHQ. On 20 May 1943, MacArthur informed Eichelberger that he "had been approached by an emissary of the War Department [and] asked if he would be willing to releases his I Corps commander for the 1st Army position. MacArthur stated that he was inclined to approve this request if "[I] wanted such a detail" but he "did not believe I would want it." Eichelberger replied very diplomatically that he preferred an army command to his present position as commander of a training corps; MacArthur responded that he understood and "would not stand in [my] way."[9]

Eichelberger believed that the matter was settled, and that MacArthur had approved his request for a transfer to the United States. When several weeks passed without any notification, however, Eichelberger became suspicious of MacArthur's intentions. He decided to write his contacts in Washington—among them Colonel Gordon B. Rogers, the Assistant Chief of Staff (G-2) of the Army Ground Forces, requesting, "If you blunder into anything about a possible detail back home for me be sure to let me know by V-mail as several rumors have reached me." He then wrote to Major General Alec D. Surles of the Bureau of Public Relations; he encouraged Surles to contact General George C. Marshall and inform him of the "peculiar circumstances" of his situation.[10]

Determined to leave nothing to chance, Eichelberger contacted General Craig in July 1943 and informed him that "naturally I would want it [the 1st Army position] for many reasons which you can well imagine." He wrote also to his old friend General Lesley McNair (commanding general of the Army Ground Forces): "If the question of my personal desire ever arises, I shall be delighted to take the above mentioned detail [command of the 1st Army] or any other detail deemed suitable by you if the offer is ever communicated to me." When McNair failed to respond to this request, Eichelberger asked his wife Emma to contact Claire McNair. "Wives often know a lot," he stated, "and she might volunteer to tell you some things."[11]

Despite his most ardent efforts, Eichelberger heard nothing more about the vacant 1st Army position until 29 September 1943. On that date, at an intimate dinner at GHQ, he learned firsthand that MacArthur "had twice refused to give me up for different jobs back home," including the command of the 1st and 9th Armies. In the discussion that followed, MacArthur explained the rationale for these decisions. These posts, he argued, would only hurt Bob, for the authorities in Washington "would always feel" that MacArthur "had gotten rid of" his I Corps commander. MacArthur also showed Eichelberger his message to the War Department, which stated that "[Bob's] services are of more value here than they could be in any assignment to which he could aspire in the United States."[12]

In December 1943, Eichelberger discovered that MacArthur had turned him down for another job—the command of an army for the Normandy invasion. MacArthur made no mention of this opening. Eichelberger learned of the position from a reliable source, who informed him that MacArthur had "turned it down [because] the officer offered [by the War Department as the replacement], General J. Lawton Collins, was too junior." In fact, Eisenhower had reportedly requested Eichelberger's services for the invasion of Europe, but MacArthur had vehemently protested the transfer, arguing that "because of [Bob's] combat experience [he] was needed here."[13]

Frustrated by his inability to get a transfer, Eichelberger complained that "if I were in any other theater I know I would be taken without question." He admitted that "[I] was very anxious to go and the question [was] on my mind constantly." "Personally," he stated, "I would have much preferred to serve under Ike who is, I believe, a solid citizen." In a moment of self-pity, he added, "If I thought that having kept me from commanding three armies as well as the Medal of Honor would be all that would be done to me I would feel better," but "I have always felt that those who have done you wrong are always glad to do it again."[14]

In the weeks and months surrounding these incidents, Eichelberger had plenty of time to decide which officers had been responsible for his frustrations. Besides the obvious choice of MacArthur, Eichelberger decided that Sutherland "had something to do" with his disappointment in his current situation. He believed that Sutherland's intense jealousy of his rank, Corps command, and combat victories had caused him to use his influence with MacArthur to deny a possible transfer.[15]

As evidence for his claim, Eichelberger argued that Sutherland "knew how to handle General MacArthur and one often could not tell whether an attitude of General MacArthur was based on his independent thought or was the result of Sutherland's presentation of the situation." The chief of staff "knew all of MacArthur's little failings, weaknesses, and foibles, and he could maneuver him and play on these characteristics like an expert plucking the strings of a fine violin." The end result was that Sutherland could "bring out in MacArthur any latent jealousy and envy in his nature."[16]

In particular, Sutherland was most successful in exploiting MacArthur's "jealousy and envy" of Generals George C. Marshall and Dwight Eisenhower.

Although Eichelberger had no evidence to explain how Sutherland was able to inflame these "jealousies," he did claim that MacArthur's prejudice against both Marshall and Eisenhower was apparent. For example, MacArthur consistently referred to Ike as "that traitor Eisenhower"; he never forgave his former aide for "walking out on him in the Philippines" before the war. MacArthur was jealous of Eisenhower's military victories. At the end of the African campaign, he complained to his staff that "Eisenhower is now made and nothing can touch him in the future." Afterwards, MacArthur imitated Eisenhower's dress; he refused to wear ribbons and a tie after "photographs came back of General Eisenhower in Africa showing him without ribbons."[17]

MacArthur's ill-feelings toward Marshall, Eichelberger claimed, had a similar background. MacArthur's prejudices against Marshall also predated the war, and were a function of his vanity and insecurity. In Eichelberger's opinion, MacArthur had been jealous of Marshall since the 1930s, when MacArthur was the Chief of Staff and Marshall had been marked as an "up-and-comer." MacArthur had seen Marshall as a potential rival for rank and glamour, and had sent him out on National Guard duty with the intention of ruining his career. When Marshall's career was revitalized before the war, MacArthur feared that Marshall would seek revenge against him from his powerful position as Chief of Staff. As Eichelberger stated, "I always felt that MacArthur was on the alert not to be treated in a similar manner by Marshall when he became Chief of Staff," because "if MacArthur had been in Marshall's position, that is the kind of thing he would have done." The end result was that MacArthur was keenly distrustful of Marshall and his intentions concerning the Southwest Pacific command.[18]

MacArthur's prejudices against Marshall and Eisenhower directly affected Eichelberger. MacArthur considered his I Corps commander both a friend and a tool of these two enemies (or so Eichelberger claimed). Eichelberger tried to reassure MacArthur on several occasions that he was only an "official acquaintance" of the two, but MacArthur did not seem to believe him. Eichelberger noted that "many times . . . General MacArthur, during a pleasant conversation, would suddenly flare up and glare at me and say, 'You are a good friend of George Catlett Marshall.'" Immediately after the Sanananda campaign, MacArthur again became suspicious when the 32d Division received a congratulatory message from General Marshall. More importantly, MacArthur had mixed feelings about the messages from the War Department requesting Bob's services in Europe; he surely knew that these requests originated from his old enemies, Eisenhower and Marshall.[19]

MacArthur's prejudices against Marshall and Eisenhower played a pivotal role in explaining Eichelberger's failure to get a transfer. Eichelberger believed that MacArthur was happy to refuse any request made by his former enemies. "My own feeling," Eichelberger stated, "was that part of his satisfaction was in saying no to George Catlett Marshall and Dwight Eisenhower"; he added, "It is my belief that MacArthur's hatred for General Marshall . . . made him glad to turn down any request of any type from Marshall."[20]

Moreover, MacArthur's distrust of his enemies caused him to fear that Marshall would attempt to replace him, that, in Eichelberger's words, MacArthur "would be ordered home [by Marshall] and taken out of the limelight." MacArthur was therefore "on the alert to see that nobody rose up in his command who could in any way" act as his replacement. Since Bob was Marshall's alleged friend with "a fine record," it was inevitable (according to Eichelberger) that he would draw MacArthur's suspicion as a potential rival for a high command in the Southwest Pacific.[21]

Eichelberger believed that MacArthur's suspicions were responsible for his difficulties in Australia and New Guinea. For example, he believed that his lack of publicity and his failure to receive the Medal of Honor were attempts by MacArthur to check the career of a potential rival. MacArthur, Eichelberger stated, "was taking no chances on my being used as a tool against him by Marshall." He concluded that "MacArthur made a God of himself and my only sin was to be his possible successor insofar as his enemies Eisenhower and Marshall were concerned."[22]

Although Eichelberger was convinced that these statements about MacArthur were correct, he had little supporting evidence besides several intermittent conversations with his chief. No other member of MacArthur's staff supported his conclusions. Most reporters felt that the I Corps commander exaggerated his own importance, at least insofar as MacArthur was concerned. The evidence of some historians, however, indicates that Eichelberger's allegations contain a kernel of truth. James, for example, states that MacArthur was capable of showing enormous vanity, insecurity, and selfishness in his dealings with his subordinates and superiors. These characteristics contributed to his preoccupation with publicity and to his "hero-martyr image." James also states that MacArthur was extremely sensitive and had an "acute persecution complex"; these factors played a large role in his negative feelings toward Marshall and Eisenhower. Nevertheless, there is no evidence from any source to indicate that MacArthur ever considered Eichelberger a serious rival. Nor is there any evidence that Marshall ever considered replacing MacArthur with Eichelberger in the Southwest Pacific.[23]

Eichelberger was convinced, however, that all of his assertions were true, and that he had finally solved the tangled riddle of MacArthur's personality. Although many of his basic assumptions about MacArthur were wrong or exaggerated, he correctly guessed that he would have to modify his behavior if he hoped to gain another combat assignment in the Southwest Pacific. In September 1943, after it became clear that his friends in Washington could not help him, he decided that it would be in his own best interests to adjust his conduct to meet the "quirky" needs of his boss. His motives were simple. He hoped to gain MacArthur's trust and, in the process, another combat command by demonstrating his willingness to "play the game."[24]

Toward this end, Eichelberger adopted a plan to discontinue his correspondence with his friends in Washington. He correctly assumed that MacArthur was threatened by his attempts to contact his powerful friends, especially since many of these letters were subtle efforts to undermine GHQ's authority. Since MacArthur was "very well informed" and undoubtedly aware of this correspondence, Eichelberger in September 1943 decided to temporarily suspend these contacts with Generals McNair, Connors, and Craig. Thereafter, he gave the impression that he was content to depend on MacArthur alone, and not Washington, for his future assignments.

As part of his new image, Eichelberger also reduced his efforts to gain publicity. His desire for fame and attention remained as strong as ever, but he now decided to use only discreet methods and to lower his national profile. For example, Eichelberger was asked to submit a biographical article for a special issue of the *Army and Navy Journal*; he politely declined with the excuse that it was "best for me not to [submit] anything." In October 1943, he wrote to Major General Alec D. Suries, the head of the Bureau of Public Relations, informing him that "I would rather you slip a rattlesnake in my pocket than to have you give me any publicity." He contacted Roy Larsen, a family relative and an influential figure in the Time-Life organization; he requested that the two publications omit any reference to the I Corps in future articles.[25]

As a substitute for this type of national exposure, he encouraged instead a more discreet form of publicity. He had his staff prepare a detailed report of the Buna campaign that was very complimentary of his role in the fighting. To ensure that this report was seen by influential people in the United States, Eichelberger sent the report to the U.S. Military Academy, the Command and General Staff School at Fort Leavenworth, and to friends at General Marshall's office in Washington. By this method, he hoped to keep a strong profile with the "people that counted," and at the same time avoid the ostentatious type of publicity that had hurt him after Buna.[26]

Another policy that Eichelberger adopted was the avoidance of any statements to reporters that could be interpreted as criticism of MacArthur. He had already aired his complaints against MacArthur to the press. In September 1943, he decided to praise MacArthur publicly and to reveal his criticisms to only a few trusted friends. After September, Eichelberger spoke glowingly to reporters about his chief's physical courage, his "brilliant" mind, and the wisdom of the "island-hopping" strategy (privately, he argued that General Stephen Chamberlin, the GHQ operations officer, was primarily responsible for MacArthur's so-called strategic genius). In private conversations with MacArthur, Eichelberger flattered and praised his boss; on one occasion, he asked for an autographed picture "to send home to Mrs. Eichelberger."[27]

In his letters to his wife, Eichelberger remained bitterly critical of MacArthur. Even here, however, he made some alterations to mask his sentiments. Fearful that MacArthur's censors would inform him of any negative comments, he decided, in the fall of 1943, to avoid using MacArthur's name directly in his letters. Instead, he began referring to his chief as "Sarah Bernhardt," (a reference to the vain French actress). Not content with this tactic, Eichelberger also decided to include some flattering comments about MacArthur in his letters; he hoped that these positive statements would be passed along to GHQ. Obviously, these statements would not be sincere. Eichelberger informed his wife that "if I use some expressions of praise which puzzle you, I may do that to present a certain picture if a stranger should read it."[28]

These deceptions were only a small part of Eichelberger's overall strategy. In October 1943, he decided to supplement these "personal policies" with some small but vital favors he would perform for MacArthur. The first of these favors involved MacArthur's struggle with the navy and the Central Pacific command. In the fall of 1943, MacArthur was competing with the navy for the right to determine overall strategy in the Pacific; he and Admiral Chester W. Nimitz clashed over the importance of the Philippines in the drive toward Japan. In September 1943, MacArthur heard rumors that the navy had a plan to attack Formosa instead of the Philippines. This plan reportedly limited MacArthur's Southwest Pacific command to a subsidiary role.

In order to confirm these rumors, Eichelberger stopped in Honolulu while on his leave and requested information about these matters from General Robert C. Richardson, the commanding officer of the Hawaiian command. This visit proved fruitful. Richardson was able to inform him that there had been "a big conference in Honolulu recently" with Admirals Ernest J. King, Chester Nimitz, and William Halsey. The navy had indeed made plans to bypass the Philippines. Eichelberger immediately sent this information to MacArthur. "The Navy considers this their show," he wrote, and "the lines of advance pass to the north of New Britain, shutting you off from the Philippines." This information was certainly appreciated by MacArthur, and undoubtedly helped him in later meetings with Admiral Nimitz and President Roosevelt.[29]

Earlier during the summer of 1943, Eichelberger had an opportunity to do his chief another favor. In June, MacArthur began talking to Eichelberger and Krueger about the possibility of running for the presidency of the United States on the Republican ticket. MacArthur was supported by a host of political leaders in the United States; they advised MacArthur to distance himself from President Roosevelt's policies and to avoid any connection with Democratic leaders. MacArthur closely followed this advice until August 1943. On 12 August, he was ordered by Washington to escort Eleanor Roosevelt, the President's wife, during a visit to Australia. This visit posed a dilemma. MacArthur was afraid that any "news articles and photographs of him with the First Lady would [be] repugnant to potential supporters among the Roosevelt haters in the States." As James points out in *The Years of MacArthur*, MacArthur's "primary considerations" were "political," for he clearly wished to avoid any association with the President and other Roosevelt Democrats.[30]

MacArthur resolved this dilemma by assigning Eichelberger the task of escorting the First Lady during her Australian visit. Offering an excuse—that his presence was needed in New Guinea, MacArthur fled to Port Moresby. Before he left, MacArthur instructed Eichelberger to avoid unnecessary publicity, to discourage the First Lady from visiting Port Moresby, and to allow Mrs. Roosevelt only a brief visit to Brisbane (the city widely known as MacArthur's headquarters). Despite these difficult orders, Eichelberger was able to successfully complete his duties without antagonizing either MacArthur or Mrs. Roosevelt. "There were a thousand ways of getting my throat cut," he stated, "and the fact that I got away with it just proves that my luck was with me again."[31]

In January 1944, Eichelberger performed yet another political favor for his boss. MacArthur was concerned about the unfavorable newspaper articles in the United States that had criticized him for failing to visit his front-line troops at Bataan and New Guinea. Fearful that these revelations would damage his image as a fighting general "during the critical period of the presidential boom," MacArthur decided that he needed some immediate "front-line" photographs to counteract this negative publicity.[32]

On 26 January 1944, MacArthur made an unscheduled visit to Eichelberger's field command post near Rockhampton, Australia. The I Corps was then engaged in a "very realistic scene" of mock jungle warfare; MacArthur insisted on reviewing the exercise in a jeep accompanied by a battery of reporters and photographers. Numerous pictures were taken of MacArthur during the tour. Eichelberger was ordered to send all photographs of the exercise to GHQ. Several weeks later, Eichelberger noticed that these same pictures appeared in newspapers throughout the United States, under the caption "General MacArthur at the Front with General Eichelberger in New Guinea."[33] Shocked and disturbed, Eichelberger nevertheless decided that it would be in his own best interest to publicly support MacArthur's "lie" and keep his personal feelings to himself.

MacArthur appreciated Eichelberger's cooperation in this matter. He noted the amenable change in attitude of his I Corps commander. Convinced that Eichelberger had finally decided to abide by his rules, MacArthur informed him, at the end of January 1944, that he would be included in operations in April. MacArthur also informed him that, if he were successful in these operations, "I [MacArthur] am going to get another Army out here [in the Southwest Pacific] and I am going to need you [to command it]."[34]

These decisions were not made on the spur of the moment; MacArthur had closely watched Eichelberger's conduct over the past five months. He was clearly pleased by the changes that Eichelberger had made in his attitudes and personal habits. But, he was not fooled into thinking that his I Corps commander had altered his desire for publicity or his views toward his boss. MacArthur was convinced, however, that Eichelberger's external reforms and favors were sufficient evidence that he had learned his lesson, and that he now understood the rules under which he was expected to perform.

Besides this newfound confidence in Eichelberger, MacArthur also had a more subtle reason for returning his Buna commander to the front lines. Since March 1943, General Krueger had been responsible for most of the combat assignments in the Southwest Pacific. MacArthur was concerned that Krueger had demonstrated a lack of aggressiveness in some of his operations. MacArthur hoped that Eichelberger's presence would spur Krueger on to greater efforts, and that the threat of being replaced would eliminate the "timidity" in Krueger's offensives.

In posing Eichelberger as a threat to Krueger, MacArthur hoped to get the best possible performance out of both men. MacArthur was fully aware that Walter and Bob did not "get along." The two men, he believed, were sensitive, jealous, and insecure. MacArthur was confident that he would be able to turn these insecurities to his own advantage. A keen student of human nature, MacArthur reasoned that the presence of Eichelberger and Krueger in the same theater of operations would cause both men to work doubly hard; each man would fear that the other was "breathing down his neck." MacArthur assumed his two subordinates would fight for his favor; both would need the support of their boss to gain additional combat assignments at the other's expense. Since MacArthur held all the advantages, he felt little concern about placing them on the same battlefield. He understood the likelihood of interpersonal conflict, but gambled that the friction would be offset by an increase in initiative and competition, even if this competition had the potential to be mean-spirited.[35]

NOTES

1. Robert Eichelberger to Emma Eichelberger, 24 March 1943, Eichelberger Papers; Robert Eichelberger to General Charles A. Willoughby, 18 September 1943, Eichelberger Papers; Robert Eichelberger to Emma Eichelberger, 10 August 1943, Eichelberger Papers.
2. Eichelberger Dictations, "Memorandum for Emmalina," 22 October 1943, 4; Eichelberger, *Our Jungle Road to Tokyo*, 100; Luvaas, *Dear Miss Em*, 66.
3. Robert Eichelberger to Emma Eichelberger, 10 February 1943 and 12 February 1944, Eichelberger Papers; Malin Craig to Robert Eichelberger, 26 Feb. 1943, Eichelberger Papers; Eichelberger Dictations (dictation refers to General Eisenhower's visit to Eichelberger in post-war Japan), no date, page 2 of dictation and 723 in notebook.
4. Robert Eichelberger to Emma Eichelberger, 2 August 1944, Eichelberger Papers.
5. Eichelberger Dictations, "Fuller, also Krueger," 29 May 1961, 1; Robert Eichelberger to Emma Eichelberger, 4 August 1943, Eichelberger Papers.
6. Oral reminiscences of Major General Charles A. Willoughby, an interview with D. Clayton James, conducted in Naples, Florida, on 30 July 1971, included in the Charles Willoughby Papers at the MacArthur Memorial in Norfolk, Virginia, Record Group 23, 11–12.
7. Barbey, *MacArthur's Amphibious Navy*, 27.

8. Robert Eichelberger to Emma Eichelberger, 26 April 1943, Eichelberger Papers; Eichelberger Dictations, "Some Phases of General MacArthur's Attitude Towards Me in my Years in the Pacific," 31 August 1959, 4.

9. Robert Eichelberger to Emma Eichelberger, 20 May 1943, Eichelberger Papers; Robert Eichelberger to Lt. General Lesley McNair, 28 May 1943, Eichelberger Papers.

10. Eichelberger Dictations, "After My Return to Australia from Buna-Sanananda," 18 April 1948, 3–5; Robert Eichelberger to Colonel Gordon S. Rogers, 2 August 1943, Eichelberger Papers; Robert Eichelberger to Major General Alec Surles, 21 October 1943, Eichelberger Papers.

11. Robert Eichelberger to General Malin Craig, 25 July 1943, Eichelberger Papers; Robert Eichelberger to Lt. General Lesley J. McNair, 28 May 1943, Eichelberger Papers; Robert Eichelberger to Emma Eichelberger, 30 August 1943, Eichelberger Papers.

12. Eichelberger Dictations, "Memorandum for Emmalina," 22 October 1943, 3; Robert Eichelberger to General Walter Krueger, 30 September 1943, Eichelberger Papers; General Douglas MacArthur to chief of staff, War Department, 26 August 1943, WD 491, RG-4: USAFPAC, correspondence, War Department, MacArthur Papers, Norfolk, Virginia.

13. Robert Eichelberger to Emma Eichelberger, 23 December 1943 and 26 December 1943, Eichelberger Papers; General Clovis Byers to Emma Eichelberger, 23 December 1943, Eichelberger Papers.

14. Robert Eichelberger to Emma Eichelberger, 6 August 1943, 26 December 1943, 30 December 1943, and 31 December 1943, Eichelberger Papers.

15. Eichelberger Dictations, "Opinions," no date, page 8 of dictation and 197 of the dictation notebook; Eichelberger Dictations, "Some Phases of General MacArthur's Attitude Towards Me in my Years in the Pacific," 31 August 1959, 1.

16. Eichelberger Dictations, "Memorandum on War Days," 20 March 1957, 4–5; Eichelberger Dictations, "Opinions," no date, page 5 of dictation and 194 of Dictation Notebook.

17. Eichelberger Dictations, no title, 5 September 1955, 1–2.

18. Eichelberger Dictations, "Some Phases of General MacArthur's Attitude towards Me in My Years in the Pacific," 31 August 1959, 2–3; Eichelberger Dictations, no title and no date, 741–42 in Dictation Notebook.

19. Eichelberger Dictations, "Some Phases of General MacArthur's Attitude towards Me in My Years in the Pacific," 31 August 1959, 2–3; Eichelberger Dictations, no title and no date, 741–42 in Dictation notebook; Eichelberger Dictations, "George C. Marshall," (no date), page 11 of dictation and 451 of Dictation notebook.

20. Eichelberger Dictations, "Opinions," no date, page 9 of dictation and 198 of Dictation notebook; Eichelberger Dictations, no date and no title, 742 of Dictation notebook.

21. Eichelberger Dictations, "Some Phases of General MacArthur's Attitude Towards Me . . .," 31 August 1959, page 3 of dictation and 572 of Dictation notebook.

22. Eichelberger Dictations, "Some Phases of General MacArthur's Attitude Towards Me in My Years in the Pacific," 31 August 1959, 4-5; Eichelberger Dictations, no title and no date, 742 of Dictation notebook.

23. James, *The Years of MacArthur, Volume II*, 429, 717-20.

24. Robert Eichelberger to Emma Eichelberger, 30 August 1943, 26 December 1943, and 7 June 1944, Eichelberger Papers; Clovis Byers to Emma Eichelberger, 23 December 1943, Eichelberger Papers; Eichelberger Dictations, "Some Phases of General MacArthur's Attitude Towards Me in My Years in the Pacific," 31 August 1959, 1-5.

25. Robert Eichelberger to Major General Alec D. Surles, 21 October 1943, Eichelberger Papers; Robert Eichelberger to Emma Eichelberger, 31 March 1944, Eichelberger Papers.

26. Robert Eichelberger to Emma Eichelberger, 9 August 1943, Eichelberger Papers; Major General F. S. Wilby (superintendent of West Point) to Robert Eichelberger, 15 July 1943 and 7 August 1943, Eichelberger Papers; Major General Karl Truesdell (commandant of Command and General Staff School) to Robert Eichelberger, 5 July 1943, Eichelberger Papers; Colonel Russell P. Reeder, Jr., to Robert Eichelberger, 14 June 1943, Eichelberger Papers.

27. Robert Eichelberger to Lieutenant Colonel C. H. Morhouse, 29 May 1943, RG-3, C-n-C correspondence, Di-Ge, SWPA correspondence, MacArthur Papers, Norfolk, Virginia; Robert Eichelberger to General Douglas MacArthur, 15 May 1944, RG-3, C-n-C Correspondence, Di-Ge, SWPA correspondence, MacArthur Papers; Eichelberger Dictations, "MacArthur," no date, pages 6-7 of dictation and 506-507 of Dictation notebook; Robert Eichelberger to Emma Eichelberger, 24 January 1944, Eichelberger Papers.

28. Robert Eichelberger to Emma Eichelberger, 24 January 1944, 26 January 1944, 1 February 1944, and 17 February 1944, Eichelberger Papers; Luvaas, *Dear Miss Em*, 69.

29. Robert Eichelberger to Douglas MacArthur, 9 October 1943, MacArthur and Eichelberger Papers; Eichelberger Dictations, "General MacArthur's . . . Conference with President Roosevelt and the Navy," 21 December 1947, 1-5.

30. James, *The Years of MacArthur, Volume II*, 427-28; Eichelberger Dictations, "General MacArthur and the Presidency . . .," 12 November 1953, 1-2.

31. Robert Eichelberger to Brig. General C. A. Willoughby, 18 September 1943, Eichelberger Papers; Robert Eichelberger to Emma Eichelberger, 10 September 1943, 15 September 1943 and 25 September 1943, Eichelberger Papers; Eichelberger Dictations, "Mrs. Roosevelt's Visit to Australia," no date, 1-8; Eichelberger Dictations, "Some Memories of Admiral Halsey," no date, pages 1-3 of Dictation and 860-62 of Dictation notebook.

32. James, *The Years of MacArthur, Volume II*, 429-31; Eichelberger Dictations, "MacArthur Lands on Beachheads, 'Mopping Up,' etc.," 24 September 1953, 2; Robert Eichelberger to Emma Eichelberger, 26 January 1944, Eichelberger Papers.

33. Eichelberger Dictations, "After My Return to Australia from Buna-Sanananda," 18 April 1948, 6.

34. Ibid.

35. Oral reminiscences of Major General Charles A. Willoughby, an interview with D. Clayton James conducted in Naples, Florida, on 30 July 1971, included in the

Charles Willoughby Papers at the MacArthur Memorial in Norfolk, Virginia, RG-23, pages 13, 24.

8

HOLLANDIA AND BIAK—
VICTORY AND CONFLICT

Although Eichelberger had indeed been informed in January 1944 that he would be allowed to take part in future operations, he did not begin preparations for his next assignment until the beginning of March. At that time, MacArthur told him that he would participate in the landing at Hollandia, an important Japanese base in New Guinea. In this operation, Eichelberger's I Corps was designated as the primary landing force, although the Hollandia task force was nominally under the command of General Krueger.

The Hollandia operation was to be an ambitious move. The Allied forces had advanced only 250 miles along the northern coast of New Guinea during the year that Eichelberger had spent on the sidelines. Hollandia was over 600 miles from the nearest Allied base, at Saidor. This operation was a bold risk for MacArthur, who still remembered the bloody lessons of Buna. After the costly Papuan campaign, MacArthur had devised a new strategy, which avoided high numbers of casualties by bypassing enemy strongpoints and attacking the rear and flanks of the enemy island defenses. Since this strategy had worked successfully during 1943 in the isolation of Rabaul and in the capture of the Marshall and Admiralty Islands, MacArthur was anxious to implement it along the northern coast of New Guinea. According to GHQ's estimation, the 600-mile advance to Hollandia would not only cut off the enemy strongpoints at Hansa Bay, Mandang, and Wewak, but would significantly accelerate the timetable for the advance to the Philippines by providing air bases and staging areas for future operations.[1]

In accordance with this strategy, Eichelberger was ordered (by MacArthur and Krueger) to make simultaneous landings at Humboldt Bay and Tanahmerah Bay, near Hollandia, and ordered to seize the three major airfields near the landing site. Then, after disposing of enemy forces in the Hollandia area, Eichelberger was to improve and widen the airfields, and to establish naval, port, and base facilities near Humboldt Bay. The speed of these operations was considered vital. The I Corps was responsible for building Hollandia into a logistical base capable of supporting the invasions of Biak island and Toem-Sarmi in New Guinea. Both these operations were scheduled for the latter part of May. Time, as well as the enemy, would be the major obstacles.[2]

On 22 April 1944, the 24th and 41st Divisions landed near Hollandia. The 24th Division, under the command of Major General Frederick Irving, landed at Tanahmerah Bay and proceeded southeast toward the Hollandia airfields. The 41st Division, under Major General Horace Fuller, landed 30 miles down the coast at Humboldt Bay, and proceeded toward the aerodromes from the northeast. Both forces advanced in a wide pincer movement along narrow paths and mountain passes, with the 24th Division having the shortest but most difficult route.[3]

These divisions were opposed by only scattered Japanese service units, instead of the three enemy regiments that MacArthur had foreseen. Faced with this weak opposition, Eichelberger's forces made rapid progress during the first three days of the operation. The 24th Division advanced 14 miles and the 41st Division nearly 20 miles. On 26 April 1944 (the fourth day of the operation), both divisions converged on the Hollandia airstrips, where they quickly scattered the defending Japanese forces. With the capture of the airfields on April 27, MacArthur announced that the operational phase of the landing was complete. The landing forces had suffered only 200 American casualties.[4]

On 28 April 1944, Eichelberger began the next phase of the operation—the building of roads, supply bases, and airfields for future operations in New Guinea and Biak. During this "big engineering phase," the I Corps widened and strengthened the surface of the Hollandia airfields and constructed a road from Humboldt Bay to the dromes. The engineer units built a huge supply base at Humboldt Bay and constructed docks, quarters, and installations for a "city" of over 140,000 men.[5]

In order to complete these tasks, Eichelberger discovered that he had to adopt the role of a factory foreman. His job was "to direct traffic and construction, and to demand speed, speed, speed." Under his direction, "sides of mountains were carved away, bridges and culverts were thrown across rivers and creeks, gravel and stone 'fill' were poured into sago swamps to make highways as tall as Mississippi levees." Hollandia rapidly became one of the "great bases of the war" with extensive roads, airfields, and harbor facilities. More importantly, all these engineering projects were completed on schedule to support the landings at Biak, Wadke, and Toem-Sarmi.[6]

Eichelberger was understandably proud of his accomplishments at Hollandia. He felt that he deserved some thanks for his enormous efforts as both a combat officer and engineer. His sentiments were shared by MacArthur, who felt that his I Corps commander had demonstrated great energy and diligence during the Hollandia campaign. After the operation had been completed in June 1944,

MacArthur thanked Eichelberger for his fine work. He hinted that "bigger things were in the works" for Bob and his staff in the near future.[7]

MacArthur's appreciation for Eichelberger's work was not shared by General Krueger. Krueger had originally been opposed to the I Corp's participation in the Hollandia campaign. His disgruntlement over this issue may have colored his judgment about Eichelberger's performance. Whatever his motives, Krueger clearly felt that he was in a better position (as commander of the Hollandia task force) than MacArthur to judge his subordinate's competence. He clearly believed that it was within his prerogative to point out several of the failings of the Hollandia campaign.[8]

In particular, Krueger argued that Eichelberger's advance was not impressive in view of the enemy's weak opposition. Most of the Japanese troops "fled ignominiously into the hills as the first shots were fired." Krueger also noted that the advance was retarded by a lack of discipline among the units; individual soldiers and even platoons stopped to search for souvenirs among captured Japanese supply dumps. Krueger was critical of the situation at Tanahmerah Bay, where he personally reprimanded soldiers for stealing booty from native huts and supply depots.[9]

In addition, Krueger believed that Eichelberger had badly bungled the supply situation. Supplies were carelessly unloaded and stockpiled at Tanahmerah and Humboldt Bay. There was a great amount of congestion and confusion at both beaches. Since there were only a few good roads to the beach supply depots, vitally needed supplies were left stranded on Humboldt Bay without the capacity to carry them inland. Furthermore, the few good roads that did exist were quickly destroyed by bad weather, continuous use, and the weight of heavy-duty vehicles. These problems contributed to a crisis at the front lines, where ammunition-depleted units had to be supplied by air despite the preponderance of material at Humboldt Bay.[10]

The vast accumulation of material on the beaches was an inviting target for enemy aircraft. The failure to properly disperse this material caused a tragedy on 23 April, when a single Japanese plane, dropping four bombs, ignited a gasoline dump at Humboldt Bay. The resulting conflagration quickly spread down the beach, causing 124 casualties and destroying over 60% of the stockpiled ammunition and rations (the equivalent of 11 LST loads of supplies). This horrible fiasco caused one supply officer to state, "Had the enemy attack from the air been in force, the loss of life and property would have probably delayed the operation for a considerable period of time."[11]

Krueger was equally appalled by this tragedy. On 28 May 1944, Krueger told Eichelberger that "his [Eichelberger's] staff had let him down in meeting our supply responsibilities." He severely reprimanded Bob for "being too easy" on his supply officers. He "ripped [Eichelberger] up one side and down the other" for other deficiencies, including the I Corps' failure to relay an "important message" to MacArthur's headquarters.[12]

Convinced that Eichelberger was making poor use of his staff members, Krueger offered to make Clovis Byers, the I Corps Chief of Staff, an assistant division commander in the 6th Army. When Byers refused—offering the excuse that he preferred to remain with Bob—Krueger took the refusal as a personal affront. He made demeaning statements about Eichelberger and his staff. He added that "Napoleon once said that the reason so few succeed in life was that most failed to recognize opportunity when it knocked."[13]

These comments did not go unnoticed by the I Corps staff. Most of the officers felt that they were being "picked on" for minor errors. Both Eichelberger and Byers believed that Krueger was jealous of their success and afraid of Bob's growing reputation as a combat officer. With the conclusion of the Hollandia operation, Eichelberger expected that his Corps would be placed "on ice," for he believed that Krueger would attempt to prevent him from enhancing his reputation in later operations.[14]

Eichelberger's fears proved to be groundless. On 14 June 1944, he was summoned to an emergency conference at Krueger's headquarters. Upon his arrival, he was informed that he would take part in the operation at Biak island. American forces had already landed at Biak on 27 May 1944. These combat units, after initial successes, had bogged down in the area of the Biak airfields; strong enemy units were lodged in the cliffs overlooking the dromes. After several weeks of aborted attacks and unsuccessful attempts to capture the airfields, MacArthur had finally grown tired of the delays and instructed Krueger to speed up the operation.

MacArthur's impatience was based on a variety of factors. First, he had promised Admiral Nimitz that he would provide air support, from Biak, for the landing on Saipan, scheduled for 15 June 1944. The delays in the capture of the Biak airfields, then, not only threatened the timetable for the Saipan operation, but served as a source of personal embarrassment for MacArthur.[15]

Furthermore, after the initial early successes of the campaign, MacArthur declared, in a communiqué on 3 June 1944, that the Biak operation was now in the "mopping up" phase. The inaccuracy of this communiqué became apparent when heavy fighting continued around the Biak airfields during the second week of June. The Australian press picked up the inconsistency and criticized MacArthur for his duplicity. This negative publicity certainly added to MacArthur's humiliation, and made him anxious to conclude the operation in the quickest possible manner.[16]

After these embarrassing incidents, MacArthur sent several messages to Krueger, inquiring whether the advance was "being pushed with sufficient determination." After a short investigation, Krueger decided that it was not. He then told MacArthur that he was sending Eichelberger to Biak to add impetus to the attacks on the airfields. Krueger's decision did not indicate any great confidence in Eichelberger's ability; he later stated that his choice was based on the fact that Bob was available and was "sitting around on [his] rear."[17]

Whatever his motivations, Krueger sent for Eichelberger on the night of 14 June and briefed him on the Biak situation. "Despite the communiqués and press stories to the contrary," he said, "things [had not gone] well. . . . Severe fighting, incredibly rough terrain, and heat and scarcity of water [had] rapidly [worn down the 41st Infantry Division]." After three weeks of hard fighting, the airfields "had not yet been secured" and "the enemy had not yet been driven far enough away from the one airfield which had been captured." Krueger ordered Eichelberger to "put some 'oomph' into" the attack, and to capture the airfields as soon as possible. He also instructed Eichelberger to replace General Horace H. Fuller and his staff "as the Task Force Command" on Biak, but to retain Fuller as commander of the 41st Division.[18]

After receiving these orders, Eichelberger flew 300 miles, from Hollandia to Biak island, on 15 June 1944. Upon his arrival, he conducted a brief reconnaissance of the front lines. He discovered that Krueger had been accurate in his description of the tactical situation—the troops were indeed tired, depressed, and worn down by weeks of attacks against strong enemy positions. Furthermore, the American units were badly scrambled. They lacked adequate information about the location and strength of the enemy's positions. Although some progress had been made in eliminating the enemy forces around the airfields, the Japanese still had the ability to move into the American rear via an underground system of interlocking caves and tunnels.[19]

Based on these conditions, Eichelberger decided on 16 June 1944 to conduct a more extensive personal reconnaissance of the battlefield areas. He deliberately chose to ignore Krueger's demands for an immediate attack on the airfields. Eichelberger had many reasons for this decision, not the least of which was his desire to avoid a painful repetition of the Buna campaign. As at Buna, he found himself in a situation where he was asked to save a stalled operation by hurried frontal attacks against strong enemy positions. This strategy had earned him bitter criticism and the title of "Bobby the Butcher" in Papua. He had no desire to repeat this experience.

From 16 June to 19 June, Eichelberger conducted a more careful examination of the American and Japanese positions on Biak. He avoided any major offensives against the Japanese caves and entrenchments. Instead, he rested and regrouped his own forces. He fixed the location of enemy units through the use of scouting and patrols. Those officers who had apparently not performed adequately during the operation were replaced; among these officers were General Horace Fuller, the commander of the 41st Division, who had in fact requested his own relief.[20]

These preparations were interrupted by a message from General Krueger on 17 June 1944. Irate that Eichelberger had not yet begun an advance against the airfields, Krueger wrote, "It is . . . vitally necessary that you promptly reduce Jap positions harassing Marshmellow [Mokmer airfield] and rush completion of

Marshmellow and Knockout dromes." Krueger reiterated, "launch your attack in Marshmellow area promptly and press it home with the utmost vigor."[21]

Eichelberger felt that Krueger had no real appreciation of the problems of the American forces. He was irritated that Krueger was not physically present at Biak to examine the situation for himself. "A combat man who is risking his life," he stated, "takes a dim view of pontifical messages coming up from those living in safety and comparative comfort." Eichelberger believed that Krueger's tough messages in fact were intended to impress MacArthur, for he was aware that Krueger was under intense pressure from his superiors to conclude the Biak operation. "In view of the fact that these messages were monitored in as far back as Melbourne," he stated, "I knew that all the people back to Melbourne including General MacArthur would know just how tough General Krueger was getting with me."[22]

Eichelberger was determined not to serve as Krueger's "whipping boy." After some deliberation, he decided to ignore, for the second time, Krueger's demand for an immediate attack. In an attempt to gain MacArthur's respect by an equal show of toughness and self-confidence, Eichelberger prepared a carefully worded response to Krueger's message and sent it over the air. This response, which admittedly contained a combination of insubordination, "bluff," and "bravado," stated the following:

> When I arrived here I was in almost complete ignorance of the situation and I was unable to controvert the statements of various officers that all possible punch was being put into the fight against the Japanese. After two days at the front, I feel that Doe with a coordinated attack on Monday can drive the Japanese back far enough to give Mokmer [airfield] reasonable protection. I am giving him Sunday in order that he may move forward part of [his forces], reorganize, rest, and prepare his troops for the drive on Monday. By Tuesday, I shall be ready if it then seems advisable to throw the Thirty-Fourth Infantry into a drive to the West and North from the vicinity of Mokmer.[23]

This response silenced Krueger, for Eichelberger was able to conduct his operations according to the terms of this message. On Monday, 19 June 1944, Eichelberger sent three battalions of the 41st Infantry Division into the rear of the enemy positions above the Mokmer airfield. These units successfully encircled the enemy caves. The Japanese forces panicked and scattered during the day's fighting. By the evening of 19 June, the tactical situation had improved dramatically. Eichelberger reported that the Mokmer airfield was now "secure from hostile ground attack."[24]

On Tuesday, 20 June, Eichelberger moved his forces toward the west in an attack on the two remaining airfields, Borokoe and Sorido. These dromes were lightly defended with the Japanese offering only slight resistance to the attacking

American units; after a few hours of sharp fighting, both dromes were in American hands. On the evening of 20 June, Eichelberger reported that units of the 41st Division were storming the ridges surrounding the captured airfields.

On Wednesday, June 21, the 41st Division attacked the Japanese forces at the Sump (also known as the West Caves), a series of underground passages and depressions located to the north of Mokmer drome. The Sump was a more difficult position to capture than the airfields; the enemy was protected by a maze of caves and tunnels that were adequately furnished with food, ammunition, and living quarters. Eichelberger attempted to eliminate this enemy sanctuary by a variety of methods, including the use of TNT, tanks, flamethrowers, bazookas, and ignited gasoline drums. But, these devices were only partially successful. It was not until the afternoon of 21 June that the 41st Division finally discovered the proper technique for destroying the Japanese subterranean bunkers. The American units "searched out crevices and cracks which led underground and poured hundreds of barrels of gasoline in them." When the gasoline was ignited, a "series of dull explosions were heard"; the enemy soldiers in the Sump were either incinerated or killed by the concussion from the blast.[25]

With this important position destroyed, Eichelberger next concentrated his efforts on the Japanese forces located to the east of the Mokmer drome. Entrenched in deep caves, most of the enemy units were located along the coastal road extending from the landing beaches to Mokmer airfield. On Thursday, 22 June, units of the 41st Division attacked these positions, encircling the Japanese units in the caves along the coastal road. With the help of the air force, which skip-bombed the cliffs along the southern coast, Eichelberger was able to destroy these pockets of Japanese resistance by the morning of June 23.

By 24 June, the bulk of the Japanese resistance on Biak was broken. Eichelberger was able to concentrate on mopping up the remaining Japanese units north of the airfields. From 25 June to 27 June, the 41st Division proceeded along the coastal road from Mokmer drome to Dedifoe, and advanced northward from Sorido to Korim on the northern coast. These operations progressed at a satisfactory pace. The few remaining pockets of enemy resistance were quickly scattered. On 27 June 1944, Eichelberger reported that the enemy was retreating throughout Biak, and was no longer capable of staging offensive operations. On 28 June 1944, Krueger declared that the situation on Biak was "stabilized"; he ordered Eichelberger to turn over the "Biak Task Force" to General Jens Doe and return to his Corps headquarters at Hollandia.[26]

Eichelberger was highly pleased with his performance during the campaign, and he returned to Hollandia on 29 June 1944 with the conviction that he had done a fine job at Biak. Eichelberger wrote his wife that "the boys [of the 41st Division] needed a kick in the pants and I had to give it to them." General Fuller had been "using little nibbling attacks that would not have gotten any place," he argued, and "the way [Fuller] had been fighting the Japanese would have ended in a victory for [the enemy]." Eichelberger stated that, unlike Fuller, he was able to earn a "speedy" victory by careful use of reconnaissance, quick flanking movements, and the willingness to try a variety of methods. He concluded that, due to his successful tactics, "it was a great break to go to Biak and it puts us in a preferential position."[27]

Historians have been less impressed with Eichelberger's victories at Biak and Hollandia. John Keegan's *The Second World War* (1989) and Guy Wint's *Total War* fail to mention either operation. Martin Gilbert's book, *The Second World War*, and John Costello's *The Pacific War* discuss the Hollandia campaign in less than a paragraph.[28]

The most complete discussions of the Hollandia operation are included in Robert Ross Smith's *Approach to the Philippines* and in Admiral Barbey's *MacArthur's Amphibious Navy*. Barbey notes that the Hollandia campaign was a great victory; MacArthur outwitted the Japanese commanders, and landed 600 miles behind the enemy lines at weakly defended Hollandia. Barbey makes no attempt to evaluate Eichelberger's performance, but notes that there was little fighting during the entire operation. Barbey does imply that Eichelberger was overcautious in his estimation of the enemy's capabilities.[29]

Smith's *The Approach to the Philippines* states that the Hollandia operation was indeed very successful, for it provided an "excellent air, naval, and logistic base from which future operations in western New Guinea were to be staged." Hollandia was captured with little fighting and only a minimal loss of American lives. Smith agrees with Barbey that there was "no strong Japanese resistance" on Hollandia. Smith makes no attempt to evaluate the performance of the American commanders, but implies that Eichelberger could be partially blamed for the supply problems along the beaches.[30]

Eichelberger fares only slightly better among historians of the Biak campaign. Ronald Spector, in *Eagle Against the Sun*, states that Biak was the scene of an intense battle. General Whitney, in his book *MacArthur*, agrees that the enemy fought "harder than usual" on Biak island. Neither author makes any attempt to evaluate the performance of the American commanders or troops, although they at least mention Eichelberger's name in connection with the fighting.[31] Smith's *The Approach to the Philippines* is the only study that makes a critical analysis of the Biak operation. Fuller's relief, Smith argues, may have been unjustified. After Fuller's departure, Eichelberger took three days to acquaint himself with the situation, and employed his units in the same manner as had Fuller. Although Smith does not condemn Eichelberger for his actions, his analysis implies that Eichelberger's performance was no better than Fuller's, and that his command decisions were something less than inspired.[32]

MacArthur, however, was impressed with Eichelberger's performance. After the Biak campaign, he informed General Clovis Byers (Eichelberger's chief of staff) that he was "very proud of what had been done" by Bob and his staff. As a token of his appreciation, MacArthur awarded Eichelberger an Oak Leaf cluster to his Silver Star, shortly after the completion of the campaign; the citation commended the I Corps commander for his "spectacular leadership" and "heroic conduct."[33]

Furthermore, MacArthur decided, after the Biak campaign, that Eichelberger was ready for additional responsibilities. At the end of June 1944, he wrote to General George C. Marshall that "the nature of the operations in this theatre . . . now require the establishment of an additional army headquarters. . . . It is contemplated that Lieut. General Eichelberger will be assigned to [this] command." MacArthur subsequently authorized the formation of the 8th Army and its transfer to the Southwest Pacific. For unknown reasons, he failed to inform Eichelberger that he would be in command of this army when it reached its final destination at Hollandia. For a period of six weeks, MacArthur allowed rumors of the planned formation of the 8th Army to filter down to the I Corps staff. He refused to either confirm or deny that Eichelberger was the chosen commander of this new unit.[34]

MacArthur's ambivalence toward the command of the 8th Army may have been caused by Eichelberger's superior, General Krueger. Krueger did not believe that there was a need for an additional army in the Southwest Pacific, nor did he feel that Eichelberger was qualified to command an army, based upon his conduct during the Biak campaign. Krueger was irked by the fact that Eichelberger ignored his orders to launch an immediate attack against the Biak airfields. He blamed "Bob's tardiness" for the 6th Army's failure to meet the timetable for the invasion of Saipan. Krueger was also displeased with Eichelberger's tactics on Biak; he complained that they were neither effective nor imaginative. As Krueger noted, Bob delayed his attacks for several days, and then "drew up new attack plans [in which his troops were] employed in the same area and in much the same manner as General Fuller had been using them." Krueger concluded that Eichelberger's presence at Biak prolonged the operation, and resulted in the relief of a fine combat officer, General Fuller.[35]

Krueger freely expressed these criticisms to his peers. But is unclear what (if any) impression they had on MacArthur. Krueger's criticisms did create a storm of controversy at I Corps headquarters; Eichelberger was convinced that Krueger was trying to destroy his reputation in the Southwest Pacific. Certain that Krueger was acting out of spite and jealousy, Eichelberger decided after the Biak operation that he would no longer tolerate "Walter's insults," but would respond with harsh words of his own.

In July 1944, Eichelberger decided to put this new policy into effect during a meeting with his superiors at Hollandia. During this meeting, Krueger brought up the subject of Fuller's relief at Biak; he blamed Eichelberger for Fuller's decision to quit. Eichelberger responded in an indignant fashion, and told Krueger that Fuller had requested his own relief because "[he] objected strenuously to the [critical] messages he was getting from Walter." After this angry outburst, Eichelberger reported that Krueger acted in an insulting manner for the next several weeks, and failed to properly congratulate him for his fine job at Biak.[36]

Relations between Eichelberger and Krueger continued to deteriorate in July and August of 1944. Eichelberger played more than a passive role in this dispute. He accused Krueger, for example, of attempting to sabotage his career by refusing to put any complimentary remarks about the Hollandia and Biak operations into his efficiency reports. Eichelberger complained that "in these reports, Krueger merely stated the names Hollandia and Biak" without "any comments," and with "nothing to indicate that I was in combat at these places." A "military man [could] realize just what was being done to me," he stated, for Krueger's actions "give you an idea of how a man would try to prevent an officer junior to him from getting any kind of a high command."[37]

Furthermore, Eichelberger accused Krueger of failing to make any preparations for the incoming 8th Army. In July 1944, MacArthur's signal officer (General Spencer Akin) informed the I Corps staff that Bob had been chosen as the commander of the 8th Army, and that the 6th Army had been ordered to prepare a camp for this unit at Hollandia (these rumors were not confirmed by MacArthur until August 1944). When Eichelberger confronted Krueger with this information, Krueger replied that Akin's remarks were only idle rumors. There was no substance, he stated, to the claim that the 8th Army was being sent to Hollandia or the Southwest Pacific.[38]

In August 1944, the advance elements of the 8th Army arrived in Hollandia. Krueger was forced to drop the pretense that the 8th Army was only a rumor. Even then, Krueger refused to cooperate in the construction of a camp. He treated the 8th Army like "an illegitimate child" that "he would like to strangle" or put "in a sack." Krueger's behavior did not surprise Eichelberger. "The truth of the matter," he stated, "was that [Walter] was frightened over the approach of his 64th birthday and was afraid that he might be sent home, and that, with the formation of a new Army, got him down."[39]

By September 1944, Eichelberger realized that Krueger could not be counted on to support the 8th Army. The 6th Army commander instead would do everything in his power to eliminate this unit as a competitor in the Southwest Pacific. Eichelberger understood that only MacArthur could protect this new command from Krueger; only MacArthur could legitimize this unit by assigning it important combat duties in the upcoming operations. Eichelberger believed, then, that he was locked in a personal duel with Krueger for MacArthur's affections.

In the fall of 1944, Eichelberger found himself in a situation reminiscent of his childhood, when he had been engaged in bitter competition with his brothers for the affection of his father. In that struggle, Eichelberger had failed to come out the victor and, as a result, had been deeply wounded and scarred. In the current competition, Eichelberger was determined not to come out second-best; he girded himself for the struggle with the determination of a "man possessed." To the 8th Army staff, the upcoming fight was a struggle for recognition and respect. For Eichelberger, it was a struggle for vindication itself.

NOTES

1. MacArthur, *Reminiscences*, 189–92; Whitney, *MacArthur*, 110–11; Luvaas, *Dear Miss Em*, 103; Eichelberger, *Our Jungle Road to Tokyo*, 100–101; Eichelberger Dictations, "Hollandia," no date, 1–2.

2. Ronald Spector, *Eagle Against the Sun: The American War with Japan* (New York: Free Press, 1985), 284–86; Barbey, *MacArthur's Amphibious Navy*, 158–68; Military Reports, "Tanahmerah Historical Report, Tanahmerah Bay Landing Force, Hollandia-Tanahmerah Campaign," no date, included in box 64 of the Eichelberger Papers, 33, 37; Eichelberger, *Our Jungle Road to Tokyo*, 104–105; Eichelberger Dictations, "Hollandia," no date, 4.

3. Spector, *Eagle Against the Sun*, 286–87; Military Report, "History of the Hollandia Operation," no date, completed at the request of General Robert L. Eichelberger, included in box 63 of the Eichelberger Papers, 1–6.

4. MacArthur, *Reminiscences*, 190–92; Military Report, "Tanahmerah Historical Report," prepared under the direction of General Fred Irving, no date, included in box 64 of the Eichelberger Papers, 112–13; Eichelberger, *Our Jungle Road to Tokyo*, 109–10.

5. Eichelberger, *Our Jungle Road to Tokyo*, 113–14.

6. Spector, *Eagle Against the Sun*, 287–88; Eichelberger, *Our Jungle Road to Tokyo*, 113–15.

7. Eichelberger Dictations, "Hollandia," no date, 9; Robert Eichelberger to Emma Eichelberger, 21 April 1944, Eichelberger Papers; cablegram, Commanding General of the Sixth Army to the Commanding General, I Corps, no date, included in Eichelberger Papers.

8. Eichelberger Dictations, "Memorandum on *The Approach to the Philippines*," 29 July 1957, page 3 or page 406 in the dictation notebook.

9. Robert Ross Smith, *The Approach to the Philippines*, (United States Army in World War II, The War in the Pacific, Washington, D.C.: Office of the Chief of Military History, Department of the Army, 1953), 55–57, 84, 99; Barbey, *MacArthur's Amphibious Navy*, 172; MacArthur, *Reminiscences*, 189–90; Eichelberger Dictations, "Memorandum on Leadership," no date, 7; Eichelberger Dictations, "Hollandia," no date, 9.

10. General Walter Krueger, *From Down Under to Nippon: The Story of Sixth Army in World War II* (Washington, D.C.: Combat Forces Press, 1953), 65; Kenney, *General Kenney Reports*, 393; Military Reports, "History of the Hollandia Operation," no date, included in box 63 of the Eichelberger Papers, 18–20, 27; Smith, *The Approach to the Philippines*, 78–82.

11. Smith, *The Approach to the Philippines*, 195; "restricted" draft included in box 71 of the Eichelberger Papers, 51–56; Barbey, *MacArthur's Amphibious Navy*, 176.

12. Diary of Clovis E. Byers, 28 May 1944, box 30—Diaries, Clovis E. Byers Papers, Hoover Institution on War, Revolution and Peace, Archives Department, Stanford University.

13. Diary of Clovis E. Byers, 29 May 1944 and 30 May 1944, box 30—Diaries, Clovis E. Byers Papers.

14. Clovis Byers to Emma Eichelberger, 30 May 1944, Eichelberger Papers; Robert Eichelberger to Emma Eichelberger, 29 May 1944 and 8 June 1944, Eichelberger Papers.

15. James, *The Years of MacArthur, Volume II*, 458–59; Luvaas, *Dear Miss Em*, 125; Eichelberger, *Our Jungle Road to Tokyo*, 135–38.

16. James, *The Years of MacArthur, Volume II*, 458–59; Luvaas, *Dear Miss Em*, 125; Eichelberger, *Our Jungle Road to Tokyo*, 135–38; Smith, *The Approach to the Philippines*, 290–341; Costello, *The Pacific War*, 474–75.

17. Eichelberger Dictations, "Memo to Milton MacKaye—The Biak Operation," 10 February 1949, 2; James, *The Years of MacArthur, Volume II*, 459–60; Smith, *The Approach to the Philippines*, 341–42.

18. Harold Riegelman, *Caves of Biak—An American Officer's Experiences in the Southwest Pacific* (New York: Dial Press, 1955), 136–37; Eichelberger Dictations, "Memorandum to Milton MacKaye," 10 February 1949, 3.

19. Military report, "History of the Biak Operation," prepared under the direction of General Robert Eichelberger, no date, 3–5, included in Eichelberger Papers.

20. Military Reports, "History of the Biak Operation," no date, 6–7, included in Eichelberger Papers; Eichelberger, *Our Jungle Road to Tokyo*, 142–45; Smith, *The Approach to the Philippines*, 343–45, 368–69; Spector, *Eagle Against the Sun*, 292; Gilbert, *The Second World War*, 542.

21. Radiogram, Commanding General Sixth Army to Commanding General, U.S. Forces, APO 920, 17 June 1944, WF 3394, included in Eichelberger Papers.

22. Eichelberger Dictations, "Background for the Biak Operation," 4 April 1948, 6–7; Eichelberger Dictations, "Fuller, also Krueger," 29 May 1961, 3.

23. Radiogram, Commanding General, U.S. Forces, APO 920 (Eichelberger) to Commanding General (Krueger), 17 June 1944, included in Eichelberger Papers; Eichelberger Dictations, "Memo. to Milton MacKaye," 10 February 1949, 7.

24. Military report, "History of the Biak Operation," no date, 8, included in Eichelberger Papers; Eichelberger Dictations, "Background for the Biak Operation," 4 April 1948, 8.

25. Smith, *The Approach to the Philippines*, 375; Eichelberger, *Our Jungle Road to Tokyo*, 151; Military Report, "History of the Biak Operation," no date, 11–14, included in Eichelberger Papers.

26. Krueger, *From Down Under to Nippon*, 101; military report, "History of the Biak Operation," no date, 15–18, Eichelberger Papers; Eichelberger, *Our Jungle Road to Tokyo*, 153; Smith, *The Approach to the Philippines*, 378–79.

27. Robert Eichelberger to Emma Eichelberger, 22 June 1944 and 30 June 1944, Eichelberger Papers; Eichelberger Dictations, "Background for the Biak Operation," 4 April 1948, 11–13.

28. Keegan, *The Second World War*; Wint and Calvocoressi, *Total War: The Story of World War II*; Gilbert, *The Second World War: A Complete History*, 519; Costello, *The Pacific War*, 473–74.

29. Barbey, *MacArthur's Amphibious Navy*, 172, 173, 178, 179.

30. Smith, *The Approach to the Philippines*, 55–57, 63–66, 78–82, 83–84.

31. Spector, *Eagle Against the Sun*, 291–94; Whitney, *MacArthur*, 111–12.

32. Smith, *The Approach to the Philippines*, 344–45, 368–69, 379.

33. Robert Eichelberger to Emma Eichelberger, 13 July 1944, Eichelberger Papers; Eighth Army General Orders No. 197, 24 December 1945, Silver Star Citation, Eichelberger Papers.

34. General Douglas MacArthur to Chief of Staff, War Department, no date, RG-4, box 17, War Department correspondence, MacArthur Papers; Robert Eichelberger to Emma Eichelberger, 8 June 1944 and 30 June 1944, Eichelberger Papers.

35. Smith, *The Approach to the Philippines*, 29 (of 1951 "restricted" draft, included in box 71 of the Eichelberger Papers); Willoughby, "Oral Reminiscences of Major General Charles A. Willoughby," 11–13, Charles A. Willoughby Papers, included with the MacArthur Papers in Norfolk, Virginia; Robert Eichelberger to Emma Eichelberger, 30 June 1944, Eichelberger Papers; Eichelberger Dictations, "Fuller, also Krueger," 29 May 1961, 4.

36. Eichelberger Dictations, "Fuller, also Krueger," 29 May 1961, 4, 5; Eichelberger Dictations, "Memo. to Milton MacKaye—The Biak Operation," 10 February 1949, 11; Robert Eichelberger to Emma Eichelberger, 30 June 1944, Eichelberger Papers; Eichelberger Dictations, "Memorandum on *The Approach To The Philippines*," 29 July 1957, page 2 of dictation, page 405 of dictation notebook.

37. Eichelberger Dictations, "Fuller, also Krueger," 29 May 1961, 6–7; Eichelberger Dictations, (no title or date), 6–7 of the Dictation, 631–32 of the dictation notebook.

38. Eichelberger Dictations, "Succession of Commands," 29 May 1961, 4; Eichelberger Dictations, "Fuller, also Krueger," 29 May 1961, 5; Eichelberger Dictations, "Background for the Biak Operation," 4 April 1948, 13; Robert Eichelberger to Emma Eichelberger, 26 June 1944 and 26 July 1944, Eichelberger Papers.

39. Eichelberger Dictations, "Memorandum to Milton MacKaye—The Biak Operation," 10 February 1949, 11; Robert Eichelberger to Emma Eichelberger, 29 July 1944, 30 July 1944 and 16 August 1944, Eichelberger Papers.

9

THE PHILIPPINES—
COMPETITION WITH KRUEGER

On 9 September 1944, Eichelberger received the official confirmation of his selection as the commanding officer of the 8th Army. He was notified that he had been released from the command of General Walter Krueger, and he also was instructed that his principal duties for the next several months would be to train and consolidate his new unit. MacArthur informed him that the 8th Army, consisting of over 200,000 troops stretching from Morotai Island to Australia, would participate in the proposed invasion of the central and southern Philippines.[1]

This information was welcome news for Eichelberger, but a very disturbing revelation for Krueger. Krueger had assumed that his 6th Army would make all the major landings in the central Philippines. The 8th Army, he believed, would be limited to training or supply duties. Krueger suddenly realized that the formation of the 8th Army had shifted the balance of power, and that he would now have to compete with Eichelberger for his assignments in the Southwest Pacific.

This revelation did nothing to improve the relations between the two men. Krueger and Eichelberger had decided months ago that they did not like each other, and the formation of the 8th Army only provided another excuse to vent their hostility. In September and October of 1944, both men engaged in a mean-spirited competition for petty advantages, with neither side willing to declare an end to their private, self-declared war.

The most obvious manifestation of this competition was the attempt by both parties to outdo each other in the construction of their camps. This competition began in September; Krueger and Eichelberger decided to build their respective headquarters near Hollandia on opposite sides of a lake. Determined to demonstrate his camp-building superiority over his former subordinate, Krueger spent a great deal of time and labor in building his headquarters. In the process, he monopolized most of the available building materials and engineer units. Within several weeks, he had built a luxurious camp in a beautiful location, complete with concrete buildings and bright spotlights to provide nighttime security.[2]

These elaborate preparations did not go unnoticed by Eichelberger, who decided from the outset that he would not be outdone by his rival. He subsequently made enormous efforts to improve the quality of the Eight Army's camp, especially to his quarters and mess. Over a period of several weeks, a large private office overlooking a lake was constructed, complete with screening, a large verandah, and an adjoining badminton court. A new Packard automobile, five boats (including two 38-foot cabin cruisers), and a plane were commandeered for the private use of the Eight Army commander. The plane, a refurbished B-17 bomber, contained an electric range and icebox, an upholstered cabin, a bed and overhead curtains, and a "grand seat out in front" in the bombardier's compartment.[3]

For his mess, Eichelberger imported a variety of foodstuffs, including a large supply of ice cream and at least 15 bottles of liquor for guests. Under his instructions, mixed vegetables, beef, pork, and lamb were flown in from Australia. In comparing his dinner arrangements with General Kenney's, Eichelberger stated that ". . . I do not believe his cook can compare with ours and certainly the Chinese do not know as much about serving as our ex-DuPont butler."[4]

Despite this accumulation of comforts, Eichelberger complained that Krueger had impeded his efforts to improve his camp and headquarters. "Walter had a battalion of engineers working on his command post for two months," he argued, with the result that the 8th Army "had to fight for every engineer we have been able to get to do any construction work." He portrayed himself as forced to send out "foraging parties" in search "of nails and other things" because Krueger had hoarded most of the construction materials. Moreover, his pleas for assistance and cooperation were largely ignored. On one occasion, Krueger reportedly remarked, "I don't give a God-damn if the Eighth Army sleeps in a swamp." Eichelberger stated that Krueger's attitude reminded him of an old childhood expression that he had used when "somebody [took] most of the candy": "Take it all, hog; I'll starve."[5]

Upset by "Walter's stinginess," Eichelberger in September 1944 decided to "get even." He criticized Krueger's ability before members of MacArthur's staff, hoping to irritate Krueger and also influence the choice of armies for the upcoming Philippine campaign.

In his weekly visits to MacArthur's headquarters, Eichelberger made frequent remarks about the inadequacies of Krueger's New Guinea operations. He suggested strongly that some "new blood" was needed in the Southwest Pacific. Believing that Generals Stephen J. Chamberlin, Charles A. Willoughby and George Kenney (MacArthur's operations officer, chief intelligence officer, and chief air officer, respectively) had the most influence on MacArthur, Eichelberger focused his attentions on these individuals. He tried to convince them that Krueger was competent but decaying in ability and vitality.[6]

The image of Krueger that Eichelberger attempted to portray was not altogether inaccurate, but it did exaggerate Krueger's more negative aspects. For example, Eichelberger emphasized that Krueger looked old and tired. This appearance, he suggested, was only natural for a person who was within a few months of his 64th birthday (the mandatory retirement age for most military personnel). Furthermore, Krueger had never "commanded anything in person," but had always been "many miles away, holding a ball bat over the fellow who has the responsibility of fighting." This style of leadership, Eichelberger argued, was acceptable for the New Guinea campaign, where the small scale of operations precluded any front-line leadership. The operations in the Philippines, however, required a commanding officer who was more in touch with conditions at the front. For this assignment, a younger and quicker officer was more qualified. Eichelberger, seven years younger than Krueger, with a reputation for front-line leadership from Buna and Biak, obviously considered himself the logical choice as Krueger's replacement. He suggested to MacArthur's staff that he was ready and able to handle the additional responsibilities. As a final argument, he stated that his staff was better equipped than the 6th Army to handle the Philippine operations. They were fresh, he argued, and "not haunted with the desire for rotation and other things which come up after officers have been out here 18 months."[7]

Not content making these arguments to MacArthur's staff, Eichelberger was determined to prove to Krueger himself that he was unfit for additional duties. On the rare occasions when the two generals met, Eichelberger casually commented on the haggard appearance of the 6th Army commander. He strongly suggested that Walter take a "long-needed" rest. He mentioned that Krueger had a "very slow step," and that Walter's poor eyesight was the mark of a "very old man." On one occasion, Eichelberger attempted to help Krueger into a boat, explaining that "it is nothing for a young fellow like myself but I thought he needed help [to get aboard]."[8]

Krueger quickly recognized Eichelberger's psychological ploys and responded to them in kind. Aware that the 8th Army commander was sensitive about his weight, Krueger commented on Bob's flabby midriff. He suggested that Eichelberger would benefit from some lighter meals and regular exercise. Krueger also commented on Bob's fondness for the media; he stated that, unlike the commander of the 8th Army, he would "never have a former newspaperman on [his] staff."[9]

More importantly, Krueger also started his own propaganda campaign among MacArthur's staff. In his visits to headquarters, he emphasized his own strengths as well as the weaknesses of his opponent. He agreed, for example, with General Willoughby's feeling that there "was no urgent necessity" for forming the 8th Army (both men believed that the 8th Army was formed only because "MacArthur was . . . influenced by Eichelberger or by the people in Washington who backed him"). Krueger also stated that Eichelberger lacked the experience to plan amphibious operations and the toughness to deal with the sister services (the navy, marines and air force). He cleverly allowed that Bob was an able officer who told good jokes and was popular with reporters. Krueger stressed, however, that these qualities were not sufficient to guarantee success in the upcoming operations; experience, and not glamour, was most essential in gaining a victory. Finally, Krueger emphasized that his own staff was far superior to the 8th Army's officers; his men had planned and staged numerous operations throughout the Southwest Pacific. The 8th Army staff, in comparison, was "brand new" from the United States (with two exceptions) and was totally inexperienced in amphibious warfare.[10]

This propaganda proved effective. At the end of September, Krueger was informed that his 6th Army had been chosen to make the initial landing in the Philippines on Leyte. The Joint Chiefs of Staff in August had given MacArthur permission to make a landing in the central Philippines; he was told that his plan to invade Luzon (in the northern Philippines) in January 1945 was dependent upon the success of the Leyte operation. MacArthur and his staff were therefore anxious for the Leyte landing to be an unqualified success, for the prestige of the army depended upon the speed of MacArthur's troops in carrying out this initial attack against the Philippines.

Although Chamberlin and Willoughby had the utmost respect for Eichelberger and his newly organized army, they agreed with Krueger's that the 8th Army staff was not used to the pressures and deadlines of amphibious planning. For this reason, they felt that it would be "safer" to allow the 6th Army to make the initial landing on Leyte in October. The 8th Army, they decided, could gradually "break in" by assuming mop-up duties on Leyte in December.[11]

This arrangement, while satisfactory to Krueger, was completely unacceptable to Eichelberger. In letters to his wife, he complained, "I was not made very happy over decisions because I see no place for myself in what one might call the big show." He added that Krueger "was trying to create the illusion that he was the only one with experience." He stated, however, that he had not yet decided to accept a subordinate role. "I shall be up close on Walter's heels always," he wrote, and if Krueger "stubs his toe . . . it is not beyond the bounds of possibility that I shall be included in the final show."[12]

Eichelberger's words proved prophetic. Krueger's troops made very slow progress during the first few weeks of the Leyte operation, and MacArthur seriously considered using Eichelberger to "bail out" the 6th Army. After the landing on the east coast of Leyte on 20 October 1944, Krueger's 6th Army made a slow but steady advance to the west; but within two weeks, the 6th Army was bogged down in the rice paddies and mountains of northern and central Leyte. The Japanese concentrated their defenses around mountain barriers such as Breakneck Ridge and Shoestring Ridge. These strongpoints successfully repulsed

THE PHILIPPINES—COMPETITION WITH KRUEGER   113

the attacks of the U.S. 32d, 7th, and 77th Divisions. Intelligence reports indicated that the advance was slow, and in "some places no forward progress was made in many days."[13]

MacArthur blamed Krueger for the 6th Army's failure to split the enemy's defenses. He told Eichelberger that he was "disappointed . . . that the troops have not moved faster"; he indicated that, if conditions did not improve, he "might have to relieve" Krueger. MacArthur commented that he "had held [Krueger] on over-age and expected him to be a driver," but that "Walter" had instead been very cautious and had made "many excuses" for his failures.[14]

MacArthur also indicated, by his actions and informal conduct, that he was displeased with Krueger's operations. On one occasion, as Eichelberger and Krueger were leaving GHQ after a conference, MacArthur "called down from his office, 'Come up and see me often, Bob!,' with no greeting to General Krueger." On another occasion, MacArthur left his office and "put [Bob] in [his] jeep to the amazement of the big-eyed soldiers and civilians passing by." This extra attention pleased Eichelberger, and indicated to him that "either . . . he [MacArthur] was through with Krueger and wanted to show his friendship for me, or . . . it was a warning to Krueger that he had better start fighting with more speed."[15]

MacArthur's true intentions were revealed at the end of November 1944, when he suggested that Krueger and the 77th Division land at the south end of the Ormoc valley. Krueger balked, arguing that an amphibious operation in this area would be exposed to heavy enemy submarine and air attack. Having heard enough "excuses" from Walter, MacArthur informed him that the 8th Army would take over the Leyte fighting on 5 December 1944, three weeks ahead of schedule. MacArthur also informed Krueger that the 8th Army would make the landing at Ormoc Bay, for Eichelberger's staff had already accepted GHQ's proposal.

Anxious not to be upstaged, Krueger agreed to make the landing after MacArthur granted him an additional three weeks to complete the operation. The date for the 8th Army takeover was pushed back to Christmas Day; meanwhile, Krueger was allowed to make a landing at Ormoc Bay on 7 December 1944. After this landing, the 6th Army advanced south along the Ormoc valley and, as MacArthur had predicted, scattered the remaining elements of organized Japanese resistance. On 25 December 1944, Krueger and MacArthur declared: "All organized resistance has ended. . . . The Leyte-Samar campaign can now be regarded as closed except for minor mopping-up." In a dramatic reversal of his previous statements, MacArthur announced that the Leyte operation "has been a magnificent performance on the part of all concerned." The "campaign," he stated, "has had few counterparts in the utter destruction of the enemy's forces with a maximum conservation of our own."[16]

These announcements were a severe jolt to Eichelberger. He felt that MacArthur had already betrayed him once by allowing Krueger to conduct the Ormoc landing. He complained, "[this] means . . . that I may sit around here until almost Christmas with nothing to do except keep in touch with" the situation. "If any of them [MacArthur or his staff] ever tell me about not wanting to hurt [Krueger's] feelings," he added, "I'll ask them why no one ever considered mine."[17]

Eichelberger also was angered by the fact that MacArthur had announced to the press that the Leyte operation was closed except for "minor mopping up." This announcement meant that the 8th Army would get no credit for their fighting on Leyte after the relief of the 6th Army; the press quickly lost interest in campaigns that had already been declared closed. Eichelberger noted that the use of the term "mopping up" did not make the 8th Army's task any easier. The "only difference between a big fight and mopping up," he stated, "is that when victory is obtained, nobody can call it that . . . [although] it is just as difficult and the bullets go by just as fast."[18]

Moreover, Eichelberger was convinced that the term "mopping up" did not adequately describe the fighting that still remained on Leyte. Although Krueger reported that the 6th Army had killed all but a few thousand of the enemy troops, Eichelberger believed that Krueger had grossly overestimated the number of enemy casualties. A large "reservoir" of Japanese combat troops, he believed, remained on the western end of the island. The so-called mop-up of Leyte would not be "any job for a boy," he wrote, and the 8th Army "will have to go at [the enemy] with hammer and tongs."[19]

Eichelberger's predictions proved to be overly pessimistic. The 8th Army met only scattered enemy resistance on Leyte after relieving the 6th Army on 26 December 1944. The weakness of the enemy defenses was caused in part by the Japanese high command; they had decided on 25 December 1944 that the Leyte campaign was lost and that the Japanese 35th Army should be transferred to other areas prior to evacuation. This order caused chaos within the Japanese ranks. Many units splintered and attempted to reach the western shore in small groups. These bands, in most cases hungry and poorly equipped, were intercepted by American combat units and destroyed piecemeal in the mountains and valleys of northwest Leyte. Eichelberger noted that the enemy troops "never seem to be in much force in any one place"; he found that he could easily destroy the Japanese units by requiring each division to send out 40 patrols daily in pursuit of the enemy. These patrols promptly destroyed the bulk of the Japanese stragglers. In mid-January, the 8th Army staff announced that the Leyte mop-up was rapidly "drawing to an end."[20]

The success of these operations did not provide any personal satisfaction for Eichelberger. He was keenly aware that he had missed out on the big show. He grumbled to his wife that the 8th Army was receiving no publicity for the Leyte mop-up, and that Krueger's 6th Army had been given the leading role for the next major operation—the invasion of Luzon. Eichelberger complained that Krueger had unjustly been declared a hero for his defective Leyte operations;

"since [Leyte] has now been called the most wonderful victory in history, [Krueger] is more or less on top again."[21]

Eichelberger voiced these complaints to MacArthur during his visits to GHQ in January 1945. He was surprised to learn that MacArthur agreed, and that he too was concerned about Krueger's slow advance on Leyte. Stating that Krueger indeed had bungled the campaign, MacArthur noted that in many ways it was "almost a pyrrhic victory." Only the successful Ormoc valley attack and the favorable publicity on the 6th Army had salvaged the operation. MacArthur was worried that Krueger's tardiness during the Leyte campaign might have been "indicative of the way [his] troops . . . [would] react later [on Luzon]."[22]

In order to alleviate this concern, MacArthur suggested that Eichelberger make plans to take two regimental combat teams into the Batangas or Lucena area of southern Luzon and "cut the Japanese lines of communication." Explaining that Krueger's 6th Army would land on Lingayen Gulf on 9 January 1945, MacArthur stated that Eichelberger's force therefore would serve as a diversion in the south for the 6th Army's northern advance. MacArthur implied that Eichelberger's southern attack would serve an added purpose; it would hopefully arouse Krueger's jealousy and "speed up the advance of the 6th Army." MacArthur had no qualms about putting Eichelberger and Krueger in direct competition against each other. He bluntly informed Eichelberger that this was his opportunity to prove that he could "out perform" the 6th Army. MacArthur told him that, unlike "Walter's" sluggish operations, this was the ideal opportunity to "be the Jeb Stuart of World War II, the George Patton of the Pacific."[23]

Eichelberger rose to MacArthur's challenge. He agreed to make the landing, provided that he could make some changes in MacArthur's plan. After consultation with his staff, Eichelberger proposed that the landing site be changed from Batangas to the Subic Bay and Nasugbu areas; he urged that the size of the force be increased from two regimental combat teams to two reinforced divisions. These alterations were approved by MacArthur in the first week of January. The 8th Army staff immediately made preparations for the scheduled landings in southern Luzon on 29 January 1945.[24]

The preparations were interrupted in mid-January by the objections of Generals Krueger, Chamberlin, and Willoughby, who were violently opposed to the details of Eichelberger's plan. They argued for either the alteration or cancellation of the 8th Army's landings in southern Luzon. General Krueger, for example, was "jealous" of the Nasugbu landing; he refused to give the 8th Army "a man, a gun or a bullet" for this operation. He also argued very strongly in favor of placing Eichelberger's Subic Bay forces under the jurisdiction of the 6th Army as soon as they "hit the beach" on Luzon.[25]

General Chamberlin was more concerned about the supply situation, particularly the shortage of ships for the Nasugbu operation. He was also alarmed by rumors emanating from the 8th Army staff, indicating that Eichelberger planned on going ashore with the leading units and conducting a "race for Manila" with

Krueger's 6th Army. In order to avoid this situation, Chamberlin reminded Bob that an officer of his rank could not personally command a unit less than a corps without MacArthur's permission. MacArthur's orders, he added, only permitted the 8th Army to "support the Central Plains operations of the 6th Army with diversionary landings in southern Luzon." In addition, Chamberlin informed Eichelberger that he was not in favor of these southern landings; there were too many risks involved and too few troops and supplies for the operation.

General Willoughby agreed with Chamberlin's assessment, and added that his intelligence reports did not look promising regarding the proposed landing sites. Willoughby was alarmed by the reports of Captain Bill Richmond, a young intelligence officer who had spent several weeks with the guerrilla forces in southern Luzon. Richmond reported that "there were two thousand Japanese around Nasugbu, twelve thousand back of those with heavy artillery and tanks, and fifteen thousand on Tagaytay Ridge [approximately 20 miles inland from Nasugbu]." Since these "figures . . . negated the chances for a successful expedition," Richmond recommended to Willoughby that the Nasugbu landing be canceled immediately.[26]

Richmond's recommendation resulted in some bitter wrangling between Eichelberger and GHQ. Eichelberger was determined to make his landing despite the protests of MacArthur's staff. He argued vehemently against Richmond, Willoughby, Chamberlin, and Krueger. He tried to prevent Richmond from making his intelligence report to GHQ and, failing this, argued that Richmond's report was inaccurate and misleading. The guerrillas, he stated, often gave exaggerated claims of Japanese strength in the Philippine islands. His own staff's estimate of the enemy numbers in the Nasugbu area, he argued, was considerably lower than Richmond's.[27]

In addition, Eichelberger claimed that Chamberlin's inadequate-supply arguments were equally misleading. There were more than sufficient troops and supplies, he argued, to conduct the Nasugbu landing. In order to ease Chamberlin's supply worries, Eichelberger told Chamberlin that he would have only one reinforced division land on Nasugbu. He also promised Chamberlin that "a 15-day supply of all classes" would be sufficient to conduct the operation, instead of the normal GHQ requirement of "a scheduled 30-day resupply." Finally, he assured Chamberlin that he had no intention of taking personal command of the landing forces, but would merely act as an observer.[28]

As for Krueger's allegations, Eichelberger argued for allowing the 8th Army to conduct at least one independent landing at Nasugbu. The 6th Army, he stated, was already overburdened by its scheduled operations in northern Luzon. Eichelberger also argued in favor of a landing at Subic Bay; he criticized Krueger's suggestion that this landing be made under the auspices of the 6th Army. The 8th Army had fewer responsibilities than Krueger's unit, and was "better equipped" to handle the Subic Bay landing without overextending its resources and manpower.[29] If problems of coordination became evident, he argued, the 8th Army could easily "turn over" the Subic Bay operation to the 6th Army within 48 hours of the initial landing.

MacArthur's staff agreed to make a compromise concerning the 8th Army's role in southern Luzon. It approved the Subic Bay landing, but allowed the 8th Army to have jurisdiction over this landing force for only 24 hours, long enough to make the initial landing. After this period, jurisdiction over this force would pass to Krueger's 6th Army. General Chamberlin decided to allow the 8th Army to make the Nasugbu landing as scheduled, with permission to advance only as far as Tagaytay Ridge. Since the intelligence reports suggested the presence there of large numbers of enemy soldiers, the operation was limited to a "reconnaissance in force." The 8th Army commander was instructed to evacuate the troops shortly after the landing if they encountered strong enemy resistance.[30]

This compromise solution was acceptable to Eichelberger, although he had no intention of stopping at Tagaytay Ridge after the landing at Nasugbu. One week after the plan was approved, Eichelberger informed his wife that he would try to get into Manila ("our old home town") before Krueger's 6th Army got there. "If the going was good," he wrote, "the only handicap given me by calling it a reconnaissance in force would be that I would have to land in column instead of with regiments abreast." He remarked, "I made up my mind that if conditions ashore were OK, I would land the rear elements not over three hours behind the others."[31]

Eichelberger knew that, by attacking Manila, he would be stretching his orders to the limit and taking big risks. He admitted that, in order to justify the landings to MacArthur's staff, he had to reduce the strength of his forces to a "shoestring" operation. The "intelligence is such," he stated, "that I do not know whether we will run into a deserted village or . . . get our pants shot off." Nevertheless, despite these risks, he was convinced that MacArthur wanted him to engage Krueger in a "race for Manila." Eichelberger's evidence for believing this was a statement by General Sutherland, indicating that "General MacArthur would like" Eichelberger to "capture Manila if possible." He interpreted these comments as oral instructions "quite at variance with the GHQ written order that my landing be a 'reconnaissance in force,'" and as "more of a . . . permission to go [to Manila] rather than a directive."[32]

Eichelberger's decision to attack Manila may also have been influenced by MacArthur's actions after the landing on Luzon. As scheduled, on 9 January 1945, Krueger's 6th Army landed on the southern coast of Lingayen Gulf, 120 miles north of Manila. On 10 January, these forces began a slow and ponderous drive southward. Casualties were light and one flank of Krueger's troops met almost no enemy opposition. After three days, MacArthur grew impatient with this "leisurely" advance. He warned Krueger that he expected the 6th Army to push rapidly forward. On 23 January 1945, Eichelberger learned from a correspondent that MacArthur was still displeased with Krueger's progress; the writer reported that he "had been laying down the law to Krueger" and "had given him an ultimatum to be in Manila by the 5th of February." During a visit to GHQ, Eichelberger was told by MacArthur that Krueger's troops were "mentally incapable but if given tremendous forces they [were] able to advance ponderously and slowly to victory."[33]

Eichelberger felt sure that MacArthur would not be displeased if the 8th Army made a drive toward Manila, especially if it incited Krueger's jealousy and encouraged the 6th Army to advance more rapidly toward the south. He ordered his leading commanders to make a "rapid advance" once they "hit the beach"; he promised them that he would "back [them] up if [they got their] pants shot off." Eichelberger wrote to his wife that "it will be a hard pull for me to beat [Krueger] out [in the race to Manila] because I have a long way to go"; but, he added, MacArthur had "invited me most heartily to get there first."[34]

Based on this "assumption," Eichelberger instructed the XI Corps of the 8th Army to land at Subic Bay on 29 January 1945. After warning General Charles Hall (the XI Corps commander) to go fast and disregard his flanks, this unit advanced over 15 miles to Olongapo in a 24-hour period. They quickly isolated the Japanese units in the Bataan peninsula. On 31 January, as prearranged, control of this force was turned over to Krueger's 6th Army. The XI Corps continued its operations in southern Luzon in coordination with the 6th Army's attack against Manila from the north.[35]

On 31 January 1945, elements of the 11th Airborne Division (7,000 combat troops) landed at Nasugbu, 45 miles south of Manila and over 60 miles southeast of the Subic Bay landing site. Unlike the Subic Bay corps, this force was scheduled to remain under the jurisdiction of the 8th Army, making it the focus of Eichelberger's hopes for a triumphant entry into Manila. Eichelberger ordered General "Joe" Swing, the 11th Airborne Division's commander, to push his troops forward relentlessly, and to take advantage of any opportunity for a fast dash into Manila.[36]

General Swing did not disappoint him. On the morning of 31 January, Swing's troops stormed ashore at Nasugbu and advanced rapidly inland. Two hours after the landing, Eichelberger decided that enemy resistance was not strong enough to dictate the withdrawal of the "reconnaissance in force"; he directed General Swing to land the remainder of the 11th Airborne Division. Detachments from this unit quickly pushed eastward. They captured several vital installations, including a small airfield, the town of Nasugbu, and the Palico River bridge. The capture of this bridge was especially important; it allowed an uninterrupted advance along the two-lane concrete Nasugbu-Tagaytay Road, one of the few passable transportation routes in the area. By sending troops and tanks down this road, the 11th Airborne was able to advance 15 miles during the first day.[37]

On 1 February, the 11th Airborne advanced an additional three miles down the Nasugbu-Tagaytay Road. At this point, with the supply and communication lines stretched to the limit, Eichelberger ordered a short rest for his leading units.

While his combat troops were resupplied and reorganized, Eichelberger sent patrols ahead to Tagaytay Ridge. He brought up reinforcements from the beaches at Nasugbu.

On 2-3 February, the 11th Airborne launched an attack against the powerful enemy positions on Tagaytay Ridge. This ridge was strategically vital; it dominated the surrounding heights, and provided easy access to a road which sloped downhill into Manila. Since Eichelberger expected enemy resistance to be strong, he supplemented the attack on this position with a flanking parachute drop and heavy air support.[38]

Almost from the start, the attack ran into serious problems. After an uphill advance of 20 miles, the 11th Airborne was nearly out of fuel. The attack almost foundered due to lack of gasoline for the tanks and self-propelled artillery. On 3 February, Eichelberger sent an emergency message to General Ennis Whitehead (the commander of the Fifth Air Force), requesting a "shipment by air" of octane gasoline "*today*"; he warned Whitehead that, without his "personal help," the 11th Airborne could not continue their attacks against the enemy positions.[39]

Eichelberger was also concerned about the planned parachute drop of the 511th Parachute Infantry Regiment behind enemy lines. Eichelberger and General Swing had originally planned this drop as a flanking maneuver to assist in the frontal assault on Tagaytay Ridge. But they had been frustrated by the lack of planes available for this mission. After some behind-the-scenes lobbying at GHQ, they had finally received the "go-ahead" for this operation, but were informed that the scarcity of planes made it necessary to transport the 511th Regiment in two separate flights instead of one. This decision caused problems on the morning of 3 February. The first flight of the 511th Regiment missed their drop zone and parachuted six miles off target. The second flight, arriving three hours later, observed the numerous chutes of the first flight on the ground; the troops jumped in the same location. This error resulted in massive confusion, and the 511th Regiment was effectively eliminated from any meaningful role in the battle for Tagaytay Ridge. This mistake also placed the regiment in potential jeopardy. The 8th Army reports stated that "stiff enemy resistance at this point might have proved disastrous, but fortunately, little opposition was encountered by our troops when they landed."

Despite these mistakes and the shortage of fuel, the 11th Airborne captured Tagaytay Ridge in two days. The success of this operation was due in part to "timely, accurate and effective" air support. The 8th Army reports indicated that "much credit for our success during this phase must be given to the air forces"; their "strafing and bombing were of immense value in destroying enemy positions and in accelerating the disintegration of his defenses."[40]

More importantly, enemy resistance simply melted away as the American troops advanced up the slopes of Tagaytay Ridge. Eichelberger later reported that "although the terrain was ideal for defense, many excellent prepared positions were taken with little or no opposition." The enemy "appeared to be demoralized" and "would not hold his ground and fight but offered only half-hearted resistance, leaving food, ammunition and personal equipment scattered along the highway as he fell back." Elements of the 11th Airborne rapidly seized the key enemy positions. All of Tagaytay Ridge was in U.S. hands by the evening of 3 February.[41]

On 4 February, the American troops moved past Tagaytay Ridge and attacked in a northward advance along Highway 17, a two-lane cement thoroughfare that served as the southern approach into Manila. In what has been described as a "half triumphal parade, half skirmishing advance," the 11th Airborne in column raced down this highway in a frantic effort to reach the suburbs of the Philippine capital. With Eichelberger at the head of the leading units, the 11th Airborne advanced 10 miles on the morning of 4 February. They were finally stopped by a Japanese strongpoint near the town of Ismus. After bypassing this position, the American units continued their advance throughout the afternoon; they reached the banks of the Paranaque River at nightfall.[42]

Eichelberger was highly excited during this period. His intelligence reports indicated that the southern approaches to Manila were unguarded and that the Japanese would abandon the Philippine capital rather than defend the city. He saw that there was a golden opportunity to sneak into Manila from the rear. His decision to do so meant that he would have to disobey his written orders to remain in the Tagaytay Ridge area, but he had few worries about such a risk. He was convinced that MacArthur would forgive him if he captured Manila ahead of Krueger's slow-moving 6th Army.[43]

He also hoped that his decision to race into Manila would gain him some extra publicity. After the landings at Subic Bay and Nasugbu, MacArthur announced in a communiqué on 31 January that the 8th Army had landed on Luzon. This communiqué, the first official announcement of the 8th Army, created a great deal of favorable press coverage back home. Eichelberger heard about this newspaper coverage from a group of reporters on 2 February. He was informed that additional articles about the 8th Army's operations would appear in newspapers throughout the United States. Eichelberger was concerned, however, that this publicity would be short-lived if the 8th Army were unable to participate in other newsworthy events. He feared that events in Europe would rapidly overshadow the Nasugbu operation unless the 8th Army captured a major city.[44]

With these considerations in mind, Eichelberger renewed his pleas for a rapid advance into Manila. On 5 February, he sent his troops across the Paranaque River in an amphibious assault. After a successful crossing, the 11th Airborne pushed forward into the suburbs of southern Manila. They advanced within 300 yards of Nichols airfield. At this point, the American units were abruptly stopped by "crossfire from pillboxes lining the highway and a barrage of heavy antiaircraft and medium artillery fire."[45]

From 6 to 10 February, the 11th Airborne hammered at these strong enemy fortifications in the Nichols Field-Fort McKinley sector. The strength of the enemy defenses was created in part by MacArthur's own communiqués, which gave the impression that an entire American army was approaching Manila from the south. In order to meet this apparent threat, the Japanese diverted some of their units from the northern defenses facing Krueger; they set them up in pre-pared positions along the Genko Line in southern Manila. This line of fortifications effectively slowed the progress of Eichelberger's units; the 11th Airborne was unable to advance beyond the suburbs of Manila.[46]

On 5 February, Eichelberger had heard rumors that Krueger's troops had increased the pace of their attacks. Elements of the 6th Army had reportedly made contact with enemy forces on the northern perimeter of Manila. On 6 February, Eichelberger was informed by GHQ that the 6th Army had breached the outer enemy defenses of Manila, and had captured Grace Park in the interior of the city.[47]

From this information, Eichelberger concluded on 7 February that the 8th Army was losing the competition to capture the Philippine capital. His own forces, he noted, were simply too weak to defeat the enemy defenses. They lacked sufficient numbers, artillery, and ammunition to compete with the 6th Army. He also noted that the 11th Airborne's supply lines were stretched dangerously thin; "our line," Eichelberger stated, "is a thousand yards wide and seventy miles long." He was informed by his supply officer that "the supply line was too long to be protected for its entire length and was subject to being cut and traffic interrupted for short periods."[48]

Despite these problems, Eichelberger refused to withdraw from the Manila area. He continued to attack the enemy positions around Nichols Field. From 7 to 9 February, he remained at the front lines, and watched as his troops suffered heavy casualties in desperate assaults against strong enemy fortifications. Although Eichelberger no longer had any hope of breaking into Manila from the south, he later revealed in a letter to his wife his reason for the continued attacks: "As long as I am here [in the suburbs of Manila], [Krueger] cannot claim exclusively that he captured Manila." He added, "I have been a part of the battle for Manila and anybody who would try to deny that fact would be laughed out of court by the newspapermen."[49]

On 9 February, Eichelberger was informed by GHQ that his units would be turned over to Krueger's 6th Army; any further attacks by the 11th Airborne would be coordinated with Krueger's drive from the north. Realizing that this order eliminated the possibility of stealing any more publicity from the 6th Army, Eichelberger decided to leave Luzon and to reassemble his staff at the 8th Army headquarters on Leyte. This task was accomplished by nightfall on 9 February 1945.[50]

Despite this premature departure, Eichelberger was excited about the role that he had played in the capture of Manila. He spent the next few days after his arrival in Leyte bragging about his good fortune during the campaign. Stating that he "had long ago given up the idea that I would have any part in the battle for

Manila," he admitted that his recent successes with the 11th Airborne seemed "as fantastic as a fairy tale." He added, "Personally I think we pulled [off] one of the most daring feats of the war."[51]

Eichelberger was also pleased that the 11th Airborne had, in his opinion, outperformed Krueger's 6th Army. Krueger's tactics "were all wrong," he argued; despite the strength of Krueger's forces, the 6th Army had demonstrated "all the dash of a circus elephant." In comparison, his own units had covered almost 70 miles in seven days, and had succeeded in paralyzing the enemy forces from Tagaytay Ridge to Paranaque. Although Eichelberger admitted that his forces had been unable to breach the Manila defenses, he still bragged: "[Krueger] can't laugh off the fact that I was sleeping in south Manila on the fourth night of February and [Krueger] hasn't done so yet."[52]

He was also pleased and flattered by the publicity that the 8th Army received following the conclusion of the Nasugbu operation. Throughout the month of February, a series of favorable articles about Eichelberger and the 8th Army appeared in newspapers and magazines in the United States. These articles praised the 11th Airborne's "dash to Manila"; they described the commander of the 8th Army as a supreme tactician, an electrifying commander, and an inspirational leader of men.[53]

In an attempt to preserve this long-awaited fame, Eichelberger wrote to his friends and relatives, asking them to send him copies of these articles. He collected them with great enthusiasm, noting: "Judging by the pictures of me that are rolling in from all over the country, I am getting plenty of publicity." In a moment of triumph, he gloated that "the headlines . . . indicate that the 8th Army almost drove the Russian attack on Berlin off the [front pages of the newspapers] for a day or so." He added that, due to his efforts at Nasugbu, the 8th Army was finally "on the map."[54]

Historians have been less impressed by the 8th Army operations. In describing the Luzon campaign, John Costello's *The Pacific War* states merely that the 8th Army "sealed off" Manila from the south. Ronald Spector's *Eagle Against the Sun* devotes two paragraphs to the race for Manila, and concludes that the 11th Airborne was "beaten out" by Krueger's 37th Division and the 1st Cavalry Division.[55]

MacArthur, in *Reminiscences*, fails even to mention Eichelberger in connection with the advance on Manila. MacArthur describes the 8th Army's contributions in a few short lines, stating that the 11th Airborne's drive from the south "formed the lower jaw of the Manila pincer movement." General Whitney, in his book *MacArthur*, barely mentions the 11th Airborne Division. He states that the XI Corps' advance (under General Hall) was the decisive move, for this attack "cut off the Bataan peninsula." Both MacArthur and Whitney agree that the 11th Airborne's attack from the south was little more than a diversion.[56]

Robert Ross Smith's *Triumph in the Philippines* includes the most complete description of the 8th Army's contributions. This study details the advance of the

11th Airborne, but is critical of Eichelberger's part in the operation. Smith criticizes the 8th Army commander for bungling the parachute drop behind Tagaytay Ridge, for "stretching" his orders, and for continuing the attack on Manila after 6 February (the 11th Airborne suffered 700 casualties in the attacks against the Genko Line). Smith concludes that the operation was a success, but not a "brilliant" or "amazing" victory, as Eichelberger believed.[57]

Historians have been even less inclined to praise the 8th Army's operations on Leyte. The most complete discussions of the 8th Army mop-up are in Samuel Eliot Morison's *Leyte, June 1944-January 1945* and in H. Hamlin Cannon's *Leyte: The Return to the Philippines*. Both authors agree that the Japanese were disorganized and dispirited by 26 December, the date of the 8th Army "takeover" from the 6th Army. The 8th Army fought adequately against weak enemy opposition, but still took over two months to clear Leyte of enemy troops.[58]

Eichelberger, however, was convinced that his forces had performed admirably on both Leyte and Luzon. This belief was supported by MacArthur. After a short meeting at GHQ in February, Eichelberger noted in his diary that "[MacArthur] expressed great satisfaction with my work with the 11th [Airborne] and said he had intentionally brought out good propaganda for the Eighth [Army] on [news] releases." In a subsequent meeting, Eichelberger was told that MacArthur would give him and his staff "a break whenever he could." MacArthur mentioned that he would recommend Bob for another Oak Leaf Cluster to his Silver Star for his gallantry and leadership during the Nasugbu campaign.[59] Eichelberger was encouraged by these promises, especially since he felt that he and his staff were finally getting the thanks and attention they deserved for their efforts in the Southwest Pacific.

The gratification quickly evaporated in late February, when Eichelberger was informed that MacArthur had recommended Krueger for a fourth star. This information was followed by rumors that an army group would be created in the Southwest Pacific; Krueger reportedly would be placed in overall command of the 6th and 8th Armies. Finally, Eichelberger was informed that the 29 January issue of *Time* magazine featured an article on Krueger, describing him as a "brilliant" general who possessed all of the "elements of greatness."[60]

Depressed and angered by these revelations, Eichelberger was particularly upset by Krueger's ability to have his picture appear in *Time* magazine. In a letter to his wife, he complained, "If [Walter] is a great General or has any of the elements of greatness then I am no judge of my fellow man." He added, "Beyond a certain meanness which scares those under him and a willingness to work, [Krueger] has little to offer." Stating that Krueger had advanced on Luzon with the speed of "old molasses in January," Eichelberger noted, "I should think *Time* would be ashamed of themselves for the write-up and play-up they gave [him].[61]

Eichelberger was also upset by the rumors that his unit would be placed in an army group under Krueger's overall command. "If that should happen," he stated,

"I will ask to be relieved and then ask to be ordered home to await retirement." He explained, "I do not intend to put up with any more of [Krueger's] insults, because after all life is a wee bit short and I do not think I could take any more."[62]

Eichelberger seriously considered requesting his relief from his post in the Southwest Pacific, but he was talked out of it by MacArthur. At this stage of the war, MacArthur had become an expert at manipulating his subordinates' emotions. He managed to soothe Eichelberger's troubled feelings by his usual assortment of promises, excuses, and half-truths. During the third week of March, MacArthur informed Bob that Krueger really had not earned his promotion, but had been recommended for a fourth star only because General Eisenhower had pushed for the promotion of General George Patton in Europe; since General Marshall was anxious to avoid the appearance of favoritism in any particular theater, Marshall had decided to approve the promotion of both Patton and the senior combat officer in the Southwest Pacific, General Krueger. MacArthur explained that this promotion did not make Krueger an army group commander; he "would never force" Eichelberger to serve under Krueger again. Stating that he was "very delighted with [Bob's] work," MacArthur promised, "from now on you will be treated with absolute parity with reference to the Sixth Army or any other army."[63]

In his typical fashion, MacArthur also appealed to Eichelberger's vanity. With the 8th Army slated for several upcoming operations in the southern Philippines, MacArthur reminded Eichelberger that he was now on an equal footing with Krueger, but that, if he were successful in these operations, it was possible that he could surpass Krueger in publicity, reputation, decorations, and even rank. MacArthur also implied that, if Eichelberger proved worthy of the task, it was possible that he would be chosen for the biggest prize of all—the leading role in the invasion of Japan.[64]

NOTES

1. Eichelberger, *Our Jungle Road to Tokyo*, 164; Eichelberger Dictations, "Arrival in the Philippines," 9 May 1948, 1–2; Eichelberger Dictations, "Formation of Eighth Army," 18 March 1948, 3–4.

2. Eichelberger Dictations, "Fuller, also Krueger," 29 May 1961, 2; Robert Eichelberger to Emma Eichelberger, 3 August 1944 and 14 August 1944, Eichelberger Papers.

3. Robert Eichelberger to Mrs. J. B. Zerbe, 31 August 1944, Eichelberger Papers; Robert Eichelberger to Emma Eichelberger, 20 September 1944 and 21 September 1944, Eichelberger Papers; Eichelberger Dictations, "Arrival in the Philippines," 9 May 1948, 1–3; Eichelberger Dictations, "Formation of Eighth Army," 18 March 1948, 1–2; Eichelberger Dictations, "Fuller, also Krueger, " 29 May 1961, 1–3.

THE PHILIPPINES—COMPETITION WITH KRUEGER 125

4. Robert Eichelberger to Emma Eichelberger, 21 October 1944, 24 October 1944, 25 October 1944, and 20 September 1944, Eichelberger Papers; Robert Eichelberger to Mrs. J. B. Zerbe, 31 August 1944, Eichelberger Papers.

5. Robert Eichelberger to Emma Eichelberger, 14 August 1944, Eichelberger Papers; Eichelberger Dictations, "Formation of Eighth Army," 18 March 1948, 2; Eichelberger Dictations, "Arrival in the Philippines," 9 May 1948, 2-3.

6. Robert Eichelberger to Emma Eichelberger, 29 September 1944 and 3 August 1944, Eichelberger Papers.

7. Robert Eichelberger to Emma Eichelberger, 15 October 1944, 3 August 1944, and 29 September 1944, Eichelberger Papers; Eichelberger Dictations, "Opinions," no date, page 8 of dictation and page 197 of dictation notebook.

8. Robert Eichelberger to Emma Eichelberger, 8 September 1944 and 26 December 1944, Eichelberger Papers.

9. Robert Eichelberger to Emma Eichelberger, 27-28 November 1944 and 26 December 1944, Eichelberger Papers; telephone interview with Robert M. White II, conducted at the request of this author on 6 June 1988, page 1 of transcript (White was a member of Eichelberger's I Corps staff from 1943 to the summer of 1944).

10. "Oral Reminiscences of General . . . Willoughby," 12, MacArthur Papers; Luvaas, *Dear Miss Em*, 249; Robert Eichelberger to Emma Eichelberger, 10 April 1945, 25 October 1944, and 3 August 1944, Eichelberger Papers.

11. MacArthur, *Reminiscences*, 211-12; M. Hamlin Cannon, *Leyte: Return to the Philippines* (Washington, D.C.: Office of the Chief of Military History, Department of the Army, 1954), 26; Eichelberger Dictations, "After My Return to Australia from Buna-Sanananda," 18 April 1948, 11; Eichelberger Dictations, "On the Eighth Army Staff," 29 August 1955, page 2 of dictation and page 242 of dictation notebook; Luvaas, *Dear Miss Em*, 195; Memorandum to Commanding General, Eighth Army, 12 October 1944, APO 343, 1, included in Eichelberger Papers.

12. Robert Eichelberger to Emma Eichelberger, 27 November 1944, 15 October 1944, 25 October 1944, 3 August 1944, and 30 December 1944, Eichelberger Papers.

13. Cannon, *Leyte: Return to the Philippines*, 1-42; Eichelberger, *Jungle Road*, 171; Spector, *Eagle Against the Sun*, 513-15; MacArthur, *Reminiscences*, 232.

14. Luvaas, *Dear Miss Em*, 176-77; Robert Eichelberger to Emma Eichelberger, 12 December 1944, Eichelberger Papers.

15. Eichelberger Dictations, "Incident in Late November, 1944," 2 January 1953, 2; Eichelberger Dictations, "After My Return to Australia From Buna-Sanananda," 18 April 1948, 7-8.

16. MacArthur, *Reminiscences*, 232-33; Samuel Eliot Morison, *Leyte, June 1944-January 1945, History of United States Naval Operations in World War II, Volume XII* (Boston: Little, Brown and Company, 1958), 394-95; Eichelberger Dictations, "Krueger and the Ormoc Bay Landing," no date, 1, 5; Eichelberger Dictations, "Some Phases of General MacArthur's Attitude towards me in my Years in the Pacific and some thoughts about Sutherland and Krueger," 31 August 1959, 7; Eichelberger Dictations, "After My Return to Australia from Buna-Sanananda," 18 April 1948, 7-8; Cannon, *Leyte: Return to the Philippines*, 275-90, 361; James, *The Years of MacArthur, Volume II*, 602.

17. Robert Eichelberger to Emma Eichelberger, 2-3 December 1944, Eichelberger Papers.

18. Robert Eichelberger to Emma Eichelberger, 27 November 1944, Eichelberger Papers; Eichelberger, *Our Jungle Road*, 181–82.

19. Eichelberger, *Our Jungle Road*, 181–82; *New York Times*, 12 June 1945, 2; Robert Eichelberger to Emma Eichelberger, 27 November 1944, 12–13 December 1944 and 15 December 1944, Eichelberger Papers.

20. Cannon, *Leyte: Return to the Philippines*, 365–68; Morison, *Leyte, June 1944-January 1945*, 394–95; R. L. Eichelberger, "Report of the Commanding General, Eighth U.S. Army, on the Leyte-Samar Operation," 8–17 (no date; included in box 78 of the Eichelberger Papers); Robert Eichelberger to Emma Eichelberger, 17 January 1945 and 25 January 1945, Eichelberger Papers.

21. Robert Eichelberger to Emma Eichelberger, 27 December 1944, 21–22 December 1944, and 14 January 1945, Eichelberger Papers.

22. Robert Eichelberger to Emma Eichelberger, 4–5 January 1945, 13–14 December 1944, 29 December 1944, 18–19 December 1944, 21–22 December 1944, 20–21 December 1944, and 27 December 1944, Eichelberger Papers.

23. Eichelberger Dictations, "Background for M-6," no date, 1; Eichelberger Dictations, "The 11th Airborne Division's Dash to Manila and Facts pertaining thereto," 2 January 1953, 2, 11; Eichelberger Dictations, "Dash with the 11th Airborne Division from Nasugbu to Manila in early February 1945," no date, 1; Robert Eichelberger to Emma Eichelberger, 22 January 1945, Eichelberger Papers.

24. Eichelberger Dictations, "The 11th Airborne Division's Dash to Manila and Facts pertaining thereto," 2 January 1953, 2–3; Eichelberger Dictations, "MacArthur," 4 November 1960, 1–2; Eichelberger Dictations, "Notes in Anticipation of Visit to Manila Area," 3 October 1960, 1–3.

25. Eichelberger Dictations, "The 11th Airborne Division's Dash to Manila and Facts pertaining thereto," 2 January 1953, 3–6, 13–15; Eichelberger Dictations, "Dash with the 11th Airborne Division from Nasugbu to Manila in early February 1945," no date, 2; Eichelberger Dictations, "Notes in Anticipation of Visit to Manila Area," 3 October 1960, 2–3.

26. Eichelberger, *Our Jungle Road to Tokyo*, 188–89; Eichelberger Dictations, "Dash with the 11th Airborne Division from Nasugbu to Manila . . .," no date, 2–3.

27. Eichelberger Dictations, "Background for M-6," no date, 3–4; Eichelberger Dictations, "Notes in Anticipation of Visit to Manila Area," 3 October 1960, 2–3.

28. General Joe Swing to Robert Eichelberger, 28 July 1948, Eichelberger Papers; Memoranda to Robert Eichelberger, written by H. C. Burgess, "Nasugbu," no date, 1–6, Eichelberger Papers; Luvaas, *Dear Miss Em*, 219–20 (footnote 19).

29. Eichelberger Dictations, "The 11th Airborne Division's Dash to Manila and Facts pertaining thereto," 2 January 1953, 3–4; Eichelberger Dictations, "Background for M-6," no date, 2; Robert Eichelberger to Emma Eichelberger, 19 January 1945, Eichelberger Papers.

30. MacArthur, *Reminiscences*, 238–46; Robert Ross Smith, *Triumph in the Philippines, The War in the Pacific, The United States Army in World War II* (Washington, D.C.: Office of the Chief of Military History, Department of Army, 1963), 221–22; Field Order 10, Eighth Army, "Operation Mike 6," 24 January 1945, 1, included in Eichelberger Papers; Eichelberger Dictations, "Notes in Anticipation of Visit to Manila Area," 3 October 1960, 2–3.

THE PHILIPPINES—COMPETITION WITH KRUEGER 127

31. Robert Eichelberger to Emma Eichelberger, 23 January 1945 and 29 January 1945, Eichelberger Papers; Eichelberger Dictations, "Background for M-6," no date, 4; Luvaas, *Dear Miss Em*, 203.

32. Costello, *The Pacific War*, 531–32; Spector, *Eagle Against the Sun*, 520–21; Samuel Eliot Morison, *The Liberation of the Philippines: Luzon, Mindanao, the Visayas, 1944–1945* (Boston: Little, Brown and Company, 1975), 193; Eichelberger Dictations, "Memorandum—Dash with the 11th Airborne Division from Nasugbu to Manila in early February 1945," no date, 3; Robert Eichelberger to Emma Eichelberger, 23 January 1945, 31 January 1945, 2 February 1945, and 16 February 1945, Eichelberger Papers; radiogram, Robert Eichelberger to Brig. General William Dunckel, 29 January 1945, APO 321, Eichelberger Papers; Smith, *Triumph in the Philippines*, 222–23.

33. Eichelberger Diary, 23 January 1945 and 23 March 1945, Eichelberger Papers; Smith, *Triumph in the Philippines*, 212; Robert Eichelberger to Emma Eichelberger, 19 January 1945, Eichelberger Papers.

34. Robert Eichelberger to Emma Eichelberger, 23 January 1945 and 29 January 1945, Eichelberger Papers; Eichelberger Dictations, "Notes in Anticipation of Visit to Manila Area," 3 October 1960, 4.

35. MacArthur, *Reminiscences*, 245; Whitney, *MacArthur*, 186–87; Spector, *Eagle Against the Sun*, 524–25; Morison, *The Liberation of the Philippines*, 187–89; Robert Eichelberger to Emma Eichelberger, 29 January 1945, Eichelberger Papers; Luvaas, *Dear Miss Em*, 204.

36. Morison, *The Liberation of the Philippines*, 182–92; Robert Eichelberger to Emma Eichelberger, 29 January 1945 and 31 January 1945, Eichelberger Papers.

37. Spector, *Eagle Against the Sun*, 522; Smith, *Triumph in the Philippines*, 224–25; Robert Eichelberger, "Report of the Commanding General Eighth Army on the Nasugbu and Bataan Operations," no date, 14–15, Eichelberger Papers; Eichelberger, *Our Jungle Road*, 189–91; Eichelberger Dictations, "Background for M-6, the Nasugbu-Manila Operation," no date, 6.

38. Smith, *Triumph in the Philippines*, 226; Eichelberger, "Report of the Commanding General Eighth Army on the Nasugbu and Bataan Operations," no date, 16–17; Radiogram, Robert Eichelberger (Commanding General, Eighth Army) to General Douglas MacArthur (CINC GHQ SWPA, Attn G-3), 2 February 1945, APO 343, included in Eichelberger Papers.

39. Radiogram, R. L. Eichelberger to General E. Whitehead, 3 February 1945 (two radiograms), Eichelberger Papers.

40. Smith, *Triumph in the Philippines*, 226–29; Eichelberger, "Report of the Commanding General Eighth Army on the Nasugbu and Bataan Operations," 17–20, Eichelberger Papers.

41. Eichelberger, "Report of the Commanding General Eighth Army on the Nasugbu and Bataan Operations," 16–22, Eichelberger Papers.

42. Ibid.; Eichelberger Dictations, "Background for M-6, Nasugbu-Manila Operation," no date, 8–11; Smith, *Triumph in the Philippines*, 230–31; Eichelberger, *Our Jungle Road*, 194–95.

43. Eichelberger Dictations, "Dash with the 11th Airborne Division from Nasugbu to Manila in Early February 1945," no date, 4; Eichelberger Dictations, "The Central Visayas Islands—Book Review of Chapter XII of *Triumph in the*

Philippines," no date, 3–4; Robert Eichelberger to Emma Eichelberger, 23 February 1946, Eichelberger Papers.

44. Eichelberger Dictations, "The 11th Airborne's Dash to Manila and Facts pertaining thereto," 2 January 1953, 4–5; Robert Eichelberger to Emma Eichelberger, 2 February 1945 and 31 January 1945, Eichelberger Papers.

45. Smith, *Triumph in the Philippines*, 231–32; Eichelberger, "Report . . . on the Nasugbu and Bataan Operations," 24, Eichelberger Papers.

46. Spector, *Eagle Against the Sun*, 522; Eichelberger Dictations, "Comments on *Triumph in the Philippines*," (two separate dictations) 21 January 1957 and 26 November 1956, pages 1 and 2, respectively.

47. Spector, *Eagle Against the Sun*, 522; Eichelberger Dictations, "Comments on *Triumph in the Philippines*," (two dictations) 21 January 1957 and 26 November 1956, pages 1 and 2, respectively; radiogram, Robert Eichelberger to Douglas MacArthur (CINC GHQ SWPA), 6 February 1945, included in Eichelberger Papers.

48. Robert Eichelberger to Emma Eichelberger, 7 February 1945 and 5 February 1945, Eichelberger Papers; Memorandum, H. C. Burgess to General Robert L. Eichelberger, no date, 1–5, Eichelberger Papers.

49. Robert Eichelberger to Emma Eichelberger, 7 February 1945, 8 February 1945, and 23 February 1945, Eichelberger Papers; radiogram, General Robert Eichelberger to General Walter Krueger, 7 February 1945, Eichelberger Papers.

50. Smith, *Triumph in the Philippines*, 268; Spector, *Eagle Against the Sun*, 522–23; Robert Eichelberger to Emma Eichelberger, 8 February 1945, 9 February 1945, 21 February 1945, and 24 February 1945, Eichelberger Papers.

51. Robert Eichelberger to Emma Eichelberger, 11 February 1945, 12 February 1945, and 5 February 1945, Eichelberger Papers.

52. Robert Eichelberger to Emma Eichelberger, 24 February 1945, 11 February 1945, and 22 February 1945, Eichelberger Papers.

53. Robert Eichelberger to Emma Eichelberger, 24 February 1945 and 17 February 1945, Eichelberger Papers (also see box 190 of the Eichelberger Papers, which includes newspaper clippings pertaining to the Eighth Army's Nasugbu operation).

54. Robert Eichelberger to Emma Eichelberger, 5 February 1945, 9 February 1946, 12 February 1945, 16 February 1945, and 24 February 1945, Eichelberger Papers; Eichelberger Dictations, "The 11th Airborne Division's Dash to Manila and Facts pertaining thereto," 2 January 1953, 5.

55. Costello, *The Pacific War*, 532; Spector, *Eagle Against the Sun*, 522.

56. MacArthur, *Reminiscences*, 245–46; Whitney, *MacArthur*, 186–87.

57. Smith, *Triumph in the Philippines*, 222–23, 227–28, 229–31, 266–67, and 268–69.

58. Morison, *Leyte*, 394–95; Cannon, *Leyte: The Return to the Philippines*, 361, 365–68.

59. Robert Eichelberger to Emma Eichelberger, 4 March 1945, Eichelberger Papers; Eichelberger Diaries, 3 March 1945, Eichelberger Papers; biographical summary of Robert L. Eichelberger, 28 January 1948, 7, included in Eichelberger Papers in "biographical" materials.

60. James, *The Years of MacArthur, Volume II*, 669; Robert Eichelberger to Emma Eichelberger, 9 February 1945, 11 February 1945, and 17 February 1945,

THE PHILIPPINES—COMPETITION WITH KRUEGER 129

Eichelberger Papers; also see the 29 January 1945 issue of *Time* for comments pertaining to Krueger.

61. Robert Eichelberger to Emma Eichelberger, 5 March 1945, 7 February 1945, and 9 February 1945, Eichelberger Papers.

62. Robert Eichelberger to Emma Eichelberger, 17 February 1945, 19 February 1945, 11 February 1945, and 19 March 1945, Eichelberger Papers.

63. Robert Eichelberger to Emma Eichelberger, 24 March 1945, 25 March 1945, and 4 March 1945, Eichelberger Papers.

64. James, *The Years of MacArthur, Volume II*, 594–95; Robert Eichelberger to Emma Eichelberger, 4 March 1945, 21 February 1945, 11 February 1945, 24 March 1945, and 25 March 1945, Eichelberger Papers.

10

VICTORY AND DISAPPOINTMENT

Even before the end of the Luzon campaign, MacArthur was making plans for future operations in the southern Philippines. He hoped to land units in rapid succession, on the island of Palawan, on the Zamboanga peninsula, and on Panay, Negros, Cebu, and Mindanao. Since Krueger's units were still fully occupied against the enemy forces in northern Luzon, MacArthur planned to make these landings in the south using elements of Eichelberger's 8th Army.[1]

Although the navy was not enthusiastic about these operations, MacArthur felt that these landings in the southern Philippines were necessary for a variety of reasons. First, it would be "immoral" to leave the Filipino natives in these areas under the control of the enemy, especially since the Japanese forces had become increasingly brutal as the war had escalated. Second, the southern Philippines contained a large number of airfields, ports and major cities, control of which was necessary to attack the Japanese oil resources in nearby Java and Borneo. Third, areas of the southern Philippines provided ideal training bases for the invasion of Japan, as well as providing adequate staging and supply bases for upcoming operations in Indonesia.[2]

More importantly, the operations in the southern Philippines were vital to MacArthur for personal reasons. Since 1944, MacArthur had been involved in an intense struggle with Admiral Chester Nimitz and the navy for overall control of the strategy in the Pacific. MacArthur had "won the battle" against Nimitz in 1944, convincing President Roosevelt and the Joint Chiefs of Staff to approve the landings on Leyte and Luzon and to reject Nimitz's argument for bypassing the Philippines. MacArthur was aware that this victory did not guarantee him the leading role for the next major operation. The Joint Chiefs of Staff could easily turn to Nimitz as overall commander for the invasion of Japan. To prevent this from happening, MacArthur was particularly anxious to do well in the southern Philippines, for he felt that a rapid and successful campaign at this juncture would convince the authorities in Washington to award him the predominant role for the final thrust against Japan. As MacArthur indicated in March 1945, his plan was to "wind up all the fighting in the Philippines and to the south as rapidly as possible and then announce to the world that [his] mission is over and ask for further instructions [i.e., pertaining to the invasion of Japan]."[3]

Eichelberger was fully aware of this plan, and understood MacArthur's desire for speed in the upcoming campaigns. He also was aware of the possible rewards to be gained from these operations, for he believed that MacArthur would be extremely grateful if he rapidly completed the operations in the southern Philippines. From private discussions with MacArthur, Eichelberger was led to believe that, if he were successful in these next operations, he in fact would be awarded the leading combat role for the invasion of Japan. From discussions with members of MacArthur's staff, Eichelberger also received a very strong indication that MacArthur subsequently would award him a fourth star and declare him the "number one fighting general" in the Pacific. His assignment seemed ideal, for he was assured by MacArthur's staff that the next operations "won't be too difficult and will look good geographically."[4]

Eichelberger thus prepared his forces for a speedy and successful campaign in the south. He correctly reasoned that the enemy in the southern Philippines lacked air and naval support, had inadequate supplies and poor communications, and suffered from disease and declining morale. He therefore concluded that his own troops could "afford to take chances," and could move with uncommon speed and audacity in their upcoming operations. At the end of February 1945, in accordance with this philosophy, Eichelberger instructed his division commanders to push forward in a rapid attack, keep the bulk of their forces near the front of their advance, maintain contact with the enemy, and disregard enemy threats to their rear and flanks.[5]

To complement these instructions, Eichelberger also devised tactics to maximize speed of movement in the southern Philippines. He planned each of his landings within 50 miles of a major port town or city, and urged his commanders to capture the port within 48 hours of the initial landing. Thereafter, they were to capture and patrol the major communication routes on the island, especially the all-weather roads and bridges, advancing beyond the range of supporting infantry fire and, if necessary, depending on airborne supplies if their communication lines were cut. Small, well-trained units were to be dropped in advance of the landing forces to capture railroad bridges and important road junctions. The Japanese then would be forced into the mountainous interior of the Philippine islands, where the enemy would be destroyed by a combination of artillery fire, Filipino guerrillas, disease and starvation.[6]

Eichelberger got his first opportunity to employ these tactics in February 1945, when his forces were assigned the task of capturing Palawan Island and the Zamboanga peninsula. Located on the extreme western flank of the Philippines, Palawan Island was a Japanese airfield and naval base used for operations south of Leyte; the Zamboanga peninsula, located on the western end of the island of

Mindanao (but separated from the rest of the island by an impenetrable mountain barrier), was used by the Japanese as a base and harbor for their naval forces in the southern Philippines. Zamboanga and Palawan were strategically important (in MacArthur's view), for American control of these areas would complete the encirclement and isolation of the Japanese-held islands in the central Philippines.[7]

On 28 February 1945, elements of Eichelberger's 8th Army (the 186th Regimental Combat Team under the command of Brigadier General Harold H. Haney) landed on the eastern shore of Palawan. From Puerto Princesa Bay, these troops advanced to the north and captured the city of Puerto Princesa, the island's only major port. After this initial success, the 186th moved cautiously inland toward the western end of the island. Eichelberger was disappointed with the progress of this unit, especially since the enemy (numbering less than 800) chose to retreat and scatter in small groups rather than stand and fight. Still, the 186th fought its way across Palawan in two weeks, and succeeded in securing the island by the end of March 1945.[8]

On 10 March 1945, Eichelberger's forces (the 41st Division minus the 186th Regimental Combat Team) began the second prong of their operation by landing at the southern tip of the Zamboanga peninsula. Overcoming moderate enemy resistance, the 41st Division moved off the beach and advanced eastward toward Zamboanga City. Within 48 hours of the initial landing, this city was captured, along with the important Dipalog and Wolfe airfields.[9]

As the American units advanced north from Zamboanga City, they were slowed by strong and stubborn enemy resistance. Unlike events at Palawan, the enemy units refused to scatter into the interior; they waged a vigorous and persistent defense from the hills overlooking the approaches to the city. In Eichelberger's words, the Japanese utilized their "ideal positions" in the coastal foothills to "harass our troops on the beaches, to set a large fuel dump on fire, and to hinder work on the airfields for days."[10]

The strength of the enemy opposition, however, failed to account for the cautious advance of the American units. Eichelberger referred to Major General Jens Doe, the commander of the 41st Division, as "a very ponderous fighter—not brilliant in any way." He believed that "the losses which Doe is taking do not indicate much heavy fighting." To accelerate operations against the 6,000 enemy troops in the Zamboanga peninsula, Eichelberger repeatedly visited Doe's headquarters and the front lines, urging greater speed and aggressiveness. Under Eichelberger's constant prodding, the 41st Division made better progress during the second week of the campaign, and succeeded in driving the Japanese from their positions overlooking Zamboanga City and the airfields. After this success, Eichelberger's troops pushed gradually northward and captured the towns of Mercedes and Pasananca; they eliminated the enemy units positioned in the foothills surrounding these towns. By 24 March, the bulk of the enemy forces in the Zamboanga peninsula had been defeated, and the campaign moved into the "mopping up" stage, although brisk fighting continued in the mountains of northern Zamboanga for the next several weeks.[11]

With the Zamboanga campaign completed, Eichelberger concentrated his efforts on the second phase of the operation—the conquest of the islands in the central southern Philippines. The invasions of Palawan and Zamboanga had successfully isolated the central islands, and had prevented the evacuation or reinforcement of the Japanese garrisons. These islands, notably Panay, Negros, and Cebu, were important to MacArthur for a variety of reasons. They were more modern and westernized than the remainder of the southern Philippines, and contained large food-producing areas, several large industrial centers, and numerous airfields. These islands also were defended by large bodies of enemy troops, including a Japanese army headquarters located on the island of Cebu.[12]

Elements of Eichelberger's 8th Army (the 40th Infantry Division under the command of Major General Rapp Brush) landed on the eastern shore of Panay on 18 March 1945. Encountering weak opposition, the 40th Division advanced eastward toward Iloilo, Panay's largest city. The 40th Division then advanced along Panay's major roads in a three-pronged attack against the mountainous interior of the island. Most of the 2,500 enemy troops on Panay scattered into the mountains, leaving the bulk of the island in American hands.[13]

Next came Negros, which the 40th Division invaded on 29 March 1945. The American forces landed just to the south of Bacolod, Negros's principal seaport and harbor. They advanced northward along Highway 1, a fine two-lane, all-weather road which encircled the coastline of the island. On the first day of the advance, a platoon of American troops, dropped onto Negros in advance of the landing forces, captured a 650-foot steel truss bridge which spanned the Bago River. The capture of this vital structure opened Highway 1 all the way to Bacolod, which fell to the Americans on 30 March 1945.[14]

From 31 March to 9 April, the 40th Division continued its advance north from Bacolod and along the coastal highway. Eichelberger's units rapidly captured most of the northern and eastern shores of the island; they slowly pushed their way into the mountainous interior. On 9 April, the 40th Division finally encountered the main line of enemy resistance in the mountains in the northern central section of the island. From 9 April to 1 May, the American forces hammered away at the prepared enemy positions. They gradually eliminated the Japanese fortifications with the assistance of well-placed air strikes and massed artillery support. On 5 May, the 40th Division broke through the enemy's defensive perimeter, and drove the remainder of the Japanese forces into the mountains on the southern end of the island. With the main enemy positions captured, Eichelberger declared on 9 May that the major fighting on Negros had ended, and that the entire coastal plain on Negros was "free of the enemy."[15]

On 26 March 1945, while the 40th Division was still fighting on Panay and Negros, Eichelberger had landed the Americal Division (under the command of Major General William H. Arnold) on the eastern shore of Cebu island, five miles south of Cebu City. Unlike Panay and Negros, Cebu posed numerous difficulties from the start. Eight of the landing craft in the first wave of the invasion force were destroyed by mines. Beach obstacles created a logjam of troops and landing craft along the shoreline. The first wave was stopped along the beach, and was unable to move inland. Eichelberger later concluded that "had the enemy chosen to man [their beach] defenses instead of withdrawing to inland hill positions, the results would have been disastrous."[16]

Despite the complications on the beach, Eichelberger's forces were able to gradually clear a path through the obstacles and to advance inland toward Cebu City, which fell on 27 March. On 28 March, the American units encountered the bulk of the enemy forces in prepared fortifications northwest of Cebu City; they began probing attacks against these positions. From 29 March to 8 April, the Americal Division suffered heavy casualties in repeated futile attempts to dislodge the enemy defenders.[17]

On 9 April, Eichelberger ordered the Americal Division to halt its frontal attacks against the enemy fortifications. Instead, he landed a regiment of reinforcements on Cebu, with instructions to make a wide, enveloping movement into the rear of the enemy defenses. This regiment, moving quietly by night, reached its destination on the morning of 12 April. They participated in a three-pronged assault against the Japanese positions. This attack caught the enemy defenders off guard; the Japanese panicked and abandoned their prepared positions.[18] Attempting to reassemble in the mountains of northern Cebu, the retreating Japanese units were rapidly destroyed by Eichelberger's patrols and the combination of American artillery and air strikes. From 12 to 19 April, the enemy forces suffered over 5,000 casualties, with the recording of only a minimal loss in American lives.[19] The success of these operations convinced Eichelberger that the enemy was soundly defeated. On 20 April, he announced that the Cebu campaign was now complete except for some minor mopping-up.[20]

Eichelberger next directed his attention to the final operation in the southern Philippines—the invasion of Mindanao. Mindanao is the southernmost and second largest island in the Philippines, with an area of over 36,500 square miles. The island is mountainous and covered by rain forests, with only a handful of major towns and harbors; the primary harbor was located at Davao City on the southern coast of the island, with other natural harbors located to the north at Macajalar Bay and to the west at Malabang and Parang.

Since most of the 50,000 enemy troops on Mindanao were stationed along the southern coastline, Davao City was made the primary objective of the American landing forces. The strength of the enemy defenses in this area, however, precluded any landing at Davao Gulf. GHQ scheduled the initial landing on Mindanao on the west coast of the island, near Parang, forcing troops to make a 110-mile march southeast to Davao City. Eichelberger was warned by GHQ that this overland advance would take several months, and that his forces would be plagued by persistent rainfall and stiff enemy opposition.[21]

Armed with this pessimistic report, Eichelberger prepared for a difficult campaign. The X Corps landed on Mindanao near Parang, on the west coast of the island, on 17 April 1945. The landing forces (consisting of the 24th and 31st Divisions under the command of Major General Franklin Sibert) moved inland in the direction of Fort Pikit and Kabakan. Using the Mindanao River as an avenue of attack and as a supply line, the 24th Division advanced over 60 miles in seven days. They captured Kabakan on the morning of 23 April. Ten days later, the division seized Davao City.[22]

While the fighting for Davao City was in progress, Eichelberger dispatched the 31st Division along the Sayre Highway in central Mindanao. Running north to south from Macajalar Bay to Kabakan, the Sayre Highway was the only major transportation route in the interior of the island and the only avenue of attack against the Japanese forces north of Davao Gulf. The 31st Division began its advance along this route on 27 April. They initially met only light enemy opposition, but as the advance continued, enemy resistance stiffened. The Japanese were successful in retarding the American attacks by destroying numerous bridges along the road. The delays caused by the destroyed bridges allowed the enemy to reorganize his forces for a stand north of Kibawe.[23]

In order to eliminate some of the pressure confronting the 31st Division, Eichelberger landed the 108th Regimental Combat Team at Macajalar Bay on the northern shore of Mindanao. Beginning on 10 May, this unit advanced down the Sayre Highway from the north, while the 31st Division continued its attack from the south. The 108th made steady progress against fanatical enemy opposition. On 23 May, it joined forces with the 31st Division near Impalutao on the Sayre Highway. The junction of the two units split the enemy forces into isolated fragments, and assured the success of the American strategic operation in Mindanao. Although substantial enemy forces remained north of Davao City and in the vicinity of Sarangami Bay, MacArthur declared on 25 May that the Mindanao operation had now been completed except for "mopping up."[24]

Eichelberger next assumed command of the mop-up of the enemy forces on Luzon. The bulk of the Japanese units had already been defeated by Krueger's forces by 1 July 1945, and on 5 July, MacArthur declared that the American operations on Luzon had been successfully completed. Despite MacArthur's announcement, approximately 70,000 enemy troops remained in the northern mountains. Eichelberger was instructed to eliminate this remaining resistance.

A tour of the front lines in early July convinced Eichelberger that the enemy forces were concentrated in two large pockets in northern Luzon—in the mountains to the east and southeast of Aparri, and in the area to the east of Baguio. Concentrating his efforts in these areas, he succeeded in rooting out the remaining resistance between 11 July and 10 August. The Japanese forces were scattered, lacked food and ammunition, and provided only token opposition

VICTORY AND DISAPPOINTMENT 137

against the attacking American troops, who were supported by artillery and air power. This superior firepower was largely instrumental in bringing a successful end to the campaign by 15 August. Over 20,000 enemy troops were killed, compared with only 600 American casualties.[25]

The termination of the Mindanao campaign in mid-August marked the conclusion of the 8th Army's operations in the Philippines, and provided an opportunity for Eichelberger to review his recent conquests in the southwest Pacific. He reported that he was extremely satisfied with the results of his rapid-fire landings. "Personally," he stated, "I do not think anyone else has equaled them for brilliance in this theater or faintly approached them." His forces had captured Cebu despite "the strongest beach defenses yet encountered in the southwest Pacific"; they had seized Davao City in "the longest and most rapid sustained drive in the history of Pacific operations." The 24th Division's 10-day march across Mindanao was "a remarkable achievement, truly one for the record books." He proudly noted that the plans for the individual landings had been largely his own. Eichelberger reported that his forces had seized all of the southern Philippines with the loss of only 2,100 American lives, "roughly one-fourth as many deaths as suffered by the Sixth Army in conquering Luzon."[26]

The campaigns in the southern Philippines were indeed inexpensive in terms of American casualties, but they were not nearly as dramatic or remarkable as Eichelberger indicated. The Japanese forces were short of food, supplies, and medicine, and suffered from poor leadership and communications. Most of the Japanese units had suffered heavy casualties on Luzon and Leyte, and had fled to the southern Philippines from the north. Beaten and dispirited, they were an easy mark for Eichelberger's well-equipped forces, and particularly for American naval power. These factors made an American victory almost inevitable, and therefore something less than "remarkable." Robert Smith supports this conclusion in *Triumph in the Philippines*, and notes that many Japanese leaders were surprised by the lack of leadership and initiative in some of the American offensives.[27]

Eichelberger had a different view of the campaign, and was much more confident as a result of these operations. In June and July of 1945, his correspondence with his wife reflected a new feeling of bravado and assurance. Unlike the Buna period, he now no longer felt any doubts about his ability as a combat commander. Believing that his victories at Cebu and Davao City were on a par with the great victories at Tarawa and Okinawa, he felt that his campaigns in the southwest Pacific compared favorably with the successes of Bradley, Patton, and Eisenhower in Europe.[28] Only his relative lack of publicity, he believed, separated him from the ranks of these more famous commanders.[29]

This bravado failed to extend to MacArthur.[30] Eichelberger remained uncertain and insecure about his standing in MacArthur's eyes, and was extremely sensitive about personal slights or any indication that MacArthur was disappointed in his performance. For example, on one occasion, Eichelberger made a visit to GHQ at Manila, and was informed by MacArthur's secretary that

MacArthur was too busy to see him. For the next two days, he fretted and worried that this refusal meant that MacArthur was angry or dissatisfied with something that he had done. William Manchester, in his book *American Caesar*, noted this incident, and stated that Eichelberger behaved "more like a worried schoolchild than a three-star general" during this period.[31]

This insecurity was caused in part by the pattern that he had established with his previous superiors. In the prewar years, Eichelberger had always enjoyed close and amiable relationships with his commanding officers; he had been successful in extending these relationships into intimate friendships. His ability to establish close contacts was important, for it helped to satisfy two very personal and vital needs—to alleviate Eichelberger's anxiety about his own performance, and to create a mentor-student, "father-son" type of relationship that provided mutual support and companionship. Lacking praise and affection from his own father, Eichelberger felt a strong need to establish intimacy with others, and seemed determined to gain in adulthood (and in his relationships with his military superiors) the love and affection that had been denied him in his childhood. Prior to 1942, he was largely successful in satisfying these needs; he was able to find older commanding officers who were receptive to his desire for close personal relationships and for mutually supportive friendships. By 1945, however, these friendships had ended or gradually deteriorated. Eichelberger was left only with a shaky relationship with MacArthur, an impersonal commander who did not desire close ties with his subordinates, had no intimate friends, and had little appreciation for the personal needs of his combat commanders. Eichelberger naturally felt frustrated in this situation, for MacArthur appeared at times to be humorless, aloof, critical, and demanding, an image that was disturbingly close to Eichelberger's views of his own father.[32]

MacArthur's distant and critical nature did not prevent Eichelberger from attempting to create a more personable type of relationship with him. Having a persistent need to feel that his commanding officer liked him or at least had some affection for him, Eichelberger used his victories in the southern Philippines as a pretext for gaining greater access to and attention from the "Big Chief." The importance of this issue became apparent in the summer of 1945, when Eichelberger noticed that MacArthur showed him special consideration "beyond what I have ever seen him show other officers [during visits to GHQ]." For example, MacArthur sent officers to the airfield to greet him, walked him out to his car, and invited him to luncheons. Eichelberger stated that, largely because of his victories in the southern Philippines, "there was no question that I was in very high favor with him [MacArthur] during that fighting."[33]

Eichelberger's psychological needs did not allow him to interpret MacArthur's actions as mere pleasantries or as rewards for a job well done. Instead, he concluded that MacArthur had a real "liking" for him, and that his victories in the southern Philippines were an excuse for MacArthur to demonstrate the personal concern and affection that he had always felt for him.

Eichelberger's thoughts on this matter were apparent in his letters to his wife. He wrote that "once in a blue moon we find someone entirely self-centered but I think the person [MacArthur] whom you are thinking about has a certain amount of real affection for me." On another occasion, he commented that "I think he [MacArthur] has a deep personal feeling for me." Even after the war, Eichelberger remarked that "I have seen General MacArthur full of praise for my campaigns in the Pacific with a show of, I believe, sincere affection."[34]

This need to believe that the "Big Chief" liked him caused Eichelberger to make excuses for MacArthur's conduct. He rationalized that Krueger and the GHQ staff, and not MacArthur, were responsible for the 8th Army's problems in the southern Philippines. During these campaigns, the 8th Army received only limited publicity, and suffered from a scarcity of building supplies and naval transport. Although all the evidence pointed to MacArthur, Eichelberger chose to believe that Krueger was somehow to blame for these problems, and that MacArthur had been misled by his staff into allowing these conditions to continue. Eichelberger also believed that, despite evidence to the contrary, MacArthur's monopolization of the press had no personal significance, but was designed to gain for the army the leading role in the invasion of Japan.[35]

These rationalizations were supported and encouraged by MacArthur, who was willing to grasp at any straw in order to deflect criticism. MacArthur was an expert at play-acting and manipulating his subordinates. As James states in *The Years of MacArthur*, he was not hesitant to use his considerable play-acting skills to split his staff, to convince each member that he alone was his personal favorite. James provides no particular examples of the MacArthur-Eichelberger relationship, but the evidence suggests that MacArthur used the full range of his skills to charm his 8th Army commander in the weeks following the conclusion of the southern Philippine operations.[36]

For example, MacArthur implied that the navy was plotting to reduce the army to a "home guard" outfit after the war; he informed Eichelberger that GHQ's public relations policies were necessary in order to uphold the prestige and honor of the army. MacArthur also informed Eichelberger that he was a great admirer of the talents that Bob had displayed in the southern Philippines, and that the meager publicity that the 8th Army received was not due to any lack of appreciation for their efforts. On the contrary, he stated that the 8th Army operations were a "model of what a light but aggressive command can accomplish in rapid exploitation." The 8th Army commander, he stated, "[ran] an army in combat just like I would like to have it done."[37] MacArthur made a variety of other flattering comments, causing Eichelberger to exclaim that "some of his praise . . . was so extravagant as to be embarrassing."[38]

In addition to this flattery, MacArthur attempted to deflect any potential criticism by exploiting Eichelberger's willingness to blame Krueger for any alleged wrongs. MacArthur informed Eichelberger that Krueger and his staff had tried to keep troops and supplies from going to the 8th Army, and had "hogged" most of the available artillery battalions. Krueger had attempted to relieve two of Eichelberger's favorite division commanders, Major Generals Frederick Irving and Rapp Brush; he had been restrained, MacArthur stated, only by the vigilance of GHQ.[39] Arguing that Krueger was "incapable of doing what [the 8th Army] had been doing," MacArthur added that the 8th Army had outperformed Krueger's troops, and had earned the leading role for the invasion of Japan. Krueger was simply too slow, wanted to change every plan, always demanded more troops, and refused to advance "as long as there [was] one Japanese behind him." MacArthur concluded that Krueger was undependable, and he declared that the 8th Army, and not the 6th, would be the "number one" fighting force in future operations.[40]

These criticisms of Krueger struck a responsive chord in Eichelberger. He believed that MacArthur would not have made these statements unless he believed them to be true and also felt a certain appreciation and affection for the 8th Army and its commander. Willing and almost eager to accept these statements at face value, Eichelberger saw them as a sign that the "Big Chief" truly liked him and had chosen him as his friend. The fact that MacArthur's criticisms were directed at Krueger, the hated rival of the 8th Army, made them only that much more pleasing, and made Eichelberger even more predisposed to believe them.

Eichelberger's wife Emma, however, was not similarly inclined. During May and June of 1945, she wrote a series of fiery letters to her husband condemning MacArthur for his alleged duplicity and double-dealing. Reminding her spouse that MacArthur had repeatedly lied to him in the past, she stated that MacArthur could not be trusted. She warned her husband that MacArthur's criticisms of Krueger were exaggerated, and were undoubtedly part of a "plot" to retain his services through flattery and emotional blackmail.[41]

These sentiments also were shared by the 8th Army chief of staff, Brigadier General Clovis Byers. Byers repeatedly told Eichelberger that the "Big Chief" was an "egotistical jackass who does things for others to please his vanity or get something more for himself." He reminded Eichelberger that MacArthur was unwilling to share the stage with any of his subordinates, and that there were "very definite efforts" to minimize the publicity of the 8th Army in the southern Philippines. Concluding that MacArthur was untrustworthy, Byers warned Eichelberger that he would be foolish to believe that MacArthur had any great personal affection for anyone but himself.[42]

Eichelberger was emotionally torn by these warnings, for he had tremendous respect for the opinions of both his wife and chief of staff. He agonized over this matter and, in an anguished letter to his wife, stated that "one must live with certain ideals and illusions and I do not want to lose the few I have with reference to certain people."[43]

In July 1945, any illusions Eichelberger still retained about the "Big Chief" were destroyed when MacArthur reneged on several key promises. At the conclusion of the Philippine operations, Eichelberger was told that the 8th Army and its commander would receive the "greatest amount of publicity" ever "awarded" for efforts in the Southwest Pacific area. MacArthur also promised him that he would be promoted for his fine efforts in the southern Philippines, and that he would receive "all decorations" that he did not "possess now."[44]

But, by July 1945, it was apparent that MacArthur had no intention of honoring these promises. Eichelberger received only a minimum amount of publicity; General L. A. Diller, MacArthur's press relations officer, "killed" an article about the 8th Army that was scheduled to appear in *Life* magazine. MacArthur took no steps to promote Eichelberger or the members of his staff, although he was urged to do so by Generals Sutherland and Chamberlin. Furthermore, MacArthur instructed his deputy chief of staff, Major General Richard J. Marshall, "that General Eichelberger [was to be] given no additional medals until after the war was over."[45] Finally, in mid-July, MacArthur awarded Krueger the role of leading the initial landing in the invasion of Japan; he selected the 6th Army to make an assault on the island of Kyushu three months prior to the 8th Army's landing on Honshu, Japan.

These events had a dramatic impact on Eichelberger. They finally convinced him that MacArthur had neither affection for him nor sincere appreciation for his efforts.[46] Realizing that his chief had merely been using him for his own cynical purposes, he complained, "There is no genuine gratitude—just what is best for them [MacArthur and his supporters]." "I wish I cared more for those for whom I must fight," he wrote his wife, adding, "I don't know why it became my fate to land among some elderly gentlemen whose motives are not always as nice as I would like to have them be."[47]

These bitter feelings lingered for several months. Eichelberger was in an angry and depressed mood when the war ended in September 1945. He could not accept MacArthur's failure to provide him with the attention and affection that he believed he deserved, and he remained painfully aware of his relative lack of medals, promotions and publicity. Feeling that MacArthur had not rewarded him for the prime years of his career, he complained that MacArthur's reluctance to share publicity and decorations had deprived him of his best opportunity to gain military honors and glory.[48] He entertained a brief hope in August that the invasion of Japan would provide a final opportunity to gain public recognition, but the explosion of the atomic bomb and the Japanese surrender quickly put an end to this hope.[49] He was subsequently informed by MacArthur that the 8th Army would play a leading role in the occupation of Japan, but it was clear that a peaceful occupation would be far less newsworthy than a wartime landing on Japan's shores.[50]

Believing that he had every reason to be depressed, Eichelberger spent the last few weeks of the war writing to his wife and describing the enormous psychological burdens that he had experienced during his service under MacArthur. "My trouble," he wrote, "was that I went through a great fight . . . to stop feeling sorry for myself and get about the business of gaining victories." He explained that his conflicts with MacArthur had affected his "whole disposition," and that his wife's constant reminders of MacArthur's unfairness had added "to this burden which I have had to bear and fight against." Stating that he periodically "went back into the dumps again," Eichelberger admitted that his emotional struggles had affected his health and sleep, and had threatened to turn his everyday existence into "a life of hate."[51]

Eichelberger had no desire to continue with this turmoil indefinitely. During the first week of August he applied for the position of Superintendent at West Point. Hoping that a different post, away from MacArthur, would improve his mental outlook, he wrote Colonel Chauncey Fenton at the U.S. Military Academy and informed him that the Superintendent's position "would be my Number One choice." During the third week of August, he learned that the position had already been filled by General Maxwell Taylor. In a galling bit of irony, he was informed that Taylor had been selected for the post because "his war record included several colorful events [which] marked him as one of the best young generals to come out of the European Theatre."[52]

This final blow made Eichelberger extremely bitter, for he found himself in a position comparable to his frustrating World War I experiences. Once again, he had missed out on the "Big Show" in Europe; he had been delegated to a secondary theater where he had struggled in relative obscurity. Worse yet, he had been forced to work under a mediocre commander, Krueger, whom he felt lacked his superior talent and abilities. And now, as a reminder of his luckless destiny, he found himself the loser in the competition for the West Point position, having come out second best to a lower-ranking "glamour boy" from Europe. As Eichelberger departed the Philippines for the occupation of Japan, he felt that there was little reason to celebrate, for it seemed that fate had again dealt him a losing hand.[53]

NOTES

1. Luvaas, *Dear Miss Em*, 222-23; Eichelberger, *Our Jungle Road to Tokyo*, 205; Ronald Spector, *Eagle Against the Sun* (New York: Free Press, 1985), 526.

2. William Manchester, *American Caesar: Douglas MacArthur 1880-1964* (New York: Dell, 1978), 500-501; Eichelberger Dictations, "Comments on *Triumph in the Philippines*, Part VII, Chapter XXIX," 29 November 1956, 2-3; Eichelberger, *Our Jungle Road to Tokyo*, 205-206.

3. Another "personal" reason for MacArthur's attack in the southern Philippines was his desire to be known as the liberator of "all" the Philippines. As William Manchester points out in his book *American Caesar*, the southern Philippines had little "strategic importance," and operations in this sector were never approved by the Joint Chiefs of Staff. Nevertheless, MacArthur carried out these operations in the south under his own authority, and thereby presented the Joint Chiefs of Staff with a fait accompli which they subsequently approved. Manchester, *American Caesar*, 500-

510; Robert Eichelberger to Emma Eichelberger, 4 March 1945, Eichelberger Papers; Eichelberger Dictations, "Comments on *Triumph in the Philippines*," 29 November 1966, 2–3.

4. General Charles Willoughby (MacArthur's chief intelligence officer) to Robert Eichelberger, 4 March 1945, Eichelberger Papers; Robert Eichelberger to Emma Eichelberger, 21 February 1945, 4 March 1945, 24 March 1945, 29 March 1945, 8 April 1945, 9 April 1945, and 10 April 1945, Eichelberger Papers.

5. Eichelberger, *Our Jungle Road to Tokyo*, 232–33; Robert Eichelberger to Emma Eichelberger, 27 February 1945 and 12 July 1945, Eichelberger Papers; Eichelberger Diaries, 13 March 1945, Eichelberger Papers.

6. Robert Eichelberger, "Report of the Commanding General, Eighth Army, on the Panay-Negros and Cebu Operations," March 1945, included in box 89 of the Eichelberger Papers, 6–9, 16–17, 27–33, 45, 56–57, 75–76.

7. Robert L. Eichelberger, "Report of the Commanding General, Eighth Army, on the Palawan and Zamboanga Operations," February–March 1945, included in box 90 of the Eichelberger Papers, pages iii, iv of introduction, 1–4, 37 of text.

8. Robert L. Eichelberger, "Report of the Commanding General, Eighth Army, on the Palawan and Zamboanga Operations," February–March 1945, included in box 90 of the Eichelberger Papers, 12, 15–16, 18, 26.

9. Robert L. Eichelberger, "Report of the Commanding General, Eighth Army, on the Palawan and Zamboanga Operations," February–March 1945, included in box 90 of the Eichelberger Papers, 46–50.

10. Robert Eichelberger, 11 March 1945 and 12 March 1945, Eichelberger Papers; Eichelberger, *Our Jungle Road to Tokyo*, 206–207; General Robert L. Eichelberger, "Report of the Commanding General, Eighth Army, on the Palawan and Zamboanga Operations," 37–40, 42, 44, 47, 49, 51–56, 58, 60, 72.

11. Robert Eichelberger to Emma Eichelberger, 20 March 1945, 10 March 1945, and 12 March 1945, Eichelberger Papers; General Robert L. Eichelberger, "Report of the Commanding General, Eighth Army, on the Palawan and Zamboanga Operations," 44, 51–55.

12. Robert Eichelberger, "Report of the Commanding General, Eighth Army, on the Panay-Negros and Cebu Operations," March 1945, included in box 89 of the Eichelberger Papers, 6–9, 12, 16–19; Eichelberger, *Our Jungle Road to Tokyo*, 207–208.

13. Eichelberger, "Report . . . on the Panay-Negros and Cebu Operations," 18–19, 21–27.

14. Ibid., 27–37; Eichelberger, *Our Jungle Road to Tokyo*, 210–11.

15. Eichelberger, "Report . . . on the Panay-Negros and Cebu Operations," 38–44; Robert Eichelberger to Emma Eichelberger, 2 April 1945 and 30 April 1945, Eichelberger Papers.

16. Eichelberger, "Report . . . on the Panay-Negros and Cebu Operations," 61–62, 75; Eichelberger Dictations, "Comments on *Triumph in the Philippines—The Central Visayan Islands*," 29 November 1956, 1; Eichelberger, *Our Jungle Road to Tokyo*, 212–21.

17. Eichelberger, "Report . . . on the Panay-Negros and Cebu Operations," 63–66; Eichelberger, *Our Jungle Road to Tokyo*, 214–15.

18. Although Eichelberger was understandably proud of this flanking maneuver, the Japanese officers were much less complimentary. After the war, a Japanese colonel stated that "the Americal Division had been inordinately slow in mounting envelopments. . . . The frontal attack in the center had been wasteful of time and lives and . . . the Americans would have done better to execute an early, strong envelopment of the Japanese left." Smith, *Triumph in the Philippines*, 616; Luvaas, *Dear Miss Em*, 275, footnote 6; General Robert L. Eichelberger, "The Amphibious Eighth," a short informal history included in box 65 of the Eichelberger Papers, 8–9.

19. Smith, *Triumph in the Philippines*, 616; Luvaas, *Dear Miss Em*, 275, footnote 6; General Robert L. Eichelberger, "The Amphibious Eighth," a short informal history included in box 65 of the Eichelberger Papers, 8–9.

20. Eichelberger, "Report . . . on the Panay-Negros and Cebu Operations," 67–69, 76; Eichelberger, *Our Jungle Road to Tokyo*, 214–15; Robert Eichelberger to Emma Eichelberger, 19 April 1945, Eichelberger Papers.

21. Eichelberger Dictations, "Background for the Mindanao Operations," no date, 1–2; Eichelberger Dictations, "Zamboanga," 16 May 1948, 4–5; R. L. Eichelberger, "Report of the Commanding General, Eighth Army, on the Mindanao Operation," 17 April 1945, included in box 96 of the Eichelberger Papers, 6–22.

22. Eichelberger, "The Amphibious Eighth," 9–11; Eichelberger, "Report of the Commanding General, Eighth Army, on the Mindanao Operation," 23–36; Robert L. Eichelberger, "Mindanao Campaign of 24th Infantry Division, April-August 1945," no date, included in the Eichelberger Papers, 3–8.

23. Eichelberger, "Report . . . on the Mindanao Operation," 38–42; Eichelberger, *Our Jungle Road to Tokyo*, 222, 224–29; Robert Eichelberger to Emma Eichelberger, 1 May 1945, 2 May 1945, 4 May 1945, and 9 May 1945, Eichelberger Papers; Eichelberger, "The Amphibious Eighth," 11–12.

24. Eichelberger, "Report . . . on the Mindanao Operation," 42–47; Eichelberger Dictations, "General MacArthur's Habit of Stating that an Operation was over when in Many Cases it had only just begun," 19 November 1956, 1–2.

25. Robert Eichelberger, "Report of the Commanding General, Eighth Army, on the Luzon Mop-Up Operation," no date, included in the Eichelberger Papers, 3–10, 12–23, 28–30, 35; Eichelberger Dictations, "Zamboanga," 16 May 1948, 1; Robert Eichelberger to Emma Eichelberger, 1 July 1945 and 4 July 1945, Eichelberger Papers.

26. Robert Eichelberger to Emma Eichelberger, 19 June 1945 and 21 May 1945, Eichelberger Papers; itinerary for MacArthur's tour of the Philippines in June 1945, dated 5 June 1945, section entitled "History of Cebu," included in Eichelberger Papers; Unit Citation for 19th Infantry Regiment, 24th Infantry Division, dated 27 April 1946, included in Eichelberger Papers; Eichelberger, *Our Jungle Road to Tokyo*, 223; James, *The Years of MacArthur, Volume II*, 748; Eichelberger Dictations, "Zamboanga," 16 May 1948, 8.

27. Smith, *Triumph in the Philippines*, 600–20; Spector, *Eagle Against the Sun*, 500–30.

28. On one occasion, Eichelberger made the unsubstantiated claim that there was "about 20 times a greater chance of getting shot at Cebu City" than at Okinawa. Robert Eichelberger to Emma Eichelberger, 23 April 1945, Eichelberger Papers.

29. Eichelberger Dictations, no title, 21 June 1955, page 4 of dictation and page 218 of dictation notebook; Robert Eichelberger to Emma Eichelberger, 6 May 1945, 25 May 1945, 8 June 1945, 9 June 1945, 3 June 1945, 15 June 1945, 23 June 1945, 28 June 1945, 29 June 1945, and 28 August 1945, Eichelberger Papers; General George S. Patton, Jr., to Robert Eichelberger, 25 May 1945, Eichelberger Papers.

30. Although Eichelberger had supreme confidence in his ability as a combat officer, he admitted that his victories in the southern Philippines had resulted more from luck than skill. In a letter to his wife, Eichelberger stated that "Your beau is a very lucky person because I could have been whipped on a number of occasions." In particular, Eichelberger noted that his drive from Parang to Digos on Mindanao could easily have ended in disaster, for his troops were spread out over 80 miles and the Japanese "knew the exact strength of [the American force]" and had 30,000 troops in the area. The enemy failed to attack, however, because the Japanese commander believed that the "overland march of the 24th" Division was merely a "prelude to an amphibious landing at Davao from Morotai." This poor decision, combined with the lack of unity and weak leadership in the Japanese high command, caused Eichelberger to remark that "no commander operating on a shoestring has ever been treated better by his enemies." Robert Eichelberger to Emma Eichelberger, 30 May 1945 and 31 May 1945, Eichelberger Papers; Eichelberger Dictations, "The Central Visayan Islands," no date, 5; Eichelberger Dictations, "Comments on *Triumph in the Philippines*," 14 January 1957, 1–2; Eichelberger Dictations, no title and no date, page 7 of dictation and page 729 of dictation notebook.

31. Robert Eichelberger to Emma Eichelberger, 6 July 1945 and 9 July 1945, Eichelberger Papers; Manchester, *American Caesar*, 466–67.

32. Manchester, *American Caesar*, 18, 21, 62, 84, 131–36; Herbert Asbury and Frank Gervasi, "MacArthur—The Story of a Great American Soldier," *Collier's*, 21 July 1945, 26, 30.

33. Eichelberger Dictations, "Some Phases of General MacArthur's Attitude towards me . . . and Krueger," 31 August 1959, 5; James, *The Years of MacArthur, Volume II*, 750–51.

34. Robert Eichelberger to Emma Eichelberger, 4 July 1945 and 20 May 1945, Eichelberger Papers; Eichelberger Dictations, "Some Phases of General MacArthur's Attitude towards me . . . and Krueger," 31 August 1959, 2.

35. Manchester, *American Caesar*, 466–67; Robert Eichelberger to Emma Eichelberger, 19 March 1945, 30 March 1945, 8 April 1945, 18 April 1945, 26 May 1945, 3 June 1945, and 28 June 1945, Eichelberger Papers.

36. James, *The Years of MacArthur, Volume II*, 425–32, 715–24.

37. Eichelberger Dictations, "Public Relations Policies of GHQ, Particularly with Reference to other Leaders besides General MacArthur," no date, 4–5; Robert Eichelberger to Emma Eichelberger, 10 April 1945, 26 May 1945, and 28 April 1945, Eichelberger Papers; Douglas MacArthur to Robert Eichelberger, 21 April 1945, Eichelberger Papers; Manchester, *American Caesar*, 510; Clovis Byers Memorandum, "Interview With General MacArthur, Saturday, 30 March 1945," Eichelberger Papers.

38. There is considerable evidence that these comments were not sincere, and were merely part of MacArthur's plan to retain Eichelberger's services by flattery and seduction. Eichelberger noted that MacArthur did not always give the impression that

he was pleased with the Eighth Army's operations in the southern Philippines. "I could tell from time to time," he stated, "that General MacArthur felt that the Japanese opposition had not been as heavy as I might have intimated." He added that MacArthur "refused to look at a list of casualties which I presented to him or at least waved these aside as unimportant." Eichelberger had his own doubts about the sincerity of MacArthur's compliments. He stated, "I have no illusions of any kind as you can imagine and I do not believe many things that I am told." In a letter to his wife, Eichelberger remarked, "I realize that some of this [praise] may not be sincere but I must live with these people" and cannot "rebuff [their] advances" when "they are friendly." Eichelberger Dictations, MacArthur as a C.O.," 21 June 1961, 4; Robert Eichelberger to Emma Eichelberger, 13 April 1945 and 27 July 1945, Eichelberger Papers.

39. General Irving was relieved by Krueger during the fighting on Leyte, and General Brush retained his command by only the narrowest of margins during the fighting on Luzon. Eichelberger believed that both men had been done an injustice by Krueger. He attempted to maintain the reputations of both officers by awarding them significant combat commands. Eichelberger made Irving the commanding officer of the 8th Army area command, and retained Brush as the commanding officer of the 40th Infantry Division. The 40th Division subsequently performed with valor and speed on Panay and Negros, causing Eichelberger to remark that "it is no surprise to me that a division which was known for its slowness under your palsy walsy [Krueger] is suddenly moving with commendable swiftness." In retaliation for Krueger's attacks on these two officers, Eichelberger decided to demote General Franklin Sibert, one of Krueger's favorites, who was indirectly responsible for Irving's relief. Although Sibert was a corps commander in the highly successful Mindanao campaign (in Eichelberger's opinion, one of the greatest operations in the history of the Pacific War), Eichelberger decided after the completion of the Philippine operations that Sibert would have to be relieved of his command. He "is good," Eichelberger stated, "but not good enough." Eichelberger later offered the excuse that Sibert was "dumb" and was responsible for some poor tactical decisions on Mindanao. Robert Eichelberger to Emma Eichelberger, 20 June 1945, 9 June 1945, and 2 April 1945, Eichelberger Papers; memorandum for McKaye, no title, 21 May 1949, Eichelberger Papers; Eichelberger Dictations, "Formation of Eighth Army," no date, 5–6; Eichelberger Dictations, "Arrival in the Philippines," 9 May 1948, 4; Eichelberger Dictations, "Comments on *Triumph in the Philippines*, Part VI, Chapter XXIII," 14 January 1957, 2.

40. Robert Eichelberger to Emma Eichelberger, 24 March 1945, 25 March 1945, 1 April 1945, 10 April 1945, 28 April 1945 and 14 June 1945, Eichelberger Papers; Eichelberger Dictations, no title, 6 March 1961, page 1 of dictation and page 635 of dictation notebook; Eichelberger Dictations, "After My Return to Australia from Buna-Sanananda," 18 April 1948, 12.

41. Unfortunately, many of Emma Eichelberger's letters to her husband were destroyed after the war. Some were lost during the 1940s and 1950s. The content and tone of her letters, however, is evident from General Eichelberger's responses and from his own letters on topics of mutual interest. In particular, see Robert Eichelberger's letters to Miss Em dated 13 April 1945, 18 April 1945, 19 May 1945,

25 May 1945, 26 May 1945, 3 June 1945, 15 June 1945, 23 June 1945, 28 June 1945, and 30 June 1945, Eichelberger Papers.

42. Brigadier General Clovis Byers to Emma Eichelberger, 2 July 1945, Eichelberger Papers; Clovis Byers Diaries, 5 July 1945, box 30, Hoover Institution on War, Peace, and Revolution, Stanford University.

43. Robert Eichelberger to Emma Eichelberger, 13 April 1945, Eichelberger Papers.

44. Robert Eichelberger to Emma Eichelberger, 10 April 1945, 28 April 1945, and 13 July 19-45, Eichelberger Papers; Eichelberger Dictations, "Background for the Mindanao Operations," no date, 5-6; Eichelberger Dictations, "MacArthur as a C.O.," 21 June 1961," pages 5-6 of dictation, 777-78 of dictation notebook.

45. Robert Eichelberger to Emma Eichelberger, 30 June 1945, 1 July 1945, 13 July 1945, plus an additional undated letter probably written in July 1940, Eichelberger Papers; James, *The Years of MacArthur, Volume II*, 750-51; James, *A Time for Giants*, 240; Eichelberger Dictations, "Opinions," no date, pages 11-12 of dictation and pages 201-202 of dictation notebook; Eichelberger Dictations, "MacArthur as a C.O.," 21 June 1961, pages 5-6 of dictation and pages 776-77 of dictation notebook; World War II military reports, "Staff Study Operations— Coronet," 15 August 1945, 1-15, included in box 102 of the Eichelberger Papers.

46. Eichelberger later confronted the "Big Chief" with this information. He asked MacArthur if it was true that he had ordered his deputy chief of staff to withhold all decorations for the 8th Army commander until after the war was over. MacArthur reportedly became quite agitated, and stated that he had recommended Eichelberger for the Silver Star. Eichelberger replied, "General, I don't want the Silver Star . . . I merely want to keep my faith in you." Eichelberger Dictations, "Opinions," no date, an addendum at the end of the "Opinions" located at or near page 202 of dictation notebook.

47. Robert Eichelberger to Emma Eichelberger, 6 July 1945, 30 June 1945, and 8 June 1945, Eichelberger Papers.

48. Eichelberger's bitter feelings, however, were not limited to his relationship with MacArthur. Eichelberger continued to feel an equal (if not greater) antipathy toward Krueger. On one occasion, when informed that General Rapp Brush would be temporarily assigned to Krueger's command, Eichelberger commented that "if I were he [Brush] I would get out even if it were necessary to invoke the question of tropical fatigue." Perhaps in response to Eichelberger's suggestion, Brush did retire and leave for the United States shortly before the end of the war. Robert Eichelberger to Emma Eichelberger, 15 June 1945, 30 June 1945, and 3 August 1945, Eichelberger Papers.

49. After the Japanese surrender, Eichelberger was assigned the task of planning and leading the initial movement into Japan, with the Eighth Army serving as the advance unit into Tokyo. This assignment led Eichelberger to brag that he was "sitting on top of the world" and that my army fought its way into the "number one position." Based on his many disappointments during this period, however, there is little evidence to support such effusive optimism, and it is more likely that Eichelberger made these statements to bolster his own sagging morale. Robert Eichelberger to Emma Eichelberger, 12 August 1945 and 18 August 1945, Eichelberger Papers.

50. Robert Eichelberger to Emma Eichelberger, 22 July 1945, 1 August 1945, 2 August 1945, 3 August 1945, 4 August 1945, 6 August 1945, and 16 August 1945, Eichelberger Papers; Robert Eichelberger to Mrs. Jerome Zerbe, 20 August 1945, Eichelberger Papers; World War II military reports, "Operations Instructions Number Four (4) with Amendments—The Military Occupation of Japan," 15 August 1945, 1–15, included in box 101 of the Eichelberger Papers.

51. Robert Eichelberger to Emma Eichelberger, 1 July 1945, 27 April 1945, and 13 April 1945, Eichelberger Papers.

52. Robert Eichelberger to Colonel Earl H. Blaik, 6 August 1945, Eichelberger Papers; Robert Eichelberger to Colonel Chauncey T. Fenton, 29 July 1945, Eichelberger Papers; Colonel Earl H. Blaik to Robert Eichelberger, 24 August 1945, Eichelberger Papers; Robert Eichelberger to Emma Eichelberger, 11 August 1945, Eichelberger Papers.

53. Robert Eichelberger to Emma Eichelberger, 23 June 1945, 9 April 1945, 2 July 1945, 30 June 1945, and 8 June 1945, Eichelberger Papers; Robert Eichelberger to George H. Eichelberger, 8 July 1945, Eichelberger Papers.

11

MILITARY OCCUPATION OF JAPAN

After the Japanese surrender on 2 September 1945, the 8th Army landed in the vicinity of Yokohama, Japan, and dispersed across the islands of Hokkaido and northern Honshu. Krueger's 6th Army landed in southern Japan, and occupied the southern half of Honshu and the islands of Shikoku and Kyushu. Krueger established his headquarters in the resort city of Kyoto. Eichelberger established the 8th Army headquarters in Yokohama, 80 miles distant from MacArthur's residence in Tokyo.[1]

Eichelberger planned on returning to the United States after a short six-month stay in Japan. Tired and worn-out from his many campaigns in the Pacific, he was eager to see his wife in Washington after many months of duty abroad. Furthermore, Eichelberger was not anxious to remain under MacArthur's command. He could not forgive or forget the many incidents of "ill-treatment," and he had no desire to prolong his suffering by serving under MacArthur during the monotonous period of the occupation. He informed his wife that he would be returning to the United States by January 1946.[2]

Not until November 1945 did he begin to have doubts about the prudence of leaving his current position. By then, a variety of events and changing circumstances made the possibility of staying in Japan more attractive. One such event was the announcement in December 1945 that General Richard (Dick) Sutherland, MacArthur's chief of staff, was quitting his position and returning to the United States. Sutherland explained that his departure was due to health reasons (high blood pressure), but Eichelberger believed that MacArthur had forced him to resign because of his continuing "affairs" with Elaine Clarke, an Australian nurse.[3] At any rate, Eichelberger was happy to see his old nemesis leave Japan. He stated that "Dick's departure" would mean a "final breaking up of the old Bataan boys who dominated the headquarters under Dick for so long." There "is no question," he added, "that the new regime under Mueller [General

Paul J. Mueller, MacArthur's new chief of staff] will be a much happier one" with a "nicer spirit than under Sutherland."[4]

In September 1945, Eichelberger received more favorable news; his other rival, General Walter Krueger, would be returning to the United States at the end of the year. Krueger's 6th Army would be transferred home in January 1946, and the 8th Army would remain as the sole American force in Japan. The departure of the 6th Army meant that Eichelberger would be the commanding officer of all Allied occupation troops, second in authority only to General MacArthur. Eichelberger wished for oblivion for his nemesis Krueger, observing "I don't believe I have ever disliked anybody more thoroughly [than Walter]."[5]

Besides the imminent departure of Krueger and Sutherland, Eichelberger was also invigorated by MacArthur's statements at the beginning of the occupation. In September 1945, he learned from a friend that MacArthur had commented, "I don't need anything more than Eichelberger. . . . When he comes to see me I don't have to pump him full of blood; . . . he has ideas and can express them." Eichelberger was also encouraged by MacArthur's statements concerning the living conditions in Japan. MacArthur promised him that he could reside in the best available quarters in Yokohama, that his wife would be allowed to join him as soon as possible, and that the 8th Army commander could use the Emperor's private train for inspection trips in Japan. In October 1945, Eichelberger received an autographed picture from MacArthur with the inscription, "No Army of this war has achieved greater glory and distinction than the Eighth." Greatly moved by this statement, Eichelberger later claimed that the receipt of this inscribed photo was "one of the greatest moments of my life." This complimentary token did not heal the deep feelings of resentment that Eichelberger felt toward his chief, but he did admit that "as I look at that [inscription], some of the bitterness that I felt sort of vanishes."[6]

Eichelberger was even more pleased by MacArthur's change in attitude toward the press. The beginning of the Japanese occupation created a deluge of media interest. MacArthur quickly realized that he would be unable to censor the press in the same manner as during the war. He therefore decided to allow greater publicity about his subordinates. His rationale was that it was preferable to allow the newspapers greater leeway in their stories than to risk criticism by attempting to monopolize the press.

As a result, MacArthur's subordinates, and particularly Eichelberger, received a much greater share of publicity than they were accustomed to getting during the war. As commander of the occupation troops in Japan, Eichelberger became a primary focus of many publications. He was featured on the covers of both *Time* and *Life*. The newspapers in the United States ran several articles about "Uncle Bob" and his Pacific campaigns. They referred to the 8th Army commander as the "Japanese expert, jungle fighter, combat fighter, political expert" and local "tough guy."[7]

Excited by this attention, Eichelberger exclaimed that "I got more publicity out of coming in here [Japan] without firing a shot than I . . . had in any of my fights." In a letter to his wife, he stated, "I am not so blasé that it doesn't startle me when I see a thing like that [his picture in *Life*] and realize that over three million copies will go out over the world." In subsequent letters, he noted that several reporters thought that he was one of a handful of officers, including Eisenhower, Patton, Bradley, and Mark Clark, who were well-known among the American public. "I have received letters . . . from George Patton and John C. H. Lee," he added, "so they must think that I have joined the fraternity of the great or near-great."[8]

This sudden fame and notoriety made Eichelberger eager to remain in Japan.[9] He feared that this wonderful publicity would end if he returned to the United States. In February 1946, he decided to remain in his current post and to bring his wife to Japan for a period of at least 12 months. In March 1946, Eichelberger made a firm commitment to MacArthur, informing his chief that he had decided to continue his present duties as commander of the 8th Army.

Eichelberger did not regret this decision. His duties in Japan were always interesting, but not unduly numerous or burdensome. Part of the reason for this palatable workload was the limited nature of the 8th Army's responsibilities. Under the existing arrangement, the main duties of the occupation were undertaken by MacArthur, the "Supreme Commander, Allied Powers" (SCAP).[10] Using the basic outlines of the Potsdam Declaration, MacArthur assumed (almost single-handedly) the task of establishing a program of reform for Japan. His program emphasized two main goals—the elimination of those elements in Japan's social, political, and economic system which were a potential menace to the peace and security of the world; and the establishment of a democratic government which reflected the ideals and principles of the Charter of the United Nations.[11]

In order to achieve these broad goals, MacArthur set specific occupation policies and announced them in the form of directives to the Japanese government. After announcing these policies, MacArthur issued instructions to the 8th Army that specified the nature and extent of their surveillance of the Japanese people. The 8th Army assumed no policy-making role, but only implemented the policies of the SCAP and reported failures of the Japanese government to comply with these directives.[12] As Eichelberger stated in his reports, the role of the 8th Army was limited to "surveillance, observe, report, [and] investigate."[13]

The 8th Army's role, while limited, was complicated by the nature and scope of its responsibilities. Each year, it assumed new duties, depending upon the changes in MacArthur's policies.[14] During each phase of the occupation, Eichelberger's forces assumed greater challenges and an ever expanding list of assignments.[15]

For example, during the first phase of the occupation, from September 1945 to January 1946, the 8th Army had the responsibility of supervising the initial "negative" tasks of the occupation, which were designed to eliminate Japan as a threat to the peace and security of the world. These tasks included the disarmament and demobilization of the Japanese military forces; the 8th Army was responsible for the destruction of 10,000 Japanese airplanes, 3,000 tanks, 90,000 fieldpieces, and one million tons of explosives.[16]

The 8th Army also unloaded and distributed army supplies and food. They provided housing, clothing, and training facilities for 250,000 American soldiers. The 8th Army liberated over 23,000 Allied prisoners of war, and provided immediate medical treatment for the sick and disabled. Finally, Eichelberger's troops repaired and restored shattered communication and logistical facilities in Japan.[17]

In order to accomplish these tasks, the 8th Army had the services of "the greatest [personnel] in history." The men were ideally suited to the tasks of the occupation. The majority were jungle veterans who were competent and businesslike; they were "not cruel nor were they overly friendly," but merely "wanted to finish their job and go home." These soldiers rarely mingled with the Japanese women, but performed their duties with discipline and efficiency. They treated their former enemies with courtesy and respect. Since these troops were battle tested and aware of the bravery of the Japanese, they had no desire to prove their courage by harassing or beating up Japanese civilians. Eichelberger had no complaints about these serious-minded "professionals"; he stated that these men were "the best representatives the American nation could have."[18]

During the second phase of the occupation (from January 1946 to January 1947), most of these "outstanding" veterans returned to the United States. They were replaced by inexperienced personnel that had not been in combat. These replacements were a different type of soldier. Most were young men who lacked "the fine disciplinary experience of being on duty in an outfit in battle." They were inclined to demonstrate their toughness by beating up helpless Japanese civilians. They had a less disciplined attitude toward appearance, saluting, and profanity. Eichelberger stated that many were black soldiers who liked "to get out at night in the Mohammedan heaven furnished by some millions of Japanese girls." He noted that the venereal disease rates among the black units were extremely high. There were numerous incidents where black recruits knifed or assaulted other soldiers for "talking to their girls." Other disciplinary problems existed within the 8th Army during this second phase, causing morale to be "at its lowest ebb."[19]

Eichelberger was forced to impose severe disciplinary regulations on his new recruits. In March 1946, he issued an order forbidding "public displays of affection." This order prohibited all American soldiers from kissing, fondling, or putting "their arms around Japanese girls." He also tightened discipline by requiring strict adherence to uniform regulations and forbidding the use of "vulgar and profane language." In addition, houses of prostitution were placed off limits. The Japanese police were required to round up neighborhood thugs, black-market traders, and Japanese prostitutes. More importantly, Eichelberger made an effort to speak personally to the soldiers under his command. Reminding them that they were serving as role models for the Japanese population, he emphasized that Uncle Sam had made the 8th Army the "best equipped, best fed, best clothed and best entertained Army in the world's history." For that reason, he argued, the country had a right to expect that the 8th Army troops would conduct themselves in an efficient and disciplined manner.[20]

These admonitions and regulations had some effect. The discipline of the 8th Army improved, and Eichelberger's forces were able to complete the duties of the second phase with some degree of success. This improvement in discipline and efficiency was very important, for the duties of the 8th Army increased dramatically during this second phase. From 1946 to 1947, the 8th Army was responsible for the supervision of the "positive" policies of the occupation; these were geared toward the creation of democratic principles and the elimination of all remaining vestiges of Japanese militarism.

For example, the 8th Army was responsible for the apprehension and prosecution of Japanese war criminals. They purged ultra-nationalists from Japan's government offices and public information agencies. Eichelberger's forces also supervised the repatriation of six million Japanese from "Nippon's lost overseas Empire," and directed the return of over one million Koreans and Chinese from Japan to their native countries. In addition, the 8th Army established military government teams in each of Japan's 47 prefectures, and set up advisory bodies of economic, political, and health experts in the major metropolitan areas.[21]

The 8th Army also supervised the establishment of a host of reforms that were controversial because of their "radical" nature. These included the release of all political prisoners, the redistribution of land from the absentee landlords to the peasants, the breaking up of the large Japanese business monopolies, and the formation of a comprehensive national welfare law. The 8th Army participated in the creation of a new Japanese Constitution (which denounced the divinity of the Emperor, renounced war, and forbade the creation of a Japanese army or navy). Other liberal reforms included the promulgation of women's suffrage, the "democratization" and decentralization of the education system, and the creation and encouragement of labor unions and collective bargaining.[22]

The implementation of these reforms was slowed by the threat of a general strike in January 1947. This threat caused a change in occupation policy. MacArthur feared that a labor shutdown would disrupt the aims of the occupation and paralyze the activities of the 8th Army. MacArthur averted a strike with a combination of promises and threats. He subsequently decided to pursue a more cautious approach in introducing changes into Japanese society.

From January 1947 to December 1948, the occupation became more conservative in tone. There was less of an effort to reform the existing political, social, and economic institutions in Japan. The changes that had already been introduced were continued, but at a reduced pace. Only a few new liberal reforms were added (including laws for better working conditions, the opening of higher education to the masses, and the establishment of free compulsory education through the secondary level). Instead, a much greater effort was made to improve the facilities of the American forces in Japan (through the establishment of service clubs, post exchanges, housing for dependents, and "rest and rehabilitation" hotels for enlisted men). The training and education of the American troops were also emphasized; over 100,000 8th Army personnel received instruction in technical, vocational, and university-level programs.[23]

During this new third phase, greater efforts were also made to improve security arrangements and to maintain law and order. The emergence of the Cold War and the deterioration of relations between the United States and the then Soviet Union were influencing events throughout the world. American leaders in Japan were alarmed by the presence of Russian troops on the nearby Kuril Islands. The U.S. State Department was concerned by the Kremlin's refusal to return over 300,000 Japanese detainees from Siberia. Many American leaders believed that the Communists were responsible for the civilian unrest in Japan, including the "Red riots" of April 1948. During these disturbances, hundreds of Koreans rioted in the cities of Kobe and Osaka; after causing extensive damage to government property, they captured and held hostage three Japanese government officials. Although the Koreans claimed that the sources of their grievances were Japanese laws which discriminated against the use of the Korean language, the majority of American officers (including MacArthur and Eichelberger) believed that the riots were Communist-inspired and were directed by the party leadership from Moscow.[24]

In order to control this new threat, Eichelberger was ordered by the SCAP in May 1948 to strengthen his security forces and to provide additional protection for American "resources" in Japan. Eichelberger increased the size of the police force and approved recommendations to arm each of the 110,000 Japanese policemen with an American .45-caliber pistol. He provided bodyguards for the Emperor and imperial family. The security forces surrounding the American bases and airfields were doubled. After inspecting each of the riot areas at Kobe, Osaka, and Hamamatsu, Eichelberger encouraged the local government leaders to "beat [the] hell out of anybody who tried to break into their offices."[25] He stated publicly that the 8th Army would provide support and protection for the elected Japanese leaders. "I will not tolerate," he added, "anyone who interferes with or attempts to push my soldiers around."[26]

Eichelberger had difficulty, however, in upholding this "hard-line" approach toward law and order. His troops were not adequately able to perform these additional duties. The 8th Army of the third phase was undermanned, although it did have some positive qualities. Most of the recruits in 1947-48 were high school graduates, and almost two-thirds (according to Eichelberger's estimate) had the desire to pursue a college education. As a result, these recruits were more motivated, intelligent, and disciplined than their predecessors; they were more inclined to "give Uncle Sam a break and to act and look like soldiers." These new troops possessed a strong military attitude and were just as capable as the old "jungle veterans," causing Eichelberger to state that "potentially, these were the finest soldiers I have ever seen."[27]

Whatever strengths Eichelberger found in the "new" 8th Army, its effectiveness was diluted by greatly diminished numbers. His army declined from a high of 250,000 men in 1945 (and a range of 100,000–150,000 in 1946-47) to only 50,000 men in 1948. This drop was caused primarily by short enlistments. A majority of the new recruits had signed on for a period of only one year or 18 months. Most of these enlistments had expired by the spring of 1948. Eichelberger claimed in April 1948 that several of his divisions were operating at a "skeleton" strength of under 4,000 men, and that the majority of his units did not have sufficient personnel to perform their duties.[28] His combat forces consisted of a cadre of only 20,000 troops; these units were scattered "in a mountainous country in which we have approximately 1,500 tunnels and bridges." Warning that the combat units were inadequately trained and understaffed, Eichelberger stated that his army was far too weak to stop a Russian attack or Communist sabotage. "The size of my Army is a top secret," he commented, "but . . . I can say that if I had to get into a fight tomorrow about my only defense would be to rise up out of a thicket and wave a night shirt while yelling 'Wah, Wah!'"[29]

The weakness of the 8th Army caused Eichelberger some anxious moments in 1948, but did not become an overriding concern until the last stages of the occupation. Prior to that time, he experienced few major problems or difficulties; he was able to enjoy his years in Japan with a minimum of stress. Part of the reason for this tranquillity was the improvement in "cooperation" between Eichelberger and MacArthur. Neither party changed dramatically, but the differences in their personalities combined in these years to form a complementary blend of leadership.

For example, MacArthur preferred to remain cloistered in Tokyo, eschewing travel, social events, or meetings with foreign ambassadors. From behind the iron gates of the American embassy, he studied the political, social, and economic problems of Japan. While frequently pacing the floor, MacArthur mentally rehearsed and debated the merits of his ideas (or expressed his "ruminations" to his favored advisors or guests). He gradually constructed, through his own efforts, the grand strategy for the democratization of Japan.[30] MacArthur preferred to formulate this strategy in the broadest possible context. His restless mind had no patience for details, and he was content to issue his directives in the form of vague generalities or nonspecific courses of action.

These directives were not the result of idle speculation. MacArthur was a strong proponent of hard work, routine, and austerity. During the occupation, he rarely deviated from his normal schedule—he rose at 7:30 AM, read his reports and the daily newspapers, left for his office in downtown Tokyo at 10:00 AM, paused for lunch and a nap at 2:00 PM, and then returned to his office at 4:00

PM, where he usually remained until late evening. MacArthur flourished under this grueling routine. He kept this pace for the duration of the occupation. MacArthur seemed to have no need for outside diversions or long vacations. He certainly felt no desire to take advantage of the "perks" of his position. He ate simply, lived modestly, and avoided parties, formal ceremonies, and social dinners. MacArthur saw few of the attractions of Japan, and rarely mingled with the Japanese people.[31] His authority, however, was unquestioned. There was no person in Japan who was unaware of his presence and the invisible hand of his power. MacArthur's hard work and pervasive influence made him the leading symbol of the occupation. The Japanese people saw him as the American equivalent of their Emperor, with comparable powers of devotion and determination.

Eichelberger, on the other hand, had a much gentler approach than MacArthur. While MacArthur was reclusive, domineering, and intellectual, Eichelberger was outgoing, friendly, and fun-loving. He enjoyed socializing, and liked to spend his evenings at dances, dinners, and other social events. Unlike MacArthur, he was not tied to his desk or office; he found paper work boring and tedious. Instead, Eichelberger enjoyed taking extensive inspection trips throughout Japan, where he was able to make contact with the Japanese people and to learn about the intimate details of their lives.[32]

During these inspections, Eichelberger enjoyed finding practical solutions to the day-to-day problems of the occupation. He had little capacity for three-dimensional thought or "theoretical" analysis, but he did possess the unique ability to assess "vague" programs and to spot difficulties in their application. He was able to observe firsthand the flaws and "gaps" in MacArthur's broad policies; he amended and reworked those that were faulty or incapable of effective implementation. Through his inspections, Eichelberger was able to provide the pragmatic solutions for many of MacArthur's "starry-eyed" programs.[33]

For example, Eichelberger provided some practical adjustments to the SCAP's political programs. MacArthur directed American units to follow a policy of strict noninterference in the Japanese campaign and election process. Eichelberger noticed in 1947, however, that the Japanese political candidates were not provided adequate food during the campaigns; during their public appearances they were frequently made the targets of abuse and violence by Communist agitators. Because these factors contributed to the inefficiency and disruption of the political process, Eichelberger provided the candidates with American bodyguards and food. Although contrary to the SCAP's announced policy, these practical adjustments eliminated the problems of the campaign process; they were belatedly approved by MacArthur and incorporated into the SCAP's political program.[34]

Eichelberger contributed to the success of MacArthur's programs in other ways. His friendly disposition made him the logical choice to entertain the multitude of visitors who arrived from the United States (including military dignitaries, politicians, writers, members of congressional committees and advisory commissions, and foreign delegations). The entertaining of these guests was normally the responsibility of the Supreme Commander, but MacArthur was unwilling to assume these social obligations. Instead, he passed them on to his outgoing and gregarious army commander.

Eichelberger talked and mingled with these visitors in a relaxed fashion. He charmed them with a blend of easy conversation, humorous anecdotes, and extreme courtesies. Attending to all the needs of his guests, Eichelberger provided each individual with plenty of souvenirs, fine foods and liquors, and free trips to the best tourist attractions in Japan.[35] In addition, he gave frank and honest answers to their questions; at every opportunity, he pointed out the results and achievements of MacArthur's programs. Most of these visiting groups, on returning to the United States, were full of praise for MacArthur and the 8th Army. Many of these individuals commented on the kind treatment that they had received from their "gracious host." General Paul Mueller, the SCAP's chief of staff, remarked that "Bob know[s] how to talk with these people" and "never [fails] to send . . . [them] away in good spirits."[36]

MacArthur himself publicly stated that Eichelberger's social and administrative skills were invaluable in Japan. These talents were a perfect complement to his own reclusive and academic tendencies. In private conversations with Eichelberger, MacArthur admitted that his extroverted army commander was "far more popular with the Japanese than he was." "Bob," he stated, "had come to represent" the "friendly face" of the SCAP's programs. MacArthur strongly believed that Eichelberger's presence in Japan was vital to the occupation's success.[37]

Historians have agreed with MacArthur's assessment, although there is a continuing debate concerning the success of the occupation. General Courtney Whitney and William Manchester, two of MacArthur's biographers, state that the occupation was an unqualified success, largely because of the "genius" of MacArthur. This conclusion is supported by Theodore Cohen's 1987 study, *Remaking Japan*; Cohen states that MacArthur, an "inspirational leader without peer," stimulated "the dynamism of the Japanese people" through his radical reforms. Justin Williams, in *Japan's Revolution* (1979), states that MacArthur "skillfully reoriented Japan's political system" and "forged the strong bond of amity and understanding that now link the United States and Japan."[38]

Other historians have been more critical. As Robert Fearey notes in *The Occupation of Japan* (1950), many conservatives have contended that MacArthur's reforms "attempt too much, go too far, are idealistic and unrealistic." Harold S. Quigley, in *The New Japan* (1956), states that the occupation's "basic objective—the advancement of democratic ideals and institutions—was realized to only a minor degree." Walter Sheldon's *The Honorable Conquerors* (1965) concludes that the occupation failed "in the area of human relationships— in making the United States and Japan friends." The *Aftermath of War* (1989), written by Howard B. Schonberger, contends that the American leaders "never agreed on what it was in prewar Japanese society that accounted for aggression in Asia and war with the United States, and hence what needed changing in Japan to achieve the objective of a peaceful democracy." As a result, the "Japanese oligarchy that [seized] power after the war managed remarkably well to thwart American policies not to their liking."[39]

Despite this controversy, almost all historians agree that Eichelberger was a valuable asset during the occupation. John Curtis Perry, in *Beneath the Eagle's Wings*, states that Bob was the only member of the SCAP's inner circle that was "active and restless"; he kept MacArthur informed by "radio, telephone, constant flow of paper, and frequent trips of inspection." Similarly, D. Clayton James states that the 8th Army commander was a "source of fresh, objective thinking." Eichelberger, James argues, was one of the few "who . . . dared to disagree with [MacArthur] and to dissent from the concurrence-seeking, 'groupthink' behavior of the . . . senior officers around the Supreme Commander."[40]

These contributions might have led to a new understanding between Eichelberger and his chief. Eichelberger, however, continued to nurse old wounds from the war; he found new complaints to make about MacArthur during the course of the occupation. These grievances continued to festered after 1946, and they finally interfered with his desire to remain in Japan.

For example, one of these grievances concerned the feasibility of some of MacArthur's programs. Eichelberger strongly disagreed with the liberal content of the SCAP's reforms during the occupation's second phase. Many of these programs (such as "trust-busting" and land redistribution) were considered "too radical and progressive" for Japanese society. He also believed that these measures weakened the Japanese political conservatives and business leaders, and created "a nice atmosphere for the breeding of communists." A staunch conservative and Republican, Eichelberger blamed MacArthur for introducing New Deal programs and ideas into Japan; these, he felt, made the Japanese schools, factories, and labor unions accessible to Communists and other radical influences.[41]

Eichelberger also disagreed with MacArthur's program for shortening the occupation. In the spring of 1947, MacArthur proposed an early withdrawal of American troops from Japan, arguing that Japan's safety could be guaranteed by a declaration of "unarmed neutrality" and by the protection of the United Nations. Eichelberger protested. The withdrawal of American forces, he felt, would leave "the Japanese . . . no alternative except to take Russia's eager and outstretched hand." Since "we deliberately disarmed the Japanese," he argued, "we have also— by all the rules of fair play—assumed the obligations of protecting her." Instead, Eichelberger recommended a 10-year occupation, with a gradual rearmament of the Japanese military. In September 1947, during a trip to Washington, he publicly announced this plan, and presented to the State Department a memorandum (written by Japan's Foreign Minister) which called for the expansion of Japan's land and sea police forces. This plan was rejected by the SCAP, but Eichelberger continued to push for the remilitarization of Japan, and strongly criticized MacArthur's proposal of "unarmed neutrality."[42]

This dispute over occupation policy was dwarfed by other, more personal, differences between Eichelberger and his chief. For example, Eichelberger felt that he deserved a promotion to full General.[43] He was convinced that MacArthur was responsible for his failure to receive a fourth star. MacArthur claimed that the "European gang" was the offending party for this slight, but Eichelberger responded "I would have been promoted within two days if [MacArthur] had recommended me anytime after the Eighth Army went wild in the Philippines."

Eichelberger also blamed MacArthur for his failure to receive more medals during the occupation. In November 1945, he was awarded the Silver Star for his courageous actions on Luzon. Nevertheless, he complained that "if I had received all the ribbons coming to me in comparison with what other people got I would have about forty." Disturbed that Krueger had received two medals (the Distinguished Service Cross and the Oak Leaf Cluster added to the Distinguished Service Medal) prior to his departure from Japan, Eichelberger grumbled that the SCAP was distributing decorations "as acts of grace and not for deeds performed."[44]

In January 1946, Eichelberger was recommended by Rear Admiral Russell Berkey for the U.S. Navy's Distinguished Service Medal. Shortly thereafter, the War Department disapproved this decoration; Eichelberger was informed that his "services had been covered on practically a day-to-day [basis] in Army awards and that there was no incident, action or operation left uncovered on which the Navy could pin its award." Unwilling to accept this explanation, Eichelberger concluded that the matter had been "referred to General MacArthur," and that the SCAP had personally vetoed the award.[45]

Frustrated by this incident, Eichelberger decided to take matters into his own hands. While he was on a short leave to the United States, he had one of his corps commanders (General "Chink" Hall, who was placed in temporary command of the 8th Army during Eichelberger's absence) recommend him to the War Department for several decorations, including the Bronze Star and the Air Medal. Then, in a "secret" ceremony in February 1946, Eichelberger presented these medals to himself along with the accompanying citations. For the next several months, he refused to wear these decorations for fear that the "SCAP might take some notice of it." He later admitted, "[I] wouldn't have done this [awarded himself medals] if the situation [with MacArthur] was not so rotten with reference to certain decorations."[46]

Eichelberger's frustration regarding the SCAP was not limited to the medal situation. He also blamed MacArthur for his failure to gain a higher position in the post-war army. In 1945 and 1946, Eichelberger had hopes of returning to the United States and replacing Dwight D. Eisenhower as Chief of Staff. These ambitions seemed to hold some promise in November 1945; Eisenhower sent a message to MacArthur requesting Eichelberger's services as deputy chief of staff.[47] MacArthur agreed to release Eichelberger for this position, but announced that he would be forced to retain Krueger as commander of the occupation forces. The 6th Army commander, he stated, "would be allowed to pick the members of [the 8th Army] staff to serve under him." This announcement caused Eichelberger a great amount of anxiety. He said that Krueger "had expressed his dislike for certain of my officers . . . such as Generals [Joe] Swing and [Clovis] Byers and I could not accept any advancement at their expense." Thus, for the benefit of his staff, Eichelberger decided to turn down the position. Nevertheless, he blamed MacArthur for forcing him into this "no win" situation.[48]

He also blamed MacArthur for other career disappointments, including his failure to become the supreme commander in Japan. After 1947, Eichelberger entertained hopes of succeeding MacArthur as the SCAP. These hopes were ostensibly supported by MacArthur, who repeatedly informed Bob that he was his preferred choice as his successor.[49] Such sentiments were also shared by General Eisenhower; Ike informed Eichelberger in October 1947 that he would be retained in Japan (past retirement age) "as an ace in the hole, should MacArthur decide to go home." MacArthur, however, expressed no desire to return to the United States; he gave no indication that he was willing to step down from his position. In April 1948, Eichelberger finally lost patience. He decided that MacArthur had deceived him, and had never intended to allow him to serve as supreme commander in Japan. Angry and embittered, he remarked, "I have no illusions [about MacArthur's intentions]," for "all the fuzz was taken off of me a long time ago in New Guinea."[50]

This disappointment, combined with his other frustrations, made Eichelberger eager to strike back against the SCAP in some way. In 1946 and 1947, he began to explore the possibility of writing about his wartime experiences, with the purpose of exposing MacArthur's "foibles" and weaknesses.[51] Eichelberger felt that the public would be interested in his chief's false claims, particularly the wartime "stories about General MacArthur at the front when [in fact] he was on the other side of a 10,000 foot mountain range," and the issuing "of his [press] releases about the small losses [suffered] because there was no hurry when we had been urged to fight to the death." "I realize that my [story] can hurt people terribly," he stated, but "if I do not do it, history is going to take some queer turns." He added, "I have a certain feeling that if I do not write that history of the Eighth Army it will never be presented to the public in the proper manner [by MacArthur]."[52]

Eichelberger's determination to write his own story was strengthened in the fall of 1947, when he discovered that MacArthur was attempting to "hog" all the credit for the accomplishments of the occupation. The most prominent visitors from the United States were briefed by MacArthur; they were informed that the 8th Army was engaged in little more than guard duty. "When General Draper (Undersecretary of the Army) was here," Eichelberger stated, "I found when I talked to him that in the briefing he had received up at [the office of] SCAP, they had not differentiated between the duties of the 8th Army and the work done in [MacArthur's headquarters]." Furthermore, General Jacob Devers (chief of the army ground forces) "had no idea of the many extracurricular duties of the Eighth Army"; he had never been informed by the SCAP that the 8th Army "operated the Military Government units throughout Japan."[53] Stunned and angered, Eichelberger complained to General Eisenhower (who had visited Japan in the spring of 1946 when he was Chief of Staff). Eisenhower advised him to "go home and write a book" about his hardships under MacArthur.[54]

Eichelberger decided to take Eisenhower's advice. In November 1947, he enlisted the help of a secretary who would take dictations about his wartime experiences. He contacted a literary agent, Gertrude Algase, and requested her advice concerning the merits of his proposed book. Encouraged by his agent to "tell his own story of the Pacific," Eichelberger was promised that his book would "gross a handsome sum of money ($50,000)," was "apt to be a best seller," and would be "the best story of the Pacific war so far told." He also was reminded that "unless you go ahead with your story, it will prey on your mind because that is only a human and normal reaction of a man who has accomplished all that you have ... without the public acknowledgment that you are entitled to."[55]

These arguments were convincing. Eichelberger decided to leave Japan and to write the "true story" of the Pacific war.[56] In March 1948, he made a formal request to return to the United States; he informed MacArthur that he planned to retire and "do a bit of writing." At the SCAP's request, Eichelberger delayed his departure until July 1948, when he finally received MacArthur's approval for his return home.[57]

On 30 July, Eichelberger traveled to the SCAP's headquarters in Tokyo, where he had his final meeting with MacArthur. As Eichelberger noted in his diary, this meeting was strained and unpleasant. It ended without MacArthur expressing any thanks or gratitude; Eichelberger left the SCAP's headquarters in an angry and resentful mood. He subsequently expressed his bitter feelings in the following words:

> Arrived at Gen MacA's at 11:30 and had to wait about 10 minutes before I could get in. Our conversation was not in very high order. He did say that I was the last of the combat commanders in the Pacific to go home and that this was the end of an epoch. I did not express any gratitude to him upon leaving him—nor regret. I did not thank him for anything. On the other hand, I must say that I don't recall any particular regret expressed by him. So ... it was 50-50. He mentioned no award of any kind which only seems ridiculous. ... This is a very interesting phase of his character that he would let an officer who has run his occupation [of Japan] for so many years and who has been in my opinion largely responsible for its success leave here without recognition of his

services. It has been unusual for him even after successful combat to praise one orally while at the same time claiming his own glory as a fighting field soldier, a thing which he certainly was not during World War II. . . . In the words of Shakespeare, "He may have been a poor player but he has certainly been a player." This boy has certainly been a player on the stage of history. A strange character who probably wonders why he has so few friends and eternally blames the other fellow.[58]

On 4 August 1948, Eichelberger boarded the U.S.S. *Buckner* for his return trip to the United States. Before his departure, he was saluted by a fine aerial and naval display. Over 50,000 people cheered his final journey from his office to the harbor. Both the Emperor of Japan and the U.S. Secretary of War expressed their thanks for his services. *Time* and *Newsweek* magazines covered his departure in front-page stories. It was the kind of "send-off" that Eichelberger had always dreamed of, but it was spoiled by the ungratefulness of MacArthur, the "one person who forgot to thank me and wish me well after six years of service in the Pacific!"[59]

NOTES

1. Military report, "Eighth Army Experience in Japan," (data prepared for the War Department in the spring of 1947 by the 8th Army public relations office), 1-4, included in the Eichelberger Papers.

2. Robert Eichelberger to Emma Eichelberger, 27 August 1945, 30 August 1945, and 17 September 1945, Eichelberger Papers.

3. In February 1946, MacArthur informed Eichelberger that Sutherland had made several unauthorized trips to Australia for the purpose of seeing his "girlfriend," and that this association, combined with "Dick's" poor health, had compromised Sutherland's ability to perform his job. MacArthur stated that, in his opinion, Sutherland had become unstable and would probably "die in an insane asylum." This proved to be an exaggeration; Sutherland's retirement years were serene and fruitful. Robert Eichelberger to Emma Eichelberger, 6 February 1946, Eichelberger Papers.

4. Robert Eichelberger to Emma Eichelberger, 4 December 1945, 14 April 1946, and 25 May 1946, Eichelberger Papers; memorandum for General Robert Eichelberger, prepared by General Clovis Byers, no title, 4 December 1945, Eichelberger Papers.

5. John Curtis Perry, *Beneath the Eagle's Wings: Americans in Occupied Japan* (New York: Dodd, Mead & Company, 1980), 57-59; Robert Eichelberger to Emma Eichelberger, 17 September 1945, 30 September 1945, and 27 October 1945, Eichelberger Papers; military report, "Statements, By Lieutenant General Eichelberger," no date, 1-2, included in Eichelberger Papers.

6. Robert Eichelberger to Emma Eichelberger, 15 September 1945, 9 October 1945, and 4 November 1945, Eichelberger Papers; Robert Eichelberger to Brig. Gen. George Honnen (Commandant of Cadets, West Point), 4 Nov. 1945, Eichelberger

Papers; Eichelberger Dictations, "Statements, By Lieutenant General Eichelberger," 1945, 4, included in Eichelberger Papers.

7. Robert Eichelberger to Emma Eichelberger, 10 September 1945, 11 September 1945, 12 September 1945, 17 September 1945, 30 September 1945, and 20 October 1945, Eichelberger Papers; *Time*, 10 September 1945, 31-35.

8. Robert Eichelberger to Emma Eichelberger, 20 September 1945, 15 October 1945, and 29 September 1945, Eichelberger Papers.

9. Eichelberger discovered, however, that there were disadvantages to being in the spotlight. In the fall of 1945, he made the offhand remark that the occupation of Japan would be completed in one year. This statement was reported by the press. Eichelberger was criticized by experts in the United States who felt that one year was insufficient to complete the goals of the occupation. Surprised by this criticism, Eichelberger had not been told that MacArthur's wartime "censorship" had been discontinued. He naturally assumed that MacArthur's public relations officers would prevent the publication of any statement that was "harmful." When Eichelberger became aware of GHQ's new "no-censorship" policy, he decided to protect himself by adopting a more antagonistic attitude toward the press. In October 1945, he decided to "keep [his] big mouth shut," avoid "big press conferences," prohibit all "direct quotes" except for those written and approved by 8th Army headquarters, and allow interviews only with "friendly" reporters. He refused to deviate from these policies. On one occasion, he canceled an inspection trip to Hokkaido because some of the reporters scheduled to accompany him were "of doubtful reliability." Ironically, the 8th Army's press regulations became very similar to MacArthur's wartime policies, which Eichelberger had criticized as unduly restrictive. Robert Eichelberger to Emma Eichelberger, 27 September 1945, 30 September 1945, 10 October 1945, 14 October 1945, 19 October 1945, 12 November 1945, and 4 June 1946, Eichelberger Papers; Robert Eichelberger to Mrs. Jerome B. Zerbe (Eichelberger's sister), 1 October 1945, Eichelberger Papers; Robert M. White II to Robert L. Eichelberger, 16 October 1945, Eichelberger Papers (box 12).

10. At the beginning of the occupation, MacArthur was directed by the President to share authority with the multinational Far Eastern Commission and the Allied Council for Japan. Largely because of the force of his personality, MacArthur was able to undermine these organizations and reduce them to advisory bodies. From 1945 on, MacArthur personally set the tone and content of the occupation. He either ignored or disobeyed "directives" from the U.S. State Department and War Department. As a result, many American officers, including Eichelberger, referred to the occupation of Japan as a "one man military government." Meirion Harries and Susan Harries, *Sheathing the Sword: The Demilitarization of Japan* (New York: Macmillan, 1987), xxx-xxxi; military report, "Eighth Army in the Military Government of Japan—Orientation," no date, 1-2, Eichelberger Papers; Manchester, *American Caesar*, 468, 470-71, 549-52; Whitney, *MacArthur*, 297-300.

11. Harries and Harries, *Sheathing the Sword: The Demilitarization of Japan*, xxx-xxxi; military report, "Eighth Army in the Military Government of Japan—Orientation," no date, 1-2, Eichelberger Papers; Manchester, *American Caesar*, 468, 470-71, 549-52; Whitney, *MacArthur*, 297-300; military report, "Education in the New Japan, Volume II," (Civil Information and Education Section, SCAP: May 1948), 6-9 of appendix, box 116 of the Eichelberger Papers.

12. Perry, *Beneath the Eagle's Wings*, 58-65; military report, "Orientation Summary," (Headquarters 8th Army: September 1947), 11, Eichelberger Papers; military report, "A Brief Progress Report on the Political Reorientation of Japan," (Government Section, SCAP: 10 October 1949), 34-35, Eichelberger Papers; Eichelberger, *Our Jungle Road to Tokyo*, 270.

13. In practice, the 8th Army had a much more active and "constructive" role. The deference of the Japanese, the vagueness of the SCAP's directives, and the remoteness of MacArthur caused the Japanese leaders to turn to the 8th Army officers for guidance, advice, and leadership. The advice of the 8th Army officers took on the force of law, particularly in the absence of any practical application of the SCAP's policies. Military report, "Eighth Army in the Military Government of Japan—Orientation," (no date), 1, 14-15, Eichelberger Papers; James, *The Years of MacArthur, Volume III*, 84-86.

14. One factor which made the 8th Army's job less complicated was the cooperation of the Japanese people. The Japanese civilians were extremely polite and deferential. They accepted, without reservation, the dictates and directives of the American leaders. The Japanese were particularly anxious to please the American officers, and went to extreme measures to ensure that the occupation leaders were treated with courtesy and respect. For example, during an inspection trip throughout Japan in 1945, Eichelberger reported that, whenever his personal train entered a village, "the entire railroad personnel of the town [were] lined up at attention on the platform." As the "train departs from the station," he noted, "the personnel remain at attention and do a sharp left or right face in the direction we are going" and "keep this immobile position until the train is out of sight." Impressed by these signs of respect, Eichelberger concluded that it was "extremely unlikely" that the 8th Army would encounter any "serious internal difficulties" during the occupation. Theodore Cohen, *Remaking Japan: The American Occupation as New Deal* (New York: Free Press, 1987), 135-36; Robert Eichelberger to Emma Eichelberger, 4 October 1945 and 27 November 1945, Eichelberger Papers; Eichelberger Dictations, "Some Reflections on the Occupation of Japan by the Eighth Army," 5 December 1960, 9-10.

15. John K. Emmerson and Harrison M. Holland, *The Eagle and the Rising Sun: America and Japan in the Twentieth Century* (New York: Addison-Wesley, 1988), 58-62; Robert Eichelberger to Brigadier General Robert E. Wood (Retired), 12 May 1947, box 16 of Eichelberger Papers.

16. The Japanese political system continued to operate from 1945 to 1948. Neither the SCAP nor the 8th Army attempted to replace the functions of the Japanese government. The SCAP informed the Japanese government of a change in policy by letter or directive, and made it the responsibility of the Japanese political leaders to carry out these changes. For example, MacArthur issued a directive providing for the destruction of Japan's military weapons in 1945. He ordered the Japanese government to provide the means and manpower in which to accomplish this end. The 8th Army was directed to supervise the destruction of this material, but the bulk of the work was completed by Japanese workers under the direction of the Japanese government. It should also be noted that the option of turning over the Japanese weapons to the Chinese Nationalist forces was discussed in 1945, but was vetoed by MacArthur and the State Department. MacArthur apparently had some reservations about the Chinese Nationalist leaders; the State Department was dissatisfied because the

MILITARY OCCUPATION OF JAPAN 165

Nationalist leaders had not cooperated in forming a joint Nationalist-Communist government in China (an option which the U.S. State Department strongly supported in 1945-46). Harold S. Quigley and John E. Turner, *The New Japan: Government and Politics* (Westport, Conn.: Greenwood Press, 1956), 90-100; Eichelberger, *Our Jungle Road to Tokyo*, 269; Manchester, *American Caesar*, 629-37, 671-72, 801-802; military report, "Eighth Army in Japan, 30 August 1945—1 May 1946," (G-3 Section: Yokohama, Japan, 8th Army headquarters, no date), 4-6, included in Eichelberger Papers.

17. Emerson and Holland, *The Eagle and the Rising Sun*, 55-60; military report, "Eighth Army in the Military Government of Japan—Orientation," no date, 2-3, Eichelberger Papers; military report, "Two Years of Occupation—August 1945 to August 1947, (Public Information Office, General Headquarters, SCAP), August 1947, 1, 5, 8, 12-14, box 130 of Eichelberger Papers.

18. Military report, "Eighth Army Experience in Japan," (data prepared for the War Department in the spring of 1947 by the 8th Army Public Relations Office), 38-39, Eichelberger Papers; Military Report, "Eighth Army in Japan, 30 August 1945—1 May 1946," (G-3 Section: Yokohama, Japan, 8th Army headquarters, no date), 1, Eichelberger Papers; Walter Sheldon, *The Honorable Conquerors: The Occupation of Japan 1945-1952* (New York: Macmillan, 1965), ix-x, 8-52; Kazuo Kawai, *Japan's American Interlude* (Chicago: University of Chicago Press, 1960), 1-17, 23-34; Justin Williams, Jr., *Japan's Political Revolution under MacArthur* (Athens: University of Georgia Press, 1979), 18-56.

19. Eichelberger Dictations, "Our Soldiers in the Occupation," no date, 2-7, 11; military report, "Eighth Army Experience in Japan," 38-40; Robert Eichelberger to General Dwight D. Eisenhower, 5 November 1946, 18 February 1947, and 28 June 1947, box 38 of the "Pre-Presidential Papers" of Dwight D. Eisenhower, Eisenhower Library, Abilene, Kansas; Robert Eichelberger to Emma Eichelberger, 17 February 1946, 1 March 1946, 5 March 1946, 7 March 1946, 20 March 1946, 10 April 1946, 25 April 1946, and 4 June 1946, Eichelberger Papers.

20. Edwin O. Reischauer, *The Pacific Rivals: A Japanese View of Japanese-American Relations* (New York: John Weatherhill, Inc., 1972), 168; Cohen, *Remaking Japan: The American Occupation as New Deal*, 131; Robert Eichelberger to Herman A. Gudger, 26 February 1946, Eichelberger Papers; Robert Eichelberger to Mrs. Jerome Zerbe, 12 November 1946, Eichelberger Papers; Robert Eichelberger to Emma Eichelberger, 23 March 1946, 26 March 1946, 3 April 1946, and 30 April 1946, Eichelberger Papers; Memorandum from General Robert L. Eichelberger to the Commanders of all 8th Army Units, "Public Display of Affection," 23 March 1946, box 13 of Eichelberger Papers; memorandum from General Robert L. Eichelberger to all unit Commanders, "Incidents Involving United States Troops," 22 June 1946, Eichelberger Papers; memoranda, General Robert L. Eichelberger to all officers, 8th Army, "Military Courtesy" and "Use of Profanity by Army Personnel," 11 July 1946 and 27 July 1946, Eichelberger Papers; Eichelberger Dictations, "Japan At The Beginning Of And During the Occupation," 10 October 1960, 2-4.

21. During this second phase, the 8th Army prosecuted over 800 Japanese for war crimes and purged over 2,000 "militarists" from national and local government agencies. Over 100 Japanese "war criminals" received the death penalty and were executed. In 1946, Eichelberger's forces distributed grain in the cities and closed down black-

market food operations. In April 1947, the 8th Army supervised the first national elections held in Japan. Robert A. Fearey, *The Occupation of Japan: Second Phase, 1948-1950* (New York: Macmillan, 1950), 17-60; Hans H. Baerwald, *The Purge of Japanese Leaders under the Occupation* (Berkeley: University of California Press, 1959), 62-78, 78-99; Edwin M. Martin, *The Allied Occupation of Japan* (Westport, Conn.: Greenwood Press, 1948), 51-59; military report, "The New Political Life of Japan," no date, 1-6, box 113 of Eichelberger Papers; military report, "Special Study of The Yokohama War Crimes Trials," (10th Information and Historical Service, 8th Army Headquarters, no date), 1-10, box 121 of Eichelberger Papers; Eichelberger Dictations, "Memoranda on War Crimes," 1 March 1948, 1-5; Eichelberger Memorandum, "Japan and Some Accomplishments of the Occupation," 4 May 1949, 1-10, Eichelberger Papers.

22. MacArthur, *Reminiscences*, 298-304; Schaller, *The American Occupation of Japan*, 38-43; Harries and Harries, *Sheathing the Sword*, 85-95; Reischauer, *The Pacific Rivals*, 131-46; Robert E. Ward, *Democratizing Japan: The Allied Occupation* (Honolulu: University of Hawaii Press, 1987), 107-27; military report, "A Brief Progress Report on the Political Reorientation of Japan," (Government Section, 8th Army headquarters, 10 October 1949), 1-58, Eichelberger Papers; Eichelberger Memorandum, "Japan and Some Accomplishments of the Occupation," 4 May 1949, 1-15, Eichelberger Papers.

23. James, *The Years of MacArthur, Volume III*, 181-82; Shigeru Yoshida, *The Yoshida Memoirs—The Story of Japan in Crisis* (Boston: Houghton Mifflin Company, 1962), 54; Whitney, *MacArthur*, 270-71; MacArthur, *Reminiscences*, 309; Fearey, *The Occupation of Japan*, 33-47; Cohen, *Remaking Japan*, 277-301; military report, "Education in the New Japan, Volume I," (Tokyo: Civil Information and Education Section, SCAP, General Headquarters, May 1948), 1-55, box 116 of Eichelberger Papers; military report, "Eighth Army Experience in Japan," spring 1947, 21-24, 35-38.

24. James, *The Years of MacArthur, Volume III*, 90-91, 235-36, 368; Eichelberger Dictations, "Student Riots in Japan," 20 May 1960, 1; Eichelberger Dictations, "Japan at the Beginning of and during the Occupation," 10 October 1960, 4-5; Emerson and Holland, *The Eagle and the Rising Sun*, 60-61.

25. Yoshida, *The Yoshida Memoirs*, 55, 177, 228-29; Eichelberger Memorandum, no title, 13 April 1948, 1, box 19 of Eichelberger Papers; Robert Eichelberger to General of the Army Douglas MacArthur, 29 April 1948, box 19 of Eichelberger Papers; Robert Eichelberger to Roy E. Larsen, 3 May 1948 and 4 May 1948, Eichelberger Papers; Robert Eichelberger to Frank Eichelberger, 10 May 1948, box 19 of Eichelberger Papers; Eichelberger Dictations, "Student Riots in Japan," 20 May 1960, 1-3; Robert Eichelberger to General of the Army Dwight D. Eisenhower, 1 May 1948, box 38 of the "Pre-Presidential Papers" of Dwight D. Eisenhower, Eisenhower Library, Abilene, Kansas; Whitney, *MacArthur*, 307-11.

26. This public announcement altered occupation policy. Prior to 1948, the United States had strictly followed the terms of the Potsdam Declaration, which "theoretically" allowed the Japanese people to overthrow their own leaders provided American lives and property were not threatened. Eichelberger Dictations, "Student Riots in Japan," 20 May 1960, 1-3.

27. Eichelberger Dictations, "Our Soldiers in the Occupation," no date, 7-8; Military Report, "Eighth Army Experience in Japan," 39-40, Eichelberger Papers.

28. The shortage of manpower in the 8th Army was alleviated by the addition of 36,000 Australian, New Zealand, British, and Indian soldiers of the British Commonwealth Occupation Force (BCOF). This unit served in Japan in 1946-48. It was placed "under MacArthur's operational control and attached to Eichelberger's command." This unit provided "a token of international flavor to the occupation," although by 1948, the size and participation of this force had declined considerably. James, *The Years of MacArthur, Volume III*, 69.

29. Manchester, *American Caesar*, 530-31; Robert Eichelberger to Houston Harte, 17 March 1948, box 19 of Eichelberger Papers; Robert Eichelberger to Major General Willard S. Paul, 6 January 1948, Eichelberger Papers; Robert Eichelberger to General of the Army Douglas MacArthur, 17 January 1948, box 19 of Eichelberger Papers; Robert Eichelberger to Lieutenant General Albert Wedemeyer (director, Plans and Operations Division, Department of the Army, Washington, D.C.), 16 April 1948 and 19 April 1948, Eichelberger Papers; Eichelberger Dictations, "Eighth Army and Variations in Strength of Eighth Army in Japan," 4 July 1955, 1-5; James, *The Years of MacArthur, Volume III*, 84.

30. Whitney, *MacArthur*, 237-39; James, *The Years of MacArthur, Volume III*, 356-57; Eichelberger Dictations, no title, 15 December 1958, 1; Harries and Harries, *Sheathing the Sword*, xxxi and xxxii; Manchester, *American Caesar*, 468, 560-68.

31. Schaller, *The American Occupation of Japan*, 23; Whitney, *MacArthur*, 229-36; Perry, *Beneath the Eagle's Wings*, 70; Eichelberger Dictations, "MacArthur as a C.O. (Commanding Officer)," 21 June 1961, 1-2; James, *The Years of MacArthur, Volume III*, 367, 369-70, 371-75; Manchester, *American Caesar*, 476-78, 557-65, 612-16.

32. Unlike MacArthur, Eichelberger never completed a comprehensive study of Japan's social, political, or economic institutions. Surprisingly, he knew very little about Japan's history. He showed no inclination to learn about Japan's language or customs. The vast majority of Eichelberger's knowledge was gathered from his inspections, travels, and 8th Army reports. His reading in Japan was limited to daily newspapers and magazines (for example, *Time* and *Newsweek*, the *Christian Science Monitor*, *New York Times*, *Baltimore Sun*, and the *Chicago Tribune*). Robert Eichelberger to Houston Harte, 17 March 1948, box 19 of Eichelberger Papers.

33. Through these inspections, Eichelberger developed a strong respect and affection for the Japanese people. He was particularly impressed by the discipline, patience, and industriousness of the villagers and townspeople. Eichelberger noticed that the Japanese people waited patiently in line, and did not push each other when "getting on street cars." He noted, "I have ridden so many times through the country by train and [have found] the people working in the fields as one awakes early in the morning, and [working] continuously until dark." Impressed that the Japanese were "busy" instead of "sitting down waiting for good times to return," Eichelberger remarked that the Japanese farmers were "not very different" from the industrious farmers in Ohio. What he observed undoubtedly made a strong impression on Eichelberger, and contributed to his decision to treat the Japanese in a just and friendly manner. Eichelberger Dictations, "Occupation of Japan," 21 February 1948, 18, 19, 23, 24; Perry, *Beneath the Eagle's Wings*, 58-59; Eichelberger Dictations,

"Memoranda on Japan—Japanese People—Yoshida, Shidehara, Emperor, etc.," 22 February 1948, 1.

34. Yoshida, *The Yoshida Memoirs*, 55, 228-29; Ward, *Democratizing Japan*, 209; Eichelberger Dictations, "Student Riots in Japan," 20 May 1960, 1-3.

35. From 1945 to 1948, Eichelberger served as host to a variety of groups, including the Far Eastern Commission, three U.S. congressional delegations, two reparations missions, one British parliamentary delegation, three groups of leading U.S. editors and publishers, a food research group, an American education mission, and an atomic bomb casualty commission. Eichelberger also entertained the following individuals—General Marshall, General Eisenhower, Secretary of the Navy James V. Forrestal, Secretary of the Interior J. A. Klug, Postmaster General Robert E. Hannegan, Secretary of War Robert P. Patterson, Undersecretary of War Kenneth C. Royall, Assistant Secretary of War Howard Peterson, Assistant Secretary of War John J. McCloy, Assistant Secretary of War Stuart Symington, Assistant Postmaster General Gael Sullivan, Assistant Secretary of the Navy William J. Kenney, General Thomas T. Handy, and former Postmaster General James A. Farloy. Eichelberger, *Our Jungle Road*, 270-80; Eichelberger Dictations, "Occupation of Japan," 21 February 1948, 3-24; Eichelberger Dictations, "Student Riots in Japan," 20 May 1960, 1-4; Eichelberger Dictations, "MacArthur as a C.O. (Commanding Officer)," 21 June 1961, 1-3.

36. Memorandum, "Memo of RLE's conversation with General Mueller on the phone," 10 September 1947, box 16 of Eichelberger Papers; Dewey Short (congressional representative of the 7th district, Missouri) to Robert Eichelberger, 28 September 1946, Eichelberger Papers; Robert Eichelberger to Mrs. Jerome Zerbe, 6 September 1946 and 26 February 1947, Eichelberger Papers; Robert Eichelberger to Emma Eichelberger, 9 March 1946 and 18 May 1946, Eichelberger Papers; General of the Army Dwight D. Eisenhower to Robert Eichelberger, 9 July 1946 and 1 March 1947, Dwight D. Eisenhower Papers, Eisenhower Library, Abilene, Kansas; Robert Eichelberger to General of the Army Dwight D. Eisenhower, 17 June 1946 and 20 September 1946, Dwight D. Eisenhower Papers.

37. James, *The Years of MacArthur, Volume III*, 370; Schaller, *The American Occupation of Japan*, 140; Eichelberger Dictations, "Some Thoughts Following General MacArthur's Visit to the Philippines in July, 1961," 17 July 1961, 4; Robert Eichelberger to Houston Harte, 17 March 1948, Eichelberger Papers; Robert Eichelberger to Emma Eichelberger, 29 May 1946, Eichelberger Papers; General "Woody" Woodruff to General Robert L. Eichelberger, 14 June 1947, Eichelberger Papers; Howard B. Schonberger, *Aftermath of War: Americans and the Remaking of Japan, 1945-1952* (Kent, Ohio: Kent State University Press, 1989), 147.

38. Whitney, *MacArthur*, 229-36, 311; Manchester, *American Caesar*, 471, 495; Cohen, *Remaking Japan*, 464-65; Williams, *Japan's Political Revolution under MacArthur*, xiv, 282; See Yoshida, *The Yoshida Memoirs*, 286-87.

39. Fearey, *The Occupation of Japan*, 99; Quigley and Turner, *The New Japan*, 90; Sheldon, *The Honorable Conquerors*, x-xiv; Schonberger, *Aftermath of War*, 10, 284; See Harries and Harries, *Sheathing the Sword*, xx-xxi.

40. Perry, *Beneath the Eagle's Wings*, 58-59; James, *The Years of MacArthur, Volume III*, 370.

41. Eichelberger's "anti-Communist" sentiments were partly the result of his World War I experiences in Siberia; he noted that the Bolshevik forces were cruel, violent, and unbelievably backward. These negative impressions were strengthened by the Cold War following World War II, and by Eichelberger's own experiences with the Communists in occupied Japan. He noticed that most of the riots and violence in Japan were caused by "Red" Koreans; these Communists seemed determined to disrupt the aims and objectives of the American occupation forces. The Russian representatives in Tokyo were also rude, insulting, and deceitful. They treated the American officers "more like enemies than allies." Eichelberger Dictations, "Halsey," 16 August 1961, 2-3; Eichelberger Dictations, "Student Riots in Japan," 20 May 1960, 1-3 (pages 590-92 of dictation notebook); Eichelberger Dictations, no title, 26 August 1957, 1-2 (pages 418-19 of dictation notebook); Eichelberger Dictations, no title, 9 November 1955, 2-3 (pages 287-88 of dictation notebook).

42. Yoshida, *The Yoshida Memoirs*, 264-66; Eichelberger, *Our Jungle Road to Tokyo*, 278; Harries and Harries, *Sheathing the Sword*, 230-33; John K. Emmerson, *Arms Yen & Power: The Japanese Dilemma* (New York: Dunellen, 1971), 63-65; Robert Eichelberger to Roy W. Howard, 26 March 1947, box 18 of Eichelberger Papers; Robert Eichelberger to Herman A. Gudger, 7 June 1947, box 18 of Eichelberger Papers.

43. In June 1946, Eichelberger did receive a promotion from Lieutenant General (temporary) to Major General (permanent rank in the regular army), but he refused to give MacArthur any credit. Instead, he decided that his nephew, Roy E. Larsen, was the responsible party. Larsen's executive position with the Time-Life organization had allowed him to give the 8th Army an abundance of publicity for their work in Japan. In a letter to his nephew, Eichelberger stated, "Maybe all the factors of my military career entered into it [the promotion], but I suspect that you, Roy, were a very large factor." Eichelberger Dictations, "General MacArthur and the Presidency," 12 November 1953, 5-6; Eichelberger Dictations, "Some Phases of General MacArthur's Attitude towards me . . .," 31 Aug. 1959, 3; Robert Eichelberger to Roy E. Larsen, 31 December 1945, Eichelberger Papers; Robert Eichelberger to Mrs. Jerome Zerbe, 9 November 1945, Eichelberger Papers; Robert Eichelberger to Emma Eichelberger, 28 Oct. 1945, 29 Oct. 1945, 31 Oct. 1945, 12 Nov. 1945, and 7 Feb. 1946, Eichelberger Papers.

44. Citation for Silver Star medal for Lieutenant General Robert L. Eichelberger, 22 November 1945, General Order No. 343, General Headquarters U.S. Army Forces (Pacific), Eichelberger Papers; Robert Eichelberger to Emma Eichelberger, 14 November 1945, 10 February 1946, and 3 April 1946, Eichelberger Papers.

45. Despite Eichelberger's suspicions, there is no evidence that MacArthur had any influence in the War Department's decision to deny this award. Rear Admiral Russell S. Berkey to Robert Eichelberger, 26 June 1946, box 14 of Eichelberger Papers; Robert Eichelberger to Rear Admiral Russell Berkey, 22 July 1946, box 14 of Eichelberger Papers; proposed citation for navy "Distinguished Service Medal" to Lieutenant General Robert L. Eichelberger, no date, Eichelberger Papers.

46. Robert Eichelberger to Emma Eichelberger, 27 February 1946, 22 March 1946 and 25 April 1946, box 14 of Eichelberger Papers; citation for "Award of the Bronze Star Medal" and "Award of the Air Medal" for Lieutenant General Robert L.

Eichelberger, 24 December 1945, General Order No. 196, Headquarters 8th Army, Eichelberger Papers.

47. In 1945, the deputy chief of staff position was considered a "stepping stone" to the Chief of Staff post.

48. Eichelberger Dictations, no title, 10 October 1960, 8 (page 633 of dictation notebook); Eichelberger Dictations, "Eisenhower in Japan, December 1945," 10 March 1954, 1-2; Cablegram, Washington to General Douglas MacArthur, 21 November 1945, Eichelberger Papers; Robert Eichelberger to Emma Eichelberger, 21 November 1945, 22 November 1945, 23 November 1945, 27 November 1945 and 29 November 1945, Eichelberger Papers.

49. Robert Eichelberger to Francis A. Gudger, 20 April 1948, Eichelberger Papers; Robert Eichelberger to Gertrude Algase, 8 March 1948, Eichelberger Papers.

50. Robert Eichelberger to Major General Clovis E. Byers, 7 October 1947, Eichelberger Papers; Robert Eichelberger to Frank Eichelberger, 10 May 1948, Eichelberger Papers; Robert Eichelberger to Emma Eichelberger, 29 November 1945 and 6 February 1946, Eichelberger Papers; Eichelberger Dictations, "Some Phases of General MacArthur's Attitude towards me in my years in the Pacific . . .," 31 August 1959, 6.

51. In 1946, Eichelberger noticed that a variety of writers were attacking MacArthur in newspapers and magazines. This critical material gave Eichelberger the idea of writing his own story. He noticed that his own experiences were more interesting and factual than the secondary accounts of the reporters. Robert Eichelberger to Ken Roberts, 31 December 1945, Eichelberger Papers; Robert Eichelberger to Emma Eichelberger, 21 March 1946, Eichelberger Papers; Dale Kramer, "The MacArthur Legend," *Salute*, December 1946, 12-14, 61-62, included in Eichelberger Papers.

52. Robert Eichelberger to Emma Eichelberger, 22 February 1946, 24 February 1946, 13 April 1946, and 4 November 1945, Eichelberger Papers.

53. Robert Eichelberger to Lieutenant General Albert Wedemeyer (director, Plans and Operation Division, Dept. of Army), 16 April 1948, Eichelberger Papers; Robert Eichelberger to General Clovis E. Byers, 17 April 1948, Eichelberger Papers; Eichelberger Dictations, "Eighth Army and Variations in Strength of Eighth Army in Japan," 4 July 1955, 2-4; Eichelberger Dictations, "Memoranda on Military Government . . . etc.," 28 February 1948, 1-2.

54. Robert Eichelberger to Emma Eichelberger, 13 May 1946 and 15 May 1946, Eichelberger Papers; Eichelberger Dictations, "Eisenhower in Japan, December 1945," 10 March 1954, 8; Eichelberger Dictations, "Public Relations Policies of GHQ, Particularly with Reference to other Leaders besides General MacArthur," no date, 5.

55. Robert Eichelberger to Milton MacKaye, 14 February 1948, Eichelberger Papers; Robert Eichelberger to Gertrude Algase, 17 March 1947, Eichelberger Papers; Gertrude Algase to Robert Eichelberger, 25 January 1946, 5 March 1946, and 27 December 1946, box 15 of Eichelberger Papers.

56. Eichelberger was reluctant to leave Japan. He truly enjoyed his job and the "perks" of his position. As Eichelberger stated to his agent, "I don't believe there is any man back home, no matter how wealthy, who can live under better . . . conditions." He cited the following benefits—A fine house overlooking Tokyo Bay, the

most efficient staff of domestics I have ever seen, the fine force of officers and men around me who make life pleasant, a fine plane when I desire to fly, a beautiful special train when I make my inspections . . . [plus] a very friendly American and foreign colony." Despite these comforts Eichelberger was ready to leave Japan in 1948. The occupation was winding down, and his "once splendid" Army had been reduced to a skeleton force. Worried by the Communist threat to Japan, Eichelberger felt that his small army was unprepared for a war in the Far East. Furthermore, he had no compelling reason to remain abroad. He was rapidly approaching the mandatory retirement age (64), and all of his former "buddies" had returned to the United States. Under these circumstances, Eichelberger thought his best option was to leave Japan and reap the financial rewards of writing his own story. He needed the money, especially since he was "making up my income tax returns for the years 1942 to 1947 inclusive and at the same time [filing] an estimate in the first quarter in 1948 under a new decision." Excited at the prospect of a "financial windfall," he remarked that "the time has about arrived when I should consider myself rather than what one might term 'one's job' or 'one's duty.'" Robert Eichelberger to Gertrude Algase, 22 July 1946, 14 January 1948, 15 January 1948, and 26 January 1948, Eichelberger Papers; Robert Eichelberger to Houston Harte, 25 May 1947, Eichelberger Papers; Robert Eichelberger to Lieutenant General Oscar W. Griswold, 14 January 1948, Eichelberger Papers; Robert Eichelberger to Francis Gudger, 25 March 1948, Eichelberger Papers; Robert Eichelberger to Ken Roberts, 19 April 1948, Eichelberger Papers.

57. MacArthur was unhappy with Eichelberger's decision. He tried every means to keep him in Japan. In March 1948, MacArthur announced that he would leave Japan during the summer. "Bob," he stated, would be his replacement as SCAP. MacArthur explained that the Republican Convention was being held in June 1948, and that he would return to the United States if he received the Republican nomination for President. Eichelberger did not believe that MacArthur would be selected. Nevertheless, he agreed to delay his departure until July on the remote possibility that his chief would be nominated as a "dark horse." Since "that job (SCAP) would give me my fourth star," Eichelberger stated, "I am willing to take the gamble." In June 1948, however, MacArthur failed to receive the nomination, and Eichelberger proceeded with his plans to leave Japan. Robert Eichelberger to General of the Army Douglas MacArthur, 6 March 1948, Eichelberger Papers; Eichelberger Dictations, "General MacArthur and the Presidency, with some remarks about General Eisenhower," 12 November 1953, 5-6; Robert Eichelberger to Gertrude Algase, 8 March 1948, Eichelberger Papers; Robert Eichelberger to Ken Roberts, 18 March 1948, Eichelberger Papers; Robert Eichelberger to Houston Harte, 17 March 1948; Robert Eichelberger to Roy E. Larsen, 22 March 1948; Robert Eichelberger to Francis Gudger, 20 April 1948; Robert Eichelberger to General Omar Bradley, 2 July 1948, all Eichelberger Papers; Robert Eichelberger to General of the Army George C. Marshall (Secretary of State), 2 July 1948, box 66 (Folder 41) of the George C. Marshall Papers, George C. Marshall Foundation, Lexington, Virginia.

58. Eichelberger Diary, 30 July 1948, Eichelberger Papers; James, *The Years of MacArthur, Volume III*, 83-84.

59. MacArthur recommended Eichelberger for the Distinguished Service Medal (Third Oak Leaf Cluster) after his departure from Japan. The citation stated the following: "By his leadership and command ability, superior devotion to duty, and keen

understanding of a conquered people, General Eichelberger contributed in marked degree to the success of the occupation mission . . ." Eichelberger received this medal shortly after his arrival in the United States. Recommendation for award of the Distinguished Service Medal, 6 August 1948, (Record Group 5: SCAP, Series 1: subseries 4: OMS, EF-EJ), Douglas MacArthur Papers, Norfolk, Virginia; Robert Eichelberger to Frazier Hunt, 23 August 1948, Eichelberger Papers; Robert Eichelberger to Major General Clovis E. Byers, 19 August 1948, Eichelberger Papers; Major General Clovis E. Byers to Robert Eichelberger, 7 September 1948, Eichelberger Papers; Robert Eichelberger to Houston Harte, 7 August 1948, Eichelberger Papers; Robert Eichelberger to Lieutenant General John C. Northcott, 7 August 1948, Eichelberger Papers; Eichelberger Dictations, "Some Reflections on the Occupation of Japan by the Eighth Army," 5 December 1960, 10; Robert Eichelberger to Charles E. Tomkins, 19 July 1948, Eichelberger Papers; Robert Eichelberger to Major General James A. Lester, 22 September 1948, Eichelberger Papers; Robert Eichelberger to Colonel A. E. Schanze, 27 August 1948, Eichelberger Papers; Robert Eichelberger to Colonel Arthur P. Thayer, 14 September 1948, Eichelberger Papers; Robert Eichelberger to Roy E. Larsen, 30 August 1948, Eichelberger Papers; Eichelberger, *Our Jungle Road to Tokyo*, 279-80.

12

Retirement—And Turmoil

Eichelberger traveled by ship from Japan to San Francisco. In August 1948, he moved to Washington, D.C. From September to December 1948, he remained in the nation's capital, where he served his final months in the U.S. military. On 31 December 1948, Eichelberger officially retired from the U.S. Army, ending 39 years of continuous service.

After his retirement, Eichelberger lived quietly as a civilian for the next 13 years. He enjoyed a variety of benefits that insulated him from the hardships of old age. His wife received a sizable inheritance from her "bachelor brother," making them financially independent.[1] Although he willingly chose to remain employed for a number of years, Eichelberger enjoyed knowing that he did not have to work. He said that it was "a relief knowing that when I awake I do not have to go to some office and plow through a basket of papers." He added, "I [suddenly] have more time for thought and reading than I have ever had in my life." He also had time to pursue his favorite hobbies, including golf, bridge, canasta, going to football games, fishing, watching TV (including his favorite show, "Gunsmoke") and "generally doing nothing." He developed a passion for travel, and visited Africa, Europe, South America, the Bahamas, Hawaii, Australia, Panama, and every corner of the continental United States.[2]

Despite these travels and his idyllic lifestyle, Eichelberger complained about a variety of frustrations during these years. Not the least was his inability to find satisfactory employment. The dissatisfaction began with his last job in the army, in which he served as an advisor at the Pentagon. Although Eichelberger was "treated wonderfully" and received a "beautiful office right near the Secretary of War," he had little to do in the new post; his only real responsibility was to make speeches for the army on the Far East. He was keenly disappointed, for he was aware that "this final position" did not allow him the authority to make a permanent mark on U.S. policy toward Japan.[3]

Eichelberger's retirement from the army in December 1948 did not eliminate his job frustrations. Secretary of Defense James Forrestal asked him to chair an advisory committee of army, navy, and air force officers. Eichelberger declined, fearing the position would entail "very difficult administrative work—lots of papers and many headaches." He also declined the offer of a United Nations peace-keeping position in Hyderabad and Kashmir, stating that he lacked sufficient knowledge of the India-Pakistan conflict. In addition, he refused an offer to become president of the University of Vermont after he discovered that the college was "full of politics" and had severe financial problems.[4]

In the fall of 1948, Eichelberger was asked by General Walter B. Smith (head of the CIA) to accept the position of "head of the CIA for the Pacific." Eichelberger felt this job "would have meant an almost immediate return to the Far East [for] a position which would not have the perquisites which I had just given up as the [commanding general] of the ground forces in Japan." He added that "without going into the details of just what my organization would be in Tokyo (Headquarters for the CIA-Pacific), I had the feeling that being independent of MacArthur would mean that I would have to fight for everything I obtained from railroad tickets on." He decided to refuse this offer, stating that the objective of the position could not possibly be successfully accomplished.[5]

In December 1948, Eichelberger considered offers to become the "head of" various chemical firms, including the "Hayden Chemical and American Potash Chemical" companies.[6] These opportunities were tempting, for the pay "would [probably] be starvation wages for the capitalists but a hell of a high salary for an Army officer." Eichelberger had always been envious of the lucrative salaries enjoyed by his two brothers in the business world; he was tempted to try his hand in the "high-powered" arena of corporate management. In April 1949, however, he reluctantly decided to decline these offers, stating that the owner of the chemical companies, Barney Armour, was a notorious "slave driver" who "worked peculiar hours."[7]

In the winter of 1949, Eichelberger finally decided to accept a position as "expert consultant" to Assistant Secretary of the Army Tracy S. Voorhees (who was in charge of providing relief to the occupied areas of Japan and Germany). This position was very attractive; it was "along the lines of the work" that Eichelberger had done in Japan, and it did not require a 40-hour workweek. Eichelberger was allowed to work as much or as little as he pleased. He noted that "Voorhees arranged everything so that I drew what was then maximum pay ($50 a day) on the days that I worked, and on the other days I drew my retired pay."[8]

Despite these advantages, Eichelberger soon "soured" on this job. He stated that "Mr. Voorhees is a pretty good single-handed talker himself and doesn't need a consultant very much." "I am not convinced," he added, "that there is anything definite for me to do which any bright college boy could not do at least as well." In the summer of 1949, he did appear before various congressional committees, where he supported Voorhees's request for an increased relief budget and answered questions about the geopolitical importance of the Far East. Even these efforts, however, were not entirely successful. Eichelberger admitted that he knew very little about the financial problems of Japan, and warned that his colleagues "would not want me to talk on economic subjects." His lack of expertise on various topics made him feel embarrassed and inadequate in his position. In March 1950, he decided to quit his advisory post and seek employment in a different field.[9]

Shortly before his departure from Voorhees's office, Eichelberger signed a contract with Clark Getts, Inc., a public relations firm that represented some of the "leading speakers in America on the lecture tour." Eichelberger was very pleased to sign with this company. He felt that he had a promising future as a public speaker. He believed that he was able to make adequate speeches "right off the cuff" with no notes. "I get some satisfaction," he added, "in talking to people of wealth and position because they are frankly scared and hang on every word." Pleased by the amount of money that could be made in this profession, he bragged that "the picture Mr. Getts (the president of Clark Getts, Inc.) gave when I signed with him was that he could get me a hundred thousand dollars a year or any amount I wanted to make."[10]

Eichelberger soon discovered that this figure was a gross exaggeration. After a few short months on tour, he noticed that the promise "'We'll pay all your expenses' always leaves me holding part of the bag, particularly when I am supposed to bring my wife." Angry that his travel schedule made him feel "harassed . . . like a shoestring drummer out of Baltimore," he complained, "My sense of humor does not permit me to sit up all night in a day coach or to use my energies living in cheap hotels and eating poor food." Citing these reasons, Eichelberger attempted to terminate his contract with Clark Getts, Inc., but was legally unable to do so. In November 1949, he decided to decline any further speaking invitations until his contract with Getts had expired.[11]

With his speaking career on temporary hold, Eichelberger decided to concentrate on his literary pursuits. Shortly after his arrival in Washington, he signed a contract with the *Saturday Evening Post* to write a series of seven articles about the 8th Army's experiences in the Pacific. During his employment under Voorhees and Getts, Eichelberger worked slowly on this project with the assistance of a ghostwriter, Milton MacKaye. After several delays, the project was completed during the summer of 1949. Eichelberger's story appeared in the August-September issues of the *Saturday Evening Post* under the title "Our Bloody Road to Tokyo."[12]

These articles received favorable reviews, and for a short time, Eichelberger became a minor celebrity. George C. Marshall informed him that the articles were "the best war stories that he had ever read." Eleanor Roosevelt commented that the series was "extremely interesting." Elated by this response, Eichelberger stated that "at one time, I had the naive impression that satisfaction should come from accomplishment and I felt pride in the numerous victories that came the hard way . . . [but] now I know it is in the widespread publication of a story that one receives credit from the public."[13]

Not all of the public reaction, however, was favorable. One former soldier complained that the articles ignored "a little Dutchman named Wally Krueger who planned and executed more amphibious operations than any other general in history." General Charles Hall, commander of the 8th Army's XI Corps, was upset that his unit was omitted in Eichelberger's discussion of the Luzon operations. More importantly, the summary of the Buna campaign offended Forrest Harding, who had been relieved by Eichelberger during the fighting in New Guinea. Speaking at a reunion of his former division (the 32d), Harding stated that "criticisms of men in 'deplorable condition, dirty and with long beards' which have recently appeared in the *Saturday Evening Post* series . . . could have been written about Valley Forge."[14]

These remarks disturbed Eichelberger, particularly since he had his own reservations about the *Saturday Evening Post* articles. He had originally intended to "take the shirt off" MacArthur by exposing him as a "vain god" who underestimated the enemy and overestimated the fighting abilities of his own troops (as he had done at Buna). After talking to several newspapermen, however, Eichelberger decided to tone down his attacks and to make his criticisms in a discreet fashion. A subtle approach was more appropriate, Eichelberger explained, for "my many friends in the Army . . . would never understand if I were raw in my criticisms of a man with whom I have served for so many years."[15]

As a result, Eichelberger criticized MacArthur indirectly in the series by "[taking him] off a few battlefields that he didn't see, but only by implication." For example, in the third article, on the Hollandia operation, MacArthur was "removed from the battlefield [and placed] on the boat for Australia the first afternoon." In "my Buna articles," Eichelberger stated, "MacArthur was taken away from personally leading the troops there, e.g., I stated in effect that every day I wrote a report to him at his headquarters in Port Moresby."[16]

Unfortunately, these subtle criticisms were negated by the photographs that accompanied the series. Eichelberger had no input in the selection of these pictures. The photos in the Buna article, for example, mistakenly "put General MacArthur on the battlefield," while the text of the article intentionally implied that MacArthur had not been present. The pictures also made Eichelberger appear healthy (and somewhat overweight), while the text emphasized that he had lost over 30 pounds during the fighting and was thin and haggard.[17]

Frustrated by these mistakes, Eichelberger decided to correct these errors and to be a bit more "hard-hitting" in a book based on the *Saturday Evening Post* articles. Even before the *Post* series was completed, he signed a contract with the Viking Press to write a book based on the same materials, with Milton MacKaye again serving as the ghostwriter. This book was scheduled to come out in March 1949 "on the heels" of the *Saturday Evening Post* articles, but problems in the writing and promotion of it delayed it for over a year.[18]

In September 1950, Eichelberger's book finally appeared under the title *Our Jungle Road to Tokyo*. This 306-page volume received favorable reviews from the critics. It was popular enough to have two American editions and one British paperback edition. Both Omar Bradley and President Harry S. Truman requested autographed copies. Professor Theodore Ropp of Duke University called it "one of the best of all of the books to come out of the Second World War."[19]

Eichelberger was somewhat less pleased with the final product. He felt it lacked the freshness and novelty of the *Post* series. He had intended to make the book more interesting by including more controversial comments, but MacArthur's continued popularity with the American public made him hesitant to condemn his former chief. The book fell short of being the hard-hitting exposé that he had intended; it included only occasional, muted criticisms of MacArthur and his abilities.[20]

Besides this shortcoming, Eichelberger was also disappointed in the efforts of his ghostwriter, MacKaye. Shortly after the completion of the project, Eichelberger confessed that "MacKaye nearly drove me nuts during preparation of the [book] because of his ill health and procrastination." MacKaye was extremely lazy, drank heavily, and preferred to "work all night with a bottle and sleep all day." These erratic work habits caused some bitter arguments between the two men. Unfortunately for MacKaye, his sensitive nature was not suited to this type of confrontation; he ended up in a hospital with a variety of stress-related ailments. These conflicts and delays eliminated much of the pleasure of completing the book. Eichelberger later commented that "I feel . . . I was wrung through a wringer in this writing game."[21]

Largely because of these frustrations, Eichelberger decided in May 1951 to "semi-retire," and to accept only temporary part-time jobs that did not demand a large commitment of time and energy. These requirements eliminated most normal employment opportunities. In the summer of 1951, he received an invitation from the army to serve as a military advisor for various Hollywood movies. He rapidly accepted; he felt this assignment would be "a lot of fun" and would provide a "much needed" vacation in California.

In the fall of 1951, Eichelberger traveled to Hollywood and served as a consultant for the movies *Francis Goes to West Point* and *The Day the Band Played*. This work was pleasant, at least at first; the participants enjoyed the sights and attractions of Beverly Hills and basked in the warm California sunshine. But Eichelberger was not pleased with all the aspects of this assignment. He complained that most of his advice was ignored and that the directors of the films were "entirely unapproachable." In February 1952, he decided to avoid any further employment "along these lines."[22]

In March 1952, Eichelberger signed a contract with *Newsweek* magazine to write book reviews and articles dealing with American foreign policy. This contract avoided most of the pitfalls of the "writing game." Eichelberger was not burdened with a ghostwriter, and he was not obligated to write on a regular basis. As Eichelberger stated in a letter to a friend, this agreement allowed "me to write about two articles a year to add to my income and yet permit[ted] me to have some leisure time."[23]

These limited obligations suited him. From 1952 to 1954, he wrote occasional articles for *Newsweek* on American policy in the Far East. These articles emphasized the same basic themes—the importance of the Far East for the security of the United States, the need for rearming Japan and revitalizing her economy, and the importance of Japan as a "first-line" defense against the advances of communism. The essays generated a sizable amount of income (approximately $1,000 to $2,000 per essay). They were generally well received by the American public. By 1954, however, Eichelberger felt that the burdens of preparation exceeded the monetary rewards. He decided to gradually reduce his literary efforts. In December 1955, he abruptly quit this occupation altogether, stating that writing "is not my forte."[24]

As a replacement for this activity, Eichelberger resumed his career as a public speaker. By June 1954, his contract with Clark Getts had expired, and he was free to set up his own schedule of public appearances. From 1954 to 1955, he made periodic trips throughout the United States; he gave a series of lectures on various military topics (including the intentions of the Russian leaders, the possibility of war in Europe, and the 8th Army's campaigns during the Second World War). Eichelberger received up to $750 per talk, although he rarely prepared his comments beforehand (he stated that "my talks are better if I do not prepare them," for "if I have no notes at all it impresses people and they seem to like the talk better even if it misses a bit of coordination"). But, by August 1955, even this activity became too burdensome. The travel was tiring and monotonous. The majority of the sponsors, Eichelberger complained, did not treat him with courtesy and respect.[25]

In September 1955, Eichelberger curtailed his schedule of speeches, and concentrated his efforts on voluntary, non-paying jobs. He had come to believe that his involvement in civic-minded functions would provide a degree of satisfaction and accomplishment that was lacking in his other professions. Unfortunately, this sense of fulfillment proved to be fleeting; Eichelberger found that he was equally frustrated in his civic pursuits.

For example, in 1955 he agreed to serve as chairman of the review board of the Asheville, North Carolina, Chamber of Commerce (which had the function of "controlling the number, kind, and extent" of money-making campaigns for charity). This position was a disappointment. Eichelberger stated that "there was too little noblesse oblige among potential" contributors. "Some residents," he complained, "have shown a lack of consideration for charity to the extent that I never want to look at them again." He decided to abandon this position, stating that "I deeply regret that I entered into this campaign in any capacity."[26]

RETIREMENT—AND TURMOIL

In 1957, Eichelberger served on the North Carolina State Ports Authority, a voluntary organization with the purpose of improving "the volume of business moving into the . . . ports of Wilmington and Morehead City." Once again, he was disgruntled with his responsibilities; he immediately took a strong dislike to the demands and obligations of the position. He quit this job as well, offering the excuse that the "state's rather meager travel allowance" did not cover his wife's expenses.[27]

In 1958, Eichelberger also discontinued his membership in the Civitan Club of Asheville, North Carolina. He arrived at this decision after he was reported "as absent" for a club event. The president of the organization (a Mr. Smith) reportedly insisted on announcing his absence. Eichelberger concluded that the president was intentionally "being discourteous" to him. "Mr. Smith," he argued, "is too bright a man to be unpleasant without deliberation."[28]

In 1960, Eichelberger accepted a position as honorary chairman of the Buncombe County Committee of North Carolina Citizens for Nixon and Gavin. This organization was formed to generate grass-roots support and money for Republican candidates. Eichelberger was enthusiastic about this group. He was a staunch conservative, and felt that the Republican candidate for President, Richard Nixon, was "far more honest and dedicated than a politician is supposed to be." During the presidential election of 1960, this organization was successful in electing several local Republican candidates; it "carried" Buncombe County for Nixon. Eichelberger, however, was somewhat disappointed in the organization's efforts. He felt that many of the volunteers "did not seem to have any particular desire to get out and work," but instead "unloaded" their duties on a few responsible individuals. The majority of the "key" political leaders "took off for Manhattan and other attractive places" after only a token effort in North Carolina.[29] Eichelberger emerged disgusted with the entire experience. He vowed not to become involved with any further activities, either paid or unpaid, that required his time and energy.

These negative "employment experiences" were emotionally frustrating, although they were not the only disappointments of Eichelberger's retirement years.[30] He had a variety of other problems, including some difficulties in adjusting to civilian life. For example, in 1948, shortly after his retirement from the U.S. Army, Eichelberger wrote that "it is a terrible feeling when one gets cut off from the life which I have led for so many years." Several months later, he remarked that his new routine could not compare favorably to his years with the army in Japan. In 1959, after 10 years as a civilian, Eichelberger still expressed a preference for military life. "In spite of quite a few mean details including Siberia and New Guinea," he stated, "I always loved the darned Army and felt it was a very honorable life."[31]

Eichelberger's preference for the army was created in part by practical considerations. Ordinary civilian tasks, such as finding adequate housing, were more difficult to accomplish than he imagined. After his retirement in 1948,

Eichelberger discovered that there were no vacancies in his preferred residence, the Kennedy-Warren apartment complex in Washington. He was forced to accept a small apartment in the Brighton Hotel, and later moved into a larger, three-bedroom apartment at 1870 Wyoming Avenue.[32]

In the spring of 1950, Eichelberger left Washington and moved to Asheville, North Carolina. He hoped to move into the former house of his wife's older brother, Herman Gudger, who had left Miss Em a half interest in his house upon his death. A family squabble, however, prevented his occupancy of this two-story structure; Miss Em's sister Ada refused to allow anyone to move in unless some provision was made for her son to live there as well. Eichelberger adamantly refused to allow it, and after some deliberation, he bought a different house in Asheville at 317 Charlotte Street. This beautifully constructed house served as the Eichelbergers' residence until 1955, when Miss Em complained that "the city fathers [failed to] properly protect [the] area by permitting the WLOS TV station to go up [and establish itself on] the street above us." In 1956, the Eichelbergers moved to 8 Fairway Place in Asheville, where they remained for the duration of their lives.[33]

These repeated moves taxed General Eichelberger's health. In 1950, immediately before his move to Asheville, his gall bladder was removed. Complications from surgery resulted in a blood clot in his lung; this delayed his recuperation for over 12 months. In later years, he suffered from hypertension and elevated blood sugar levels, which limited to some extent his ability to walk and travel.[34]

Medical problems were only a part of Eichelberger's worries. A variety of interpersonal stresses and strains contributed to his physical complaints. By 1950, for example, Eichelberger and General Horace Fuller, a friend and former classmate, were no longer on speaking terms. Fuller felt that Bob was indirectly responsible for his relief at Biak in 1944. Upset by this estrangement, Eichelberger was puzzled that Fuller had expressed no anger or resentment toward him during the war. Nevertheless, in December 1951, he sadly noted that "[Fuller] has had a bit of hurt feelings . . . [against him in regard to] Biak and I have never been able to get him to talk to me frankly since my return [from Japan]."[35]

Eichelberger was also upset that another former classmate, General Edwin F. Harding, retained some "bad feelings" from the war. During the 1950s, he learned from various sources that Harding felt that he was grossly mistreated in New Guinea; Bob, he believed, had acted "harshly" and "unnecessarily" in relieving him of his Buna command. This issue was a troubling one for Eichelberger. He could never decide in his own mind whether he had treated Harding unfairly during the extreme stress of the campaign. Even if he had, he was never given the chance to apologize or express his feelings. Friends of both parties warned the two men to stay apart, fearing a "clash" if they should meet. Eichelberger avoided most of his West Point class reunions, stating that "I would like to see a lot of various classmates,'" but "[obviously] not all of them [i.e., not Harding]."[36]

These lingering disputes caused Eichelberger a considerable amount of emotional distress.[37] He was particularly troubled by the allegation that he was responsible for the relief of his old schoolmates. He believed it was unfair to blame him for the decisions made in the heat of battle.[38] Furthermore, if anyone was to blame, Eichelberger felt that MacArthur was the responsible party. MacArthur, he believed, had indirectly ordered the relief of these officers, and then "covered his tracks" by blaming others (in particular, Eichelberger). Indeed, as his retirement years progressed, Eichelberger became convinced that MacArthur had let him "take the fall" for many of his decisions in the Southwest Pacific.[39]

During the fall of 1948, Eichelberger made several speeches in New York, where he met members of an organization called the American Council for Japan. This council was a small but influential group dedicated to altering MacArthur's occupation policies in Tokyo. The members believed that the SCAP's programs were "inefficient, corrupt and radical," and were supervised by a "bureaucratic, inefficient, dictatorial, vindictive, and at times corrupt" military administration. MacArthur's policies, they felt, had disillusioned the Japanese people; it was feared that Japan would turn to communism as an alternative solution. To prevent this, the council advocated some drastic changes in SCAP's programs, including the streamlining of MacArthur's bureaucratic administration, the rapid revitalization of the Japanese economy, and the rearming of the Japanese defense force.[40]

Agreeing with the aims of this organization, Eichelberger joined the group in October 1948. He toured the country in the organization's behalf, and gave speeches in support of the council's goals and principles. In December 1948, in a series of speeches in Washington, Eichelberger criticized MacArthur for his failure to allow the Japanese any means of self-defense against external threats. He argued that MacArthur's plan to make Japan the unarmed "Switzerland of the Pacific" was dangerous and unrealistic. As an alternative, he proposed the creation of a 150,000-man national Japanese defense force, in part to protect against the expansionist designs of Communist Russia.[41]

This proposal generated wide publicity. It drew the attention of Assistant Secretary of the Army Tracy S. Voorhees (whom Eichelberger was serving as a consultant and who was a close friend of MacArthur). In November 1949, Voorhees called Eichelberger into his office. He informed him that MacArthur had asked his department to prepare a draft of a peace treaty between the United States, Japan, and the Soviet Union. Voorhees told Eichelberger it was decided that he would not be allowed to work on the portions of the treaty dealing with Japanese rearmament; Eichelberger, Voorhees explained, "had publicly expressed his own opinions in this area," and his position "was in opposition to General MacArthur's views." Voorhees added that Eichelberger's "[opinions] were well known and had been ably presented throughout the country in talks, which was all right," but that he didn't feel "that . . . [Bob] should in his office run counter to General MacArthur's ideas."[42]

Enraged by this discussion, Eichelberger felt that his former chief was responsible for Voorhees's decision. In a memorandum written after this meeting, he indicated that he felt no remorse in opposing the views of the SCAP. The "United States," he said, "was much greater than General MacArthur." In his opinion, MacArthur was "anxious to get out [of Japan] on a 'fait accompli' in any way that would bring honor to him"; this is what explained the SCAP's insistence on an early peace treaty. "It [is] very evident," complained Eichelberger, "that the love feast has been successful and that anybody that gets in the way of General MacArthur is liable to get tramped on."[43]

In subsequent months, Eichelberger gained some revenge by criticizing his former chief in statements to the press. For example, in March 1950, he publicly announced that MacArthur's plan for an early peace treaty would not guarantee the security of the Far East, but would only undermine the ability of Japan "to rearm defensively." This argument was repeated in the last chapter of Our *Jungle Road to Tokyo* (published in 1950). "It is easy," he wrote, "to sympathize with the sentiments of General MacArthur [when he says that] 'the Japanese deserve a peace treaty,' but the world situation is shaky and explosive and major shifts in policy . . . should be undertaken with the greatest caution." Eichelberger was less diplomatic in letters to his friends. He boldly stated that SCAP's views were "wrong," adding that MacArthur was "not one of my favorite gods even though he does think that he can walk on water."[44]

Eichelberger's comments became even more critical once the Korean War began in June 1950. He felt that the SCAP made a mistake in recommending the intervention of American troops in Korea; the available U.S. forces in Japan were not adequately trained or equipped for this assignment.[45] And he believed that MacArthur's advance to the Yalu River in September-November 1950 was a strategic error. "Every mile marched to the northward," he argued, "meant a deeper and deeper penetration into enemy territory and an ever closer march toward . . . the [Chinese] hydroelectric plants" along the Korean-Chinese border. The threat to these vital plants forced the Chinese to attack the American units along the Yalu River, causing the retreat of MacArthur's forces from North Korea. This disorganized retreat was more in the nature of a "rout"; it was, in Eichelberger's words, the "worst defeat the American Army has ever suffered." The U.S. forces in fact outran their Chinese pursuers, and continued their withdrawal until General Matthew Ridgway reinstituted some fighting spirit into the 8th Army. Eichelberger believed that MacArthur was entitled to little or no credit for the stabilization of the American lines, and was solely responsible for the preceding errors which caused this "horrible tragedy."[46]

Furthermore, Eichelberger believed that his former chief covered up these errors, and deliberately deceived the American public by "censoring" and "manipulating" the press. He said the "average citizen" was never informed that MacArthur had his headquarters in Tokyo and was rarely present during the fighting in Korea. The "reading public" also was unaware of MacArthur's "great defeat on the Yalu"; indeed "the retreat with the loss of tremendous amount of material was called a withdrawal." Eichelberger noted that "it was even said [by several of MacArthur's communiqués] that the Chinese numbered millions instead of [200,000-300,000], the real number which originally attacked the 8th Army."[47]

It was because of these "distortions," Eichelberger believed, that the "mass of the public" reacted with anger and bitterness when MacArthur was sent home by President Harry S. Truman.[48] The American people had little knowledge of the many errors made by the high command in Korea, and did not understand Truman's decision to fire General MacArthur in 1951. This action by an "unpopular President" was, in Eichelberger's words, the "greatest break [MacArthur] . . . ever had"; it rescued SCAP from an "unwinnable" war and prevented a dispassionate review of his tactical mistakes.[49] In Eichelberger's opinion, Truman's actions helped make his former chief into a "martyr" and a "great hero."[50] Eichelberger believed this to be the "picture which [MacArthur] had been building up in the minds of the American public for many years."[51]

Historians have been more charitable in evaluating MacArthur's role in the Korean conflict. David Rees, in *Korea: The Limited War* (1964), states that MacArthur performed his duties in an exemplary fashion, although he clearly misread the intentions of the Chinese. This conclusion is supported by Matthew B. Ridgway's *The Korean War* (1967) and John W. Spanier's *The Truman-MacArthur Controversy and the Korean War* (1959). Other books, including the most recent histories of the Korean War, are critical of MacArthur's contributions. For example, Joseph C. Goulden, in *Korea: The Untold Story* (1982), argues that MacArthur was "a blend of Caesar and Caligula, skittering along the thin line between brilliance and eccentricity." Richard Whelan, in *Drawing the Line: The Korean War* (1990), states that MacArthur was an "egregious egotist" who deliberately manipulated the information sent to Washington. Although these two authors support some of Eichelberger's conclusions, they find a redeeming quality in MacArthur's "genius." Both authors agree that the landing at Inchon was a "brilliant" operation, one of the finest in American military history.[52]

Eichelberger, however, was not interested in praising MacArthur, even faintly; he was concerned only with diminishing the stature of his former chief. He was greatly disappointed in MacArthur's emergence as a war hero following his dismissal from Korea. He was shocked by the number of festivities attending MacArthur's return to the United States in April 1951, and by the outpouring of public praise and adulation that greeted his arrival. In order to escape the publicity surrounding the SCAP's return, Eichelberger fled to the Bahamas on a fishing trip. He later admitted that "I resisted full time pressure from the

Pentagon [to] ride in the parade with MacArthur . . . and sit in front of him . . . when he made the famous 'Old soldiers never die' speech." He also refused to make any excuses for his absence. "Maybe I am no Christian," he stated, "but at least I make a better friend if I do not like my enemies."[53]

Following these festivities, Eichelberger became concerned that his former chief would use his surging popularity to win the presidency of the United States. Having witnessed MacArthur's spectacular victories in the Pacific, he felt it was very possible that his former boss could "work his magic" to gain the nation's highest office. Eichelberger decided to do everything in his power to thwart MacArthur's ambitions. He announced in October 1951 that he would not support MacArthur's bid for the presidency, stating that "I would . . . be an Eisenhower man instead of a MacArthur man if the choice came of one of these two as a Presidential candidate." In the following months, Eichelberger wrote to key political leaders in Pennsylvania and Michigan; he urged the nomination of General Dwight D. Eisenhower. In March 1952, he wrote a personal note to Ike himself, warning that "in the background is my old chief who is the best hater that I have ever seen—he doesn't change from year to year, except to get worse."[54]

In June 1952, Eichelberger publicly denounced the SCAP's press releases, particularly MacArthur's comment that "it would be a tragic development" to elect a "military man as President." He labeled this statement "hypocritical." MacArthur, he argued, still retained hopes of capturing the presidency for himself, and believed that these comments did not "rule out his own candidacy."[55] Eichelberger warned that MacArthur had a strong antagonism towards his former aide, Eisenhower, and was seeking to erode support for Ike by disclaiming the presidency for any military officer. Finally, Eichelberger stated that MacArthur's promises could not be trusted by any politician, either friend or foe. Any candidate that "gets in bed with him," he stated, "[is likely to] . . . emerge barefooted in the snow.[56]

These bitter comments were repeated even after Eisenhower's presidential victory in November 1952. Eichelberger remained cautious; he believed that his former chief posed something of a threat to Ike even after the election. His concern became apparent in June 1954, after he discovered that his old boss had been invited to the White House.[57] Convinced that MacArthur would somehow turn the occasion to his own advantage, Eichelberger wrote Eisenhower the following precautionary message:

> What impressed me particularly was how little you seemed worried about the impending visit of your old friend [MacArthur]—before going to the dinner I had rather hoped for your sake that you would cancel the arrangements so that you could rest up for the arrival of the world's most prominent night owl.[58]

RETIREMENT—AND TURMOIL

By 1955, Eichelberger's concerns about MacArthur had become much larger than the issue of the presidency; they had developed into a painful, haunting obsession. Even Eichelberger's sleep was marred by thoughts and memories of his former chief. Every insult, every battle, every perceived slight was replayed over and over again in his mind, until he was constantly plagued by bitter thoughts that "rise like cream on milk." In letters to his friends, he stated that "there is so much in the past which rises up before me with little or no business." He added, "I have been impressed with memories which recur (usually in the middle of the night) about events or attitudes which [seem to be connected to the war]."[59]

Eichelberger had no ready explanation for these haunting memories. He had the vague feeling that his anguish was tied to the "sins" of MacArthur, and that his troubles would cease as soon as he punctured the "MacArthur myth." Eichelberger believed that much of his personal bitterness stemmed from the SCAP's success in hiding his faults and defeats from the American public. As he angrily noted, "I know of no other figure in history who has been able to surround himself with so much [distortion and] mystery."[60]

Eichelberger eventually came to the conclusion that he would not achieve any peace of mind until he had shattered the "myths" surrounding the SCAP's "greatness." He therefore adopted several strategies. He wrote letters to his friends and acquaintances, describing the many defects in MacArthur's campaigns.[61] He poured out a litany of complaints, and fully reviewed MacArthur's failures in Korea and the Pacific. Eichelberger criticized MacArthur for the loss of the Philippines in 1942, for his errors in judgment during the Pacific campaigns, and for his defeats near the Yalu River during the Korean War. He also chastised MacArthur for his premature announcements of victories, for his jealous monopolizing of the press, and for his failure to visit the front lines except for occasional "media blitzes." Furthermore, Eichelberger blasted his former chief for the errors of the Buna campaign. He felt that MacArthur had committed his greatest crimes during this operation. In particular, Eichelberger condemned MacArthur for the statement that "time was not a factor"; if this were true, he argued, then "we suffered casualties at Buna which were unnecessary."[62]

Eichelberger chastised MacArthur on a variety of other issues and events, but most of his letters emphasized the same basic theme: that MacArthur was not a "great" leader or military commander, but merely a superb offensive-minded strategist who understood neither his own troops nor the enemy. Eichelberger wrote that his former chief "knew less about enlisted men and what makes them tick than any high ranking officer I have ever known." He explained that MacArthur's "great trouble was that he started his service with soldiers too near the top"; it "would have helped if he had marched a few hundred miles and helped train the small units in his younger days." He added that MacArthur was "not in any sense an experienced leader of units, either large or small—talking on a high level, walking the floor, taking newspaper men up to some comparatively safe place for a few minutes—this doesn't constitute [true] leadership."[63]

Unfortunately for Eichelberger, most of these caustic remarks were ignored by his friends. The majority of his closest associates "patched up" their differences with MacArthur after the war. Clovis Byers and "Red" Blaik, two of Eichelberger's closest friends, resumed cordial relations with the SCAP in 1954, and attended the celebrations surrounding MacArthur's annual birthday party. Both these men encouraged Eichelberger to do the same.[64] Byers, in particular, made special efforts to get Eichelberger to overcome his prejudices. He warned him that a continuation of this negative criticism would affect MacArthur "in no way," but would only allow the "mud slingers to besmirch the distinguished position you now enjoy as a result of your outstanding . . . leadership."[65]

Eichelberger, however, was not disposed to accept Byers's advice; he instead looked for alternative methods of tarnishing MacArthur's reputation.[66] In 1956, he began to skim newspapers, magazines, and book lists, and to read those publications that dealt with MacArthur and the Pacific campaigns; his purpose was to find material that exposed the "MacArthur myth" and that told the "full" story of Eichelberger's contributions in the Pacific.[67]

Unfortunately, most of the books that were published in the early-to-mid 1950s failed to meet Eichelberger's expectations. For example, George C. Kenney's book, *General Kenney Reports*, gave the impression that the air force had won the war single-handedly in New Guinea; it disputed Eichelberger's contention that MacArthur had told him, "Take Buna or don't come back alive!" Similarly, H. W. Blakeley's *History of the 32nd Infantry Division* questioned the accuracy of these remarks, and placed the responsibility for Harding's relief squarely on Eichelberger's shoulders. Frazier Hunt's biography of MacArthur, *The Untold Story of Douglas MacArthur*, also failed to place any blame on the SCAP for the errors of the Papuan campaign. Hunt attributed the success of the Pacific operations solely to the "brilliance" of the "Army's top military commander."[68]

The government publication *Pictorial Record: The War Against Japan* followed a similar theme. It emphasized the contributions of MacArthur and Nimitz in the Pacific; it virtually ignored the efforts of the subordinate commanders. Eichelberger complained, "I was amazed to see no reference to [the subordinate army] commanders and no photographs of officers." He added that "maybe there is some good explanation [for this omission] but none is readily available."[69]

Beginning in the late 1950s, other books were published that were more compatible with Eichelberger's views. These provided a more critical analysis of MacArthur and the Pacific war. For example, Eichelberger was delighted with Louis Morton's *The Fall of the Philippines*. This book criticized MacArthur for his erroneous claim that he would "meet the Japanese on the beach and destroy them," for his infrequent trips to the front lines during the fighting at Bataan, and for the destruction of American planes on the ground at Nichols airfield. Overjoyed by Morton's comments, Eichelberger stated, "I have always looked forward to the day when somebody would tell the essential facts about the Southwest Pacific."[70]

Eichelberger was also pleased with Dudley McCarthy's *Southwest Pacific Area: First Year*, an Australian history of the fighting in New Guinea in 1942-43. McCarthy's book, he felt, was "the first written indication that I have seen of adverse Australian military sentiment towards General MacArthur." In addition, Eichelberger was impressed with Samuel Eliot Morison's *The Liberation of the Philippines*. He noted that "[this author] does better than any historian I have ever read on our own [campaigns]." Eichelberger praised Morison for his extensive coverage of the operations in 1944-45, and for his recognition of the 8th Army's dominant role in the Philippines during the latter stages of the war.[71]

Eichelberger's greatest compliments, however, were reserved for Samuel Milner's *Victory in Papua (VIP)*. This publication was an army study of the fighting in New Guinea. Eichelberger stated that "VIP is a wonderful book and the best report on jungle fighting that I have ever seen." In a letter to Milner, he wrote that "your great work has been to recognize the Buna fight as one of the terrible fights of the war, not the 'skirmish' described by MacArthur in the press." Milner's book, he added, was the only publication that correctly blamed his former chief for the "needless losses" of the Buna campaign, and the only study "to bring some element of reality into the MacArthur question."[72]

None of these publications, however, were totally satisfactory to Eichelberger. He noted that even Milner's fine book failed to reveal the complexity and duplicity of MacArthur's personality.[73] Furthermore, none of the current books arrived at the conclusion that Eichelberger so desperately wanted to prove: that "MacArthur's outstanding accomplishment was to be able to control the press to the extent that many [praiseworthy] things were published which were not true." As early as 1949, Eichelberger toyed with the idea of "correcting these misconceptions" by writing his own book on MacArthur. "I do not believe," he stated, "that anybody in the world has known SCAP as I have seen him in action." From 1949 to 1956, this idea became gradually more attractive, particularly as he recalled the events and tragedies of the war. By 1957, Eichelberger had become convinced that a book on MacArthur was his only means of redressing the supposed imbalances and injustices of the Pacific campaigns.[74]

Eichelberger had another reason for pursuing this project; he felt that a "tell-all" book would provide an ideal opportunity to gain revenge against his old rivals, Krueger and Sutherland. He never forgave Krueger for the "many insults and personal problems" of the war. In 1953, many of these bitter feelings resurfaced with the publication of Krueger's book *From Down Under to Nippon*. Asked for his reaction, Eichelberger said, "About all Walter could tell, if he keeps to the truth, is what the maps looked like as he stuck pins in them." In the early 1950s, Eichelberger had planned "to refute this book" by writing his own article on Krueger. He eventually decided against it, stating that "there are not enough adjectives to cover him properly," and "it would probably kill" the "mean old so-and-so" to discover that MacArthur "had intended to relieve him at least a dozen times." By the late 1950s, Eichelberger no longer cared about Krueger's feelings.[75] He took pleasure in reports that his former nemesis was old, feeble, and nearly blind. He stated that he would "never" forgive "Walter" for making his "way difficult" while he was "in the presence of the enemy," adding "I have no intention of speaking to him [Krueger] in heaven or hell."[76]

Eichelberger felt no better toward Sutherland. In 1949, he reported, "Sutherland came to Washington and tried to talk to me . . . [but] I refused to see him." He explained that he "had nothing to say to the man" who "indulged in the luxury of trying to cut [his] throat while [he] was trying to fight a deadly enemy." These bitter feelings persisted and intensified throughout Eichelberger's retirement years. In 1956, he stated that "it might be appropriate" to include some observations about Sutherland in his proposed book. He commented, "I hope Dick is still alive when he reads excerpts from my diaries in which MacArthur . . . [considered replacing him] because he . . . made himself persona non grata by succumbing to the wiles of a more or less attractive female."[77]

In 1957, Eichelberger decided that any book considered critical of Sutherland, Krueger, and MacArthur would have to be written after his death. "Some of the material in my diaries," he stated, "is just solid dynamite and cannot be used while I am alive." He began to look for a ghostwriter who would be willing to handle the more controversial elements of his story, particularly MacArthur's "flawed" personality, the MacArthur-Marshall feud, the MacArthur-Eisenhower controversy, and the issue of Sutherland's girlfriend. At first, Eichelberger preferred Milton MacKaye; he eventually changed his mind when he recalled MacKaye's drinking and erratic work habits. He next considered a variety of other writers (including Ken Roberts, a close friend and noted author), but eliminated all of them for various reasons. In October 1957, he settled on Jay Luvaas (a young and enterprising historian who had persuaded Eichelberger to donate his papers to Duke University). Eichelberger convinced Luvaas to "do something" with his letters and diaries, and to write "some sort of book" on his experiences in the Pacific with MacArthur, Krueger, and Sutherland.[78]

In preparation for this project, Eichelberger dictated hundreds of memorandums from 1957 to 1961, covering every aspect of his service under MacArthur. With each passing year, these memorandums increased in number and stridency. Most of these dictations emphasized MacArthur's flaws as a person and military leader. Believing that these dictations would be "priceless" in the preparation of the book, Eichelberger expected Luvaas to use them as the background for an exposé of his former chief.[79] By 1958, he could think of little else; the last years of his life were devoted to the preparation of the sources that "hopefully, would destroy the MacArthur myth forever."[80]

In September 1958, Eichelberger submitted some of these memorandums to various publishers. He received a tentative agreement from the University of

Chicago Press to publish a book based on these materials. That month, he also decided that it would be appropriate if Luvaas worked on the book "both before and after" he died. "I have finally agreed," he stated, "to let this work be done while I am still alive and can make suggestions."[81] In the following weeks, Eichelberger urged Luvaas to organize the source materials and microfilm his diaries. This work was delayed by Luvaas's trip to England in 1959 (where he studied under Basil Liddell Hart and did research on various aspects of World War II). Nevertheless, Luvaas kept in contact with Eichelberger by mail; he promised to apply for some grants so that he could resume work on the book upon his return to the United States.[82]

In August 1961, Luvaas visited Eichelberger at his home in Asheville, and spent several days talking with him about the proposed book.[83] Luvaas suggested the possibility of writing two books (or, at least, two versions of the same book), one based on Eichelberger's letters to his wife, and the second based on his memorandums and his attacks against MacArthur.[84] Eichelberger reluctantly agreed to Luvaas's proposal, although he was clearly more interested in the latter project.[85]

Three weeks after this meeting, Eichelberger informed Clovis Byers that he was "going in the hospital [for some surgery]." "This will be a minor operation," he stated. "I have as my . . . doctor Irby Stephens who is a John Hopkins man and one of the best." Nevertheless, Eichelberger made preparations in the event of his death; he sent a copy of his self-prepared obituary to the local paper, the *Asheville Citizen Times*.[86]

On 25 September 1961, Eichelberger underwent exploratory prostate surgery at Memorial Mission Hospital in Asheville. He survived the operation, but suffered from post-operative pulmonary complications that quickly developed into pneumonia. He died quietly in the hospital the next day.[87]

On 29 September 1961, Robert L. Eichelberger was buried at Arlington National Cemetery. In the days following his death, newspapers around the nation recalled his splendid achievements. They commemorated his career with glowing tributes. Ironically, Eichelberger's greatest epitaph came from Douglas MacArthur. In front-page headlines, he declared that Bob was "one of the Army's most brilliant commanders. . . . His Eighth Army was a vital factor in the defeat of Japan in the Pacific War." MacArthur concluded, "I hold him in outstanding esteem and admiration and mourn him deeply."[88]

In his own way, Eichelberger returned the compliment. The first line of his obituary (prepared personally before his death and carried by dozens of newspapers throughout the world) proclaimed that "General Robert L. Eichelberger [had been the] top ground commander under General Douglas MacArthur in the Pacific . . ."[89]

As for Eichelberger's intended legacy—his proposed books—the hopes for these publications were only partially fulfilled. In 1972, Luvaas edited Eichelberger's letters to his wife and published *Dear Miss Em*, a relatively non-controversial book about his experiences in the Pacific. The other book, the exposé that was to shatter the "MacArthur myth," was never written.[90]

NOTES

1. By 1950, Eichelberger also had over $30,000 invested in stocks and bonds, over $10,000 in his savings account, plus a retirement pension of over $700 a month. Robert Eichelberger to C. Emory Glander (tax commissioner), 5 May 1949, box 24 of Eichelberger Papers; Robert Eichelberger to Herman A. Gudger, 4 September 1948, Eichelberger Papers; Herman A. Gudger to Robert Eichelberger, 4 April 1947, Eichelberger Papers.

2. Robert Eichelberger to Houston Harte, 25 March 1950, Eichelberger Papers; Robert Eichelberger to Lieutenant General G. W. Griswold, 31 August 1954, Eichelberger Papers; Robert Eichelberger, "Notes for talk on 'Why I Like Asheville,'" 1957, 1, box 36 of Eichelberger Papers; Eichelberger Dictations, "Retired Life in Asheville," 6 July 1959, 2–4.

3. Robert Eichelberger to Mrs. Douglas MacArthur, 24 September 1948, Eichelberger Papers; Robert Eichelberger to General James A. Lester, 22 September 1948, Eichelberger Papers; Robert Eichelberger to Brigadier General George D. Shea, 15 November 1948, box 22 of Eichelberger Papers.

4. Robert Eichelberger to George Adams Ellis, 12 May 1949, Eichelberger Papers; Robert Eichelberger to Major J. J. Gibbons, 22 July 1949, Eichelberger Papers; Eichelberger Dictations, "Post-War Opportunities," 15 June 1959, 1–2; Eichelberger Dictations, "Forrestal," 4 August 1958, 1–2; Eichelberger Dictations, "Various Positions Offered Me on my Return from Japan in 1948," no date, 1.

5. Eichelberger Dictations, "RLE Offered Position as Head of CIA-Pacific," 15 September 1961, 1–2.

6. Even before his return from Japan, Eichelberger was asked about his availability for certain jobs. In 1946 and 1947, several friends inquired if he was interested in becoming the ambassador to Australia or the president of Texas A & M University. Although Eichelberger was extremely interested, no official offer was ever made. In 1947, Eichelberger was asked to head a joint American-Brazilian War College, but he declined on the basis that he lacked sufficient knowledge of the culture and the language of Brazil. Robert Eichelberger to Emma Eichelberger, 23 November 1945 and 1 April 1946, Eichelberger Papers; Robert Eichelberger to Houston Harte, 25 May 1947 and 16 June 1947, Eichelberger Papers; Houston Harte to Robert Eichelberger, 16 May 1947, Eichelberger Papers.

7. Robert Eichelberger to B. R. Armour, 11 April 1949, Eichelberger Papers; Robert Eichelberger to Major General James A. Lester, 22 September 1948, Eichelberger Papers; Eichelberger Dictations, "Post War Opportunities," 15 June 1959, 1; Schonberger, *Aftermath of War*, 147.

8. Robert Eichelberger to Roger Baldwin, 8 March 1949, Eichelberger Papers; Robert Eichelberger to Major J. J. Gibbons, 16 March 1949, Eichelberger Papers; Eichelberger Dictations, "Post War Opportunities," 2–3.

9. Robert Eichelberger to John Fennelly, 23 March 1949, Eichelberger Papers; Robert Eichelberger to Harold Houston, 19 March 1949, Eichelberger Papers; Robert Eichelberger to Major General Edward M. Almond, 21 February 1950, Eichelberger Papers; Robert Eichelberger to Jean MacArthur, 1 March 1950, Eichelberger Papers; Robert Eichelberger to Harry Kern, 24 March 1950, Eichelberger Papers; Robert Eichelberger to Major General Charles A. Willoughby, 28 March 1950, Eichelberger Papers; Robert Eichelberger to General Dwight Eisenhower, 11 March 1949, Dwight D. Eisenhower Papers, Eisenhower Library, Abilene, Kansas.

10. Robert Eichelberger to Clark H. Getts, Inc., 5 December 1949, Eichelberger Papers; Robert Eichelberger to Major General Edward Almond, 8 November 1949, Eichelberger Papers; Robert Eichelberger to Mrs. Douglas MacArthur, 11 December 1948, Eichelberger Papers.

11. Robert Eichelberger to Major General Edward Almond, 8 November 1949, Eichelberger Papers; Robert Eichelberger to Mrs. Douglas MacArthur, 11 December 1948, Eichelberger Papers; Robert Eichelberger to J. Howard Andrews, 30 September 1949 and 8 February 1950, Eichelberger Papers; Robert Eichelberger to Clark H. Getts, 14 March 1949, 16 May 1949, 23 March 1949, and 5 December 1949, Eichelberger Papers.

12. Eichelberger was paid $35,000 by the *Saturday Evening Post*. His story appeared in a series which ran from 13 August to 24 September 1949. Robert Eichelberger to Ken Roberts, 11 April 1949, Eichelberger Papers; Ben Hibbs to Robert Eichelberger, 29 June 1949, Eichelberger Papers; Robert Eichelberger to Colonel John K. Reinoehl, 14 September 1949, Eichelberger Papers; Robert Eichelberger to Mark C. Houston, 28 September 1949, Eichelberger Papers.

13. Ben Hibbs to Robert Eichelberger, 29 June 1949, Eichelberger Papers; Robert Eichelberger to Ben Hibbs, 11 August 1949 and 20 September 1949, Eichelberger Papers; Robert Eichelberger to Roy E. Larson, 21 September 1949 and 30 September 1949, Eichelberger Papers; Robert Eichelberger to Milton MacKaye, 23 August 1949 and 24 August 1949, Eichelberger Papers; Robert Eichelberger to General John Northcott, 10 October 1949, Eichelberger Papers; Robert Eichelberger to W. L. Guthrie, 30 August 1949, Eichelberger Papers.

14. Anders, *Gentle Knight*, 305; George Robinson to Robert Eichelberger, 21 September 1949, Eichelberger Papers; Colonel George Jones to Robert Eichelberger, 2 November 1949, Eichelberger Papers; Robert Eichelberger to Colonel George Jones, 21 November 1949, Eichelberger Papers.

15. Roy Larsen to Robert Eichelberger, 16 September 1948, Eichelberger Papers; Eichelberger Dictations, "MacArthur a 'great soldier?,'" 12 November 1954, 5; Robert Eichelberger to Milton MacKaye, 14 February 1948 and 4 February 1948, Eichelberger Papers; Robert Eichelberger to Miss Gertrude Algase, 8 May 1948, Eichelberger Papers; Robert Eichelberger to Roy Howard, 25 August 1948, Eichelberger Papers.

16. Robert Eichelberger to Mrs. K. T. Nichols, Jr., 12 July 1949, Eichelberger Papers; Robert Eichelberger to Major W. J. Fitzmaurice, 25 August 1949, Eichelberger Papers.

17. Robert Eichelberger to Milton MacKaye, 8 August 1949, Eichelberger Papers.

18. Robert Eichelberger to Kenneth Roberts, 11 April 1949, Eichelberger Papers; Robert Eichelberger to Major W. J. Fitzmaurice, 6 October 1948, Eichelberger

Papers; Robert Eichelberger to Gertrude Algase, 30 January 1950, Eichelberger Papers.

19. Theodore Ropp to Robert Eichelberger, 7 October 1954, Eichelberger Papers; Harry Kern to Robert Eichelberger, 24 September 1950, Eichelberger Papers; Rose A. Conway (administrative assistant to President Harry Truman) to Robert Eichelberger, 26 September 1950, Eichelberger Papers; General Omar Bradley to Robert Eichelberger, 2 October 1950, Eichelberger Papers.

20. Robert Eichelberger to Colonel B. E. Kendall, 31 August 1954, Eichelberger Papers; Robert Eichelberger to Kenneth Roberts, 5 December 1949, Eichelberger Papers.

21. Robert Eichelberger to Ken Roberts, 11 April 1949 and 5 December 1949, Eichelberger Papers; Robert Eichelberger to Gertrude Algase, 4 December 1948, 16 March 1949, 30 January 1950, and 6 June 1950; Robert Eichelberger to Mark C. Houston, 28 September 1949; Robert Eichelberger to Roy E. Larsen, 30 September 1949; Robert Eichelberger to Major J. J. Gibbons, 22 July 1949; Robert Eichelberger to Frank Eichelberger, 22 November 1948; Robert Eichelberger to Major General George D. Shea, 23 March 1949, all Eichelberger Papers.

22. Robert Eichelberger to John Horton, 13 February 1952, Eichelberger Papers; Robert Eichelberger to General Dwight D. Eisenhower, 11 March 1952; E. A. Brown to Robert Eichelberger, 20 September 1956; Robert Eichelberger to Major J. J. Gibbons, 22 July 1949, all Eichelberger Papers.

23. Eichelberger Dictations, "Retired Life in Asheville," 6 July 1959, 1; Robert Eichelberger to Harry F. Kern (*Newsweek*), 9 November 1953, Eichelberger Papers; Shizue Tomikawa to Robert Eichelberger, 29 February 1951, box 30 of Eichelberger Papers; Harry F. Kern to Robert Eichelberger, 24 September 1950 and 28 April 1951 (a copy of Eichelberger's *Newsweek* article is included with this 1951 letter), box 30 of Eichelberger Papers; Robert Eichelberger to Major J. J. Gibbons, 22 July 1949, Eichelberger Papers.

24. Robert Eichelberger to Lieutenant Colonel William H. Zierdt, Jr., 5 December 1955, box 33 of Eichelberger Papers; Robert Eichelberger to Harry Kern, 10 January 1952 (Eichelberger's *Newsweek* article on the "Korean offensive" is enclosed with this letter), box 31 of Eichelberger Papers; Harry Kern to Robert Eichelberger, 24 September 1950, Eichelberger Papers; Shizue Tomikawa to Robert Eichelberger, 28 February 1951, Eichelberger Papers; Robert Eichelberger to Frank Eichelberger, 29 June 1949, Eichelberger Papers.

25. Robert Eichelberger to General Clifford Bluemel, 22 August 1955, box 33 of Eichelberger Papers; Robert Eichelberger to Samuel Milner, 6 January 1955, Eichelberger Papers; Eichelberger Dictations, "Post War Opportunities," 15 June 1959, 3–5; Robert Eichelberger to Frank Eichelberger, 22 November 1948, Eichelberger Papers; Robert Eichelberger to Robert Parker, 4 December 1948, Eichelberger Papers.

26. Robert Eichelberger to Otto Fesitmann, 23 November 1955, box 35 of Eichelberger Papers; Robert Eichelberger to W. Fleming Talman (president of the Asheville Chamber of Commerce), 13 January 1958, box 35 of Eichelberger Papers.

27. Luther H. Hodges to Robert Eichelberger, 31 October 1957, box 37 of Eichelberger Papers; Robert Eichelberger to General Clovis E. Byers, 25 November 1957, Eichelberger Papers; Robert Eichelberger to General Mark Wayne Clark, 30

December 1957, Eichelberger Papers; "Memorandum for Robert Eichelberger," 19 November 1957, included in box 37 of Eichelberger Papers; Robert Eichelberger to G. Aiken Taylor, 21 October 1960, Eichelberger Papers.

28. Robert Eichelberger to Al Fris, 17 November 1958, box 39 of Eichelberger Papers.

29. Eichelberger Dictations, "Politics, 1960," 11 November 1960, 1-3; Robert Eichelberger to Lindsay Harkness, 11 December 1959, Eichelberger Papers; Robert Eichelberger to General Clovis Byers, 2 September 1960, 7 November 1960, and 30 November 1960, Eichelberger Papers; Robert Eichelberger to General David Sarnoff, 30 September 1960, Eichelberger Papers; Robert Eichelberger to R. M. White II, 29 July 1960 and 11 November 1960, Eichelberger Papers; Robert Eichelberger to W. B. Persons, 29 Aug. 1960, Eichelberger Papers; Robert Eichelberger to Richard M. Nixon, 18 July 1960, Eichelberger Papers; Robert Eichelberger to General Sir Edmund F. Herring, 3 August 1959, box 41 of Eichelberger Papers.

30. Eichelberger did have a pleasant experience with one volunteer organization—the John and Mary Markle Foundation. During the 1950s, this foundation selected "highly qualified doctors of experience for expensive fellowships in medical research." Eichelberger was a member of the group's executive board. He was impressed by the fine work which this organization accomplished. Eichelberger Dictations, "Retired Life in Asheville," 6 July 1959, 2-3; Eichelberger Dictations, "Post War Opportunities," 15 June 1959, 5; Eichelberger Dictations, "RLE Offered Position as Head of CIA-Pacific," 15 September 1961, 1-2.

31. Robert Eichelberger to General Clovis Byers, 22 July 1960, Eichelberger Papers; Robert Eichelberger to Jean MacArthur, 1 March 1950, Eichelberger Papers; Robert Eichelberger to Brigadier General George D. Shea, 15 November 1948, Eichelberger Papers; Robert Eichelberger to Major General Joseph M. Swing, 21 September 1948, Eichelberger Papers.

32. Eichelberger Dictations, "Post War Opportunities," 15 June 1959, 3-4; Robert Eichelberger to Milton MacKaye, 1 September 1948, Eichelberger Papers; Robert Eichelberger to Brigadier General E. B. Colladay, 17 September 1948, Eichelberger Papers; Robert Eichelberger to Mrs. George H. Eichelberger, 6 October 1948, Eichelberger Papers; Robert Eichelberger to Mrs. Douglas MacArthur, 22 October 1948, Eichelberger Papers; Robert Eichelberger to Rosie Wagner, 3 December 1948, Eichelberger Papers.

33. Eichelberger Dictations, "Retired Life in Asheville," 6 July 1959, 1-2; Robert Eichelberger to Frank Eichelberger, 23 December 1949; Robert Eichelberger to Raymond D. Knight, 19 January 1950; Robert Eichelberger to Harold A. Brand, 27 April 1956, all Eichelberger Papers; Robert Eichelberger to President Dwight D. Eisenhower, 8 June 1956, box 34 of Eichelberger Papers; Robert Eichelberger to Francis Gudger, 21 February 1950, Eichelberger Papers.

34. Eichelberger's family also experienced some health-related problems during this period. In 1948, George (the oldest brother) died of a heart attack. In 1955, Frank (the middle brother) was diagnosed with bone cancer. Frank's illness was particularly devastating to the harmony of the family. Prior to his death, he had accused Eichelberger of being a "tightwad" and refusing to undertake the expense of visiting his home in the Pacific Northwest. Eichelberger finally agreed to make the trip, but there is no indication that the two brothers resolved their differences before Frank's

death in 1956. Frank Eichelberger to Mrs. Jerome B. Zerbe, 29 July 1955, Eichelberger Papers; Robert Eichelberger to Fred Eichelberger, 10 February 1966 and 13 July 1966, Eichelberger Papers; Robert Eichelberger to Lieutenant R. H. Stetson, 7 September 1956, Eichelberger Papers; Robert Eichelberger to Mrs. Jerome Zerbe, 25 October 1956, Eichelberger Papers; Robert Eichelberger to Harold Houston, 28 August 1948, Eichelberger Papers; Eichelberger Dictations, "Retired Life in Asheville," 6 July 1959, 1; Robert Eichelberger to Christopher McDaniel, 9 June 1958, Eichelberger Papers; Robert Eichelberger to Douglas Mueller, 8 January 1951, Eichelberger Papers.

35. Robert Eichelberger to Samuel Milner, 19 December 1951, box 30 of Eichelberger Papers; Eichelberger Dictations, "Fuller, also Krueger," 29 May 1961, 1–4; Robert Eichelberger to Francis Gudger, 23 November 1949, Eichelberger Papers.

36. Robert Eichelberger to Clifford Bluemel, 25 August 1958, Eichelberger Papers; Anders, *Gentle Knight*, 305, 313; Robert Eichelberger to Robert B. Parker, 29 June 1949, Eichelberger Papers; Robert Eichelberger to Samuel Milner, 4 July 1957 and 11 July 1957, Eichelberger Papers.

37. The conflict with Harding influenced Eichelberger's decision to give his papers to Duke University. He had originally intended to donate his letters to West Point, but he later feared that Harding and his friends would use this correspondence to write a history critical of his Pacific campaigns. In 1954, he decided to give his correspondence to Duke's Flowers Memorial Collection after receiving the following warning from Clovis E. Byers, his former chief of staff: "Your sending them [the Eichelberger Papers] to Duke University appears to be a very wise decision. . . . Professional jealousy and personal prejudice might . . . result in their receiving far less intelligent consideration had you permitted them to be taken to West Point." Clovis Byers to Robert Eichelberger, 12 November 1954, Eichelberger Papers; Daniel K. Edwards to Robert Eichelberger, 19 June 1964, Eichelberger Papers.

38. Despite these personal problems, there was one piece of good news during this period. In July 1954, Congress voted to award a fourth star to "those individuals who, over a period of time, were either Army commanders in combat or had the tremendous responsibility of commanding Army Ground Forces during World War II." Eichelberger was eligible for his fourth star under this legislation. He received his long-awaited promotion to full General during a ceremony at Fort Jackson (South Carolina) in November 1954. Robert T. Stevens (Secretary of the Army) to Robert Eichelberger, 4 August 1954, Eichelberger Papers (also included is a copy of the relevant House bill, S. 2468); "101st Airborne Division Review in honor of General Robert L. Eichelberger," 5 November 1954, 1–10, Eichelberger Papers.

39. Robert L. Eichelberger to Samuel Milner, 4 July 1957 and 11 July 1957, Eichelberger Papers; Robert Eichelberger to Robert B. Parker, 29 June 1949, Eichelberger Papers.

40. Schaller, *The American Occupation of Japan*, 139–40; Harry F. Kern to Robert Eichelberger, 30 October 1948, Eichelberger Papers; Robert Eichelberger to Harry F. Kern, 3 December 1948, Eichelberger Papers; Comptom Packenham to Harry F. Kern, 20 May 1949, Eichelberger Papers.

41. Harries and Harries, *Sheathing the Sword*, 230–31; Eichelberger Dictations, no title, 27 September 1957, 1 (pages 427–28 of dictation notebook); William J.

RETIREMENT—AND TURMOIL   195

Sebald and Russell Brines, *With MacArthur in Japan: A Personal History of the Occupation* (New York: W. W. Norton & Company, 1965), 248–49; Robert Eichelberger to DeWitt Wallace, 6 June 1950, Eichelberger Papers; *Nippon Times*, "Urges Strong Police Force," 16 December 1948, 1 (copies of this article and other articles pertaining to Eichelberger's ideas on the rearmament issue are attached to a letter from T. Suzuki to Robert Eichelberger, 7 January 1949, Eichelberger Papers); M. Kambe to Robert Eichelberger, 22 December 1948, Eichelberger Papers.

42. MacArthur's proposal of an early peace treaty based on Japan's neutrality was rejected by the army and the Department of Defense. Instead, in March 1954, Japan signed a "mutual defense pact" with the United States.

43. Memorandum prepared by Robert Eichelberger, no title, 16 November 1949, Eichelberger Papers; Robert Eichelberger to Roy E. Larsen, 9 December 1949, Eichelberger Papers; Robert Eichelberger to DeWitt Wallace, 6 June 1950, Eichelberger Papers; Douglas MacArthur to Tracy S. Voorhees, 9 October 1950, Eichelberger Papers.

44. *The Mainichi*, "May Have to Allow Japan to Rearm, Says Eichelberger," 4 March 1950, 1 (a copy is included in the Eichelberger Papers); Eichelberger Memorandum, "Memorandum for the Board of Directors of Common Cause, Inc.," 14 February 1950, 1–2, Eichelberger Papers; Eichelberger, *Our Jungle Road*, 288–89; Robert Eichelberger to Francis Gudger, 23 November 1949, Eichelberger Papers; Robert Eichelberger to DeWitt Wallace, 1 December 1949, Eichelberger Papers.

45. For the first nine months of this conflict, Eichelberger's illness (complications from his gall bladder operation) prevented him from commenting on MacArthur's actions in the Korean War. Only in April 1951, after the U.S. lines had stabilized near the 38th parallel, did Eichelberger feel well enough to make public statements. All of Eichelberger's criticisms of MacArthur, therefore, were made after the bulk of the fighting had been completed, with the added advantage of perfect "hindsight."

46. Eichelberger Dictations, "Some Phases of the Korean War," 26 August 1957, 1; Joseph C. Goulden, *Korea: The Untold Story of the War* (New York: Times Books, 1982), xx–xxiv; Eichelberger Dictations, "Memorandum on the Advance to the Yalu," 26 August 1959, 1–3; Eichelberger Dictations, "Remarks Following Reading of Speech by General MacArthur on Philippine Independence Day," 7 July 1961, 4; Eichelberger Dictations, no title, 5 September 1955, 3–4 (pages 246–47 of dictation notebook); Robert Eichelberger to George Folster, 28 August 1950, Eichelberger Papers; Eichelberger Dictations, "Thoughts on the MacArthur-Truman Incident," 27 May 1957, 1; Eichelberger Dictations, no title, 17 February 1956, 11–13 (pages 300–302 of dictation notebook).

47. Eichelberger Dictations, "MacArthur," 18 March 1959, 1; Richard Whelan, *Drawing the Line: The Korean War, 1950-1953* (Boston: Little, Brown, and Company, 1990), 191, 248–49; Eichelberger Dictations, no title, 28 April 1961, 3 (page 748 of dictation notebook); Eichelberger Dictations, "Memorandum on the Advance to the Yalu," 26 August 1959, 2.

48. Eichelberger felt that MacArthur used the same "tricks" during the Korean War that he had initially employed during World War II. For example, in Korea, MacArthur split his forces into two separate commands, the 8th Army under General Walton Walker and the X Corps under General Ned Almond. Eichelberger felt that this separa-

tion was unnecessary; he believed that "the reason for these two separate commands was to enable General MacArthur to . . . sleep in Tokyo all the time" and still claim that he was in direct command of American units in Korea. Eichelberger also claimed that MacArthur awarded himself medals for making brief trips to the front. In 1950, General Frank Bowen, Jr., (commander of the 187th Paratroopers and Eichelberger's former operations officer) made a successful jump behind enemy lines north of Pyongyang. MacArthur observed this operation by plane, and subsequently awarded himself a Distinguished Flying Cross (MacArthur also awarded Silver Stars to those officers who had accompanied him). General Bowen, on the other hand, received no medals for this operation or for his activities behind enemy lines. This incident was verified by members of MacArthur's staff. Robert Eichelberger to General Sir Edmund Herring, 26 August 1959, Eichelberger Papers; Eichelberger Dictations, (no title), 17 February 1956, 2–3 (pages 291–92 of dictation notebook); Eichelberger Dictations, "Memorandum on the Advance to the Yalu (as told to me by Major General Frank S. Bowen, Jr., on Sunday, August 23, 1959)," 26 August 1959, 1–3; Max Hastings, *The Korean War* (New York: Simon and Schuster, 1987), 64–66; Burton Kaufman, *The Korean War: Challenges in Crisis, Credibility, and Command* (Philadelphia: Temple University Press, 1986), 70–71.

49. Instead of firing MacArthur, Eichelberger stated that it would have been better if Truman had "ordered him home to become a consultant with beautiful offices, flags, MP's, etc., in the Pentagon." This method would have removed MacArthur from Korea, curtailed any criticism of Truman's motivations, and prevented MacArthur from becoming a "martyr" to the American public. Answers dictated by General Robert L. Eichelberger to questions presented by R. F. Campbell of the *Winston Salem Journal and Sentinel*, 13 October 1955, 3 (Eichelberger's response to question 10), Eichelberger Papers.

50. Eichelberger was also frustrated by other events surrounding MacArthur's relief. After MacArthur was sent home, Eichelberger was asked by General George C. Marshall to attend a private meeting in Washington, D.C. Although the purpose of this meeting was not specified, Eichelberger believed that he was being considered as a replacement for MacArthur in Japan (leaving Ridgway as commander of the fighting forces in Korea). During the meeting, however, Eichelberger was not offered the position as SCAP, ostensibly because he was still "showing the effects of this gall bladder) operation." He later commented, "I believe that if I had not been extremely thin [25–30 pounds lighter than normal] following an operation for gall bladder, I would have been sent to Japan to take MacArthur's place and that would have been some satisfaction to me." This event is not mentioned in Marshall's papers or any of his biographies. Eichelberger Dictations, "George C. Marshall," (no date), 10–11 (pages 150–51 of dictation notebook); Eichelberger Dictations, "Some Phases of General MacArthur's Attitude towards me," 31 August 1959, 4; Eichelberger Dictations, "RLE Offered Position as Head of CIA-Pacific," 15 September 1961, 2 (see the addition to this page).

51. Robert Eichelberger to Mrs. Ben K. Bare, 23 April 1951, Eichelberger Papers; Eichelberger Dictations, "Thoughts on the MacArthur-Truman Incident," 27 May 1957, 1–2; John W. Spanier, *The Truman-MacArthur Controversy and the Korean War* (Cambridge: Harvard University Press, 1959), 211–17; Eichelberger Dictations,

no title, 12 September 1955, 2 (page 249 of dictation notebook); Bevin Alexander, *Korea: The First War We Lost* (New York: Hippocrene Books, 1986), 410–13.

52. David Rees, *Korea: The Limited War* (New York: St. Martin's Press, 1964), 1–24; Spanier, *The Truman-MacArthur Controversy and the Korean War*, 3–12, 30–35, 81; General Matthew B. Ridgway, *The Korean War: How We Met the Challenge* (Garden City, N.Y.: Doubleday and Company, 1967), 31–32; Goulden, *Korea: The Untold Story of the War*, xx; Whelan, *Drawing the Line: The Korean War*, 248–49; see James L. Stokesbury, *A Short History of the Korean War* (New York: William Morrow and Company, 1988), 67–68; and Hastings, *The Korean War*, 64–66, 99.

53. David Crenshaw to Robert Eichelberger, 13 April 1951, Eichelberger Papers; Robert Eichelberger to Mrs. E. B. Colladay, 23 April 1951, Eichelberger Papers; Robert Eichelberger to Ralph (the last name was not specified), 19 December 1958, Eichelberger Papers.

54. Robert Eichelberger to General Dwight D. Eisenhower, 12 July 1952 and 11 March 1952, Eichelberger Papers; Robert Eichelberger to Mrs. Ken K. Bare, 23 April 1951, Eichelberger Papers; James, *The Years of MacArthur Volume III*, 649; Robert Eichelberger to Governor John S. Fine (Pennsylvania), 18 June 1952, Eichelberger Papers; Robert Eichelberger to Arthur J. Sommerfield, 24 June 1952, Eichelberger Papers; Robert Eichelberger to Mrs. John Y. Huber, 3 October 1951, Eichelberger Papers.

55. In May 1952, MacArthur gave a speech before the Michigan legislature. He stated, "It would be a tragic development indeed if this generation was forced to look to the rigidity of military dominance and discipline to redeem it from the tragic failure of a civilian administration."

56. Press release, no title, 23 June 1952, 1–3, Eichelberger Papers (also included in the 23 June 1952 issue of the *New York Times*); Robert Eichelberger to Tracy S. Voorhees, 30 June 1952, Eichelberger Papers; Sam Lebowitz to Robert Eichelberger, 30 June 1952, Eichelberger Papers; Tracy S. Voorhees to Robert L. Eichelberger, 28 June 1952, Eichelberger Papers; Eichelberger Dictations, "General MacArthur and the Presidency, with some remarks about General Eisenhower," 12 November 1953, 7–8; Robert L. Eichelberger to Dwight D. Eisenhower, 4 July 1952, Eichelberger Papers; Dwight D. Eisenhower to Robert L. Eichelberger, 28 June 1952, Eichelberger Papers.

57. Eichelberger truly believed that MacArthur would be victorious in his bid for the White House. Even after the election, he stated, "my own opinion is that if the Presidential election had been in the year 1951 (following MacArthur's "triumphant" return to the U.S.) instead of 1952, MacArthur would have been President." In reality, MacArthur's chances were much slimmer than Eichelberger had feared. MacArthur never publicly announced his candidacy. He hoped that he would be drafted as the nominee during the Republican National Convention, but this was never a strong possibility. As James notes, the MacArthur movement lacked "leadership, local organizational contacts and funding, and never posed a threat to the forces of Eisenhower and [Senator Robert] Taft in any state where a spring primary was . . . held." Eichelberger Dictations, "MacArthur and his Presidential Ambitions," 29 May 1961, 2; James, *The Years of MacArthur, Volume III*, 648–49; Robert Eichelberger to John Horton, 13 February 1952, Eichelberger Papers.

58. Robert Eichelberger to President Dwight D. Eisenhower, 28 June 1964, Eichelberger Papers; Eichelberger Dictations, "Memorandum for file on General MacArthur's Speech," 2 August 1957, 1–3.

59. Robert Eichelberger to Samuel Milner, 5 January 1955, Eichelberger Papers; Robert Eichelberger to Clovis E. Byers, 23 October 1959, Eichelberger Papers; Robert Eichelberger to Jay and Mrs. Luvaas, 13 January 1961, Eichelberger Papers.

60. Robert Eichelberger to Samuel Milner, 26 May 1958 and 24 October 1958, Eichelberger Papers; Eichelberger Dictations, no title, 12 September 1955, 1–4 (pages 248–51 of dictation notebook).

61. Robert Eichelberger to Samuel Milner, 6 January 1955 and 26 May 1958, Eichelberger Papers; Clifford Bluemel to Robert Eichelberger, 2 September 1958, Eichelberger Papers; Robert Eichelberger to Admiral Samuel Eliot Morison, 26 May 1961, Eichelberger Papers.

62. Robert Eichelberger to Frank S. Bowen, Jr., 8 April 1955 and 10 March 1961, Eichelberger Papers; Robert Eichelberger to Major Edward T. Lauer, 17 October 1953, Eichelberger Papers; Robert Eichelberger to Lt. Colonel William H. Zierdt Jr., 11 November 1955, Eichelberger Papers; Robert Eichelberger to Clovis E. Byers, 27 February 1959 and 28 September 1959, Eichelberger Papers; Robert Eichelberger to Samuel Milner, 8 March 1954, 6 January 1955, and 24 October 1958, Eichelberger Papers; Robert Eichelberger to General Clifford Bluemel, 25 August 1958 and 12 September 1958, Eichelberger Papers; Robert Eichelberger to Colonel L. C. Harkness, 3 April 1959, Eichelberger Papers.

63. Robert Eichelberger to Clifford Bluemel, 12 September 1958, Eichelberger Papers; Robert Eichelberger to Harry F. Kern, 29 December 1952, Eichelberger Papers; Eichelberger Dictations, no title, 11 November 1960, 5 (page 653 of dictation notebook); Eichelberger Dictations, "MacArthur," 18 March 1959, 1–3.

64. Robert M. White II, a former member of the I Corps staff, also encouraged Eichelberger to end his feud with MacArthur. On several occasions, White informed Eichelberger that he was only "hurting himself" by refusing to make peace with his old chief. It was "wrong," he argued, to hold on to these vindictive feelings. Telephone interview with Robert M. White II, conducted at the request of this author on 6 June 1988, page 1 of transcript.

65. Robert Eichelberger to F. S. Bowen Jr., 8 April 1955, Eichelberger Papers; Clovis Byers to Robert Eichelberger, 12 February 1959, Eichelberger Papers; Robert Eichelberger to Clovis Byers, 7 November 1960, Eichelberger Papers.

66. Despite Eichelberger's prejudices, there is no evidence to suggest that MacArthur ever criticized Bob or responded in an angry fashion. In 1959, Eichelberger learned from several sources that MacArthur frequently asked about him, and, on occasion, instructed his associates to convey his "warmest regards" to his "grand old" 8th Army commander. Eichelberger admitted, "Every time anyone whom I know sees General MacArthur, he always says good things about me." Robert Eichelberger to Colonel George G. Dunn, Jr., 4 May 1959, Eichelberger Papers; General Clovis Byers to Robert Eichelberger, 12 February 1959, Eichelberger Papers; Robert Eichelberger to Colonel R. M. White II, 27 February 1961, Eichelberger Papers.

67. Eichelberger's "normal' sources of information were limited to *Life*, *Time*, and *Newsweek*, "conservative" newspapers such as the *New York Times*, the *Wall*

Street Journal, and the *New York Herald Tribune*, and major television news shows (the CBS "World News Report" and the NBC "Huntley-Brinkley News"). Robert Eichelberger to Mrs. Lindesay Parrott, 1 February 1950, Eichelberger Papers; Robert Eichelberger to Colonel R. M. White II, 6 June 1960 and 29 July 1960, Eichelberger Papers; Robert Eichelberger to General F. S. Bowen Jr., 10 March 1961, Eichelberger Papers.

68. Kenney, *General Kenney Reports*, 157-66; General H. W. Blakeley, *History of the 32nd Infantry Division in World War II* (manuscript, 1953), 56-60 (a copy is included in the Eichelberger Papers in box 66); Robert Eichelberger to Samuel Milner, 8 March 1954, Eichelberger Papers; General Clovis E. Byers to Robert Eichelberger, 12 November 1954, Eichelberger Papers; Robert Eichelberger to Major Edward T. Lauer, 17 October 1953 and 15 March 1957, Eichelberger Papers; Eichelberger Dictations, "Explanation of Certain Statements During the Buna Period Carried in the 'History of the 32nd Infantry Division in World War II,'" 17 October 1953, 1-7 (this dictation is attached to the 17 October 1953 letter sent to Major Lauer); Robert Eichelberger to Jay and Mrs. Luvaas, 13 January 1961, Eichelberger Papers; Frazier Hunt, *The Untold Story of Douglas MacArthur* (New York: Devin-Adair Co., 1954), 102-200.

69. *Pictorial Record: The War Against Japan* (Washington, D.C.: Office of Chief of Military History, Department of the Army, 1952), 1-200; Robert L. Eichelberger to H. O. Werner (United States Naval Institute), 3 February 1953, Eichelberger Papers (Eichelberger's three-page review of the *Pictorial Record: The War Against Japan* is attached to this letter).

70. Robert Eichelberger to Samuel Milner, 16 July 1957, Eichelberger Papers; Robert Eichelberger to Colonel L. C. Harkness, 3 April 1959, Eichelberger Papers; Louis Morton, *The Fall of the Philippines* (Washington, D.C.: Office of Chief of Military History, Department of the Army, 1953), 1-250; Eichelberger Dictations, no title, 17 February 1956, 1-7 (pages 290-97 of dictation notebook).

71. Dudley McCarthy, *Southwest Pacific Area: First Year—Kokoda to Wau* (Canberra: Australian War Memorial, 1959), 1-200; Robert Eichelberger to Edmund F. Herring, 8 December 1959, Eichelberger Papers; Robert Eichelberger to Samuel Eliot Morison, 13 March 1961, Eichelberger Papers; Morison, *The Liberation of the Philippines*, 1-250; Robert Eichelberger to Frank S. Bowen Jr., 10 March 1961, Eichelberger Papers.

72. Robert Eichelberger to Samuel Milner, 4 July 1957, 11 July 1957, 16 July 1957, and 22 July 1957, Eichelberger Papers; Robert Eichelberger to Jay Luvaas, 10 August 1959, Eichelberger Papers; Milner, *Victory in Papua*, 204-11, 375-76.

73. Eichelberger wrote to all of the authors who had criticized MacArthur; he became quite familiar with their personal backgrounds and books. In 1961, Eichelberger was amused to discover that one of the authors (Dudley McCarthy, who wrote *Southwest Pacific Area* partly to satisfy his Ph.D. requirements) was denied his doctorate because he was "not critical enough" of MacArthur in his dissertation. On another occasion, Eichelberger wrote to Samuel Milner, and inquired when *Victory in Papua* would be published. After he was informed that the book had been delayed, Eichelberger commented, "I have no exact knowledge but I am convinced that the delay in issuing the book is because it is critical of General MacArthur." After it was finally published, Eichelberger became Milner's greatest supporter. He encouraged

him to continue his writings about the Southwest Pacific (particularly on those topics that would help to explode the MacArthur "myth"). Eichelberger later attempted to get a favorable review of *VIP* in *Time* magazine. He successfully helped Milner win a Guggenheim Fellowship for additional projects. Robert Eichelberger to Samuel Milner, 4 July 1957, 16 July 1957, 24 October 1958, and 8 March 1954; Samuel Milner to Robert L. Eichelberger, 13 April 1959; Robert Eichelberger to Colonel Fred V. Brown, 26 June 1961; Robert Eichelberger to Clovis E. Byers, 26 May 1961; Robert Eichelberger to Major Edward T. Lauer, 15 March 1957; Robert Eichelberger to Jay Luvaas, 10 August 1959, all Eichelberger Papers.

74. Robert Eichelberger to Kenneth Roberts, 9 November 1949 and 5 December 1949, Eichelberger Papers; Robert Eichelberger to Ben Hibbs, 11 August 1949, Eichelberger Papers; Robert Eichelberger to Samuel Milner, 8 March 1954, Eichelberger Papers; Robert Eichelberger to Jeannette E. Hopkins, 15 February 1957, Eichelberger Papers; Eichelberger Dictations, no title, 28 April 1961, 4 (page 749 of dictation notebook).

75. It is difficult to understand why Eichelberger persisted in his hatred of Krueger, particularly since the two men never met or exchanged any letters after the war. (Eichelberger also never met MacArthur after his return from Japan, and only exchanged one or two letters with his former chief during the course of his retirement.) Major General Charles A. Willoughby had some feelings on this topic, and made some observations about Eichelberger's attitudes toward Krueger during the post-war years. Willoughby felt that, if anyone had reason to be bitter after the war, it was Krueger, not Eichelberger. Willoughby stated that "MacArthur gave Eichelberger every consideration," while Krueger was frequently criticized and scolded. Eichelberger was obviously "jealous" of Krueger, he noted, adding, "When a man . . . reaches a certain age or level of experience, he ought to be able to adjust that feature [jealousy]." Oral reminiscences of Major General Charles A. Willoughby, 30 July 1971, included in the Charles Willoughby Papers at the MacArthur Memorial in Norfolk, Virginia, RG-23, 12-13.

76. Robert Eichelberger to Clovis E. Byers, 17 February 1961, 28 September 1959, and 23 October 1959, Eichelberger Papers; Robert Eichelberger to Colonel George A. A. Jones, 21 November 1949, Eichelberger Papers; Robert Eichelberger to Lee Van Atta, 31 August 1949, Eichelberger Papers; Robert Eichelberger to General Hanford MacNider, 9 November 1949, Eichelberger Papers.

77. Robert Eichelberger to Mrs. E. S. Colladay, 23 April 1951, Eichelberger Papers; Robert Eichelberger to Mrs. Douglas MacArthur, 22 October 1948, Eichelberger Papers; Robert Eichelberger to Samuel Milner, 14 June 1957, Eichelberger Papers; Robert Eichelberger to Colonel R. M. White II, 27 February 1961, Eichelberger Papers; Robert Eichelberger to General Clovis E. Byers, 6 September 1961, Eichelberger Papers; Eichelberger Dictations, "Additional Memoranda on Some Phases of Victory in Papua," 31 May 1957, 1-2; Eichelberger Dictations, "Memorandum on War Days," 20 March 1957, 3-5; Eichelberger Dictations, "Memorandum to Accompany Carbon Copies of My Buna Letters to MacArthur and Sutherland," 31 May 1957, 1.

78. Robert Eichelberger to Jeannette E. Hopkins, 15 February 1957, Eichelberger Papers; Robert Eichelberger to Samuel Milner, 21 March 1958, Eichelberger Papers; Robert Eichelberger to Ken Roberts, 9 November 1949 and 5 December 1949,

RETIREMENT—AND TURMOIL 201

Eichelberger Papers; Robert Eichelberger to Milton MacKaye, 14 February 1948, Eichelberger Papers.

79. Eichelberger started dictating these memorandums in the late 1940s, when he first considered writing a book on MacArthur. By the late 1950s, this activity had become a part of his routine; Eichelberger dictated memoranda to his secretary (Virginia Westall) on almost a daily basis. Eichelberger Dictations, "Retired Life in Asheville," 6 July 1959, 2; Robert Eichelberger to Ben Leonard, 21 June 1954, Eichelberger Papers.

80. Jay Luvaas to Robert Eichelberger, 12 September 1958, 26 June 1954, 30 July 1954, and 1 April 1955, Eichelberger Papers; Robert Eichelberger to Jay Luvaas, 23 November 1959 and 19 June 1961, Eichelberger Papers; Robert Eichelberger to Major General R. W. Stephens, 1 March 1957, Eichelberger Papers; Robert Eichelberger to Samuel Milner, 21 March 1958, Eichelberger Papers; Robert Eichelberger to Carroll G. Bowen, 10 April 1958, Eichelberger Papers; Robert Eichelberger to General Clovis E. Byers, 27 February 1959, Eichelberger Papers; Robert Eichelberger to General Clifford Bluemel, 6 September 1961, Eichelberger Papers; Eichelberger Dictations, "MacArthur a 'Great Soldier?,'" 12 November 1954, 1–5.

81. On the surface, Luvaas was not an ideal choice for the proposed book; he was a young historian still working on his dissertation, and he had little available free time. Eichelberger, however, was not deterred. He noted that Luvaas was "a college professor with a growing reputation [as an author]." More importantly, he liked and admired Jay. Eichelberger felt that Luvaas could be trusted to write a book that would portray him in a sympathetic manner (unlike some of the older and more established historians, who seemed more concerned with expanding MacArthur's already overblown reputation). Furthermore, Luvaas felt somewhat obligated to write the book; he had promised Eichelberger that, if he gave his personal papers to Duke University, they would "be the subject of a biography." (When Luvaas left Duke University to accept a teaching position at Allegheny College, Eichelberger considered pulling his papers out of Duke; he changed his mind only after Luvaas assured him that "your original reasons for giving your papers to Duke University are still good.") Telephone interview with Jay Luvaas, conducted at the request of this author on 29 December 1989, 1–2 of written transcript; Jay Luvaas to Robert Eichelberger, 26 June 1954, Eichelberger Papers; Robert Eichelberger to Thomas B. Doe, 5 September 1958, Eichelberger Papers; Robert Eichelberger to Clovis Byers, 6 September 1961, Eichelberger Papers.

82. Robert Eichelberger to Captain Thomas B. Doe, 5 September 1958, Eichelberger Papers; Robert Eichelberger to Carroll G. Bowen, 10 April 1958, Eichelberger Papers; Jay Luvaas to Robert Eichelberger, 31 August 1959 and June 1959 [exact date unknown], Eichelberger Papers; Robert Eichelberger to Jay Luvaas, 19 June 1961 and 14 August 1961, Eichelberger Papers; Robert Eichelberger to General Clifford Bluemel, 6 September 1961, Eichelberger Papers.

83. In a telephone interview (conducted by this author in 1989), Luvaas stated that Eichelberger never mentioned the proposed book until their last meeting together in 1961. He stated that he was unaware that Eichelberger intended to write a book condemning MacArthur. The evidence suggests otherwise. From 1957 to 1961, Eichelberger wrote over 30 letters that referred specifically to the book. Many of

these were written to Luvaas (during this same period, Eichelberger prepared over fifty dictations in preparation for this project). Furthermore, Eichelberger clearly stated the purpose and intention of his book: to attack MacArthur and to provide some balance to the "MacArthur story." The letters also indicate a lively correspondence between Luvaas and Eichelberger concerning the project; they discussed whether the book should be written either before or after Eichelberger's death. The letters clearly indicate that Luvaas was to be the author. It appears likely, however, that there was a misunderstanding between the two men, and that Luvaas did not fully appreciate the depth of Eichelberger's hatred toward MacArthur. Luvaas admitted that Bob was an "astute army politician" and was adept at keeping his true feelings guarded. Eichelberger was sensitive about his public image; he was anxious to avoid giving the impression that he was a "hothead" in his attitude toward MacArthur. Eichelberger may have couched his criticisms of his former chief in diplomatic terms, giving Luvaas the impression that he was not overly concerned about criticizing MacArthur. The letters, however, give the opposite impression, and indicate that Eichelberger was clearly intent on cutting his former chief down to size. Robert Eichelberger to Jay Luvaas, 1 April 1957, 11 April 1957, 30 May 1958, 10 August 1959, 23 November 1959, 19 June 1961, and 14 August 1961, Eichelberger Papers; Jay Luvaas to Robert Eichelberger, 12 September 1958 and June 1959, Eichelberger Papers; Robert Eichelberger to Captain Thomas B. Doe, 5 September 1958, Eichelberger Papers; Robert Eichelberger to Samuel Milner, 21 March 1958, Eichelberger Papers; Robert Eichelberger to Carroll G. Bowen, 10 April 1958, Eichelberger Papers; telephone interview with Jay Luvaas, 29 December 1989, pages 1–2 of transcript.

84. Robert Eichelberger to General Clovis E. Byers, 6 September 1961, Eichelberger Papers; Robert Eichelberger to Jay Luvaas, 19 June 1961 and 14 August 1961, Eichelberger Papers; Robert Eichelberger to General Clifford Bluemel, 6 September 1961, Eichelberger Papers.

85. After this last meeting, Eichelberger reportedly stood at the window for a long time and watched Luvaas drive away. He then turned toward his wife and said, "That's the last bit of business that we have to deal with [regarding the book]—I'm not coming back from the hospital." Telephone interview with Luvaas, conducted at the request of the author on 29 December 1989, pages 1–2 of transcript.

86. Robert Eichelberger to General Clovis E. Byers, 22 September 1961, Eichelberger Papers; Robert Eichelberger to Charles K. Robinson (of the *Asheville Citizen Times*), 18 September 1961, Eichelberger Papers.

87. Demaree Bess to Emma Eichelberger, 26 September 1961, Eichelberger Papers; *New York Herald Tribune*, 27 Sept. 1961, 43 (copies of this obituary, along with other obituaries of Robert L. Eichelberger, are included in box 197 of the Eichelberger Papers).

88. *Urbana Daily Citizen*, "Gen. R. L. Eichelberger Dies," 26 September 1961, 1 (included in box 197 of Eichelberger Papers); *Urbana Daily Citizen*, "Memorial Rites Are Set at City Hall as Nation Mourns Gen. Eichelberger," 27 September 1961, 1, 7; *New York Herald Tribune*, 27 September 1961, 43; *New York Times*, 27 September 1961.

89. *Asheville Citizen Times*, "Eichelberger, War Hero, Dies," 27 September 1961, 1A-1B (box 197 of Eichelberger Papers).

90. As indicated in note 82, Luvaas did not feel obligated to write a book criticizing MacArthur. He was not convinced that Eichelberger desired revenge against his former chief (although, as this author has indicated, the evidence strongly suggests that this was precisely Eichelberger's motive). Even if Luvaas had been convinced that Eichelberger desired such a book, however, it is unlikely that he would have followed through on the project. Luvaas truly liked and respected Bob; he had no desire to see Eichelberger's reputation tarnished by a vindictive book published solely to satisfy a personal grudge. Telephone interview with Jay Luvaas, 29 December 1989, pages 1–2 of transcript.

Conclusion

Robert L. Eichelberger had a distinguished and prominent career. His accomplishments approached a level of greatness, although he was never accorded the honors that crowned the careers of the truly great officers, such as Patton, Bradley, and Eisenhower. Eichelberger died with the painful realization that, despite his many victories, he had never captured the attention of the historians and his peers; he had somehow been accorded less status than his more noteworthy counterparts in Europe.

This book suggests that Eichelberger's status as a near-great but not truly great officer can be explained by four key factors. One was Eichelberger's failure to achieve a special competence among his peers. As Morris Janowitz states in *The Professional Soldier*, officers "who wanted to rise [in rank and prestige] had to establish a reputation based on their skill or on their heroic qualities." For example, Patton fit the ideal prototype for the "heroic leader"; Eisenhower and Bradley were prime models of the "military manager." Eichelberger conformed to neither model, although Janowitz states that he "conformed more to the military manager image."[1]

Indeed, Eichelberger's image in the years preceding World War II was ambiguous and ill-defined. He was known more for his ability to get along with his superiors than for any recognized talent or skill. He was perceived as a "rising star" among his peers and classmates, but his rapid advancement was generally attributed to the generous support of his well-connected superiors, as opposed to any outstanding accomplishments or talents.

Eichelberger's reputation, or lack thereof, proved to be a major detriment from 1935 to the end of his military career. His rapid advancement through the ranks in the late 1930s attracted negative attention from his peers; they felt he was being unjustly advanced over possibly more qualified candidates. His transfer to the infantry in 1937 only intensified these suspicions. Many of his fellow officers were aware of Eichelberger's connections, and felt that he had gained a line position only because of his willingness to exploit his well-known contacts in Washington.

These perceptions hurt Eichelberger during his service in the Southwest Pacific. MacArthur was suspicious of his penchant for contacting prominent friends in the United States. Furthermore, members of MacArthur's staff (such as General Charles A. Willoughby) harbored doubts about his competence. They noted with disfavor the methods that he had used to gain promotions and advancement. Willoughby felt that Krueger, a self-made leader, was a better and more qualified officer. This feeling was certainly shared by Krueger himself. Although Eichelberger later disproved these sentiments by his excellent performances, lingering doubts about his abilities persisted; they continued to plague him even after the war. These doubts and suspicions, whether well founded or not, certainly tainted his achievements, and soiled to some extent the superb reputation that he had earned in the Pacific fighting.

Eichelberger's reputation also was damaged by factors that were beyond his control. There is no doubt that luck played a prominent role in his diminished stature, and contributed in some measure to his relative lack of publicity, awards, and recognition. In 1918, Eichelberger had the misfortune of being sent to Siberia, after having lost out at the last moment on a promising assignment in France. In World War II, he was denied (at the last hour) an exciting role in Europe (as a corps commander in Operation Torch); he was instead sent to the Southwest Pacific, a decidedly less glamorous and publicized theater of operations. Once there, he had the further misfortune of serving under General Douglas MacArthur, a brilliant but self-serving officer who intentionally degraded his subordinates and hogged the publicity for the successes in the Southwest Pacific.[2] For over six years, Eichelberger suffered under this selfish leader. He was repeatedly denied medals, decorations, and publicity for his achievements. Indeed, Eichelberger firmly believed that he had been dealt a fatal blow when he was sent to serve under MacArthur, and that this factor alone accounted for his reduced stature after World War II.

It is more likely, however, that other factors worked to diminish his status, and that the seeds of his demise were planted long before his service under MacArthur. For example, Eichelberger's reputation might have been more resilient if he had placed a higher value on learning and education. Numerous authors have conceded that education is a critical element in an officer's career; indeed, it may be the most important factor in developing a favorable reputation. As Dwight D. Eisenhower noted in *Crusade in Europe*, Omar Bradley's high standing was based in part on his "reputation as a sound, painstaking, and broadly educated soldier."[3]

Unlike Bradley, Eichelberger was not a "broadly educated" officer. He did not place a high priority on learning and academic study. Although Eichelberger did well in the military schools, he was motivated solely by a desire for promotion and advancement, not by any commitment to the values of education. For the vast majority of his career, he did very little to supplement his military schooling. He read almost nothing in the fields of history, literature, foreign languages, and political science. Eichelberger preferred to learn by observation and personal experience. This pattern became painfully obvious in Siberia and Japan, where he chose to travel around the countryside instead of undertaking an in-depth study of the culture and history of his environment.

His preference for experience over education damaged Eichelberger's reputation, particularly during the latter portions of his career. In the early-to-mid 1940s, he became known as a "can-do" type of officer who was an excellent administrator and a courageous leader of troops. Although he received numerous accolades for these qualities (from MacArthur and Marshall, among others), he received no special compliments for his intelligence or range of knowledge. None of his peers commended him for any superior aptitude or mental skill.

Eichelberger's lack of intellectual depth, however, was more of a personal handicap than a professional one. As one reporter remarked, "Bob's distaste" for education was combined with an extreme aversion to "boredom and introspection."[4] This combination of traits was an unfortunate one, for he had no incentive to explore his own personality. Eichelberger's lack of intellectual curiosity made him unwilling and unable to examine the depths of his own demeanor, and made him incapable of discovering the forces that ruled his inner being.

Indeed, Eichelberger's principal problem, and the greatest impediment to his growing reputation and stature, was the destructive nature of his own personality. For almost all of his career, he was ruled by sinister forces that had originated in his youth. Largely stemming from his relationship with his father, these forces included feelings of inferiority, a desperate need for attention and approval, and an overwhelming drive for the trappings of success, especially acknowledgment of his achievements and self-worth.

Eichelberger was able to control these forces as long as he served under the protective influence of men such as Malin Craig and William Connor, surrogate-father figures who were willing to provide the affection and attention that he needed. However, when he fell under the control of Douglas MacArthur, a cold and demanding figure (not unlike his own father), Eichelberger began to act erratically; he attempted to capture the approval that earlier had been denied him. When MacArthur refused (or was unable) to provide the requisite assurances and support, Eichelberger became engaged in a meaningless struggle with Krueger for the SCAP's affections (a struggle reminiscent of his childhood battle with his brothers for his father's approval). This struggle eventually became a consuming and compulsive one. It dominated Eichelberger's thoughts for the last 18 years of his life.

The toll exacted by these internal problems was devastating. Eichelberger came into conflict with Richard Sutherland. He lost the respect of Walter Krueger. As a means of winning the competition for MacArthur's affections,

Eichelberger placed his troops in needless jeopardy and suffered unnecessary losses (that is, on the outskirts of Manila). He exaggerated his own victories and, in a burst of grandiosity, shamelessly sought publicity and medals for his important, but relatively modest, contributions.

More importantly, Eichelberger's internal difficulties shattered his personal life. His preoccupation with publicity and his problems with MacArthur dominated his thoughts and emotions; these feelings made him dissatisfied with his own awards and achievements (which, by most standards, were quite impressive). He became increasingly bitter. He eventually focused all of his hate on MacArthur, the one man (besides his father) who had frustrated all of his attempts to gain love and attention.[5]

Unable to tame these unresolved conflicts, Eichelberger spent the last years of his life with unhappy memories, inner turmoil, and angry vendettas. His retirement years certainly lacked any mark of greatness, for he felt no contentment with his importance or place in history. Instead, he felt only deep distress. He bore the wounds of a man suffering from a fatally flawed personality. If a man's golden years are any indicator of his true merit, Eichelberger's behavior certainly removed him from the list of the truly great, and marked him as a figure worthy more of pity than emulation.

NOTES

1. Morris Janowitz, *The Professional Soldier: A Social and Political Portrait* (New York: Free Press, 1971), 161.

2. Eichelberger felt that MacArthur's vanity would have required him to overshadow any subordinate. He once stated that "a Patton serving under MacArthur would have been the 'Unknown Soldier.'" Eichelberger Dictations, no title, 12 September 1955, 4 (page 251 of dictation notebook).

3. Janowitz, *The Professional Soldier*, 144-45, 170-71; Dwight D. Eisenhower, *Crusade in Europe* (Garden City, N.Y.: Doubleday and Company, 1948), 215.

4. Associated Press dispatch, "Eighth Army Boss Looks Beyond Stars on Shoulder to G.I. Joe" (by Hal Boyle), 29 October 1945, included in box 190 of Eichelberger Papers.

5. Eichelberger believed that his life would have been much more satisfying if he had been allowed to serve in Europe under Eisenhower. This author respectfully disagrees. Eichelberger demanded an enormous amount of attention and approval. It is not likely that any wartime commander could have completely satisfied him (particularly if Eichelberger were forced to compete for assignments with the equally vainglorious George S. Patton).

SOURCES

The central focus of this study is the life and career of Robert L. Eichelberger. As noted in the Introduction, there are few secondary sources on this topic. In fact, most of the secondary works on World War II and the occupation of Japan omit any discussion of Eichelberger. Furthermore, many of the autobiographies (and biographies) of prominent military leaders fail to include any reference to the Eighth Army commander. This study, therefore, has been forced to rely heavily on manuscript sources, primarily the personal papers of Robert Eichelberger and Douglas MacArthur.

MANUSCRIPTS AND OTHER UNPUBLISHED SOURCE MATERIALS

The unpublished materials used in the preparation of this study were drawn from a number of collections, including the Robert L. Eichelberger Papers, the Douglas MacArthur Memorial Archives, the Dwight D. Eisenhower Papers, the George C. Marshall Papers, the Clovis E. Byers Papers, the General Henry H. Arnold Papers, the Edwin M. Watson Papers, and the Mark W. Clark Papers. Materials used from each of these collections are described in detail below.

Robert L. Eichelberger Papers (William R. Perkins Library, Duke University, Durham, North Carolina)

The Robert L. Eichelberger Papers constitute the prime source for this study. Consisting of 251 boxes, this collection includes a wide variety of valuable materials. Boxes 1–45 include Eichelberger's letters, both personal and official. Boxes 46–50 contain notebooks of dictations (in shorthand) on assorted subjects.

Boxes 51 and 52 include certificates of distinction and personal military service records. Boxes 53–158 consist of army intelligence summaries, military reports, and special studies on World War II, the Siberian expedition, and the occupation of Japan. Maps, speeches, and personal bills are included in boxes 159–68. Boxes 169–87 contain notebooks of typed dictations, press releases, and personal diaries. Finally, boxes 188–251 contain newspaper clippings, personal scrapbooks and albums, memorabilia of various types, and pictures of Eichelberger from his days at West Point to his retirement.

The most valuable of these materials are the letters (boxes 1–45). For most of his career, Eichelberger kept up a lively correspondence with his friends and colleagues. During World War II, he wrote to his wife every day. He fully intended that these letters be kept as an official record of his services. As early as 1941, he informed his wife that his career would be valuable to historians. and that these letters would serve as the primary source of his biography.

While somewhat self-serving, these letters form a complete record of Eichelberger's activities from 1942 until his death. They include what he thought, what he ate, and the nature of his relationships with his wife and peers. Frankly written, they reflect his up-front approach in regard to his own thoughts and frustrations. A scrupulous "saver," Eichelberger also retained most of the correspondence that he received during his years in the military. This included letters from his friends, family, military superiors, and peers, plus a majority of the official correspondence that passed his desk during his assignments abroad.

This correspondence, while extremely valuable, has several shortcomings. Only three boxes of letters exist for the period 1905–41. Furthermore, most of the letters that Miss Em wrote her husband are not included in the collection. Many were lost during World War II; those that were saved were destroyed at Miss Em's request shortly after Eichelberger's papers were donated to Duke University.

Next in importance are the dictations and memorandums. These are included in boxes 169–78. Eichelberger dictated most of these during his retirement, although some were written during his service under MacArthur in World War II and in Japan. The dictations include Eichelberger's most severe criticisms of MacArthur, Krueger, and Sutherland. Most of the comments are covered in the letters; the dictations and memorandums, however, provide short, concise summaries of Eichelberger's opinions. For the historian with only limited time to review the collection, these materials are probably the most valuable source.

The dictations are organized in bound notebooks. The notebooks are not titled. Each dictation page has two numbers—one number representing its order in the dictation, and another number representing its order in the dictation notebook (i.e., page 4 of the dictation "Eichelberger in Japan," but page 174 of the dictation notebook). For purposes of clarity, I have included both numbers in the notes.

Third in importance are the military reports on the Siberian expedition, on World War II, and on the occupation of Japan (boxes 53–133). These include Eighth Army reports, intelligence reports, special studies, reports by the commanding general of the Eighth Army, terrain studies, and operations instructions. These are valuable in describing the military activities of the I Corps and the Eighth Army at Buna, Hollandia, Biak, and Manila, and in the southern Philippines. Poorly written but detailed, these sources are particularly useful in fleshing out the activities of individual combat units. The most important are the "Report of the Commanding General, Buna Forces—History of the Buna Campaign," and "Report of the Commanding General, Eighth Army, on the Nasugbu and Bataan Operations."

Other materials in the collection are of less interest. His diaries are disappointing; they include only short references to his activities. The letters are far more useful in providing a daily log of events and his personal observations. The pictures, scrapbooks, albums, and memorabilia are entertaining, but provide little additional information. The speeches and press releases (boxes 163–68, 186–98) are an important source; they provide a comprehensive collection of Eichelberger's public statements.

Papers of Douglas MacArthur (MacArthur Memorial Library and Archives, Norfolk, Virginia)

Materials relating to Eichelberger are scattered throughout the MacArthur Papers. Most of the materials are concentrated in Record Group 3 (personal correspondence), and Record Group 4 (War Department correspondence). Also of interest are Record Group 23 (papers and interviews of General Charles Willoughby) and Record Group 30 (papers of Lieutenant General Richard Sutherland).

Most of the correspondence is official. MacArthur reveals almost nothing of his personal feelings toward Eichelberger in his papers. The most pertinent sources are the telegrams that MacArthur and George Marshall sent to each other; these provide some clues as to the nature of the MacArthur-Eichelberger relationship.

Most of Eichelberger's letters to MacArthur are included in Record Group 3. MacArthur rarely, if ever, responded. These letters give an accurate description of Eichelberger's sentiments toward his chief, but provide no clue about MacArthur's feelings.

Dwight D. Eisenhower Papers (Dwight D. Eisenhower Library, Abilene, Kansas)

Most of the Eisenhower correspondence concerning Eichelberger is found in box 38 of the "Pre-Presidential Papers." This includes the letters that Eichelberger wrote to Eisenhower from 1945 to 1952. During this period, the two men exchanged chatty letters about conditions in Japan and about the American political situation. This correspondence is particularly valuable in describing the problems of the Eighth Army in occupied Japan.

George C. Marshall Papers (George C. Marshall Research Library, Lexington, Virginia)

The bulk of the correspondence between Marshall and Eichelberger is included in box 66 (folder 41) of the "Personal Correspondence" file. Eichelberger wrote to Marshall intermittently from 1939 until the end of the war. Marshall rarely replied. The most informative letters are the ones Eichelberger wrote in the early 1940s, in which he attempted to persuade Marshall to give him a field command.

Clovis E. Byers Papers (Hoover Institution on War, Revolution and Peace, Archives Department, Stanford University, Stanford, California)

The most relevant portions of the Byers Papers are the diaries (box 30). These describe the Eighth Army staff's feelings toward MacArthur and General Walter Krueger. Surprisingly, the Byers Papers include little information about Eichelberger. Although the two men were close friends and wrote often, few of their letters to each other are included in this collection.

General Henry H. Arnold Papers (Library of Congress, Washington, D.C.)

The most pertinent information from Arnold's papers is found in box 12 containing "General Correspondence, 1939–1946." Arnold and Eichelberger had a lively correspondence in 1941 concerning the establishment of flight training at West Point. The two men also exchanged letters about the West Point football program.

Edwin M. Watson Papers (Alderman Library, University of Virginia, Charlottesville)

Most of the relevant information is found in boxes 4, 5, 7, 9, and 27. These are divided into memorandums, requests, reminders, and personal correspondence. Most of the information dealing with Eichelberger refers to the establishment of the football program at West Point. Other letters refer to Watson's efforts to get Eichelberger a field command in 1942.

Mark W. Clark Papers (The Citadel, Archives-Museum, Charleston, South Carolina)

There are only a handful of pertinent letters in this collection. The only one of major interest is a commendation that Eichelberger sent to Clark in May 1940.

Other sources of interest include the efficiency records of Robert L. Eichelberger. These are found at the National Personnel Records Center in St. Louis. Brief but interesting, these records include evaluations of Eichelberger's character, and numerical ratings of his personal attributes (such as initiative). These were useful in evaluating Eichelberger's career prior to World War II, particularly his performance as a field commander in the early 1940's.

Personal interviews also were helpful. These included interviews with Robert White II, a member of the I Corps staff, and with Jay Luvaas, a historian. Both men knew General Eichelberger well, and were able to provide a wealth of information. In particular, they provided valuable evidence about Eichelberger's retirement years.

PUBLISHED MATERIALS

Published materials utilized in this study fall into two groups—primary source materials, such as autobiographies, and secondary materials.

Published Primary Sources

Two primary sources deserve special note. These are Robert Eichelberger, *Our Jungle Road to Tokyo* (New York: Viking Press, 1950), and Jay Luvaas, *Dear Miss Em: General Eichelberger's War in the Pacific, 1942-1945* (Westport, Conn.: Greenwood Press, 1972). Eichelberger's book is not an autobiography. It covers only his experiences in the Pacific during World War II. While somewhat self-complimentary, it provides an honest and straightforward account of his impressions during the Pacific War. Most of the comments concerning MacArthur, however, are cryptic; Eichelberger was wary of criticizing his former chief, and is very diplomatic in his treatment of MacArthur. The book is useful as a beginner's tool in studying Eichelberger's wartime experiences, although it is sorely lacking in historical background.

Dear Miss Em is an edited compilation of Eichelberger's letters during World War II. The majority of these letters were written to Miss Em, Eichelberger's wife. Luvaas organizes the letters chronologically, and makes intermittent comments and observations in each chapter. The book is a valuable introduction to the Eichelberger Papers, although it fails to include some of the most controversial correspondence.

There are few other important primary sources. Dwight D. Eisenhower's *Crusade in Europe* (Garden City, N.Y.: Doubleday and Company, 1949) and *At Ease: Stories I Tell to Friends* (Garden City, N.Y.: Doubleday and Company, 1967) are significant only insofar as their discussions completely neglect Eichelberger. Similarly, George S. Patton, *War As I Knew It* (Boston: Houghton-Mifflin Company, 1947) and Omar N. Bradley, *A Soldier's Story* (New York: Henry Holt, 1951) fail to include any discussion of the I Corps and Eighth Army commander. Surprisingly, Douglas MacArthur's *Reminiscences* (New York: McGraw-Hill, 1964) makes only sparse mention of his chief subordinate. MacArthur gives Eichelberger only cursory attention in the discussion of the Pacific campaigns, and fails to mention his contributions at Buna, Hollandia, and Biak. This study also provides almost no information concerning the MacArthur-Eichelberger relationship.

More helpful are George C. Kenney, *General Kenney Reports* (New York: Duell, Sloan, Pearce, 1949), and General Walter Krueger, *From Down Under to Nippon: The Story of Sixth Army in World War II* (Washington, D.C.: Combat Forces Press, 1953). Both include some discussion of Eichelberger's contributions in the Pacific. Kenney's book makes favorable comments about Eichelberger's role in the Buna campaign. Krueger's book is less favorable, but includes a detailed description of the I Corps' activities during the Hollandia and Biak operations. Krueger's study fails to include any personal observations about other officers, and is disappointing in its failure to shed more light on the Krueger-Eichelberger conflict.

The best source on the Krueger-Eichelberger controversy is Admiral Daniel E. Barbey's *MacArthur's Amphibious Navy* (Annapolis, Md.: U.S. Naval Institute, 1969). As the naval officer for most of the I Corps operations, Barbey had the opportunity to witness firsthand the relations between Eichelberger and his superiors. In his book, he offers insightful observations concerning Eichelberger's personality, the feud with Krueger, and the problems with MacArthur following the Buna campaign. Barbey's book is one of the few sources to offer frank comments on these issues.

Also of interest are Shigeru Yoshida, *The Yoshida Memoirs—The Story of Japan in Crisis* (Boston: Houghton Mifflin Company, 1962), and William S. Graves, *America's Siberian Adventure, 1918-1920* (Salem, N.H.: Ayer Publishing Company, 1931). Yoshida was the prime minister of Japan in 1946-47 and 1949-55. He worked closely with Eichelberger during the occupation. In his memoirs, he analyzes the differences in style between Eichelberger and MacArthur, and comments favorably on Eichelberger's contributions in post-war Japan. Graves's book is a personal history of the Siberian expedition. As commander of the American contingent, Graves was keenly aware of Eichelberger's activities. He makes several brief comments about the contributions of his young subordinate. The book, however, inadequately describes the role of the American officers, and is more of an attempt to explain Graves's own participation in this controversial mission.

Published Secondary Sources

Two secondary sources deserve special mention. One is D. Clayton James, *The Years of MacArthur* (Boston: Houghton Mifflin Company, 1975). This three-volume work is the best biography of MacArthur. James details the Pacific campaigns, MacArthur's career, and his relationship with his subordinates. He does not include a lengthy discussion of the MacArthur-Eichelberger conflict, but does mention briefly some of the problems inherent in their relationship. In a half-dozen scattered pages, he offers cogent reasons for Eichelberger's bitterness toward his chief. James makes liberal use of the Eichelberger Papers, and includes quotes from the Eighth Army commander in most chapters. This study is an invaluable source, and a must-see for any author interested in MacArthur's subordinates.

Also of importance is John F. Shortal, *Forged By Fire: Robert L. Eichelberger and the Pacific War* (Columbia: University of South Carolina Press, 1987). Originally a Temple University dissertation, Shortal's book describes Eichelberger's Pacific campaigns during the Second World War. It is not a biography. Shortal makes only limited use of the Eichelberger Papers, and glosses over much of the material that is critical of Eichelberger's actions in the Southwest Pacific. Flattering and uncritical, this study is more concerned with resurrecting Eichelberger's reputation than presenting an objective appraisal of his career (as the author indicates in the introduction). Although of limited value, it presents a useful analysis of Eichelberger's training methods with the I Corps and the Eighth Army.

The other secondary sources can be divided by subject. There are no outstanding sources on the Siberian Expedition. Most have a political agenda, and are concerned more with condemning the American involvement than providing a factual analysis. These include Betty M. Unterberger, *American Intervention in* the *Russian Civil War* (Lexington, Mass.: D.C. Heath and Company, 1969); Ernest M. Halliday, *The Ignorant Armies* (New York: Harper and Brothers, 1960); Arthur Bullard, *The Russian Pendulum* (New York: Macmillan, 1919); John Albert White, *The Siberian Intervention* (Princeton, N.J.: Princeton University Press, 1950); Paul Dotsenko, *The Struggle for a Democracy in Siberia, 1917-1920* (Stanford, Calif.: Hoover Institution Press, 1983); Carl W. Ackerman, *Trailing the Bolsheviki* (New York: Charles Scribner's Sons, 1919); Richard Goldhurst, *The Midnight War: The American Intervention in Russia, 1918-1920* (New York: McGraw-Hill Book Company, 1978); and George Kennan, *Russian and the West under Lenin and Stalin* (Boston: Little, Brown, 1960). Many of these studies are based on personal observations, and lean heavily toward the conclusion that American participation in Siberia was wrong and immoral.

Other sources, although equally argumentative, also provide valuable background information. Russell E. Snow, *The Bolsheviks in Siberia, 1917-1918* (London: Associated University Presses, 1977), and Canfield F. Smith, *The Bolsheviks in Siberia, 1917-1918* (Seattle: University of Washington Press, 1975) provide excellent summaries of the last months of the expedition. Michael Jabard Carley, *Revolution and Intervention: The French Government and the Russian Civil War* (Montreal: McGill-Queen's University Press, 1983) explains in detail the participation of the European governments in Russia. Another source of interest is Sylvian G. Kindall, *American Soldiers in Siberia* (New York: Richard R. Smith Company, 1945), which explores the dilemmas confronting General Graves as commander of the American forces.

Only a few sources pertaining to the interwar years were valuable. Russell F. Weigley, *Towards an American Army: Military Thought from Washington to Marshall* (New York: Columbia University Press, 1962) provides an excellent account of the changes in the U.S. Army following World War I. Harry P. Ball, *Of Responsible Command: A History of the U.S. Army War College* (Carlisle Barracks, Penn.: Alumni Association of the United States Army War College, 1984) explores the changes in leadership and curriculum in the Army War College during the 1920s and 1930s. Also of interest is Forrest C. Pogue, *George C. Marshall: Organizer of Victory* (New York: Viking Press, 1966), which provides valuable information about the army's preparation for war immediately prior to World War II.

There are a number of important sources on the Pacific operations during the Second World War. The best study of the Buna campaign is Samuel Milner's *Victory in Papua* (Washington, D.C.: Office of the Chief of Military History, Department of the Army, 1957). Well written and comprehensive, this study discusses the fighting done by individual units, the suffering and privations of the participants, and MacArthur's role in each of the tactical decisions. Milner describes Eichelberger's role in the campaign, particularly his participation in the decision to relieve General Harding. Milner's study covers Buna from every angle, and is the only book that addresses the controversies surrounding this operation.

Another important source is Lida Mayo, *Bloody Buna* (Garden City, N.Y.: Doubleday and Company, 1974). While less comprehensive than *Victory In Papua*, Mayo's book provides detailed information about the hardships facing the American troops. It also provides a good summary of Eichelberger's activities in Papua.

Other sources worthy of special mention are Leslie Anders, *Gentle Knight: The Life and Times of Major General Edwin Forrest Harding* (Kent, Ohio: Kent State University Press, 1985) and Major General Courtney Whitney, *MacArthur: His Rendezvous with History* (Westport, Conn.: Greenwood Press, 1977). Anders's excellent biography of Harding includes a detailed account of the Buna campaign. Anders concludes that Harding was treated unfairly in Papua, and that Eichelberger performed poorly (or at least no better than Harding) at Buna. Well documented, this study challenges Eichelberger's interpretation of events, and provides interesting new insights into the Buna fighting.

Whitney's biography of MacArthur is flattering and self-serving, but provides excellent coverage of the operations in Papua. It is particularly useful in explaining MacArthur's strategy during the early fighting in New Guinea. Whitney covers in some detail the events in Port Moresby, including Eichelberger's arrival at GHQ and MacArthur's orders: "Take Buna or don't come back alive."

Other sources are noteworthy only because they completely neglect the Buna operation. These include Martin Gilbert, *The Second World War: A Complete History* (New York: Henry Holt and Company, 1989); Peter Calvocoressi and Guy Wint, *Total War: The Story of World War II* (New York: Pantheon Books, 1972); and John Keegan, *The Second World War* (New York: Viking Press, 1989). Major-General S. Woodburn Kirby's *The War Against Japan: India's Most Dangerous Hour* (London: Her Majesty's Stationery Office, 1958) discusses Buna in two brief pages, but fails to even mention Eichelberger's name.

The best source on the Hollandia operation is Robert Ross Smith, *The Approach to the Philippines* (Washington, D.C.: Office of the Chief of Military History, Department of the Army, 1953). Smith's study is comprehensive, and includes an impressive discussion of the events leading up to this operation. It covers particularly well the supply problems of the I Corps after the landing.

Also of interest is John Costello, *The Pacific War* (New York: Rawson, Wade, 1981). Well researched, this general history offers excellent summaries of the Southwest Pacific campaigns. It is surprisingly complete. Costello covers many of the commanders and landings that have been omitted by other authors. This book provides a brief but useful history of Hollandia, particularly MacArthur's role in the operation.

There are few adequate studies of the Biak landing. The best is Harold Riegelman's *Caves of Biak: An American Officer's Experiences in the Southwest Pacific* (New York: Dial Press, 1955). This study is subjective and poorly documented, but is one of the few books totally devoted to Biak. Riegelman adequately explains the events leading up to the operation, General Fuller's relief, and Eichelberger's arrival. The dispositions of the Japanese troops and the difficulties of the American forces are amply discussed.

Also of importance is Ronald Spector, *Eagle Against the Sun: The American War with Japan* (New York: Free Press, 1985). Perhaps the best single volume of the Pacific war, this study is splendidly written and well researched. Spector provides a useful summary of the Biak campaign, and is the only author to criticize MacArthur for his handling of the operation.

There are several good sources on the Leyte campaign. The most comprehensive are M. Hamlin Cannon, *Leyte: The Return to the Philippines* (Washington, D.C.: Office of the Chief of Military History, Department of the Army, 1954) and Samuel Eliot Morison, *Leyte: June 1944-January 1945* (Boston: Little, Brown, 1958). Both provide excellent accounts of the strategic planning, the tactical movements of the troops, and actions of the leading American combat commanders. The Eighth Army's mop-up is covered in some detail. Both are particularly good in describing the dispositions of the American and Japanese units.

Robert Ross Smith's *Triumph in the Philippines* (Washington, D.C.: Office of the Chief of Military History, Department of the Army, 1963) is the leading authority on the Luzon operation. This provides a superb summary of the Nasugbu landing and of the Eighth Army's race for Manila. Detailed and carefully written, Smith's study covers the preliminary planning for the landing, a day-by-day account of the fighting, the dispute surrounding Eichelberger's decision to attack Manila, and the problems of the American units at each stage of the operation. Smith combines these elements masterfully, and tells his story in a compelling fashion.

Other valuable sources on the Luzon and Leyte campaigns have already been cited, including Douglas MacArthur's *Reminiscences*, Walter Krueger's *From Down Under to Nippon*, Courtney Whitney's *MacArthur*, John Costello's *Pacific War*, and Ronald Spector's *Eagle Against the Sun*.

The number of useful sources on the southern Philippines is disappointing; this topic has received much less attention than it deserves. The best source is, once again, Smith's *Triumph in the Philippines*. This should be read in conjunction with Samuel Eliot Morison, *The Liberation of the Philippines: Luzon, Mindanao, the Visayas, 1944-1945* (Boston: Little, Brown, 1975). Both provide adequate coverage of the Eighth Army's landings on Panay, Negros, Cebu, Palawan, and Mindanao. Smith's study is somewhat better in describing Eichelberger's role in these operations, while Morison provides a more detailed analysis of the fighting on each island. Both are excellent in describing the strategic planning at GHQ and at Eighth Army headquarters.

Another source of importance is William Manchester's *American Caesar: Douglas MacArthur 1880-1964* (Boston: Little, Brown, 1978). While not critical of MacArthur, Manchester's book provides an excellent overview of the operations in the southern Philippines. It is particularly helpful in describing MacArthur's strategy for the landings south of Leyte.

The occupation of Japan has received increased attention in recent years. Much of the current literature, however, is biased. For example, some studies ignore the problems in Japan, and argue that the occupation was an unqualified success. These include Theodore Cohen, *Remaking Japan: The American Occupation as New Deal* (New York: Free Press, 1987); Justin Williams Jr., *Japan's Political Revolution under MacArthur* (Athens: University of Georgia Press, 1979); and John K. Emmerson, *Arms, Yen & Power: The Japanese Dilemma* (New York: Dunellen Publishing Company, 1971). Others focus exclusively on the negative aspects, and argue that the occupation was a dismal failure. These include Howard B. Schonberger, *Aftermath of War: Americans and the Remaking of Japan, 1945-1952* (Kent, Ohio: Kent State University Press, 1989); Howard S. Quigley and John E. Turner, *The New Japan: Government and Politics* (Westport, Conn.: Greenwood Press, 1956); and Robert A. Fearey, *The Occupation of Japan, Second Phase: 1948-1950* (New York: Macmillan, 1950). Both kinds of studies fail to provide balanced analyses, and sacrifice detail in favor of subjective interpretations.

The most balanced sources on the occupation are Kazuo Kawai, *Japan's American Interlude* (Chicago: University of Chicago Press, 1960), and Edwin O. Reischauer, *The Pacific Rivals: A Japanese View of Japanese-American Relations* (New York: John Weatherhill, 1972). Although somewhat dated, both studies provide concise but detailed information concerning the occupation reforms and the reaction of the Japanese people. Equally important are John Curtis Perry, *Beneath the Eagle's Wings: Americans in Occupied Japan* (New York: Dodd, Mead, 1980), and Russell Brines, *With MacArthur in Japan: A Personal History of the Occupation* (New York: W. W. Norton, 1965). These provide excellent summaries of Eichelberger's contributions from 1945 to 1948. Also of value, mostly as general reference materials, are Edwin M. Martin, *The Allied Occupation of Japan* (Westport, Conn.: Greenwood Press, 1948); Robert Wolfe, *Americans as Proconsuls: U.S. Military Government in Germany and Japan* (Edwardsville: Southern Illinois University Press, 1984); John K. Emmerson and Harrison M. Holland, *The Eagle and the Rising Sun: America and Japan in the Twentieth Century* (New York: Addison-Wesley Publishing Company, 1988); Hans H. Baerwald, *The Purge of Japanese Leaders under the Occupation* (Berkeley: University of California Press, 1959); Meirion and Susie Harries, *Sheathing the Sword: The Demilitarization of Japan* (New York: Macmillan, 1987); Robert E. Ward, *Democratizing Japan: The Allied Occupation* (Honolulu: University of Hawaii Press, 1987); and Michael Schaller, *The American Occupation of Japan* (Oxford, England: Oxford University Press, 1985).

There are several fine sources on the Korean War. The best is David Rees, *Korea: The Limited War* (New York: St. Martin's Press, 1964). Although somewhat dated, Rees's book provides the best summary of the conflict's military, political, and diplomatic components. Equally important are Joseph C. Goulden, *Korea: The Untold Story of the War* (New York: Times Books, 1982), and Max Hastings, *The Korean War* (New York: Simon and Schuster, 1987). These studies provide new information on the police action, and question MacArthur's competence as commander of the UN forces. General Matthew B. Ridgway, *The Korean War: How We Met the Challenge* (Garden City, N.Y.: Doubleday, 1967), and General Mark W. Clark, *From the Danube to the Yalu* (New York: Harper and Brothers, 1954) are valuable sources; both authors played pivotal roles in Korea, and provide an insider's perspective on the conflict. Also of interest are Richard Whelan, *Drawing the Line: The Korean War, 1950-1953* (Boston: Little, Brown, 1990), and Roy E. Appleman, *Disaster in Korea: The Chinese Confront MacArthur* (College Station: Texas A&M University Press, 1989). These represent a new generation of authors who are highly critical of MacArthur's actions after Inchon. Important background sources include John W. Spanier, *The Truman-MacArthur Controversy and the Korean War* (Cambridge, Mass.: Harvard University Press, 1959); Callum A. MacDonald, *Korea: The War Before Vietnam* (New York: Free Press, 1986); Burton I. Kaufman, *The Korean War: Challenges in Crisis, Credibility, and Command* (Philadelphia: Temple University Press, 1986); James L. Stokesbury, *A Short History of the Korean War* (New York: William Morrow and Company, 1988); and Bevin Alexander, *Korea: The First War We Lost* (New York: Hippocrene Books, 1986).

Morris Janowitz's *The Professional Soldier: A Social and Political Portrait* (Glencoe, Ill.: Free Press, 1960) is an excellent analysis of the political, social, and ideological roots of American military leaders. It provides valuable insights into the background and training of the elite leaders of the World War II generation.

Magazines, Journals, and Newspapers

There were a handful of helpful magazines and journals used for this study. These include the *Saturday Evening Post*, *Newsweek*, the *Army and Navy Journal*, *Collier's*, *Time*, *Life*, *Reader's Digest*, and *Salute*. *Newsweek* and the *Saturday Evening Post* provided invaluable information on Eichelberger's retirement years.

The newspapers consulted for this study included the following—the *New York Times*, *New York Herald Tribune*, *Philadelphia Inquirer*, *Chicago Tribune*, *Columbus* (Ohio) *Dispatch*, *Urbana Daily Citizen*, *Asheville Citizen Times*, *Winston-Salem Journal and Sentinel*, *Nippon Times*, and *The Mainichi*. The *New York Times* and *Chicago Tribune* are the best sources overall, while the *Nippon Times* and *The Mainichi* provide the most complete information on Eichelberger's role in the occupation. Many of these newspaper articles are included in boxes 188–205 of the Eichelberger Papers.

INDEX

Adjutant General's Corps (AGC), 31–32, 34, 39
Akin, Spencer (General), 104
Algase, Gertrude, 161
Allied Council for Japan, 163n
Almond, Ned (General), 195n
American Council for Japan, 181
American Expeditionary Force (Siberia, 1918–20), 15–25; *see* Eichelberger, Robert L., experiences in Siberia
Anderson, Roy, 30
Anti–Comintern Pact, 39
Arlington National Cemetery, 189
Armour, Barney, 174
Army War College, 31–33, 46
Arnold, Henry "Hap" (General), 47
Arnold, William H. (General), 134
Asheville, North Carolina, 178–80, 189
Atomic Bomb Casualty Commission, 168n

Bacolod (Negros, Philippines), 134
Baker, Newton D. (U.S. Secretary of War), 16, 19
Barbey, Daniel E. (Admiral), 83, 102
Barnes, Julian F. (General), 53
Berkey, Russell (Rear Admiral), 159
Bernhardt, Sarah, 88
Biak Island, 96, 98, 99, 100–104, 111, 180
Blaik, Earl "Red," 47–48, 55n, 186
Blakeley, H. W., 186
Blamey, Thomas A. (General–Australia), 52–53
Bolsheviks, 15–18, 21–22, 24, 169n
Bowen, Frank, Jr. (General), 196n
Bradley, Omar (General), ix, 137, 151, 177, 205
Breckenridge, E. L. (Captain), 9
Brest–Litovsk, Treaty of, 15
Brett, George H. (General), 53
Brook, Alan (Field Marshall), 51
Brown, Philip E. (General), 67
Brush, Rapp (General), 134, 140, 146n, 147n
Buna, New Guinea, 57–75, 81, 83, 88, 91, 95, 99, 111, 137, 176, 179, 185–87
Burnett, Frank (General), 43
Byers, Clovis (General), 74, 98, 102, 140, 160, 186, 189, 194n

Calvocoressi, Peter, x, 64
Camp Columbia (Australia), 83
Camp E. S. Otis (Panama), 8
Camp Pike (Arkansas), 8
Cannon, H. Hamlin, 123
Cebu City (Cebu, Philippines), 135, 144n

Central Intelligence Agency (CIA), 174
Chamberlin, Stephen (General), 88, 110, 112, 115–17, 141
Churchill, Winston (Prime Minister-Great Britain), 49–52
Clark, Mark (General), 45, 48–50; Eichelberger compares self to, 151
Clark Getts, Inc., 175–178
Clarke, Elaine, 149
Cohen, Theodore, 157
Collins, J. Lawton (General), 85
Collins, James (Sergeant), 8, 10
Command and General Staff School (Fort Leavenworth), 30–34, 46, 88
Connor, William D. (General), 33–34, 37–38, 43, 207
Coronet, Operation (Proposed invasion of Japan), 141
Costello, John, 72, 102, 122
Craig, Malin (General), 36–38, 43–44, 53, 57, 82, 84, 88, 207

Davao City (Mindanao, Philippines), 135–37, 145n
Davis, Robert C. (General), 31–33
Devers, Jacob (General), 161
Diller, L. A. (General), 141
Doe, Jens (General), 100–101, 133
Draper, William H. (Undersecretary of Army), 160
Drum, Hugh (General), 34
Duke University (Durham, N.C.), x, 177, 188, 194n, 201n

Eichelberger, Emma (mother), 1–4
Eichelberger, Emma (wife), 12, 44, 81, 84, 88–89, 137, 140, 146–47n, 180, 189
Eichelberger, Frank, 2, 4, 193–94n
Eichelberger, Fred, 2, 4
Eichelberger, George Maley, 1–5, 7
Eichelberger, George, Jr., 2–4, 193–94n
Eichelberger, Robert L.;
childhood of, 1–3; relations with father, 1–5; entrance into West Point, 5; experience as a cadet, 7–8; promotion to first lieutenant, 8; to captain, 8; to major (temporary), 21; to lieutenant colonel (temporary), 21; to lieutenant colonel (permanent), 34; to full colonel, 44; to brigadier general, 45; to major general (temporary), 49; to lieutenant general (temporary), 57; to major general (permanent), 169n; receives fourth star, 194n; assignments immediately after graduation from West Point, 8–12; considers flying school, 12; marriage, 12; experiences in Siberia, 15–25; decorations and medals, 22, 69, 74–75, 87, 102, 123, 141, 147n, 159, 171–72n, 208; desire for publicity, 22, 69–71, 73–74, 87, 90, 120–23, 132, 137, 141–42, 150–51, 208; conflicts with P. O. Robinson, 22–23; early impressions of Japanese military, 24; as intelligence officer in Manila, 29; ordered to China as intelligence officer, 29–30; failure to make "General Staff eligible list," 30; participation in Washington Disarmament Conference (1921–22), 30–31; transfers to Adjutant General's Corps (AGC), 31–32; attends Command and General Staff School, 32; attends Army War College, 33; appointed secretary to the War Department General Staff, 34–39; impressions of Douglas MacArthur as Chief of Staff, 35–36; relations with General Malin Craig (Chief of Staff), 36; efficiency reports, 38, 104; techniques of dealing with superiors, 37–39; transfers to infantry, 42–43, 205–206; commands 30th Infantry Regiment, 43–45; as Superintendent of West Point, 46–

49; preoccupation with football, 47–48; assumes command of 77th Division (1942), 49–51; assumes command of I Corps, 50; conducts corps demonstration for Winston Churchill, 49–52; sent to Southwest Pacific as corps commander under Douglas MacArthur, 52–53; Buna campaign, 57–63; relieves General Harding at Buna, 59–60; Sanananda campaign, 63–64; differences with General E. Harding, 65–67, 176, 180–81, 194n; antagonism towards General Richard Sutherland, 67–68, 85–86,149–50, 187–88; conflicts with MacArthur after Buna, 68–75, 84–87; placed under General Walter Krueger's command, 81; conflicts with Krueger, 81–84, 91, 97–100, 103–104, 109–14, 123–24, 139–40, 147n, 150, 159, 187–88, 200n; applies for transfer to European theater, 84–85; alters behavior after Buna operation, 88–90; Hollandia operation, 95–97; Biak operation, 98–102; formation of Eighth Army, 103; competes with Krueger for operations in Philippines, 114–22; Leyte operation, 114; Nasugbu landing, 115–18; suffers unnecessary casualties, 121, 207–208; operations in southern Philippines, 131–37; desire to please MacArthur, 137–39, 150; antagonism towards MacArthur, 139–42, 149, 158–62, 176, 181–90; hopes to succeed MacArthur as SCAP, 160; occupation of Japan, 151–62; duties in Japan, 151–57; working relationship with MacArthur, 157–59; returns to U.S., 161–62; decides to write book on MacArthur and SW Pacific, 160–61; final meeting with MacArthur, 161–62; retires from U.S. Army, 173; retirement years, 173–90, 208; literary pursuits, 175–78, 187–90, 200n; charitable work, 178–79, 193n; political activities, 179, 184; adjustment to civilian life, 179–80; obsession with MacArthur and WW II, 184–90, 208; death and funeral, 189–90

Eichelberger, Sue, 2, 4

Eighth Army, 103–104, 109–24, 131–41, 145–47n, 149–55, 157, 160–61, 163–64n, 167n, 169n, 171n, 175–76, 178, 181, 183, 187, 195n, 198n

Eisenhower, Dwight D., ix, xi(n), 32, 34, 37, 38, 45, 50–51, 67, 70–71, 85–87, 124, 159–61, 168n, 184, 188, 205, 208n; Eichelberger compares self to, 137, 151

Far Eastern Commission, 163n, 167n
Farloy, James A., 167n
Fearey, Robert, 157
Fenton, Chauncey (Colonel), 142
Forrestal, James V. (Secretary of Navy), 167n, 174
Fort Benjamin Harrison (Indiana), 8
Fort Benning, 43–44, 51
Fort Dix, 30
Fort Douglas (Utah), 8
Fort Jackson (S.C.), 49, 194n
Fort Lewis (Washington), 45
Fort Ord (California), 45
Fort Porter (New York), 8, 11
Fort Willis, 47
Fuller, Horace (General), 57, 96, 99, 101–103, 180

Gilbert, Martin, x, 64, 102
Goethals, George (Colonel), 9
Goldhurst, Richard, 18
Goulden, Joseph C., 183
Gowen, James (Captain), 9, 12
Graves, Sidney, 21
Graves, William S. (General), 8, 12, 15–16, 18–25, 30, 37, 43
Greene, Henry A. (Colonel), 9–11

Griswold, Oscar W. (General), 53
Guadacanal (Solomon Islands), 64
Gudger, H. A. (Judge), 11–12
Gudger, Herman, 180

Hall, Charles "Chink" (General), 118, 122, 159, 176
Halsey, William (Admiral), 89
Handy, Thomas T. (General), 52, 168n
Haney, Harold H. (Brig. General), 133
Hannegan, Robert E. (Postmaster General), 168n
Harding, Edwin F. (General), 57–60, 65–67, 176, 180–81, 194n
Hewitt, Henry K. (Admiral), 52
Hitler, Adolf, 39
Hodges, Courtney B. (General), 45
Hollandia (New Guinea), 95–99, 101–103, 109, 176
Hollywood (California), 177
Howard, Michael, x
Humboldt Bay (Hollandia), 95–97
Hunt, Frazier, 186

Iloilo (Panay, Philippines), 134
Impalutao (Mindanao, Philippines), 136
Inchon (Korea); landing at,183
Irving, Frederick (General), 96, 140, 146n

James, D. Clayton, 153, 175, 182, 295, 337–38, 389 (f 57)
Janowitz, Morris, 409
Johnson, Louis (Assistant Secretary of War), 74

Kabakan (Mindanao, Philippines), 136
Kahn, E. J., 66–67
Keegan, John, 64, 102
Kemper Military School (Boonville, Missouri), 8, 11
Kennan, George F., 18
Kenney, George C. (General), 58, 68, 110, 186
Kenney, William J. (Assistant Secretary of Navy), 168n

King, Eddy (General), 32
King, Ernest J. (Admiral), 89
Klug, J. A. (Secretary of Interior), 168n
Kolchak, Alexander (Admiral), 17–19, 21, 24
Korean War (1950–53), 182–83
Krueger, Walter (General), 75, 81–84, 88, 91–92, 95, 97–101, 103–104, 109–24, 131, 136, 139–42, 149–50, 159–60, 176, 187–88, 200n, 206
Kuril Islands, 154

Larsen, Roy, 88, 169n
Lavarak, John (General), 57
Lear, Ben (General), 52
Liddell Hart, Basil (Sir), 189
Lingayen Gulf (Philippines), 115, 117
Louisiana Maneuvers, 82
Luvaas, Jay, xi(n), 188–90, 201–203n

MacArthur, Douglas (General), ix, 57–58, 65–68, 138, 149, 206–208, 208n; fails to mention Eichelberger in his postwar books, xi(n); as a captain, 12; as Chief of Staff, 35–36; with Dwight Eisenhower as senior aide, 37; impressions of Eichelberger's abilities, 38, 206; requests a new corps command in SW Pacific, 52–53; develops reputation for being hard to get along with, 53; briefs Eichelberger upon arrival in Australia, 57; sends Eichelberger to Buna, 58; unhappy with progress of Buna operation, 58, 61–63; commends Eichelberger for Buna success, 63; mistakes in Buna campaign, 64; and Sutherland, 67–68, 85–86, 162n; and Eisenhower, 70–71, 85–87; Buna controversies, 72–75; control of the press, 69–71, 69–74, 90, 120–23, 139–40, 150–51, 163n, 182–84; replaces Eichelberger with Krueger after Buna, 81–84; refuses Eichelberger's request for a transfer,

84–85; and George C. Marshall, 85–87; notes Eichelberger's change of attitude, 90; places Eichelberger and Krueger in competition, 91; and Hollandia operation, 95–97, 102; and Biak operation, 98–103; formation of Eighth Army, 103; plays off Eichelberger and Krueger, 104, 114–22, 139–40; and advance on Manila, 117–18; and southern Philippines, 131–37; emotional manipulation of Eichelberger, 123–24, 141–42, 150, 207; as Supreme Commander, Allied Powers (SCAP) in Japan, 151, 154, 156–61, 164–65n; desire to be President, 171n, 184, 197n; Eichelberger's attempts to destroy the reputation of, 176, 181–90; and Korean War, 182–83; reaction to Eichelberger's death, 189
McCarthy, Dudley, 187, 199n
McClernand, John (General), 4
McCloy, John J. (Assistant Secretary of War), 168n
MacKaye, Milton, 175–77, 188
McKinley, James (General), 33–34, 38, 43
McNair, Lesley J. (General), 48–53, 84
Manchester, William, 138, 142–43n, 157
Manila (Philippines), 29, 115, 117–23
March, Peyton (General), 29
Marley, Bill (General), 52
Marshall, George C. (General), ix, 12, 35, 37–38, 44–53, 84–88, 103, 124, 175, 188, 207
Marshall, Richard J. (General), 141
Mathues, William, 7
Mayo, Lida, 64, 66–67, 72
Milner, Samuel, 64, 66, 70, 72–73, 187, 199–200n
Morison, Samuel Eliot, 123, 187
Morton, Louis, 186–87
Moss, Wentworth, 7
Mott, John (Colonel), 59–60, 65

Mountbatten, Louis (Lord Vice-Admiral), 50
Mueller, Paul J. (General), 149–50, 157

Nasugbu (Philippines), operations at, 115–20, 122–23
New Deal, 158
Newsweek, 162, 177–78, 198–99n
Nimitz, Chester (Admiral), 89, 98, 131, 186
Nixon, Richard, 179
Normandy (France), invasion of, 85

Occupation of Japan; structure, 151; phases, 151–54; heads of occupation, 155–57; evaluation of, 1564–58
Ohio State University, 3, 4
Ohio Wesleyan University, 1, 3, 4
Okinawa, 137, 144n
Open Door policy, 15
Our Jungle Road to Tokyo, 176–77, 182
Overman, John (Senator–North Carolina), 11

Panama Canal, 8–12
Pan-American Exposition (1901), 2, 5
Parang (Mindanao, Philippines), 134, 136, 145n
Patterson, Robert P. (Secretary of War), 168n
Patton, George S. (General), ix, xi(n), 34, 45, 115, 124, 205, 208n; Eichelberger compares self to, 137, 151
Pearl Harbor (Hawaii), 49
Perry, John Curtis, 158
Peterson, Howard (Assistant Secretary of War), 168n
Peterson, V. L. (General), 72
Philippines, operations at; Leyte, 112–15, 123; Luzon, 112, 114–18, 122–23; Southern Philippines planning, 131–32; Palawan, 131–34; Zamboanga Peninsula, 131–34; Panay, 131, 134–35; Negros, 131,

134–35; Cebu, 131, 134–35, 137; Mindanao, 131, 133, 135–37
Phillipson, Irving J. (Colonel), 44
Port Moresby, 57–58, 64, 67, 69, 71, 90, 176
Potsdam Declaration, 150, 166n
Presidio (San Francisco), 43–45, 48
Puerto Princesa (Palawan, Philippines), 133

Quigley, Harold S., 157

Rees, David, 183
Richardson, Robert C. (General), 52–53, 89
Richmond, Bill (Captain), 116
Ridgway, Matthew B. (General), 182–3, 196n
Roberts, Ken, 188
Robinson., P. O. (Colonel), 20, 22–23
Rogers, Gordon (Colonel), 74–75, 84
Roosevelt, Eleanor, 89–90, 175
Roosevelt, Franklin D., 37, 46, 71, 89, 131
Roosevelt, Theodore "Teddy," 5
Ropp, Theodore (Professor), 177
Royall, Kenneth C. (Undersecretary of War), 168n
Russell, Mathew (General), 52

Saipan, 98, 103
Sanananda (New Guinea), 63–65, 70, 73, 82, 86
Saturday Evening Post, 175–76
Schmidt, Frederick (Sgt.), 8, 10
Schoeffel, John B. (Captain), 9–10
Schonberger, Howard B., 157–58
Sheldon, Walter, 157
Sherman, William T. (General), 33
Shortal, John, x
Siberian Railroad, 17–18
Sibert, Franklin (General), 136, 146n
Simonds, George S. (General), 36–38, 43
Sixth Army, 75, 80–82, 98, 103–104, 111–18, 120–23, 140–41, 149–50, 160

Smith, Robert Ross, 102, 122–23, 137
Smith, Walter B. (General), 174
Smithsonian Institution, 2
Spanier, John W., 183
Spector, Ronald, 102, 122
Stephens, Irby, 187
Stevens, John F., 9
Stilwell, Joseph (General), 30, 45
Stimson, Henry (Secretary of War), 53
Subic Bay (Philippines), 115–18, 120
Sullivan, Gael (Assistant Postmaster General), 168n
Sun Yat Sen (President of China), 30
Surles, Alec D. (General), 84
Sutherland, Richard K. (General), 58, 67–70, 72, 85–86, 117, 141, 149–50, 162n, 187–88, 207
Sweeney, W. C. (General), 45
Swing, Joseph (General), 118–19, 160
Symington, Stuart (Assistant Secretary of War), 168n

Taft, Robert (Senator), 197n
Tagaytay Ridge (Luzon, Philippines), 116–20, 122–23
Tanahmerah Bay (Hollandia, New Guinea), 95–97
Tarawa, 137
Taylor, Maxwell (General), 142
Texas A & M University, 190n
Thompson, Charles (General), 51
Tokyo (Japan), 149, 155, 161, 168n, 174, 181, 183, 195–96n
Torch, Operation, 52, 206
Truman, Harry S., 177, 183, 196n

United Nations, 151, 158, 174
Units (corps size or smaller); I Corps, 57, 67–68, 74–75, 81–82, 84–88, 90, 95–98, 103, 104, 198n; XI Corps, 118, 122, 176; 11th Airborne Division, 118–23
Unterberger, Betty M., 18
Urbana College, 4
Urbana (Ohio), 1–5, 11

Van Deman, Ralph H., 29
Vermont, University of, 174
Viking Press, 176–77
Villa, Pancho, 11–12
Voorhees, Tracy S. (Assistant Secretary of Army), 174–75, 181–82

Waldron, Albert (General), 60
Walker, Walton (General), 196n
Warnock, William R. (Judge), 4, 5
Washington Disarmament Conference (1920–22), 30–31
Watson, Edwin "Pa" (General), 37–38, 46–49
Weigley, Russell F., ix
West Point, ix, 5, 7–8, 11, 32–34, 37–38, 45–49, 65, 83, 88, 142, 177, 180–81, 194n
Westall, Virginia, 200n

Whelan, Richard, 183
White, Robert M., II, 198n
Whitehead, Ennis (General), 67, 119
Whitney, Courtney (General), 102, 122, 157
Williams, Justin, 157
Willoughby, Charles A. (General), 82–83, 110–12, 115–16, 200n, 206
Wilson, Woodrow, 16, 18–19, 24
Wint, Guy, x, 102
Woodring, Harold (Secretary of War), 36
Works Progress Administration (WPA), 44

Yalu River (Korea), 182–83, 185
Yokohama (Japan), 149–50

Zamboanga City (Philippines), 133

About the Author

PAUL CHWIALKOWSKI is Visiting Assistant Professor of History at The University of Toledo and a specialist in modern American military history.

**Recent Titles in
Contributions in Military Studies**

"Mad Jack": The Biography of Captain John Percival, USN, 1779-1862
David F. Long

Military Helicopter Doctrines of the Major Powers, 1945-1992: Making Decisions about Air-Land Warfare
Matthew Allen

Joint Military Operations: A Short History
Roger A. Beaumont

Iron Brigade General: John Gibbon, A Rebel in Blue
Dennis S. Lavery and Mark H. Jordan

Looking Back on the Vietnam War: A 1990s Perspective on the Decisions, Combat, and Legacies
William Head and Lawrence E. Grinter, editors

The Search for Strategy: Politics and Strategic Vision
Gary L. Guertner, editor

Paying the Premium: A Military Insurance Policy for Peace and Freedom
Walter Hahn and H. Joachim Maitre, editors

Imperial Spies Invade Russia: The British Intelligence Interventions, 1918
A. J. Plotke

Uneasy Coalition: The Entente Experience in World War I
Jehuda L. Wallach

Peacekeepers and Their Wives: American Participation in the Multinational Force and Observers
David R. Segal and Mady Wechsler Segal

The American Revolution, Garrison Life in French Canada and New York
Translated by Helga Doblin and edited with an introduction by Mary C. Lynn

Edwards Brothers Malloy
Thorofare, NJ USA
October 12, 2012